D1058281

BRITISH PREËMINENCE IN BRAZIL
ITS RISE AND DECLINE

BRITISH PREËMINENCE IN BRAZIL
ITS RISE AND DECLINE

A Study in European Expansion

By

ALAN K. MANCHESTER, PH.D.

1964
OCTAGON BOOKS, INC.
NEW YORK

Reprinted 1964
by special arrangement with The University of North Carolina Press

OCTAGON BOOKS, INC.
175 FIFTH AVENUE
NEW YORK, N. Y. 10010

LIBRARY OF CONGRESS CATALOG CARD NUMBER: 64-24848

Printed in U.S.A. by
NOBLE OFFSET PRINTERS, INC.
NEW YORK 3, N. Y.

TO

J. Fred Rippy

SCHOLAR, TEACHER, FRIEND

FOREWORD

In September of 1922 the commercial secretary of the British Embassy at Rio de Janeiro wrote to his government that Great Britain since the World War had been overtaking slowly but surely its American rival and that the official statistics for the first quarter of the current year showed that Great Britain once more occupied "its original position as the most important of Brazil's suppliers."[1] A year later he ignored the United States altogether and warned his government that Germany was now the "most serious competitor of Great Britain in the Brazilian markets."[2] But his satisfaction over England's recovery after the war period was shortlived, for in 1924 the United States surpassed Britain's sales to Brazil by two hundred thousand pounds sterling. In 1925 the lead was increased to two millions sterling; and by 1926 the United States was selling to Brazil one and a half times as much as England.[3]

Great Britain's loss was serious. For one hundred and sixteen years, with the single exception of the World War period and the post-war readjustment, England dominated the markets of Portuguese America. Shortly after the middle of the nineteenth century the United States began to *purchase* more from Brazil than did any other country, and it has maintained that position ever since. But England has not made a question of absorbing Brazilian exports: its efforts have always been directed toward maintaining the supremacy of English goods in Brazilian markets. Not once from 1808 until the World War did Great Britain lose its position, but in 1922 England regained it only to lose it again to the United States. The loss is

[1] Great Britain, *Diplomatic and Commercial Reports*, 1922, Department of Overseas Trade, "Report on Economic and Financial conditions in Brazil," by E. Hambloch, p. 23.

[2] *Ibid.*, 1923, p. 40.

[3] Brazil, Directoria de Estatistica, *Commercio Exterior do Brasil*, 1927, pp. 8-13.

more striking in view of the predominance of English capital in Portuguese America. In 1927 there was four times as much British as American money invested in Brazil and over one and a half times as much as all other foreign capital combined.[4] In Central America and in other parts of South America, England lost first place in the markets to the United States before the World War period; but it took the catastrophe of 1914 to pry Britain loose from dominance in Portuguese America. Brazil occupies half the territory and includes over half of the population south of Panama.[5] Supremacy in that market is a valuable prize.

The importance of Brazil to English exporters has been demonstrated by two missions which Great Britain has sent to South America within the last few years in an effort to promote the consumption of British goods. The first of these was the D'Abernon mission of 1929, which visited Argentina, Uruguay, and Brazil with the purpose of studying markets and consulting with British and native importers in the countries visited. The second of these missions occurred in the spring of 1931 when the Prince of Wales and his brother toured South America. With all the pomp and ceremony of the British Empire the two princes were sent with the frankly avowed purpose of regaining markets for English articles. Their reception in Brazil demonstrated the importance of British interests in that country.

Although the population of about forty-two millions does not possess a high purchasing power, the consumption of native products, both raw materials and manufactured articles, is increasing steadily. Tobacco, which at one time was grown principally for export, is now being consumed within the country itself, the amount exported being reduced to one-half of the production. Only a very small percentage of the sugar produced is sent out of the country and packing houses utilize the greater part of the production of fresh meat for home con-

[4] *South American Handbook for 1928*, p. 188. The estimate was made by Wileman's *Brazilian Review*.

[5] Funk and Wagnalls, *Atlas of the World and Gazeteer, 1924*.

sumption. Almost the entire production of cotton, which until recently has been one of the principal exports, is being absorbed by the textile industry in home manufacturing.[6]

Brazil, therefore, with its forty millions of population offers an economic market of domestic consumption, a condition which is favorable to the investment of foreign capital and the growth of foreign enterprise in Brazil itself. The growing foreign trade[7] is enhancing the value of the shipping business and the increasing purchasing power of the population invites international rivalry in the contest for control of the markets of Brazil. Until 1914, British capital, British enterprise, British shipping, and British goods predominated in the economic life of Brazil. To-day Great Britain is still supreme in the amount of capital invested and in the carrying trade of Brazil; but the United States has won the markets for North American goods and Yankee enterprise is challenging the traditional British supremacy.

In the words of the Prince of Wales, "the prestige of Britain as a manufacturing country" is "no longer what it used to be in South America. . . ." So great has been that change, the prince pointed out, that only by a personal visit of inspection is it possible "to realize the extent to which the influence of the North has penetrated into the industrial and commercial life of the South."[8] In Brazil this waning of traditional economic preëminence is in startling contrast to the absolute mastery enjoyed by British interests for over a century.

The winning of half of a continent as a virtual economic colony and the maintenance of that position for one hundred years constitute a British achievement which suggests several interesting problems. How was that position of preëminence secured? To what extent did Great Britain dominate the economic and political life of Brazil? What were the factors which

[6] Max Winkler, *Investments of United States Capital in Latin America*, p. 81.

[7] The foreign trade of Brazil increased thirty-three per cent. between 1913 and 1926 (*ibid.*).

[8] The *New York Times*, May 22, 1931, Sec. I, pp. 3, 13. The quotations are from a speech delivered by the Prince of Wales before three thousand members of the Manchester Chamber of Commerce, May 12.

tended to undermine England's influence in Portuguese America? In what way and to what extent was British preëminence threatened by foreign competitors? How did it happen that a European power could win for itself the dominant political and economic position in half the continent of South America?

The attempt to answer these questions disclosed the fact that there was a line of continuity in Anglo-Brazilian relations which originated in the European background of the Anglo-Portuguese Alliance. The foundations of British preëminence in Brazil, laid in Europe prior to 1808, were transferred to South America when the exigencies of war forced the flight of the Portuguese court to Rio de Janeiro. Two chapters (I, II), therefore, are devoted to the establishing of British preëminence in Portugal; four chapters (III, IV, VII, VIII) explain the manner in which that supremacy was transferred to the independent empire of Brazil between 1808 and 1827; three chapters (IX, X, XI) discuss the decline of British political preëminence in Brazil; and a concluding chapter (XII) deals with the rise of competitors who were to challenge Britain's economic supremacy. Two chapters (V, VI) are concerned with the attitude of the British Foreign Office toward the intricate problems created by the determination of the Rio court to annex and hold the eastern bank of the Rio de la Plata.

The study does not pretend to be an exhaustive discussion of Anglo-Brazilian relations. The objective has been rather to discover how Great Britain, a European power, established its preëminence in Brazil, a New World nation, and how and to what extent that preëminence has declined.

The writer wishes to express sincere gratitude for the very careful revision and personal inspiration of Professor J. Fred Rippy, by whose kindly coöperation this project was made possible. Grateful acknowledgment is made also of the fertile suggestions and helpful criticism of Professor W. T. Laprade, particularly with reference to the first two chapters. Both Professor Rippy and Professor Laprade read the entire manuscript. Professor Percy A. Martin was kind enough to examine the manuscript also and to offer valuable suggestions. The map reproductions are the work of Mr. Ben F. Lemert of Duke University. The writer is indebted for many courtesies received from the authorities and personnel of the Public Record Office, the British Museum, and the Pan-American Union, and from the staffs of the Library of Congress, the Iberian Library of the Catholic University of America, and the library of Duke University. Much valuable material was received from Dr. Mario Behring, Director of the Bibliotheca Nacional of Brazil. And lastly, it is a pleasure to acknowledge the debt incurred from the assistance of my most helpful co-worker, my wife.

Alan K. Manchester

February, 1933

TABLE OF CONTENTS

BRITISH PREËMINENCE IN BRAZIL
ITS RISE AND DECLINE

CHAPTER I

THE BASIS OF ENGLISH SUPREMACY IN PORTUGUESE COMMERCE

FROM 1147 when English Crusaders helped the young Affonso Henriques of the House of Burgundy, first king of the new state,[1] to capture Lisbon from the Moors, until the first quarter of the nineteenth century, when D. João VI was shorn of the best of his overseas dominions, Portugal was an important pawn on the chessboard of European history. Never much larger than the modern state of Panama, it demanded the attention of Spain, France, Holland, and England by virtue of its strategic position in Europe and its overseas possessions. England's interest in the country was greatest from 1654, when British merchants and shipping interests made of Portugal practically an English commercial vassal, to 1825 when the colony of Brazil won its independence.

England secured a dominant influence in Portuguese commerce by the triple complementary treaties of 1642-'54-'61. Some foundation on which to base these treaties had been laid, however, in the five hundred years previous. Other crusading expeditions called at Portugal after the first detachment and helped Affonso's successors to round out the kingdom, while the Patent Rolls[2] reveal much commerce between the two countries in King John's time. Henry III[3] issued fresh letters patent in the middle of the thirteenth century. These friendly relations continued down to the reign of Edward III when the

[1] J. P. Oliveira Martins, *Historia de Portugal*, I, 53-78, 82-86.

[2] Violet Shillington, "The Beginnings of the Anglo-Portuguese Alliance," *Transactions of the Royal Historical Society*, New Series, XX, 111-112.

[3] *Patent Rolls*, 42, Henry III, m. 13, p. 613. In 1258.

first written treaty[4] between the two kingdoms was signed by Edward on behalf of his people and by Alfonso Martin Alho, a citizen of Portugal, on behalf of the merchants of Lisbon and Oporto. The agreement, among other things, guaranteed the safety of subjects of one country trading in the territory of the other. The first political alliance[5] was signed by Edward and Fernando in 1373, with an eye to Spain. Later John of Gaunt, whose wife, Constance, was the daughter of Peter the Cruel of Castile, attempted to grasp that crown for himself after Peter's death; but succeeded only in getting his daughter, Phillipa, married to João of Aviz and the two recognized as sovereigns of Portugal by the effective aid of English land and sea forces.[6] The Treaty of Windsor[7] in 1386 guaranteed safe-conduct to subjects of both countries, ceded commercial privileges, and stipulated mutual defense. Phillipa's son, Prince Henry the Navigator, preferring his Portuguese ships to the captaincy of Henry VI's armies, turned Portugal into a nation of maritime explorers in advance of the other European peoples.[8] Henry VII[9] conferred the Order of the Garter on João II and confirmed the Treaty of Windsor.

In 1580 Philip II brought Portugal under Spanish domination but in 1640 the Duke of Bragança initiated a revolt to free his country from the control of Spain.[10] Striving for independence and distracted by the inroads the Dutch were making on the rich booty coming from the colonies, Lisbon turned to England for help and sent a commission to London to negotiate a treaty which would recognize the newly proclaimed independence. The instructions sent by João IV to his ambassadors, Antão d'Almada and Andrade Leitão, are illegible in the only known copy, but the objects sought by Portugal are given in the "Capitulações" which the ambassadors addressed to

---

[4] T. Rymer, *Foedera*, III, pt. i, p. 88. In 1353.

[5] *Ibid.*, pt. iii, p. 8. June 16.

[6] *Ibid.*, pp. 175-177.

[7] *Ibid.*, p. 200.

[8] *Ibid.*, IV, pt. iii, p. 5.

[9] *Ibid.*, V, pt. iii, p. 194, pt. iv, pp. 4-5.

[10] Oliveira Martins, *Historia de Portugal*, II, 109-149.

Charles on April 1, 1641.[11] They proposed peace and amity and abstention from aiding the enemy of either contracting party; permission for English subjects to serve in the Portuguese army and navy with their own persons, munitions, and ships; free commerce subject to customary duties; and the *status quo* in India. On April 8, they obtained a public audience, and commissioners were appointed to treat with them. News leaked out of the treaty signed between Portugal and Holland on June 12, and the merchants of London presented to the Lords Commissioners eighteen articles for "better benefit and accomodation of" the treaty.[12] The Portuguese ambassador protested against five of these demands, refusing to concede to the English freedom of religion and exemption from the power of the Inquisition; the right of Englishmen to sail in British ships hired by Portugal for her colonial trade, without the express license from the king to trade with the colonies; the right to reëxport goods from Portugal without paying additional duties; the right to trade with all Portuguese dominions—Africa, America, and the East Indies—on the same footing as Portuguese subjects; and the payment of import and export duties as fixed in the time of Sebastião and Henry of Portugal with exemption from all taxes levied since then. The merchants replied to his protest, reasserting these demands and adding others. A ten page "Remonstrance for the continuance of Trade from England for Portugal" by merchants begging Charles to arrange a treaty is included in this bundle of treaty papers.[13]

These demands by British merchants demonstrate the importance of Portuguese trade to English commerce. The points

---

[11] Capitulações que á magestade do serenissimo Carlos Rey da Grã Bretanha propoem os ambaixadores do serenissimo dom João Rey de Portugal. Signed by Leitão. Great Britain, Public Record Office, State Papers, Foreign, Treaty Papers, 103/57. In view of the great number of citations from the Public Record Office, dates will be given only in cases where the absence of a number on a dispatch requires a date for identification or where the date is considered necessary for a more complete understanding of the text.

[12] S. P. For., Treaty Papers, 103/57. The group cited is dated 1640 on the back of the packet. The records of the negotiations are largely undated and are in disorder.

[13] *Ibid.*

to which the Portuguese ambassador objected, with the exception of the religious demands which were partly commercial, deal exclusively with the question of colonial trade. Portugal was the "staple" for two streams of commerce; one from the Portuguese colonies through the mother country to England and one from England through Portugal to the colonies. The British merchant desired control of this *entrepôt* business and a share in the carrying trade resulting from these two streams of commerce. The treaty of 1642[14] was a decisive step in that direction.

The treaty was negotiated by England in a time of turmoil. Strafford was executed during the month of the public audience granted to the newly arrived Portuguese ambassadors; the five members were impeached January 3, 1642; the king came for his "birds" the next day; and seven days later Charles left London. On the twenty-ninth the signed treaties were exchanged. The English commissioners kept a cool head during the excitement for the agreement left England with everything to gain and little to lose, while on Portugal's side the concessions were exorbitant and the advantages attenuated.

By the twenty-one sections of the treaty England secured religious toleration for her subjects resident in Portugal, said residents being largely merchants, and protection from primary losses resulting from action by the Inquisition; most favored nation status commercially; a limited but effective extra-territorial jurisdiction under its own consul and immunity from Portuguese laws for English subjects. Commissioners were to be appointed to treat of concessions to the British in Brazilian commerce, the first formal knock by the English at the door of Portuguese South America. One searches in vain for an economic clause in behalf of the Portuguese. All they obtained was recognition of independence and England's friendship, which was not a very stable commodity in 1642.

[14] J. F. Borges de Castro, *Collecção de Tratados*, I, 82-101. Signatures: Antão d'Almada and Francisco de Andrade Leitão for Portugal and Arundel & Surrey, John, Count of Bristol, W. Say & Seale, and Falkland for England. Signed January 29, 1642. Renewed by Article XXVI of theTreaty of 1810.

The treaty came to nothing for the time being, but it served twelve years later as the basis of Cromwell's sledge-hammer demands. It was, in fact, the basis of all subsequent treaties.

D. João helped his friend Charles loyally, more sincerely even than France or Spain.[15] Letters, money, and supplies were smuggled to Charles by Antonio de Souza de Macedo, Portuguese ambassador in London from 1642 to 1646.[16] Portugal was the first to protest against the Regicides, the first to recognize the Commonwealth and send an ambassador, and the first to renew relations with Charles at the restoration; or, as it were, it was first in war with the Puritans, first in peace with Cromwell, and first in friendship for the Stuarts.

In the meantime, the British merchants in Lisbon were submitting to D. João and his auditor, Nicolau Dias Tinoco, who was also judge conservator of the English, a complaint against the non-execution of privileges justly theirs with certain papers showing the nature of these privileges. Arranged chronologically, these documents were: a charter dated August 10, 1400, by which D. João I conceded to the English the same privileges as had been conceded to the Genoese; a charter dated October 29, 1450, by which D. Affonso V conceded to the English the right to a special judge in all commercial cases which should arise between them and the Portuguese; a charter dated March 28, 1452, by D. Affonso V, granting the right to Englishmen to live and move about at will within the Portuguese kingdom; and the letter patent, dated February 7, 1495, by which D. Manuel granted special privileges to merchants from certain German cities.

In consequence of the petition Tinoco issued an order dated May 11, 1645, commanding that "no other officer of ours, either disturb or meddle with them [the English merchants], or anything that belongs to them, except [through] their said

---

[15] Guernsey Jones, "The Oldest European Alliance—England and Portugal, 1640 to 1661," American Historical Association, *Reports*, 1916, pt. I, p. 411.

[16] Macedo's residence in England is given in: *Quadro Elementar*, XVII, 27-38; S. P. For., Portugal, 89/4, fl. 220; Birch MS. 4155, fl. 250; *Commons Journals*, II, III, IV; Edgar Prestage, *Diplomatic Relations of Portugal with France, England and Holland from 1640 to 1668*, pp. 99-108.

judges, or any [Portuguese officer] by their order." In case of the necessity of imprisonment, the English were to be conducted to the castle by their said judge, or by his bailiff, in person and not by the servants or followers of these officials. The English might carry arms, and no other officer of justice might enter the house of English merchants without an order from the English conservator. The petition with its enclosures and the order were approved by D. João on November 4, 1647. These documents constituted the famous Charter of English Privileges in the Portuguese Dominions,[17] and served to uphold Cromwell's demands in 1654.[18]

After the execution of Charles, Portugal waged a feeble war on the English, doing its greatest damage by sequestering the property of English merchants and imprisoning them. Prince Rupert, son of the ex-king of Bohemia and a Stuart fire-brand, used Lisbon as a place of refuge for his fleet and was bottled up by Admiral Blake.[19] When D. João despite his attitude of ostensible neutrality refused to drive the prince out into the jaws of the Puritan fleet, Admiral Blake wrote[20] to Charles Vane in Lisbon to tell the king that he "should take it far better at his hands that he did openly declare for Prince Rupert against us than by such indirect policies to undermine us, and by uncertain and equivocal pretenses of amity to entertain us and to lead us along by the nose any longer with an opinion of neutrality, when we may clearly perceive by that order[21] to his forts the contrary is intended."

[17] *Privileges of an Englishman in the Kingdoms and Dominions of Portugal*, London, 1736, pp. 51-73. The compiler copied these papers from the original certificate in the office of the scrivener of the Spanish Conservatory in Lisbon. These documents of English privileges were found in the archives of the Spanish Conservator because in 1691 a decree granted to the Spaniards the same privileges as those enjoyed by the English (*Relação de Leis Extravagantes*, No. 11, fl. 243). Borges de Castro, *Collecção de Tratados*, I, 204ff. gives the "Charter of English privileges." He points out errors in the documents: the 1400 charter should be 1427 and D. Fernando, not Affonso, granted the 1450 charter.

[18] See Article III of the Treaty of 1654.

[19] See Historical Manuscripts Commission, *Portland MSS.*, I, 520-542.

[20] *Ibid.*, p. 522.

[21] The order reinforced the garrisons of the forts commanding the port and the English fleet.

Two facts deterred the wily D. João from openly declaring for Prince Rupert. The first of these was the cogent argument of Dunbar. Whitelock states[22] in December of 1650 "that upon news of Parliament's victory in Scotland, the King of Portugal released" the English merchants whom he had seized and "resolved to send an ambassador to England to the Parliament." D. João de Guimarães therefore was authorized by the king to treat of all points of difference between Portugal and England and to attempt to confirm the treaty of 1642.[23] The second fact which deterred João from breaking definitely with the Roundheads was a real anxiety for his overseas dominions. The English council of state, in view of Rupert's extended stay in the neutral port, had ordered Admirals Popham and Blake to blockade Lisbon and by letters of marque to prey on Portuguese shipping and take "all and sundry,"[24] with the result that in October, Blake had captured rich booty from the annual Brazilian fleet as it attempted to enter Lisbon. Dunbar and his lost ships convinced D. João, and Guimarães was dispatched to England the next month.

His was a luckless mission. His troubles began as soon as he landed in Portsmouth, when the council of state demanded to know whether he was an ambassador or only an agent and what powers he had to treat of the damages done the English. He made a conciliatory speech before the committee of Parliament, seeking presentation; he extolled the past services of England to Portugal and requested that the sale of the Portuguese goods seized by Blake be arrested until his mission could be accomplished.[25] A third petition by Guimarães for admittance before Parliament and for the suspension of the sale of the goods received the reply that "England was getting redress in one way for wrongs suffered but that it would be ready to take it in another if he were sufficiently authorized for the purpose."[26]

---

[22] *Memorials of English Affairs*, p. 484.

[23] Hist. Mss. Com., *Portland Mss.*, I, 540-541; *Commons Journals*, VI, 530.

[24] *Portland Mss.*, I, 527-528; *Commons Journals*, VI, 525.

[25] *Portland Mss.*, I, 552; *Commons Journals*, VI, 523.

[26] *Portland Mss.*, I, 555; *Commons Journals*, VI, 529.

Parliament then presented six articles for Guimarães' acquiescence before it would treat of any further accord, and the Portuguese agent was unable to find out from the stiff-necked House of Commons what further demands or possible compensations he would receive if he consented.

All English persons concerned in the murder of Blake's sailors in Lisbon and the attempt on Blake's flagship by an infernal machine were to be punished; all ships brought into Portuguese waters by Rupert were to be turned over, reparation being made for all English ships seized by the Portuguese; and over two hundred thousand pounds sterling (later reduced to one hundred and eighty thousand) was to be paid by Portugal to cover the expenses of Blake's fleet during the blockade.[27] Guimarães, with no money or sufficient authorization from D. João, fought for time to soften these demands, by what the committee of Parliament called "ambiguous and insignificant answers to draw the business into length upon pretense of difficulties."[28] In desperation Guimarães finally accepted all six, but could not guarantee the execution of them for want of the proper authorization. Instead he pawned "his head and person for his majesty's putting into execution all and every of the Six Articles,"[29] and suggested a commercial treaty. Parliament gave him three days to present security other than his head.[30] When Guimarães pleaded for time to return to Portugal for the king's consent, Parliament gave him fourteen days to set out with a one way passport and ordered the council of state to supply any deficiencies in the matter of prize-taking among the Portuguese trade.[31]

Guimarães was followed by an important personage, the king's chamberlain, D. Rodrigo de Sá e Menezes, Conde de Peneguião, ambassador extraordinary with an imposing train. On September 28, 1652, he forwarded his credentials to Par-

[27] *Portland Mss.*, I, 565-566; *Commons Journals*, VI, 539, 558-560.

[28] Council of state to Parliament, April 1, 1651, *Commons Journals*, VI, 565.

[29] *Ibid.*, p. 568.

[30] *Portland Mss.*, I, 569-572; *Commons Journals*, VI, 570.

[31] *Commons Journals*, VI, 574-575. See John Thurloe, *Collection of the State Papers of John Thurloe*, I, 141-142, 145, 168, for various side lights on these incidents.

liament and requested an audience.[32] He agreed to all six articles after gracefully reducing the indemnity demands to fifty thousand pounds sterling, by pointing out a "slight error in arithmetic made by Parliament." Thereupon he proposed a revival of the treaty of 1642. During the ensuing negotiations the English merchants interested in the Portuguese trade gave the committee a list of thirty-six articles of additional privileges and concessions which they thought desirable,[33] and got them all.

The treaty which resulted was the great charter of English liberties in Portugal.[34] It confirmed, strengthened, and extended rights previously granted, removed petty annoyances, extended extra-territorial jurisdiction and religious freedom, gave English merchants freedom of trade with Brazil and the west coast of Africa on terms of equality with Portuguese subjects, and provided that Portuguese customs duties to be paid by the English should never be raised above the current rate without the consent of two English merchants residing in Portugal and chosen by the English consul.[35] Thirteen of the twenty-eight articles of the treaty[36] were ratifications of the 1642 document with amplifications, and the rights conceded in the Charter of English Privileges were incorporated in the agreement. Again England limited her obligations to professions of friendship with no expressed liabilities for military assistance, while Portugal became virtually England's commercial vassal.

Cárdenas, Spanish ambassador, wrote Philip IV on December 21/31, 1654, that the treaty had been agreed upon fifteen months before. His information was correct, for the negotiations had been concluded and now the agreement depended solely on Peneguião's signature. He had hesitated to sign, how-

---

[32] *Portland Mss.*, I, 663.

[33] Papers of the Com. of Eng. Council of State, Add. Mss. 4192.

[34] Guernsey Jones, "The Oldest European Alliance," p. 413.

[35] This last provision was in a secret article appended to the treaty.

[36] George Chalmers, *Treaties*, II, 267-286. Done at Westminster. Between Oliver Cromwell and João IV. Ratified by Portugal at Alcántara, June 9, 1656. Reaffirmed by Article XXVI of the Treaty of 1810.

ever, despite the undercurrents which swirled about him. Spain had worked feverishly for an alliance with England but the religious clauses demanded by Protestant England, when submitted to the Inquisition for an opinion, had been rejected and any possibility of an Anglo-Spanish alliance had vanished. The Portuguese envoy had circulated verses written in red letters to the dishonor of Holland,[37] and the Dutch ambassadors had refused to visit the Portuguese minister and had returned a pipe of wine and a cellar of strong waters sent them by the Portuguese envoy.

Peneguião still hesitated while his king failed in an offer at the Hague of an offensive and defensive alliance to be sealed by the marriage of one of his daughters to the king with four millions of florins as dowry.[38] But personal reasons soon after forced his signature. His nineteen year old brother, D. Pantaleão de Sá, after a scuffle in the Arcade in the New Exchange south of the Strand, returned with fifty men and in the brawl shot and killed one Greenway, an innocent bystander who was attempting to protect his sister and fiancée. Pantaleão was tried, convicted, and sentenced to be beheaded, and Cromwell refused to interfere. On July 10, 1654, the morning of the execution, Peneguião signed the treaty and fled in horror. Whitelocke adds[39] that the luckless ambassador was arrested at Gravesend by some London merchants to whom he owed great sums of money. His goods were attached and he left for Portugal to get the treaty ratified. As a guaranty for the fifty thousand pounds due the English under the six preliminary articles, half of the duties paid by the English merchants in Portugal were to be held in pledge.[40]

---

[37] Thurloe, *State Papers*, I, 317, 324; Whitelocke, *Memorials*, p. 559. July 4 and 11, 1655 (N. S.).

[38] Thurloe, *State Papers*, II, 50. February 4, 1654 (N. S.).

[39] *Memorials*, p. 598.

[40] Thurloe, *State Papers*, II, 200-201. Sources for Peneguião's mission are: Birch Ms. 4192; Lansdowne Ms. 223, fl. 117; Add. Ms. 15170, fl. 295; *Commons Journals*, VII, S. P. For., Port., 89/4; *Portland Mss.*, I. Fragmentary accounts of Pantaleão's trial are given in Howell's *State Trials*, V, and a statement by him is given in *Harleian Miscellany*, III, 285.

The treaty had thus been negotiated but ratification was delayed due to the clauses conceding to the English merchants and seamen the free exercise of worship in their ships and houses, the same article which had been refused at Madrid. Philip Meadows was sent[41] to Lisbon therefore to demand signature without the change of a syllable. D. João offered to submit the religious clause to the Pope[42] for a decision, but Cromwell took the suggestion as an insult and became incensed when he learned from Langland, English agent at Leghorn, that it was "credibly reported in Italy that Spayn and Portugal ar as good as agreed, which may hapilly be a reason why the latter seeks to fly off from the agreement made with the Protector's hyhness."[43] Cromwell by way of reply ordered Blake and Montague from Cádiz to Lisbon with the fleet. When an attempt was made to assassinate Meadows,[44] the ambassador came off with a shattered hand but a steady head. The talk at Lisbon centered around the religious article, but Meadows divined the trouble to be the fifty thousand pounds since the Pope had not recognized D. João as king of Portugal after his revolt from Spanish domination in 1640 and there was only one bishop in the kingdom. D. João died soon afterwards, however, and Meadows, playing a shrewd hand with the high trump of the arrival of the British squadron to capture the overdue annual Brazil fleet with its rich booty, obtained D. Affonso VI's consent to the treaty on May 31. He shipped the fifty thousand pounds compensation on board the fleet[45] and the full ratification was signed finally on June 9, 1656.

The treaty thus finally ratified was a diplomatic triumph for the Commonwealth, for by it great commercial and religious advantages were secured from Portugal which had been sought from Spain and refused while in return the Portuguese obtained only what concerned peace and mutual amity. It gave a con-

[41] He was commissioned February 19, 1655 (Thurloe, *State Papers*, IV, 546).

[42] *Ibid.*, p. 759.

[43] *Ibid.*, p. 566.

[44] The attempted assassination was in vengeance for Pantaleão's execution (*ibid.*, V, 28, 35, 124).

[45] Whitelocke, *Memorials*, p. 649.

vincing proof of the ascendency of England, whose subjects trading with or residing in Portugal, were for the future in a better situation than the Portuguese themselves.[46] Britain here laid the foundations of its privileged position in Portuguese overseas dominions.

When in the summer of 1657 news reached Lisbon that France, Sweden, and England were resolved to join in the league against Spain, Portugal sent the Marquez de Sande to London with public and secret instructions ordering him to ask for the inclusion of his government in the negotiations.[47] Portugal, he suggested, would serve admirably as a southern base—naval as well as land— for the northern league against Spain, a potent argument in favor of his country for the succeeding one hundred and fifty years. His plea was successful, for in October the council appointed a committee of seven to treat with him. Although Mazarin blocked the league and deserted Portugal by the Treaty of the Pyrenees, the Portuguese Marquis signed an agreement with the English council of state, in April, 1660, authorizing Portugal to enlist twelve thousand infantry and to buy twenty-five hundred horses and arms.[48] He was ready to sail to secure ratification when the Restoration came in May.

The agreement was reached just in time to have Charles II return and catch his old friends, who had suffered so much for the Stuart cause, red-handed in collusion with the murderers of his father. Charles was sensitive on this point; he dispatched unceremoniously, the French ambassador, Bordeaux, for his too great intimacy with Cromwell, and for a time the rumor spread that he would not receive any ambassador who had treated with the preceding government. Portugal was in despair over this last blow of a malignant fate.

Several forces were working beneath the surface, however,

---

[46] Prestage, *Diplomatic Relations of Portugal*, p. 132.

[47] *Quadro Elementar*, XVIII, 160 ff., under date of July 10, 1687, an error made by Santarem which Ribello da Silva did not correct.

[48] *Ibid.*, XVII, 118. Little is given about this part of his mission in English sources, due to the domestic turmoil in 1659-1660. The treaty was never ratified.

that were to have bearing on the play of the pawn. France had abandoned its ally in the treaty of the Pyrenees, ending its twenty years of conflict with Spain and gaining a breathing space of peace. During the war, France had protected the House of Bragança in its secession from the empire of the Philips; now, although nominally at peace with Spain and no longer an ally of Portugal, France had no idea of allowing Spain to wreak retarded vengeance. As to England, if the Mediterranean naval policy adopted by Cromwell and demanded by English merchants was to be continued, a base of operations had to be retained in southern Europe. Portugal fitted the bill precisely: her empire was vast and overflowing with riches which were only in part fabulous and imaginary; her ports were ideal for bases in South European Atlantic and Mediterranean waters; and she was an irritating and effective foil to be used against Spain. From England's point of view she would also serve equally as well as a base of operations against France.

At the moment, Portugal was further backed by two forceful arguments: Jamaica, which Cromwell had taken from Spain, and the lure of India with its "most beneficialest trade that ever our nation enjoyed." Moreover, if Charles were to reverse Cromwell's policy of supporting Portugal against Spain, he would have to run counter to Louis XIV and to the merchants in the City. The argument was conclusive, and the negotiations for the 1661 agreement were begun.

In October the Marquis left for Portugal to obtain full powers to complete the treaty which was to be sealed by the marriage of Charles to Catherine of Bragança. Since the negotiations were a deep secret, Sande departed with his whole household as if discontented in order to deceive the diplomatic world.[49] He secured the approval of the Portuguese court to his plans and returned in February of 1661, as Conde da Ponte, the

[49] Sande's first mission is found in: State Papers, Domestic, 1657-8, 1658-9, and 1659-60; S. P. For., Port., 89/4 and 5; *Quadro Elementar*, XVII, 114 ff. One of Sande's letterbooks, January, 1659-July, 1660, is at the Instituto Historico in Rio de Janeiro, cod. no. 1158.

title to depend on the fulfillment of the marriage proposals. Batteville, the Spanish ambassador, and Mazarin opposed his project, and the London court seethed with intrigue.

The subsequent negotiations are given in detail by Clarendon in the secret letters[50] exchanged in cipher between him and M. Bastide in France. In March, 1661, Clarendon anxiously inquired how Louis XIV viewed the proposed Anglo-Portuguese alliance and whether he thought a wedding in Spain would be of better advantage. Bastide replied that he had the authority to assure Charles that the king of France was of the opinion that no wedding would do so well as one in Portugal.[51] In April, Bastide urged the wedding and promised the aid of Louis if such assistance were kept secret. Charles needed help, for the Spanish ambassador in London was creating trouble.[52] But since Batteville was not a man of "great dexterity in treaties," his propaganda in favor of a Protestant marriage with the Princess of Saxe, or any other, with the king of Spain adopting her and giving as large a dowry as England should demand, was making little headway. When Bastide repeated an offer of money if Charles should need it at the meeting of Parliament, Clarendon asked for fifty thousand pounds.[53]

In May the Privy Council unanimously voted for the marriage. Bastide at the same time warned Clarendon of the anti-marriage propaganda getting under way to upset the scheme. The opposition, he said, planned to "raise the Protestants and make a party at home by showing them that the King of England is so little concerned for their religion, that being in capacity to make choice betwixt many protestant matches, all of an equal advantage, by reason of the King of Spain's proffers,

[50] Edward Hyde, Earl of Clarendon, *State Papers*, III, Supplement. The correspondence was known to only six persons: Clarendon; his son, who carried the dispatches; M. Bastide, who had been secretary of the French embassy at London in 1652 and who was again sent to London by Louis in 1662; the two kings; and, later, M. d'Estrade, French ambassador in London at the time of the correspondence.

[51] *Ibid.*, Supplement, i.

[52] Prestage, *Diplomatic Relations of Portugal*, p. 46, gives Batteville's activities in detail.

[53] Clarendon, *State Papers*, III, Supplement, ii-v.

he is more inclined to betake himself to a Catholic, who is so far from affording him any considerable countenance or greater advantages than others could do, that it is like to bring him a Great War, the undoing of trade, and thereby of the whole nation, and hurt the Merchants of London in their very heart."[54] The propaganda was good but there were two obstacles of importance in the eyes of these merchants which prevented any acceptance of Spain's offers: Dunkirk and Jamaica, taken from Spain by Cromwell in time of peace, would have to be returned. Jamaica with her sugar and rum weighed heavily on the side of Portugal.

The Conde was informed of the decision of the Council and told to hurry the project along as it would soon be made public. On May 21, Charles announced the proposed marriage to an enthusiastic Parliament. One member wrote to the Conde that this was the only business of importance that he had ever seen treated by Parliament without any opposition whatsoever.[55] Bastide promised that although Louis could not show his joy over the marriage due to his peace with Spain, he would be indifferent and not oppose it, while Louis himself was sarcastic over Spanish offers since not one penny of the Spanish dowry of his wife had ever been paid.[56] On June 23, the treaty was signed.

By one line the basic treaty negotiated so obstreperously during the Cromwellian régime was declared valid, for the first article stated that "All treaties since 1641 are hereby reaffirmed." Tangier was ceded with proper precautions taken for the transfer without riots. Due arrangements were specified for the safe conduct to England of the lady involved in the treaty, and for her reception there. Portugal presented two million crowns[57] dowry, a sufficiently attractive palliative to accompany a princess torn from a convent; and due precau-

[54] *Ibid.*, III, Supplement, vi.

[55] Francisco de Mello e Torres, *Relaçam da Embaixada*, Lisbon, 1661. In a collection of *Relações de Embaixadas*, in the British Museum.

[56] Clarendon, *State Papers*, III, Supplement, ix.

[57] In 1688 the value of one crown was about five shillings gold (R. Holme, *Armory*, III, 28/2. Given in *New English Dictonary*).

tions were taken as to her privileges, financial and religious. The Portuguese guaranteed the English trade in the East Indies against the Dutch, and ceded Bombay permanently, while the English fleet was to aid the Portuguese in maintaining order in its East India possessions. England was granted the privilege of having resident merchants in Gôa, Cochim, and Dio in the East; in Bahia, Pernambuco, and Rio de Janeiro in Brazil; and in all the Portuguese West Indies. Any town or territory formerly belonging to Portugal which England might capture was to remain in its possession, except Mascate or a part of Ceylon, which were to be handed over to the original owners. In return England, for the first time in this series of treaties, promised more than its friendship, for troops and ships were to be furnished; the British guaranteed help if Lisbon or Oporto should ever be besieged, and a pledge was made never to make a treaty with Spain which would interfere with this promised assistance to Portugal. Nor would England ever deliver Dunkirk or Jamaica back to Spain, or refrain from aiding Portugal even to the extent of war with Castile. A secret clause promised to defend Portuguese possessions against all enemies.[58]

By the treaty of 1654 Portugal had become the virtual commercial vassal of England; by the present treaty that relation was maintained and concrete fruits were added. Bombay, with Madras and the station on the Hoogli, was to from one of the three points of the triangle whence the East India Company was to spread over India. The Portuguese East and West Indies trade was thrown open to the English and further advance was made in Brazil, while Charles was to get two millions of crowns pocket money, the largest dowry ever conferred in a European marriage settlement to that date. The price to be paid was a Catholic queen on the throne of England, two regiments of soldiers, and ten ships in Portugal, and a guaranty

---

[58] Chalmers, *Treaties*, II, 286-296. June 23, 1661. Reaffirmed by Article XXVI of the Treaty of 1810. For these negotiations see also; Prestage, *Diplomatic Relations*, p. 142-147; Guernsey Jones, "Oldest European Alliance," pp. 414 ff.; S. P. For., Port., 89/4 and 5; *Quadro Elementar*, XVII. The best source for the Conde da Ponte's activities between February 17 and May 15, 1661, is his letterbook in the Iberian Library of the Catholic University at Washington, D. C.

of armed support against any enemy which might attack—a good bargain which had revealed an amazing paradox; for Spain and the English Catholics had urged Charles to espouse a Protestant queen while Clarendon and the Puritans had zealously supported the cause of a Catholic.

In the meantime, Lord Sandwich in Portugal was hastening arrangements there. "Things have been dispatched here," he wrote,[59] "with greater haste than this people (I believe) have been known to make (though not so fast as I have desired and urged them into)." But when the princess reached Portsmouth,[60] trouble arose in regard to the form of the marriage ceremony since the queen was a Catholic and Charles an Anglican. Over Lord Russel's vehement protest, the king took her by the hand and declared her to be his wife; she did the like for him, declaring him her husband, and afterwards the Bishop of London read the words written on a piece of paper.[61] The Bishop of London declared the marriage legal and the king said that the question did not interest him, if the queen was satisfied.[62] On June 23, the treaty was declared ratified.

The agreement was consummated but, as before, dissatisfaction reigned. Queen Catherine led a dog's life, held up to ridicule by Charles and forced to accept the king's mistress, the Countess of Castlemain, as her own Lady of the Bedchamber. In former treaties Portugal had shown reluctance in paying fifty thousand pounds; now the two million crowns were slow of payment. Robert Southwell, sent three years after the treaty was signed as agent to Portugal, returned only after fifteen years of arduous service to claim his reward. By virtue of his signal service in recovering so effectively the residue of the marriage portion—sixty thousand pounds having entered, with the rest coming in every day—the king ordered the Duke of

[59] Clarendon, *State Papers*, III, Supplement, xx.

[60] *Quadro Elementar*, XVII, 236-256, devotes twenty touching pages to the picture of Catherine leaving Lisbon.

[61] Doctor Douglas, who saw the paper before it was destroyed, said the words were those of the Liturgy in joining the hands of the parties (Clarendon, *State Papers*, III, Supplement, xxi).

[62] *Ibid.*, xxi. The Earl of Portland to Clarendon, May 20 and 21, 1661.

Ormond to discharge Southwell of his quitrents in Ireland.[63] Moreover, mutiny broke out in Bombay; the soldiers complained and did more harm than good; Tangier was a costly gift to maintain; and the Portuguese Conde got froward and captious.

Nevertheless, Spain recognized Portugal as an independent state in 1668[64] and England forced the Dutch to leave Portugal alone.[65] The doors to the East and West Indies and to South America were opened to England while a base and a lucrative market in a strategic point in southern Europe were obtained. The alliance more than justified itself in the long run.

General opinion names the Methuen Treaty of 1703 as the principal alliance formed between England and Portugal, and it was customary in after years to refer to this treaty as the beginning of England's dominance over her ally and of the lucrative profit from her Portuguese relations. The seeds had been sown, however, in the complementary treaties of 1642-'54-'61 with profitable results for half a century. The importance of Portuguese affairs was enhanced by the Methuen Treaty in a way which would attract attention, as it created a new vested interest which became vociferous throughout the remainder of the century at any suggestion of a rapprochement with France. Portugal entered local English politics and got itself allied with a strong element in the City which would lose its lucrative business if England should turn from Portugal to France. In the former treaties of 1642-'54-'61, England could unite with France in negotiating and maintaining the clauses specified therein, but the Methuen Treaty decisively ran counter to France and would continue to do so as long as it was in force. The importance of Portugal was enhanced by the dignity of its opponent.

The Methuen Treaty was signed only after the customary vacillation on the part of the king of Portugal and the usual

[63] Warrant to James, Duke of Ormond, Lieut.-Gen. and Gov.-Gen. of Ireland, in Hist. Mss. Com., *Egmont Papers*, II, 89-90. The quitrents amounted to £75 a year.

[64] Borges de Castro, *Tratados*, I, 357 and 410.

[65] *Ibid.*, pp. 444 ff.

trump card of the English fleet. A base for operations in the Mediterranean and Spain was necessary to the allies then engaged in the War of the Spanish Succession, but Portugal had agreements with Spain and France and maintained a strict neutrality. In March of 1702, Anne declared her intention of waging war on a large scale both by sea and land, much to the relief of the Grand Alliance which had been formed against the Bourbons. In the middle of the next month, John Methuen, who was well versed in Portuguese affairs from long residence at the court of Lisbon, was dispatched to demand a positive answer of the king of Portugal whether he would recede from his alliance with France and Spain or persist therein.[66] War was declared at London and at the Hague in May, and Marlborough crossed to the Continent with the British army.

Methuen found no easy task on his arrival in Lisbon. For some time the French minister had been very importunate with his Portuguese Majesty to recognize the Pretender, James Edward, as the Prince of Wales, but his efforts had obtained no reply from the king other than "I have acknowledged one King of England already, and so long as he lives I shall acknowledge no other. I seek repose and love peace."[67] Little chance had he to enjoy peace with two kings centering the play around his section of the chessboard! Yet he stoutly affirmed his neutrality and maintained it so resolutely that even until the moment of the final presentation of the treaty in London by Methuen, rumor had it that he had refused to sign.[68] He sincerely endeavored to keep peace with both sides, for in February, 1702, before Methuen's arrival in Lisbon all of the ministers who had been turned out of his council for opposing the earlier treaties with France and Spain were restored to favor again,[69] while at King William's death the king of Portugal wrote Queen Anne that he intended to maintain inviolable his old treaties with Holland and England.[70]

---

[66] Narcissus Luttrell, *A Brief Historical Relation of State Affairs*, V, 163.

[67] *The Present State of Europe*, XIII, 35.

[68] Luttrell, *Historical Relation*, V, 265, 282, 286, 289-90.

[69] *Ibid.*, p. 78.

[70] *Ibid.*, p. 190.

A rift in the Portuguese-French relations appeared in July, however, when only four galleys and some few brigantines appeared instead of the forty men-of-war promised by France to protect the Portuguese coast. The king told the French ambassador to take them back home and called to mind Mazarin's desertion at the Treaty of the Pyrenees.[71] But as Portugal still refused to allow the English and the Dutch to use its harbors, clubs were declared trumps by England, and the fleet at the Isle of Wight was ordered to be victualled and to sail at once.[72] Fresh news from the south soon mentioned a noticeable change in the state of affairs in Lisbon due to Methuen's activities, although the Portuguese subjects still insisted on neutrality to protect their trade. Porto Carrero, the Spanish minister at Lisbon, after the manner of Batteville at the court of Charles II, helped Methuen by overplaying his hand, and sneered that "it was no more than could be expected from a rebel Duke of Bragança."[73]

In September Lord Godolphin wrote to Robert Harley that "the letters from our English Merchants at Lisbon as well as those from Methuen say that the King has publicly signified himself free from all engagements from France and resolved to live in entire friendship with England, so I reckon if we succeed at Cádiz, it will be our own fault if we do not come to an alliance with the rest of our confederates."[74] Unfortunately Sir George Rooke and the Duke of Ormond failed disgracefully in the attack on Cádiz. On the way home news came to them that the treasure galleons from the West Indies with a score of French and Spanish warships had slipped into Vigo. By an extraordinary feat of arms the British stormed the forts, broke the boom, destroyed the great fleet,[75] and wiped out the disgrace of Cádiz.

The argument was a sound one in the ears of the king of Portugal, for Vigo is a short day's trip (nowadays) north of

---

[71] Luttrell, *Historical Relation*, V, 280-281.

[72] *Ibid.*, p. 180.

[73] *Present State of Europe*, XIII, 321 and 433.

[74] *Portland Mss.*, IV, 46.

[75] G. M. Trevelyan, *England Under the Stuarts*, p. 483; Luttrell, *Relation*, V, 231.

Lisbon, and a victorious English fleet added weight to Methuen's point of view. Rumors were current in Lisbon by December that a treaty between the Grand Alliance and Portugal had been reached, and the breach between the court of Portugal and those of France and Spain was widening.[76] Yet when Methuen returned to England with the treaty, the belief was still current in London that the king of Portugal had resolved to stand neutral.[77] Unlike the previous treaties the Methuen agreement was negotiated and ratified in Lisbon before it was presented at London, and with such secrecy that even the best informed circles of London had no hint of the provisions stipulated. The final ratification was given by the queen at Windsor on July 12, 1703.[78]

The treaty renewed for another and a longer lease of life the system of alliance between Portugal and Britain originated by the triple agreements of 1642-1661. Old treaties were reaffirmed; the king of Portugal espoused the cause of Charles of Austria as king of Spain and agreed to maintain fifteen thousand men and accept subsidies for thirteen thousand more; he received twelve thousand auxiliary troops from abroad to swell his army. Various arrangements as to money, horses, men, munitions, and the command of the combined armies and navies occupied twenty articles of the defensive and twenty-nine of an offensive agreement in favor of Charles. The upshot of the treaty was simply that Portugal joined the Alliance and would serve as a base in southern Europe against Spain and France.

Had this been all, the Methuen Treaty would have no importance except in so far as it bore on the strategic operations of the war. Another element of great significance entered however. Between 1662 and 1701 the woolen export from England had increased[79] by over a million pounds sterling, or more than

[76] *Present State of Europe*, XIII, 472; XIV, 37, 78, 158, 196.

[77] Luttrell, *Relation*, V, 289.

[78] Chalmers, *Treaties*, II, 296-305 (Renewed by Article XXVI of the Treaty of 1810); *Commons Journals*, XIV, 224-226.

[79] The figures which follow are from a report by a special committee on the "Account of the trade of this Kingdom since the last session of Parliament," laid

fifty per cent. In 1698 woolen goods lacked but little of accounting for exactly one-half of the total value of the general exports. The wool business was important. But in 1700, despite the fact that the general exports increased, the woolens decreased in value. Complaints by producers of wool and by clothiers proclaimed the fall of the price of goods and their imminent ruin. Importation of wool from Ireland had jumped seven hundred per cent between 1693 and 1701; importation of superfine Spanish wool had increased; the demand for woolen articles on the Continent had decreased; and two and a half pages of closely typed words lamented the growth of manufactures in the colonies with the resultant fall in the demand for the English commodity. The Turkey Company reported[80] to a select committee in November that the importation of silks from India was the greatest enemy of their trade in Turkey as it killed the trade in woolens which amounted to more than two-thirds of the business of the company. The East India Company was bringing in silk enough for the whole kingdom, but India would not buy wool cloth. Woolens continued to decrease in value of exportation during 1702.[81] The woolen industry was facing a serious crisis.

In the meantime commerce with Portugal was undergoing another transition. In the early part of the seventeenth century, Brazilian tobacco and sugar shipped to England through Portugal supplanted spices from Portuguese Asiatic colonies as the principal articles sent to England. Virginia tobacco with the aid of the navigation laws gradually forced the Brazilian product from the English market, leaving sugar as the mainstay of Portuguese exchange. The planter of Brazil, using low marsh lands with horses, Negroes, and cattle much cheaper than could be had in English plantations, conveying his wood, canes, and sugar by water and grinding by the same power—conveniences not to be had on English plantations—was able to produce

before the House, November 20, 1702 (*Lords Journals*, XVII, 169, and Hist. Mss. Com., *Mss. of House of Lords*, 1702-4, V, 66-73) and signed by Dartmouth, Ph. Meadows, Wm. Blathwayt, Math. Prior, and others, to wit, the Board of Trade.

[80] *Mss. House of Lords*, V, 73.

[81] *Ibid.*, p. 334.

sugar thirty per cent. cheaper than the English planter.[82] But as the British sugar colonies developed under the navigation laws, the last product exportable in any great quantity from Portugal to England was cut off. By 1669 only 705 tuns of white sugar, worth £38,480, were brought from Portugal, not one-tenth of what had been the yearly importation before the rise of the English sugar plantations.[83] By 1690 the trade was limited to not more than two thousand chests of finest Brazilian sugar, worth about forty thousand pounds. One-quarter of the sugars received in exchange for English manufactures was not brought to England at all, but was carried to other European markets in British ships.[84] By 1700 the stream of commodities from the Portuguese dominions, flowing to England through the ports of Lisbon and Oporto, was well-nigh choked off.

English shipments of commodities to Portugal had remained practically the same from 1500 to 1700, textiles, hardware, and provisions being the staples. As the woolen industry rose toward the end of the seventeenth century, textiles became of paramount importance. But Portugal, imitating England's sugar policy, imposed a protective tariff, and began to develop a cloth industry of its own,[85] thus adding to the already serious woes of the English industry. The privileges gained so obstreperously by the triple treaties of 1642-1661 were of advantage only in case the Englishman could find a profitable interest in the Portuguese trade. These privileges could not create commerce; their purpose was to give England a commanding advantage in case such a trade existed. In 1700 it appeared that the active exchange which had gone on between the two allies for over two hundred years was about to cease, and this at the very time when the mines of Brazil were beginning to send a golden stream of riches across the seas to Lisbon.[86]

---

[82] *Tracts Relating to Various Trades,* Item 265, "The State of the English Sugar Trade with that of Portugal," British Museum. The tract dates about 1689.

[83] *Ibid.,* Item 266, "The Case of their Majesties Sugar Plantations," also undated, but about 1689. See also: A. B. W. Chapman, "Commercial Relations of England and Portugal, 1487-1807," *Trans. Roy. Hist. Soc.,* 3rd. Series, I, 164-169.

[84] *Tracts,* "State of English Sugar Trade."

[85] Chapman, *Commercial Relations,* 164-169, *passim.*

[86] J. P. Oliveira Martins, *O Brazil e as Colonias Portuguezas,* pp. 78-82.

There was one commodity, however, which could substitute for sugar as a basis of Portuguese shipments to England. Wine, "the nerve of commerce between England and France," had been prohibited[87] entrance into England during the wars, and Portuguese wines had been substituted. In 1697, English traders, judging that there would be a renewal of commerce with France, diminished their wine orders in Portugal with the result that exportation of English manufactures to that country likewise diminished. The next year wine orders increased, and so did the value of articles exported to Portugal. If the wine trade were extinguished, which would result if French wines were admitted on a par with Portuguese vintages, England's "so flourishing trade" in manufactured articles "must needs be extinguished" also, which would be "of ill consequence" in view of the fact that only one-fourth of the value of all English manufactures exported to Portugal was returned in goods and three parts in money. "What trade can be more coveted by England?"[88]

John Methuen met the crisis by his famous treaty concluded at Lisbon December 27, 1703,[89] a momentous document, refreshing in its brevity and simplicity. Portugal was forever to admit into Portugal the woolen cloths and the rest of the woolen manufactures of the Britons free of duty; in return for this concession, England was forever thereafter to "admit Portuguese wine into England in such a manner that even in war between England and France, or in peace, no greater duties or customs or charges by whatever title should be imposed on Portuguese wine than is demanded of French wine with one-third reduction."

The woolen business was saved, and the long argument over heavy Portuguese port wine and the lighter French vintage,

[87] I. W. & M. c. 3, 4.

[88] S. P. For., Foreign Ministers, 100/37, "Reflexions on the importance of trade with Portugal." Unsigned, undated document attached to document dated April 21, 1699, from the Portuguese ambassador in London. It was written in 1699.

[89] S. P. For., Treaty Papers, 103/58. Ratification by Portugal, December 27, 1703; by England, May 6, 1704. A copy of the treaty in Portuguese (and Latin) is given in Castro, *Tratados*, II, 192-198.

which lasted throughout the century, was begun. A stream of woolens was to flow from England to Portuguese possessions through the gateway of Lisbon and Oporto, where trade was admitted. In time, Brazil came to absorb the greater part of the stream. The return came to England largely in the shape of wines from Portugal and gold from Brazil. By the treaties of 1642-'54-'61 England secured its privileged position in Portuguese commerce; by the Methuen Treaty Portugal tied England to its side and an economic basis for commercial exchange favorable to both contracting parties was worked out. Britain could not renounce Portugal without running counter to the wool and wine interests; yet as long as it hung on to its ally, France was irritated. England manoeuvred itself into a position wherein it was forced to choose between Portugal and France instead of being free to favor either as occasion demanded. Portugal and England were united against France by new ties of commercial advantage and new vested interests arose.

CHAPTER II

A PERIOD OF STRESS AND READJUSTMENT
1703-1800

By the opening of the eighteenth century, England had established its preëminence in Portuguese commerce. The strong English economic interests, strengthened by the treaty of 1703, were enjoying special privileges obtained by the series of agreements concluded during the previous half century. The next hundred years, however, witnessed a conflict between certain forces which tended to destroy those firmly intrenched interests and other influences of a military and economic nature which tended to maintain the Portuguese alliance. During the first decades of the eighteenth century the economic forces of union triumphed decisively in the rejection of the French Commercial Treaty of 1713; by 1786 economic pressure reversed that decision, and England chose France in preference to Portugal; but at the turn of the century, war and new economic forces brought reconciliation between the old allies. The colony of Brazil was an important factor in this conflict.

John Methuen won Portugal to the Grand Alliance in 1703 by treaties of offense and defense. During the entire war the Portuguese ports served as bases for the English navy in its operations in the Mediterranean and South-Atlantic waters.[1] From a naval standpoint, Portugal was a success; but as military allies, the Portuguese were a constant tribulation to English commanders and ministers.[2] When Portugal began treating secretly for a separate peace with France[3] in 1711, the English

[1] Able Boyer, *Annals of Anne*, IV, 137; V, 314; VII, 178-179.

[2] *Ibid.*, IV, 130, 163; V, 308-309; VI, 31; VIII, 93-95; IX, 110-117; Hist. Mss. Comm., *Bath Papers*, I, 71, 84, 176; Cobbett, *Parliamentary History*, VI, 936-993.

[3] Able Boyer, *The Political State of Great Britain*, II, 313-316.

withdrew their troops, leaving the Portuguese "to stand on their own bottoms." The Marquis of Bey, seeing his opportunity, broke into Portugal with a formidable Spanish force, at a time when that country was destitute of its main support. But the Portuguese defended themselves more vigorously than at any time during the war and drove the Spaniards out by the battle of Campo Mayor. Almost simultaneously with the arrival of the news of this victory at Lisbon, the Brazil fleet reached port, very richly laden, and an heir was born to the throne. In Portugal the war ended in a blaze of happiness.[4]

At Utrecht Portugal fared well.[5] At the end of the conference, besides the usual terms such as those relating to the exchange of prisoners and return of property and territory seized, Portugal secured from France the renunciation of its claims to the north bank of the mouth of the Amazon and to any rights of navigation on that river.[6] This clause, which was of the utmost importance to Brazil, was guaranteed directly by England.[7]

Equally as significant was the sixth article of the treaty exchanged with Spain at Utrecht, which provided that Colonia do Sacramento should be ceded forever to the Crown of Portugal.[8] Colonia, a town on the north bank of the River Plate above the present site of Montevideo and almost straight across from Buenos Aires, had been a thorn in the flesh of the Spanish governors of that region. The Brazilians had founded the colony mainly to establish rights to all land north of the river, but it also served admirably as a place of secure deposit in the very heart of the Spanish colonies for the smuggling trade of Portugal, England, France, and Holland. In 1701 Portuguese pro-

[4] *Ibid.*, IV, 342 ff.

[5] The conference adjourned for three days of celebration when the news of the birth of the heir reached Utrecht (Boyer, *Political State*, V, 25).

[6] David MacPherson, *Annals of Commerce*, III, 35.

[7] Article XXIV of Treaty of Peace and Friendship with France concluded at Utrecht, March 1-April 11, 1713. Chalmers, *Treaties*, I, 385.

[8] Bernard Moses, *Spain's Declining Power in South America, 1790-1806*, p. 29. For the history of Colonia, from its founding in 1680 to 1713, see: José de Charlevoix, *Historia del Paraguay*, Tomo IV, Libro 13, pp. 67-96, 197-203; Robert Southey, *History of Brazil*, II, 570-573; Calvo, *Collección completa de los tratados de la América Latina*, I, 114 and II, 53.

tests, backed by England and France, forced Spain to return the colony, which had been seized by the Spanish governor of Buenos Aires. During the war it had again fallen into Spanish hands; but England, at the insistence of its ally and mindful of the commercial advantages which the possession of the place afforded, urged that the town with enough territory for its defense be given up to the Portuguese. Philip V was forced to consent, and Portugal obtained the special guaranty of England to the terms of the treaty with Spain.[9]

In this manner Portugal reaped its reward for signing the two treaties of offense and defense negotiated by John Methuen in 1703. The two famous commercial articles concluded in December of the same year had a more spectacular fate, for they were largely instrumental in defeating the important Anglo-French treaty of commerce of 1713.

At first glance it is surprising that a country only a little larger than Scotland and decadent almost to stagnation after a glorious colonial period, should have competed successfully for British trade against France. A more careful scrutiny, however, reveals important factors supporting Anglo-Portuguese trade relations.

In the first place, there was a fairly brisk trade between Portugal and the English colonies in America. Lisbon was a good market for pitch, for early in the war several gentlemen of the Pennsylvania Company petitioned the Commissioners of Trade and Plantations for a bounty on some four hundred barrels of pitch and tar which they might have sold in Portugal for fifty shillings a barrel when their ship stopped on its way from the Carolinas. In England, they complained, they could not afford to sell for less than forty shillings per barrel unless her Majesty helped them.[10] By 1714 a yearly average of six thousand barrels of rice was shipped from the Carolinas directly to Portugal.[11] Lisbon lay on the regular route of ships

---

[9] Chalmers, *Treaties*, II, 306-307; Calvo, *Collección*, II, 115; Southey, *History of Brazil*, III, 131-140; R. Altamira, *Historia de España*, III, 179 ff. and IV, 110.

[10] *Journal of Commissioners for Trade and Plantations*, I, 156.

[11] *Ibid.*, p. 156.

going from England to the British colonies in America and served as a provisioning station.[12] In addition, the fish trade between Newfoundland and Portugal in the first years of the century was considerable,[13] and a free trade in everything except enumerated articles could be carried on between the English colonies in America and the Portuguese Madeira Islands, since these were considered to be in Africa and did not fall within the application of the navigation laws. Consequently Madeira wine poured into the colonies, until by 1775 the taste for it was general; the English officers returning after that date set the fashion for it in England.[14] South Carolina alone took yearly 230 to 250 pipes of wine from the islands.[15] In exchange any surplus of corn in the plantations went to the Madeiras.[16] Usually one-half of the bill for wines was paid in British goods and the other half by bills of exchange on Lisbon,[17] although sometimes the proportion rose to two-thirds payment in English woolens and only one-third in letters of exchange.[18]

Besides this trade in naval stores, rice, woolens, and fish from the English plantations in America to Portugal, there was a lucrative export business of lumber from the northern colonies,[19] and six to ten thousand hogsheads of tobacco a year passed through England to Portuguese ports.[20] Considerable quantities of wine, brandy, salt, oil, French linens, and other articles, were carried to Newfoundland by English ships that fetched salt from Portugal. On the banks these commodities were exchanged for tobacco, sugar, and other enumerated articles, brought there by New England vessels. This contraband was then carried back to Lisbon.[21] Also salt was obtained on the Portuguese Islands of May and Bonavista, a trade which required the full time of some 120 English vessels in 1713.[22]

In the second place, the direct trade between England and

[12] *Ibid.*, pp. 69, 395.

[13] *Ibid.*, p. 427.

[14] W. Cunningham, *Growth of English Industry and Commerce*, Modern Times, I, 460.

[15] *Jour. of Comrs. Trade*, IV, 202.

[16] *Ibid.*, II, 74.

[17] *Ibid.*, IV, 210.

[18] *Ibid.*, IV, 300.

[19] *Ibid.*, II, 274; IV, 328.

[20] *Ibid.*, I, 251.

[21] *Ibid.*, I, 465.

[22] *Ibid.*, III, 94.

Portugal was important. An economic basis for a commercial exchange which was favorable to both of the contracting parties had been worked out in the 1642-1703 period. On the one hand, the Portuguese proprietors of vineyards and manufacturers of wine, who were prospering under Methuen's solution to the crisis of 1700, supported the activities of the British merchants in Portugal. On the other hand, while Portugal itself absorbed a large amount of English woolens, the passage of goods between England and the Portuguese colonies through the ports of Portugal where trade was permitted was favorable to the establishment of English factories at these points.

The complementary treaties of 1642-'54-'61, by granting an extraordinary amount of liberty to these organizations of British merchants, had become the Magna Carta of the Portugal trade. After consultation with the Portugal merchants, one Milner, whose brother was consul general at Lisbon, insisted in 1714 before the Commissioners for Trade and Plantations that these merchants emphatically desired the confirmation of the whole treaty of 1654.[23] These factories developed rapidly until they became a powerful group with influence in Portugal and London.[24] As a matter of fact, at the beginning of the eighteenth century practically all of the carrying trade of Portugal was done through English hands.[25] In view of the extensive commerce between Lisbon and her colonies, this was a lucrative business for the Britisher.

After 1703 business with Portugal increased amazingly. From 1675 to 1696 France sent an average of fifteen thousand tuns of wine[26] to England, and Portugal only three hundred. In 1712

[23] *Jour. of Comrs. Trade*, II, 535.

[24] As early as 1654 the claims sent in by these factories for damages during Admiral Blake's blockade amounted to £10,000 from Lisbon companies and £12,500 from Oporto companies for damages to their business. One company alone entered a claim for £5,000. Claims for English ships engaged in their trade and seized by Blake amounted to £23,614. With allowance for exaggeration, these figures indicate a real prosperity for these companies.

[25] Chapman, "Commercial Relations of England and Portugal, 1487-1807," p. 168.

[26] 31½ old wine gallons to the barrel, two barrels to the hogshead, two hogsheads to the pipe, and two pipes to the tun.

England imported 585,954 tuns of Portuguese wines and a little over eight thousand of French wine.[27] The export of English woolens quadrupled in a few years and included colored cloths, druggets, hats, and such manufactures as had been excluded formerly.[28] Duties imposed by Portugal were evaded by abatements and other means until they "were reduced very low and the merchants made very easy therein,"[29] while English families, settled by special permission in Brazil as resident traders, were of great advantage to English commerce.[30] In the ten years of the war English exports to Portugal jumped from three hundred thousand pounds sterling a year to over a million whereas the imports from Portugal grew from two hundred thousand to a maximum of four hundred thousand.[31] By gold brought from Brazil the Portuguese made up the difference between the four hundred thousand pounds worth of goods sent to England and the million due for merchandise received. Under the conditions of trade existing after 1703, Portugal was shipping from five hundred thousand to a million pounds sterling of gold a year into England. One estimate places the amount of bullion imported from Portugal as high as fifty thousand pounds a week.[32] It is apparent that with such a trade there would be created a powerful set of interests intent on maintaining their business.

The woolen industry was the basis of this trade, and its ramifications were many. The merchants and shipping interests were at the top of the pyramid. Beneath them were the manufacturers of woolen cloths such as bays, broadcloths, draperies, and white goods; the dyers, packers, and setters; the manufac-

---

[27] Oscar Browning, "The Treaty of Commerce between England and France in 1786," *Trans. Roy. Hist. Soc.*, N. S., II, 352.

[28] Chapman, "Commercial Relations," p. 171.

[29] *Jour. of Comrs. Trade*, II, 535.

[30] *Ibid.*, III, 179-180.

[31] Chapman, "Commercial Relations," p. 171. Ireland carried on an export trade to Lisbon of over £200,000 a year (*Jour. of Comrs. Trade*, I, 427).

[32] Cunningham, *Growth of English Industry*, I, 460-461. In Ireland the gold currency was said to consist almost entirely of Portuguese pieces, received in exchange for cattle, bacon, linen, and dairy produce, staples of Irish trade with Portugal (Chapman, "Commercial Relations," p. 172).

turers of rugs, stockings, belts, hats, blankets, and serges. Behind these interests were the large landowners whose profits from raw wool mounted with the price of the manufactured article. Linked with both the manufacturer and the wool producer was the newly created banking group. These interests were scattered in the city of London, and its vicinity; in the towns of Plymouth, Gloucester, Leeds, and Worcester; in counties such as Essex, Devon, Suffolk, and Norfolk.[33] Together their influence possessed something of the power of a Standard Oil Company or a United States Steel Corporation of to-day.

A third factor tending to favor Anglo-Portuguese trade relations was British fear of French competition in the home market. In the time of the Stuarts the English court had favored[34] trade with France for the sake of the large revenue which a tariff on importations would bring. Under William and Mary, however, a bill was passed prohibiting all trade with France for "it hath beene found by long experience that the Importing of French Wines, Vinegar,] Brandy, Linnen, Silks, Salt, Paper, and other Commodities of the Growth, Product, or Manufacture of France or of the territories or Dominions of the French King, hath much exhausted the treasure of this Nation, lessened the value of the native commodities and manufactures thereof, and greatly impoverished the English Artificers and Handycrafts and caused great detriment to this Kingdom in generale. . . ."[35] This complete prohibition lasted until 1710. Houblon and Papillon drew up a document in support of the bill, showing that England, besides suffering disastrous competition in her home markets, was the loser by a million pounds sterling a year in her trade with France.[36] Colbert began his

[33] *Commons Journals*, XVII. See various petitions, pp. 315 ff.

[34] James had removed (I James II, cc. 6, 7) the prohibition set on French trade under Charles II (29, 30 Ch. II, c. par. 70).

[35] I W. & M. c. 3, 4.

[36] This document was published again in 1713 at the time of the French treaty crisis, by Boyer in his *Political State*, V, 419. Sir John Houblon (died 1712) was a merchant interested in the Spanish trade and was the first governor of the Bank of England. He served in various governmental positions such as member of the Admiralty Commission, the Victualling Office, and others. Thomas Papillon (died 1702) was a merchant who served on the Board of Trade and on the Direct-

revival of French commerce soon after 1661, imposed his prohibitory tariffs six years later, and put his rigid mercantilist theory of commerce into practice during the succeeding years.[37] Wars aggravated the rivalry. By 1713 the commercial and industrial interests of England were as opposed to French trade as they were enthusiastic for Portuguese commerce.

Thus in 1713, due to the trade carried on between Portugal and the British colonies, the advantages of the direct trade between England and the Portuguese possessions through Lisbon and Oporto, and the fear of French competition in the English markets, the opinion was firmly intrenched among a powerful class of Englishmen that the Portugal trade was "at present the most advantageous that we drove anywhere."[38] Methuen had opened a large foreign demand for manufactured goods and stimulated employment of labor at home, and returns from Portugal came to England largely in the form most necessary for restoring the currency and most convenient for carrying on the great European conflict.

A fourth factor in the crisis of 1713 was the state of English politics, for the Opposition used these economic forces as an instrument with which to attack the ministry. Any attempt to explain the decisive triumph of the Portuguese trade over its French rival which fails to take into consideration the struggle going on for the control of the English Government will be wide of the mark. The Opposition defeated the French treaty by arousing the fears of that powerful class which were profiting by an economic situation based on trade with Portugal.

On May 8, 1713, the queen's message respecting the treaties of peace and commerce which had been concluded at Utrecht was read to the Commons and the agreements presented. The forty-one articles of the French treaty of commerce were "in

---

orate of the East India Company. He also served as Victualler for the Navy (*Dict. Nat. Biog.*).

[37] L. B. Packard, *The Commercial Revolution. 1400-1776*, pp. 71 ff.; Cunningham, *The Growth of English Industry*, I, 458 ff.

[38] Cobbett, *Parl. Debates*, VI, 1211. MacPherson quotes contemporary opinion which stated that the Portugal trade was the "very best branch of all our European commerce" (*Annals*, III, 30).

the customary form" except for the eighth and ninth articles which were so "extraordinary in themselves" and "occasioned so great a stir and uneasiness at that time, as to bring the whole treaty of commerce to miscarry then, and ever since."[39] Article 8 gave most favored nation privileges to France in England; by the ninth a law was to be passed that no higher duties should be paid for goods brought from France than those payable on like goods imported from any other country in Europe.[40] The high protective tariff wall erected against France in favor of English manufacturers and traders was to be demolished, and the foundation of the Portuguese trade as established by the commercial articles of the Methuen Treaty destroyed. Henry St. John, Lord Bolingbroke, secretary of state, who represented England in the negotiation at Paris, demonstrated in the terms of the treaty his inclination toward the Church and the gentry and his opposition to the moneyed class. The activities of the war, favorable to the profiteers of the war party, made difficult the position of the ministry under Robert Harley, Earl of Oxford. The land and malt tax weighed on the landed men, and a swarm of duties on the necessaries of life came home to every household. Harley's majority in the Commons was based in large measure on a wave of feeling hostile to the war and the moneyed class and favorable to the Church. Attention had to be paid to the feelings of this group in making the treaty. To strengthen their position St. John and Harley hoped to create a mercantile group in their own interest in the City, then largely hostile to them.[41] As a result, the existing economic system, which was pro-Portuguese and anti-French, was seriously threatened.

The project aroused immediate opposition. Article 9 of the treaty called for a law to reduce the tariff on French goods to the level of duties levied on the goods of any other country. On

---

[39] MacPherson, *Annals*, III, 472-473.

[40] Chalmers, *Treaties*, I, 390-424. Articles 8 and 9, pp. 396-398.

[41] St. John to Harley, October 11 and November 6, 1708, Hist. Miss. Comm., *Bath Papers*, I, 191-94; Keith Feiling, *History of the Tory Party, 1614-1714*, pp. 433, 405, 429; Trevelyan, *England under the Stuarts*, p. 511.

the same day that a bill to this effect was introduced for the first reading,[42] a petition against the measure was presented by the powerful Levant Company. On June 4, the day set for the second reading, thirteen petitions from London, Worcester, Gloucester, Trowbridge, Liverpool, and the counties of Essex and Suffolk came in. From then on an ever-increasing volume of objections came up from every side.

The arguments against the project as shown in the petitions were more or less the same. The export of woolens to Potrugal depended on the importation of Portuguese wines; if the French treaty went through, Portuguese wines would be supplanted both because the Englishman liked French wines better[43] and because the distance would add freight charges that would make the Portuguese wines dearer than the French. Portugal in retaliation, would renew its woolen industries and prohibit the entrance of English goods. If French silks were allowed to enter, the English silk industry, grown up under protection, would go to the wall, carrying with it the Italian and Levant trades, for the basis of that commerce was the exchange of raw silk for manufactured woolens. A still worse calamity threatened, for the French woolen industry, developed under French protection and carried on with cheaper labor and less expensive raw materials, would compete successfully with English goods in the home market. And finally a trade with Portugal which brought in from four hundred thousand to a million pounds sterling of gold and silver a year would be exchanged for a trade with France which would drain over a million out of the country in the same length of time. Moreover "many thousands of poor Manufacturers would be undone . . . and many thousands of poor Families must become a Burthen to their respective parishes, and the value of lands of England would sink to a great degree and taxes rise."[44]

---

[42] *Commons Journals*, XVII, 386.

[43] Swift to Stella, *Journals*, February 18, 1711; Earl Stanhope, *History of the Reign of Queen Anne*, p. 112.

[44] See various petitions presented to the House of Commons, *Commons Journals*, XVII, 391-429; Cobbett, *Parl. Debates*, VI, 1211-1213.

As a matter of fact, that pyramid of special interests built up under protection against France and based on the woolen trade with Portugal and its ramifications, was seriously menaced. Using that threat as an incentive, the Opposition found little difficulty in setting up a hue and cry against the bill and the ministry. Such momentum was acquired that when the crisis came on June 18, the debate lasted from three in the afternoon till eleven at night. The turning point came when Sir Thomas Hanmer changed sides and took with him two members holding government positions. The City representatives, who had been elected as supporters of the ministry, and the Scotch members voted against the bill irrespective of party. On a vote to engross the bill, the tellers for the Noes counted 194 and the Yeas 185. And so it passed in the negative.[45] That night the London drapers, mercers, and weavers, "overjoyed at the failure of the bill," staged a big celebration with illuminations and bonfires.[46]

Thus the Portugal trade, chartered under the triple treaties of 1642-'54-'61 and founded on the two short articles of the Methuen Treaty of 1703, was largely instrumental in defeating the commercial agreement with France and furnished the club with which the Opposition belabored Harley's ministry. The economic forces of the period tended toward union between England and Portugal, and the triumph was decisive in maintaining what to-day is the oldest existing European alliance.

The treaty of commerce with France in September, 1786, offers a curious parallel to the projected agreement of 1713.[47] In both, the Portugal trade was the chief factor used in oppo-

---

[45] For details of the political battle which arose over the treaty, see: *Jour. Comrs. Trade*, II, 34, 68, 355-357, 371-372; Cobbett, *Parl. History*, VI, 1170, 1211-1213; *Commons Journals*, XVII, 310, 314-315, 347-358, 386; Swift, *Journal to Stella*, April 7 and 8, 1713; Feiling, *A History of the Tory Party*, pp. 417-423.

[46] Cobbett, *Parl. Debates*, VI, 1223-1224; *Commons Journals*, XVII, 429-430; Boyer, *Political State*, V, 444.

[47] Twice in the intervening seventy-odd years Portugal demanded England's attention: In 1735-'37 Walpole prevented a war between Portugal and Spain which would have involved England. In 1762 Portugal was forced into the Seven Years' War and fared well at the Peace of Paris. In both of these cases the Spanish-Portuguese frontiers in America played important parts. See Chapter V.

sition to the legislative action needed to make the terms of the treaties effectual. On both occasions a coalition party fallen from power attempted to drive out the ministry by defeating the commercial policy adopted by the agreements. In both cases a long economic development which determined the outcome preceded the crisis. In 1713 the opposition won and the Portugal trade triumphed. In 1786 the ministry was easily victorious and England turned from Portugal to France. The reversal was due in the first place to the changing state of England's commercial relations with Portugal during these seventy years, and in the second place to the rise of a new group of vested interests in England, whose profit dictated a new commercial policy.

Although in 1713 the opinion was quite universal that the Portugal trade "was the very best branch of all" England's "European commerce,"[48] friction between the two countries soon developed. Frequent complaints came up before the Commissioners for Trade and Plantations. Two years after the peace, the factors of Blackwell Hall complained that their shipment of coarse woolens to Portugal had fallen off to one-fifth of what it had been formerly.[49] Before the war was over the English merchants in Lisbon sent in repeated representations against the Irish traders in that city for their refusal to contribute toward the expenses of the factory while they enjoyed the benefits of that institution.[50] The Assiento Contract with Spain (1713) suggested a similar arrangement with Portugal, and that matter was well discussed by the Commissioners.[51] Since Portugal refused to grant a monopoly of the slave traffic to Portuguese possessions, participation by England in that trade in which so many nations already shared, could result only in increasing the number of Negroes carried to Brazil, with the consequent fall in the price of slaves. The Brazilian sugar planter could then undersell the product of the British sugar colonies in European markets. The Commissioners therefore decided against any agitation to share the Portuguese slave

[48] MacPherson, *Annals*, III, 30.
[49] *Jour. Comrs. Trade*, III, 95-96.
[50] *Ibid.*, II, 269, 271-272, 287.
[51] *Ibid.*, II, 490, 491, 492.

trade.[52] By 1726 the English African Company was demanding forts as protection against the Portuguese whose jealousy of the growing strength of that company had led them to destroy the English fort at Cabinda.[53] Moreover, after the discovery of gold and diamonds in Brazil, Portugal tightened its restrictions on contacts between the colony and other nations with uncomfortable results to the resident foreigners. The offer of Portugal to expel the French traders resident in Brazil, if the British would withdraw voluntarily,[54] was rejected by the Commissioners for Trade and Plantations, however, and English families continued to live in Brazil under rights acquired by the 1654 treaty despite Portugal's desire to "abridge" the English "as much as possible."[55]

In fact, the fabulous quantities of gold and diamonds arriving at Lisbon from Brazil[56] incited the English to import the metal and stones clandestinely. In 1732 the king of Portugal ordered all the letters arriving by the Brazil fleet to be opened "under pretence of discovering who had brought gold in a clandestine manner . . . which put the People of Business in great fear."[57] The king got 2880 pounds weight of gold and many diamonds. The penalty for smuggling gold was confiscation with banish-

---

[52] *Jour. Comrs. Trade*, II, 491-492.

[53] *Ibid.*, V, 234, 237-238, 242, 268.

[54] S. P. For. Port., 89/64. Letter of August 22, 1766. Resident merchant privileges in Brazil had been granted the French by the treaty of 1667.

[55] *Jour. Comrs. Trade*, III, 179-180.

[56] Oliveira Martins estimates that D. João V (1706-1750) received about 130,000,000 cruzados (over $50,000,000) from gold works and 40,000,000 cruzados ($16,000,000) from diamonds (*Hist. de Port.*, II, 151). The fifths due the crown rendered about $2,000,000 annually; some think double that sum (Oliveira Martins, *O Brazil*, p. 84, footnote). Fifths were paid on about half the production, the rest leaving Brazil clandestinely (*ibid.*, p. 83, footnote). The fleet from Rio in 1753 was thought to have brought gold, and silver, and goods worth $15,000,000 (Keller, *Colonization*, p. 166, note). See Oliveira Martins *O Brazil*, Chap. VII and Keller, *Colonization*, pp. 149-153, 165-167 for brief discussions of Brazilian gold mines. Humboldt estimates that from the date of discovery to 1803, there came in gold from Portuguese America, 6,290,000 gold marcs (Castilian weight) and from Spanish America, 3,625,000 gold marcs (*Essai Politique sur le Royaume de la Noveau Espagne*, II, 645).

[57] Hon. Charles Compton to Lord Wilmington, Lisbon, January 12, 1732, Hist. Mss. Comm., *Marquis of Townshend Papers*, pp. 351-352.

ment or the gallows, yet the English escaped by relying on the judges conservators.

The friction which arose between the two countries from these minor sources became acute during the administration of one of the strongest men Portugal has ever produced, F. José de Carvalho e Mello, of humble parentage but later Marquis of Pombal. Made secretary of state for foreign affairs and of war on August 2, 1750, three days after the death of D. João V, he soon became absolute head of the government with complete ascendancy over D. José, the new king.[58]

The man who was to rule Portugal for twenty-seven years after the manner of Cardinal Richelieu in France held decided views in regard to the English alliance and influence. He wrote that, at the time of the Lisbon earthquake,[59] the

> Portuguese Monarchy was at its last gasp. The English had firmly bound the nation in a state of dependence. They had conquered it without the inconvenience of a conquest. . . . Portugal was powerless and without vigour, and all her movements were regulated by the desires of England. . . . In 1754 Portugal scarcely produced anything towards her own support. Two-thirds of her physical necessities were supplied by England. . . . England had become mistress of the entire commerce of Portugal, and all the trade of the country was carried on by her agents. The English were at the same time the furnishers and the retailers of all the necessaries of life that the country required. Having a monopoly of everything, no business was carried on but through their hands. . . .
>
> The English came to Lisbon to monopolize even the commerce of Brazil. The entire cargo of the vessels that were sent thither, and consequently the riches that were returned in exchange, belonged to them. . . . These foreigners, after having acquired immense fortunes, disappeared on a sudden, carrying with them the riches of the country.[60]

[58] Mello was born 1699 and died 1782. He became Conde de Oeiras in 1759 and Marquis of Pombal in 1770. He was ambassador to London, 1738-1745. He was dismissed from office, March 4, 1777, by D. Maria I, successor to D. José. For a brief sketch of his life see *La Grande Encyclopédie*, XXXVII, 177-178.

[59] November 1, 1755.

[60] John A. Smith, Count da Carnota, *Memoirs of the Marquis of Pombal*, I, 85, 112-116.

Cromwell's treaty, negotiated before the discovery of gold in Brazil, continued, in the opinion of the minister, to bind Portugal to England after the gold mines had brought European prominence to Pombal's country. The "former manufactures of Portugal were destroyed. . . . Every article of clothing the" Portuguese nation "required was drawn from England, to the amount of twenty millions of cruzados annually."[61] When the rush to the mines began, Brazil ceased to send agricultural products to supply the needs of the mother country, allowing England to take over the provision trade in addition to the clothing business. "Every measure of political change was predetermined by the Cabinet of London."[62]

Moreover the marquis could see no advantage to his country from the influx of gold from Brazil.

> Gold and silver are fictitious riches . . . the more they are multiplied, the less is their real value. . . . The Negroes that work in the mines of Brazil must be clothed by England, by which the value of their produce becomes relative to the price of cloth. To work the mines, it is necessary to have a large capital expended on slaves. If this sum be twenty millions, the interest, which is one million, independent of the cost of extraction, must be the first money paid for this produce. Add to this the food and clothing for more than an hundred thousand persons, blacks and whites, which the mines carry to Brazil, which food is not to be had in the colony, but must be purchased from foreigners. Lastly, to supply the physical wants of the country, which since the discovery of the mines had lost its arts and manufactures, all the gold became the property of other nations. What riches, great God! the possession of which involves the ruin of the state![63]

These words of the man who ruled his country with an iron hand present a vivid picture of England's supremacy in the dominions of Portugal during the first half of the eighteenth century. With due allowance made for exaggeration by one who was pleading a cause, it is clear that Portugal was the vir-

---

[61] About £10,000,000, according to Smith's estimate, given in footnote (Smith, *Memoirs of Pombal*, I, 117).

[62] *Ibid.*, I, 117-120.

[63] *Ibid.*, I, 123, 125-126.

tual commercial vassal of England. To a man of Pombal's intelligence and spirit, such a condition could not continue. As soon as he rose to power, he began his effective struggle to curtail England's power in Portuguese dominions.

By the law of October 30, 1752, the English judge conservator was forbidden to grant mandates to impede the execution of writs or orders issued by the ordinary courts, under penalty of suspension from office for six months. Pombal thus repealed the right granted by the Charter of English Privileges in 1647 and confirmed by the treaty of 1654, whereby the English subject could not be arrested without the consent of the judge conservator.[64] The new trading companies of Grão Pará and of Pernambuco, the Alto Douro Wine Company, and the statutes of the newly organized *Junta do Commercio*, created Portuguese judges conservators whose authority superseded that of the English conservator. The power of these new courts was so extreme that Britishers had first to litigate extensively as to jurisdiction—whether the case lay in the British or the new conservatorial courts—before they could bring suit even for debt.[65] In this way Pombal struck at the very roots of the privileges of the English in Portugal. He now turned to commerce.

By a decree dated June 7, 1755, the Portuguese trading company of Grão Pará and Maranhão was established. Every ship which sailed from Portugal to the Brazilian provinces of Grão Pará and Maranhão had to belong to the company and had to sail from Lisbon; no ship but that of the company could enter or leave any port of these provinces; no person who did not belong to the company could send, take, or introduce any goods whatever into them, although the company was prohibited from selling by retail in the colonies; and the exclusive right to import slaves was granted to the company.[66] In 1759 another company was instituted on the same basis to trade with the provinces of Parahiba and Pernambuco.[67] Both or-

[64] S. P. For., Port., 89/64.

[65] *Ibid.*

[66] Ignacio de Freitas, *Collecção Chronologica de Leis Extravagantes*, III, 432-465. Capitulações 17, 20, 28, 29, and 30 of the *alvará*.

[67] S. P. For., Port., 89/64.

ganizations had conservators to decide cases arising from action by the companies under their statutes.

The year following the establishment of the Company of Grão Pará, Pombal set up a *Junta do Commercio*.[68] It had power to regulate all affairs connected with commerce, to prevent and punish smuggling, and to grant or refuse license for opening retail shops. The members of the *junta* had power to visit and inspect those retail shops already open, in order to check abuses of smuggling and the ownership of two or more shops by the same person. In many cases the shops, operating under different names, really belonged to one individual and he a foreigner, although such double ownership was contrary to law. This measure was directed especially against the English, because they carried on the principal commerce and engrossed much of the profit of the retail trade.[69] As the *junta* maintained a conservatorial court with authority superior to the English tribunal and as the matters falling under the cognizance of the *junta* involved English merchants, a clash between the two courts was inevitable.

To curtail further the trade enjoyed by the English, the *junta* declared contraband a long list of articles.[70] Tanned leather was prohibited entrance in 1758. New duties were added, such as an additional two per cent. at Oporto to pay for the Portuguese frigates which accompanied the ships of the Alto Douro Wine Company on their voyage to Brazil. British merchants complained that the king granted royal letters of protection or moratoriums to his subjects who owed money to the English and prevented the latter from bringing suit for recovery. The Portuguese government often seized goods for the king's troops,

---

[68] Ignacio de Freitas, *Collecção*, III, 541, gives the *alvará*, dated December 16, 1756. The statutes defining the powers and duties of the *junta* follow, pp. 543-582. The *junta* was substituted for the old Board of Trade, dismissed by Pombal for inefficiency and corruption, at the time of the organization of the new *junta*.

[69] Smith, *Memoirs of Pombal*, I, 298-299.

[70] The Pragmatick or Sumptuary Law of 1749 prohibited the importation into Portugal of certain articles named as luxuries. The *junta* now used this law as grounds for prohibiting importation of many articles which the English did not consider as coming under the title of luxuries. S. P. For., Port., 89/64.

or household, and even for convents and monasteries, from the English proprietor, who received no pay or payment only after an extended delay, while accounting houses and homes of the English were entered by common officers of the law without the proper order from the British conservator.[71] Pombal thus conducted a vigorous campaign against English privileges and English commercial supremacy.

There yet remained one branch of commerce which Pombal considered to be in need of regulation. The establishment of the Portuguese wine business on a firm basis had been Portugal's share in the bargain of 1703. Yet by the middle of the century English merchants, established at Oporto, bought the wines directly from the farmer at prices set by themselves and so reaped the profit from that trade.[72] A delegation of the principal husbandmen of the Upper Douro region and some inhabitants of Oporto delivered to Pombal in 1756 a statement of the conditions of the wine trade. By holding a monopoly of the middleman and shipping business, the commission asserted, the English had pushed the price so low that utter misery resulted for the wine growers.[73] Consequently after an investigation, the marquis issued the *alvará* establishing the Alto Douro Wine Company[74] (August 31, 1756) for the purpose of regulating the wine business of that region. As the Alto Douro district was the center of the vineyard areas of Portugal, the company in reality was to regulate the wine business of the country.

By sections 29, 30, and 31 of the statutes of the company, the exportation of wines from Portugal was limited to the production of the Alto Douro area. Only wine with a permit could be sent down from Alto Douro to the port of Oporto;

---

[71] S. P. For., Port., 89/64. The complaints are taken from a memorandum of merchants living in Lisbon, dated November 29, 1764.

[72] Thomas Hay, English ambassador at Lisbon, to secretary of state for foreign affairs, March 18, 1763. The letter is given by Smith in *Memoirs of Pombal*, II, 47.

[73] From "An Account of the Establishment and Progress of the Oporto Wine Company," written by Pombal after his retirement from the ministry (Smith, *Memoirs of Pombal*, I, 143 ff).

[74] Ignacio de Freitas, *Collecção*, III, 488-517. There are fifty-three sections to the regulations of the company.

failure to secure the permit resulted in confiscation of the wine by the agents of the company. Permits were issued by official tasters who approved for exportation or condemned for home use at their own judgment. The tasters were employees of the wine company, which was a competitor of the British merchants, and no appeal from their decisions was permitted. The only sale possible for wine belonging to English merchants which had been condemned was to the wine company itself, as section 28 said that only the company could sell to any one within a radius of three leagues of Oporto, and sale beyond that limit became "exportation." The English merchant therefore was forced to accept for his condemned wine whatever price the company set, while the employees of the company possessed the power to condemn any amount they adjudged advisable. By section 19, the company obtained a monopoly of the export of wines, brandies, and vinegars to Brazil. By sections 7 and 8 the judge conservator of the company could commandeer all means of conveyance, warehousing, and all artificers needful for the wine trade of the company. By such drastic regulations, Pombal tried to retrieve the wine business from the hands of the English.

Practically all of the measures adopted by the minister to combat English supremacy were contrary to the treaty stipulations existing between England and Portugal. It was plain that his design was to establish an active trade among the subjects of Portugal, and to make the foreign merchant useless. Yet Thomas Hay, British ambassador at Lisbon, could add to this declaration of Pombal's purpose that he did not know a more upright man than Pombal and that he was sure that the minister firmly believed that he had advised only what every sovereign had a right to do, independent of treaties, within his own dominions.[75] Pombal was not an enemy of England; he was attempting to retrieve his country from a condition of virtual vassalage to a foreign state.

The result of this policy soon became obvious, for England's

[75] Hay to sect. of state for foreign affairs, March 18, 1763, Smith, *Memoirs of Pombal*, II, 49, 50.

trade with Portugal fell off decisively after the Peace of Paris. In 1765 the woolen trade was half what it had been ten years earlier. Fish from Newfoundland had diminished by one-fourth; and the silk export to Portugal, begun so prosperously, had been checked by the rise of home manufactures and importation from Spain and Italy. French and Dutch woolens were competing favorably with the English article while the silk stocking trade was equally divided between France and England. Twenty years earlier there arrived annually at Lisbon six or seven hundred English vessels which were the almost exclusive carriers of Portuguese trade in the Mediterranean. Now due to Dutch and Swedish competition the number of English vessels had shrunk to less than four hundred.[76]

In summing up their findings, certain commissioners appointed to study Anglo-Portuguese trade relations reported in 1767 that what appeared to them to be by far the most important phase of all that had come under their consideration was the situation of the trade with Brazil. They unanimously concurred with the reports which came up yearly from Lisbon representing that the improvement or diminution of Great Britain's commerce with Portugal depended on the trade with the South American colony. Now the exclusive trading companies and the *Junta do Commercio* instituted by Pombal threatened to deprive England of participation in Brazilian colonial commerce, which, in the opinion of the commissioners, was by far the most important element in Anglo-Portuguese commercial relations.[77]

In 1774 the trade with Portugal "usually so highly extolled" was "sunk down to less than half of what it used to be formerly."[78] In 1781 the Portuguese, after strictly prohibiting the importation of cotton goods from England, now refused to ad-

---

[76] MacPherson, *Annals*, III, 425-426. From 1748 to 1755, 1294 British ships entered Oporto. From 1756 to 1763, the number was reduced to 757 (S. P. For., Port., 89/64, Annex 2). Another annex gives total value of exports and imports to and from Portugal by years from 1750 to 1765. Exports diminished steadily after 1761, except for 1764 immediately after the Peace of Paris.

[77] S. P. For., Port., 89/64, pp. 118-119.

[78] MacPherson, *Annals*, III, 560; Smith, *Memoirs of Pombal*, II, 254.

mit woolen goods and printed linens from Ireland.[79] In 1760 the balance of trade was nearly a million pounds sterling in favor of England; by 1770 it was down to two hundred thousand; by 1780 there was a balance against England of nearly one hundred thousand pounds. In 1760 only Holland and Germany took more English goods than did Portugal; but fifteen years later, Holland, Germany, Spain, Italy, and Flanders pushed Portugal to sixth place among Britain's foreign traders, while Africa, the East Indies, Ireland, and the American colonies far outstripped the Portuguese as buyers of British merchandise.[80]

It is evident from the foregoing discussion that the Portugal trade underwent a radical change between 1713 and 1786. The irritation from minor causes became acute under the Marquis of Pombal's anti-English policy; the income of gold resulting from a favorable balance of trade shrank from over a million sterling to little or nothing; and the trade itself fell from being "the most advantageous that" England "drove anywhere" to an humble sixth place among the foreign nations buying from England. Economically Portugal had lost its paramount importance.

Coincident with this change in the Portugal trade, there arose a new group of vested interests in England, whose profit dictated a new commercial policy. Before the rise of the new class, the productive resources of England were mainly in the hands of the landlords who controlled the national resources, and of merchant princes who based their business on a monopolistic commercial system. The great manufacturers, who rose to power in the first half of George III's reign as a consequence of the transition to mechanical production, did not maintain themselves by a monopoly either of raw materials or of trade artificially acquired by protective laws at home and special concessions abroad. By virtue of their new machines, they could produce more goods at less cost for sale at prices under those of any competitor. Trade restrictions on those articles in

---

[79] MacPherson, *Annals*, III, 685.

[80] *Ibid.*, III, 339, 500, 673.

the production of which they excelled the world were not necessary.[81]

One of the principal articles which benefitted from the invention of machinery was cotton. In 1769 only some fifty thousand wheels were employed in spinning, but twenty years later the number was around two millions. Manchester and Birmingham developed as centers of the new interests. Woolens suffered from competition of cotton cloths and from the slowness with which the woolen manufacturers gave up their old methods and adopted the new machine system.[82] The tide of fashion which had been so long in favor of French goods in England now turned strongly in the contrary direction, with the result that English manufactures of almost all kinds were in such demand in France that shop-keepers wrote over their doors "*Marchandises d'Angleterre.*" England could buy raw cotton from France, work it up under double freights, send it back to France under 12½ per cent. duty, and still undersell the French fabric by twelve to twenty per cent.[83]

Leagued with the cotton group were the pottery and iron manufacturers. Josiah Wedgwood, of pottery fame, testified before a committee of the House of Lords that "there are articles of the utmost consequence to the manufacturers of this kingdom, as they enable us to baffle all competition with foreign markets. . . . These are the machines, presses, dies and tools, in which the manufacturers of Great Britain excell all the world."[84]

The ramifications of the new power were as far-reaching as the woolen business of 1713, with an even larger number of people "called from idleness to comfortable independence" by

---

[81] For the best discussion of the rise of the great manufacturers of England, 1760-1790, see Witt Bowden's book of that title. See also MacPherson, *Annals*, IV, 79-83, 132-134.

[82] Bowden, *Rise of the Great Manufacturers*, pp. 35-37. In West Riding of Yorkshire, however, the transition to machines in wool manufacture followed quickly on the revolution in cotton manufacturing.

[83] Bowden, *op. cit.*, p. 39; MacPherson, *Annals*, IV, 82; Oscar Browning, "Commercial Treaty between England and France," p. 359.

[84] Bowden, *op. cit.*, pp. 41, 79.

increased demands of labor.[85] The new interests were able by their organization and finances to ship their own foreign trade and to search out new markets. They made money quickly, for one cotton lord cleared seventeen thousand pounds sterling a year for two successive years, and various manufacturers paid twenty to twenty-six thousand pounds excise tax in 1785.[86]

These new industrialists felt the need of wider markets for their increased output. "It was now (and, strange to say, not till now) discovered that France was capable of being a most valuable commercial connection to Great Britain, and that a trade with twenty-four millions of people, possessing many valuable commodities which we stand in need of and wanting many valuable articles which we manufacture and having moreover a currency of near ninety millions sterling of real gold and silver money, was likely to be an object of greater importance to a manufacturing and commercial people than a trade with any other nation of inferior population and opulence."[87] At the time when England's market was narrowing down, the creation of new outlets was becoming imperative. Against this need of new markets to soak up the surplus of manufactures produced in England, Portugal closed its doors and revived its own industries. On the other hand France turned from Colbert Mercantilism to faith in the physiocrats and was ready to offer liberal terms to English commerce.[88]

When in October, 1785, England had not yet acted in regard to article 18 of the treaty of Versailles,[89] France forbade the importation of a number of British manufactures and indicated that it intended to turn to Holland.[90] William Pitt, then prime minister, was thus prodded into action. He had learned by the failure of his Irish project that any measure

---

[85] MacPherson, *Annals*, IV, 133. [86] Bowden, *Rise of the Manufacturers*, p. 62.

[87] MacPherson, *Annals*, IV, 11.

[88] Cunningham, *Growth of English Industry*, I, 602; Hist. Mss. Comm., *Dropmore Papers*, I, 261, Buckingham to Grenville, May 17, 1786.

[89] 1783. The article called for a commission to be appointed by England and France to draw up a new arrangement of commerce between the two countries on the basis of reciprocity.

[90] Browning, "Treaty of Commerce between England and France," pp. 349-363.

dealing with commerce must have the approval of the new industrial lords.[91] He therefore cleverly chose William Eden from the opposition to negotiate with France,[92] with instructions to remain in constant communication with the members of the General Chamber of Manufacturers.[93] Before he left for Paris, Eden spent days in consultation with both the old and the new style manufacturer, but his results show that he heeded the advice of the cotton, hardware, and pottery groups, which made up the new interests.[94] The chamber, through its individual members, exerted a profound influence on the terms of the treaty, with Josiah Wedgwood and the Birmingham and Manchester groups controlling the action of the manufacturers.[95] The treaty was signed on September 26, 1786, and on January 26 following, a copy was placed before the House of Commons.[96]

---

[91] Witt Bowden, "The Influence of the Manufacturers on Some of the Earlier Policies of Wm. Pitt," *American Historical Review*, XXIX, 615 ff.; Hist. Mss. Comm., *Dropmore Papers*, I, 248-254, Earl of Mornington to W. W. Grenville, April 1, May 20-31, August 13, 1785.

[92] George Tomline, *Memoirs of the Life of William Pitt*, II, 220 and footnote; Stanhope, *Life of Pitt*, I, 287; *Correspondence between Pitt and the Duke of Rutland, 1781-1787*, p. 136.

[93] The Chamber had been organized March 14, 1785, by the manufacturers to oppose Pitt's Excise Tax and Irish Resolutions. It had modified the first and caused the defeat of the second project.

[94] Add. Ms. 34,462, Evidence for the Commercial Treaty with France taken before the Board of Trade, 1785-1786. Eden attended every one of the twenty-four meetings held between January 4, and March 16, 1786. The committee examined representatives from manufacturers of linens, woolens, iron, cutlery, and plated work; cotton goods of all kinds, leather goods, printed calicoes, pottery and china; glass, hardware, hats, paper, and gauze. Merchants and bankers dealing with Portugal and wine merchants in general were examined. With very few exceptions these groups demanded that trade be opened with France. They had no fear of French competition and they needed the new market badly. *Journal and Correspondence of William, Lord Auckland*, Chapters V and VI, gives some letters bearing on the negotiations leading to the signing of the treaty.

[95] Witt Bowden, "English Manufacturers and the Treaty of 1786," *Amer. Hist. Review*, XXV, 28-30; Add. Ms. 34,420 ff. 253-4, Letter from Josiah Wedgwood to Eden, December 13, 1785; *ibid.*, ff. 280-281, Knox to Eden, December 19, 1785; *ibid.*, ff. 296 ff., Sheffield to Eden, December 28, 1785; *ibid.*, ff. 348 ff. gives résumé of information obtained through the widespread inquiry made by the government among manufacturers as to their opinion on Anglo-French commerce. Little mention is made of Portuguese trade.

[96] *Commons Journals*, XLII, 266 ff.; Cobbett, *Parl. Debates*, XXVI, 235 ff.

The most important of the forty-seven articles was the sixth which specified the duties to be charged on goods imported into the two countries. The first division of this article stated decisively that "the wines of France, imported directly from France into Great Britain, shall in no case, pay any higher duties than those which the wines of Portugal now pay." The duties on vinegar and brandies were reduced while those on olive oils were made equal to the most favored nation. These clauses were clearly detrimental to the Portuguese trade. On the other hand, hardware, cutlery, cabinet ware, and iron; steel, copper, and brass works; cotton manufactures and pottery interests secured the advantages which the members of those groups desired, while cotton or woolens mixed with silk were absolutely prohibited. The most favored nation clause was guaranteed each, with the right of each crown to reserve the special concessions granted respectively to Spain and to Portugal by the French Compact of 1761 and the Methuen treaty[97] of 1703.

Pitt intended to reserve all of England's rights under the Methuen Treaty, "in case Portugal makes it worth our while to agree with it," and he was going to "*insist* on Ireland's having the full benefit of the Methuen Treaty, *if it is to be preserved at all*."[98] The 1703 treaty was to continue, but as a matter of fact, its effect was destroyed. French wines had paid ninety-nine pounds a tun duty while Portugal paid only forty-six.[99] By the reduction of the duties to less than half the former rate, French wines would become cheap enough to lie within the reach of the average buyer and permit the general popularity of French over Portuguese wines to overbalance the relatively cheaper price paid for the latter. The French treaty was a renunciation of the Portuguese trade in favor of France, although by virtue of the clause which reserved the right to preserve the special concessions granted to Portugal in 1703, the letter of the Methuen treaty was not violated.

---

[97] Article VII.

[98] Pitt to Rutland, Downing Street, August 19, 1786, *Correspondence*, pp. 159-160.

[99] Browning, "Treaty of Commerce Between England and France," p. 358.

Charles James Fox with seventy faithful followers attempted to revive the drama of 1713. From January 29 to February 21, he labored, by rallying the Opposition around the banner of Portugal, to defeat the French treaty. The minister emphasized the manner in which Portugal had been departing from the very treaties which Fox was holding up as the idol of English commerce, while Pitt insisted that whether the Portuguese trade survived or collapsed, it was better to agree quickly with France. Numerous accounts of the state of all branches of the trade of Great Britain with Portugal, France, and the world at large, were loaded on the table for the perusal of the members of the House of Commons, who thus came to realize the changed conditions of Anglo-Portuguese commerce. Only one petition was presented against the bill. A discontented minority of the General Chamber of Manufacturers pleaded for delay on the treaty without advancing any argument against it.[100] But Fox's effort was futile,[101] as Pitt had spiked the guns of any opposition when he gave heed to the wishes of the new class who stood to profit by a different commercial policy for England. The Portuguese trade was a broken reed for the Opposition. On April 4, 1787, the bill for repealing the duties and customs necessary to put the treaty into effect was carried, 119 to 43, and the treaty became a fact.[102] The decision of 1713 had been reversed.

But at the very time when English commercial policy so decisively turned against Portugal, a new element was developing in the economic relations of the two countries. In his efforts to free Portugal from its dependence on England, Pombal had

[100] Eden had kept in touch with the members of the Chamber which, in December after the signature of the treaty, had approved the terms negotiated. Opposition developed among the older manufacturers and at a separate meeting the futile petition was prepared and signed (Bowden, *Rise of the Manufacturers*, pp. 72-79).

[101] For a detailed account of the efforts of the Opposition to defeat the treaty, see: *Commons Journals*, XVII, 278-279, 299-307, 365-367, 375, 379, 386; Cobbett *Parl. Debates*, XXVI, 260-268, 343-351, 357, 358, 361-378, 381-408, 408-468; Hist. Mss. Comm., *Rutland Papers*, II, 373, Daniel Pulteney to Rutland, February 16 and 20, 1787.

[102] Cobbett, *Parl. Debates*, XXVI, 894-913.

fostered plantations in preference to mines in the colony. Under his influence, the culture of cotton, rice, indigo, coffee, and cacao began to spread rapidly through Brazil. By 1806 from 136,000 to 140,000 bales of cotton (of four arrobas—32 lbs. to an arroba—each) entered Lisbon from the colony; and Pombal's huge warehouses, constructed in the market place of Lisbon amid the jeers of his enemies, were now insufficient to hold the cotton, coffee, sugar, and indigo flowing in from Brazil.[103] Between 1789 and 1792 importation at Lisbon of cotton from Brazil increased from 38,243 to over sixty thousand bales of from 140 to 200 pounds each.[104]

Coincident with this increased supply of raw cotton from Brazil, there came an increased demand for it on the part of the new manufacturers of England who had turned their backs on the Portuguese trade. In 1786, of the twenty millions of pounds imported into England, less than six millions were from British domains. Eight years later the empire supplied no more than one-sixth of the amount needed.[105] On the other hand, the old stream of gold from Brazil through Portugal to England was replaced by the flow of raw cotton. From less than one hundred thousand pounds sterling worth in 1785, the importation of raw cotton from Portugal to England grew to over six hundred thousand pounds in value in 1791.[106] In that year there was a balance of trade in favor of Portugal of nearly £252,000, and English gold was shipped through Portugal to Brazil.[107] This was before the wars started on the Continent.

In 1792 only Russia, the United States, and Italy sold more merchandise to England than did Portugal. The war, starting in 1793, by closing the markets of France to Great Britain and

---

[103] *Biographie Universelle*, XXXV, 371, footnote.

[104] Add. Ms. 9252, ff. 101-102.

[105] Bowden, "English Manufacturers and the Treaty of 1786," pp. 25-26.

[106] General Statement made by the factory at Lisbon at request of the English ambassador, dated Lisbon, November 12, 1792. Of the cotton exported from Lisbon in 1791, nearly 4,800,000 lbs. came from Pernambuco and about 3,000,000 from Maranhão. The rest came from Pará, Bahia, and Rio de Janeiro (Add. Ms. 9252, ff. 101-102).

[107] Add. Ms. 9252, fl. 98, reverse.

preventing the operation of the stipulations of the treaty of 1786, drove England's shipments to her old ally beyond the million pounds sterling mark, whereas Britain's bill for goods received, contrary to former times, did not lack much of reaching the same amount.[108]

The swing of the pendulum back toward Portugal was accelerated by the French Revolution. War with France, as of old, drove England and Portugal together. On February 1, 1793, France declared war on England; on September 26, Grenville signed a short but significant treaty with Portugal. All old treaties were reaffirmed, and Portugal promised to help England against France. The trading vessels of each nation were to be considered as of the same nationality and to be so treated in the ports of each country; Portuguese ports were to be closed to French war vessels and privateers and to all trade in munitions with that country. If France should attack Portugal, the latter would at once close her ports to all classes of French ships, and England was to come to the aid of its ally.[109] The short treaty of six articles prophesied clearly the struggle between Napoleon and England for control of the Portuguese ports, the importance of which lay in their strategic and commercial value.

The European situation of 1703 was being repeated in an aggravated form. Raw cotton and provisions from Brazil now surpassed in importance the wine provision of Methuen's treaty, although England was again dependent on Portugal for its liquors. The new market opened in 1786, and still urgently needed by British manufacturers, was closed by the French wars; but Portugal would serve as a gateway for the entrance of such articles to the Continent, and to the colony of Brazil. Strategically, Portugal was necessary to England as a land and naval base. At the turn of the century the Anglo-Portuguese Alliance was firmly reëstablished.

---

[108] MacPherson, *Annals*, IV, 262, 536.

[109] *Commons Journals*, XLIX, 10; J. Debrett, *A Collection of State Papers*, I, 25-27. The treaty was presented to the Commons together with the treaties with Spain, the two Sicilies, Prussia, and the Emperor (Cobbett, *Parl. Debates*, XXX, 1048).

CHAPTER III

THE TRANSFER OF THE PORTUGUESE COURT TO RIO DE JANEIRO

Portugal, caught like a shellfish in a tempest between the waves of England's seapower and the rock of Napoleon's armies, wavered in its allegiance to the English treaty of 1793. In Lisbon Queen Maria hovered between lucid intelligence and complete insanity, with the fat, irresolute, silent D. João waiting to become João VI. Pombal had been dropped overboard when D. Maria succeeded José in 1777, and D. João had married D. Carlota Joaquina, sister of the future Ferdinand VII of Spain. Pombal's efforts to play Richelieu and create a strong court group ceased at his fall, and now a decadent court surrounded a half-insane queen and an obese prince royal who suffered from a chronic case of indecision.[1]

In 1796 D. Maria declared Lisbon a free port[2] under certain conditions, and four months later she announced that Portugal was neutral.[3] In Paris D. Antonio d'Araujo e Azevedo, who eighteen years later at Rio de Janeiro was to cause the recall of Minister Strangford, concluded a secret peace[4] with Talleyrand which closed the ports of Portugal to English vessels.[5] But

---

[1] This picture of João VI is given by Tobias Monteiro, *Historia do Imperio, A Elaboração da Independencia, passim.* A more sympathetic picture is given by J. M. Pereira da Silva, *Historia da Fundação do Imperio Brazileiro*, I, 50-51, 57-68.

[2] F. Martens, *Recueil des Traités des Puissances e États de l'Europe Depuis 1761*, VI, 604-608.

[3] *Ibid.*, VII, 140.

[4] *Ibid., Recueil*, VII, 201. Signed August 20, 1797.

[5] Lord Malmesbury, English peace envoy, called Araujo a "very strange man . . . partial to revolutionary principles and modern philosophy." Hist. Mss. Comm., *Dropmore Papers*, III, 355, Malmesbury to Grenville, Lille, August 22, 1797.

Lord Grenville demanded that Lisbon disavow the negotiations and the treaty was not ratified.[6] Diplomacy had failed to win Portugal to France.

By 1801 the overflowing warehouses of Lisbon, the trade with England mounting to the two million pounds sterling mark, and the strategic position of Portugal in the Peninsula could no longer be overlooked by Napoleon. Hence he peremptorily demanded that the Portuguese close their ports to the English, send him fifteen to twenty million livres, and cede him the Guianas in South America; if they refused, Spain, under the unconscionable Godoy, Príncipe de la Paz, would oblige them to obey.[7] The Portuguese refused, and were forced to sign the disastrous treaty of Badajoz with Spain, the second article of which specified that the Portuguese ports in all the possessions of the kingdom were to be closed to all English ships.[8] A French treaty negotiated by Lucien Bonaparte on the same occasion, although it was apparently very stringent in its demands, failed to please Napoleon, and a second agreement was forced on the Portuguese by the Treaty of Madrid, September 29, 1801. The ports were closed; no help of any sort was to be given to the enemies of France; French Guiana was enlarged; the original payment of one million livres monthly till fifteen millions were paid was increased by five more millions;[9] and Lannes, one of Napoleon's most brilliant generals, was ordered to Lisbon to "hold the bridle on the Portuguese."[10]

By the Treaty of Amiens which soon followed, the integrity of Portuguese territory was guaranteed by England, but the French did not return the gains in Guiana nor did Spain re-

[6] For the Araujo-Malmesbury negotiations and the reaction of Pitt and Grenville, see: Hist. Mss. Comm., *Dropmore Papers*, III, 282, 355, 359, 373; Cobbett, *Debates*, XXXI, 1422; J. Debrett, *A Collection of State Papers*, V, 173-212, VI, xvi-xx and 136; Malmesbury, *Diaries and Correspondence of James Harris, Ist Earl of Malmesbury*, III, 460-467, 488-496; Pereira da Silva, *Historia do Imperio*, I, 54-57. After the time limit of six months had expired, João, fearing a French invasion, did send a ratification which was rejected by France.

[7] A. Sorel, *L'Europe et la Révolution française*, VI, 106.

[8] Martens, *Recueil*, Supplement, II, 340 ff.; Sorel, *op. cit.*, VI, 153.

[9] *Ibid.*, II, 589 ff.; Monteiro, *Historia do Imperio*, p. 3.

[10] A Sorel, *L'Europe et la Révolution française*, VI, 175.

linquish the territory won by the Treaty of Badajoz.[11] At the moment of the crisis in the Portuguese affair of 1801, England was forced to choose between Egypt and its old ally. By withdrawing its forces from Portugal and concentrating on Egypt in accordance with a plan agreed upon by both countries, England left Portugal exposed to the advance of Godoy, Prince of Peace. In return, the English ministry voted the Portuguese a subsidy to help pay the twenty millions of francs demanded by Napoleon. The additional articles forced on Portugal requiring the closing of the ports and the loss of territory were unfortunate, but could not be helped.[12]

About the middle of June, 1803, João, now prince regent ruling in place of his demented mother, declared his country would be neutral if war broke out among his allies and friends, which included both France and England. In addition, remembering the outcome of the 1801 affair, he prohibited the entrance into Portuguese ports of privateers, war vessels, and prizes, a stipulation which was detrimental to England's interests.[13] In March of the next year he secured the guaranty of France to Portuguese neutrality by signing a convention whereby the former agreed to convert the obligation of the treaty of Madrid into a subsidy of sixteen million francs payable in monthly installments.[14] Quite sure that he had brought his country into safe harbor just in time to escape the tempest of war which broke out afresh in 1803, D. João dismissed the affairs of Europe from his mind, and the Portuguese nation rejoiced in the prospects of peace.[15]

But D. João was resting in false security, for "after Tilsit the one great gap in Napoleon's barrier was Portugal."[16] Closely allied to England economically and politically and preoccupied with its colonial possessions, Portugal was reluctant to

---

[11] Martens, *Recueil*, Supplement, II, 566.

[12] Speech by Lord Hawkesbury, Cobbett, *Debates*, XXXVI, 665; also speech by Chancellor Addington, *ibid.*, XXXVI, 667-668.

[13] Martens, *Recueil*, Supplement, III, 536 ff.

[14] Monteiro, *Historia do Imperio*, p. 4; Pereira da Silva, *Historia do Imperio*, I, 57-61.

[15] Pereira da Silva, *op. cit.*, I, 60-61.

[16] A. D. Innes, *A History of England and the British Empire*, IV, 37.

enforce the restrictions of the continental blockade. Yet Napoleon believed it necessary, if England was to be starved out, to stop British trade with Portuguese ports. "For the moment he dreamed of but one thing; that was to secure in the Peninsula the severest restrictions on British commerce and to obtain the submission of Portugal to his vast designs."[17]

When, in 1806, Talleyrand warned England that the emperor intended to take possession of Portugal unless England made peace with France, the Portuguese minister in London reported to his government that the warning was only a threat to frighten the English government into concluding peace. The Portuguese cabinet thereupon refused the offer of ten thousand English troops and frowned upon the British fleet which was ordered to Lisbon by England in reply to Talleyrand's threat.[18]

In view of the critical situation, the English government sent the energetic Percy Clinton Sydney Smythe, Viscount Strangford, to Lisbon to hold Portugal fast to the English alliance.[19] There he found two groups in the Portuguese court, each striving for control over the prince regent. One party, led by Antonio d'Araujo e Azevedo, then minister for foreign affairs, leaned toward France. Napoleon, Araujo said, had given a positive promise not to allow Spain to attack Portugal by land, and France had guaranteed the neutrality of Portugal. His group, however, would be guided by the example of Denmark, which was then neutral; if Bonaparte should respect that neutrality, Portugal would also be spared. Resistance to France, he argued further, was futile, for what Prussia had failed to do, Portugal could never accomplish.[20] But to counteract Spanish intrigues at the emperor's court, Araujo established his former secretary as a special Portuguese agent in Paris.[21]

This party was in the ascendency when Strangford arrived.

---

[17] M. A. Thiers, *Histoire du Consulat et de l'Empire*, VIII, 20.

[18] Pereira da Silva, *Historia do Imperio*, I, 99-100.

[19] F. O., 63/54, from Strangford, Nos. 1-5.

[20] *Ibid.*, Strangford to Howick, No. 5.

[21] *Ibid.*, No. 21.

The other group, led by Rodrigo de Souza e Coutinho, brother of the Portuguese minister at London, was intriguing against Araujo. Souza Coutinho favored active military measures and a strong alliance with England in the face of Napoleon's demands.[22] From this group Strangford received valuable information and support.

The two groups and the British minister centered their activities on the prince regent, where lay the final decision regarding whatever course might be chosen. In their efforts to influence D. João, these conflicting elements faced a provoking difficulty. Toward the end of 1805 the prince regent had discovered a plot to declare him insane and seat D. Carlota on the throne. The fact that the leader of the conspiracy was his wife drove D. João into retirement at the convent at Mafra six leagues from Lisbon. He rarely received visitors, still more rarely came to Lisbon, and began to suffer from attacks of vertigo. He saw treason in every corner and mistrusted everybody and everything.[23] Thus during the critical months of 1807, the man in whom rested the ultimate authority and responsibility for the Portuguese nation permitted only a meager contact with his ministers and the diplomatic corps at Lisbon and remained out of touch with developments in Europe.

Immediately on his arrival, Viscount Strangford was faced by the hostility of Spain. Spanish rowboat privateers were seriously damaging British commerce on the Portuguese coasts,[24] and the Spanish minister at Lisbon complained in a nasty way that it was only in consequence of supplies received by British ships from Brazilian ports that England could maintain its system of hostilities against the colonial possessions of Spain.[25]

---

[22] F. O., 63/55, Strangford to Canning, No. 54.

[23] Pereira da Silva, *Historia do Imperio,* I, 65-68.

[24] The rowboats could escape into Portuguese ports where British warships could not follow, due to Portugal's declaration of neutrality. Strangford said that there were portions of the Portuguese coast more dangerous to British subjects than any equal extent of coast in possession of England's enemies (F. O. 63/54, Strangford to Howick, No. 23).

[25] F. O., 63/54, Strangford to Canning, Nos. 27, 28; F. O., 63/55, Strangford to Canning, No. 41.

Strangford appealed to the Lisbon cabinet for aid against the rowboat privateers and urged that a proper national defense be prepared.[26] The inroads made by the Spanish on British commerce led him to send home a long dispatch in which he discussed the whole question of Anglo-Portuguese trade relations. He suggested that a remodeled Methuen Treaty be signed whereby Portugal was to admit English cotton manufactures at twenty per cent. ad valorem duty while England was to give preference to Portuguese raw cotton from Brazil.[27] Although the suggestions were fruitless, the dispatch demonstrates the minister's preoccupation with the economic relations of the two countries.

On August 12, 1807, Portugal received notice that Talleyrand's warning of the previous year was more than a threat. A joint note signed by France and Spain was delivered on that date, demanding that Portugal declare war on England by withdrawing its minister from London and requesting the recall of the English representative at Lisbon; that the ports of Portugal be closed to British war vessels and merchantmen; and that English residents in Portugal be imprisoned and their property confiscated. A reply was to be made by September, and failure to comply with the demands would mean war.[28]

Neutrality was no longer possible; Portugal had to choose sides before the end of the month, but the cabinet was split, and the prince regent was hiding in Mafra. Orders were sent to the Chevalier de Souza in London to inform the English government that the very existence of the Portuguese monarchy depended on England's making peace with Napoleon, and that D. João would not confiscate the property of English subjects under any hazard. Strangford believed that Portugal

[26] F. O., 63/54, Strangford to Howick, Nos. 17, 23; Strangford to Canning, No. 33.

[27] *Ibid.*, Strangford to Canning, No. 33.

[28] F. O., 63/55, Strangford to Canning, No. 46. Also 63/57, *Letters and Papers from Chev. de Souza, Portuguese Minister, and Others*, extract of dispatch of D. Lourenço de Lima, Portuguese minister at Paris, to Araujo, August 7, 1807, and the certified copy of the French minister's note of August 12, delivered at Lisbon. The copy was sent to Souza with orders to show it to the English foreign minister. These papers are in some confusion and are not numbered.

would accede to all of the other demands however.[29] On August 20, news from England dispelled any hopes of salvation through peace between Britain and Napoleon, and the Portuguese court in despair begged England to be merciful. Strangford suggested to the Foreign Office in the dispatch which conveyed this plea for mercy, that in the situation which was rapidly developing an opportunity would be presented for England to secure concessions from Portugal such as the establishment of English commercial houses in Brazil,[30] the importation of British cotton manufactures into Portuguese dominions, and the amending of the treaty of 1654 and of the Charter of Privileges to the advantage of England.[31]

On the nineteenth the council of state formally refused to confiscate British property and imprison British subjects. Time was to be gained until an "apparent system of hostility" could be worked out with England. Portugal required only that England should not destroy Portuguese colonies and commerce. War would be declared and England could seize all Portuguese warships which should operate against the British (although Portugal would prevent such operation by their vessels) and no letters of marque would be issued by Lisbon to Portuguese subjects. Strangford added to his report of this astounding proposal of a simulated state of war between Eng-

---

[29] F. O., 63/55, Strangford to Canning, No. 46; F. O., 63/57, Minister Souza to George Canning, August 28, 1807.

[30] Pereira da Silva, *Historia do Imperio*, I, 79-80, gives the following statistics for the trade of Portugal with foreign countries and with its colonies for 1806; imported from all foreign countries, 16, 440: 921$781 (read 16,440 contos 921 mil 781 reis); exported to all Portuguese colonies, 11,314:313$554; exported to Brazil, 8,426:-097$899; exported to all foreign countries, 23,255:505$141; imported from all colonies, 16,103:966$250; imported from Brazil, 14,153:752$891. These figures, which he quotes from Balbi, *Statistique du Portugal*, demonstrate the importance of Brazil in Portuguese commercial exchange. Strangford, F. O., 63/55, Strangford to Canning, No. 67, states that of the £657,510 worth of merchandise which England imported from Lisbon as an annual average for the five year period ending 1792, nearly £427,000 was produce of Brazil. His figures were taken from the books of the English factory at Lisbon. It would be advantageous to English commerce with Portugal to eliminate the *entrepôt* of Portugal and establish commercial houses in Brazil with direct Anglo-Brazilian trade.

[31] F. O., 63/55, Strangford to Canning, No. 47.

land and Portugal that, in truth, no military means could save Portugal from French invasion as the army was thoroughly incapable. Lisbon could be saved by means of the British fleet, but English property at Oporto, which was defenseless, was five times as valuable as that at Lisbon.[32]

Five days before the expiration of the time limit set for this reply, the council voted to take no action until the opinion of the English cabinet could be secured.[33] This opinion, as given by Strangford, was for the court to move to Brazil immediately, finding refuge beyond the reach of Napoleon's armies.[34] Active preparations were begun in the ship yards and the minister was told that D. João would appreciate help from England in case the flight took place.[35] The Portuguese foreign minister asserted that a great and powerful empire, protected in its infancy by the naval power of England, was to be established in America. Strangford, at this point in his report of the interview, gleefully interjected that, in such a case, nothing could prevent the granting to England of an exclusive trade to the ports of Brazil. By the decision of the council of state, the eldest son of the king was to leave for the colony at once as a warning to Spain and France that in case Portugal did fall into their hands, the Portuguese monarchy would remain intact to threaten Spanish colonies and fatten British commerce. If French troops should enter Portuguese territory, the prince regent would follow his son, and although France would gain Portugal, England would gain Brazil.[36] The English minister expressed himself as being well content with this plan, and noted

[32] F. O., 63/55, Strangford to Canning, No. 48. The minister enclosed a statement of the value of British property in Oporto in Dispatch 67. He estimated the value of the movable property, houses and land, and debts due English residents in Oporto to be 2,900:000$000, the factory to be £20,000, the burying ground, £2,000, while debts due British manufacturers for goods of all kinds reached the amount of £250,000. 1$000 was worth something over three shillings in 1800.

[33] *Ibid.*, No. 50.

[34] *Ibid.*, Canning urged the same solution (F. O., 63/56, Canning to Strangford, Nos. 9, 11).

[35] F. O., 63/55, Strangford to Canning, No. 51.

[36] *Ibid.*, No. 55. Council meeting of September 2, 1807.

with approval that thirty-nine Portuguese warships of all classes were collected in the harbor of Lisbon with this policy in view.[37]

Toward the end of September Strangford secured a decree allowing English merchants to withdraw all goods from the customs houses free of duties and expenses, as an emergency measure to prevent the seizure of British property by the French in case of invasion.[38] A day or so later the French minister repeated his demands, to which he had as yet received no reply although almost a month had elapsed since the time limit had expired. A five day limit was set this time.[39] The Portuguese offer, in reply, to close the ports to the English was not satisfactory, and both the Spanish and French ministers demanded their passports. A courier was sent to General Junot who was waiting at Bayonne with a French force, and Strangford was certain that the French troops would advance at once.[40]

In the meantime full powers had been sent to the Chevalier de Souza, Portuguese minister in London, to conclude a secret treaty whereby England was to be compensated for the closing of the Portuguese ports.[41] By the secret convention of October 22,[42] which was the result of the ensuing negotiations, England secured the right to occupy the Madeira Islands as soon as France made a hostile move or Portugal closed its ports to English vessels[43]; the prince regent promised not to let any part of his naval or mercantile fleet fall into French hands[44]; England pledged an escort in case the royal family fled to Brazil,[45] and guaranteed never to recognize as king of Portugal any prince who was not the legitimate heir of the house of

[37] The list of the warships is appended to Dispatch 55.

[38] F. O., 63/55, Strangford to Canning, No. 60.

[39] *Ibid.*, No. 62. The dispatch is dated September 25. The original demand of confiscation of British property was modified to sequestration; otherwise the demands were identical (*ibid.*, No. 64).

[40] *Ibid.*, No. 64.

[41] F. O., 63/57. The instructions are dated September 27, 1807.

[42] F. O., 93, Treaties and Protocols, 37/1B, Portugal. The convention is given also in Borges de Castro, *Collecção de Tratados*, IV, 236.

[43] Preamble and Articles I and III.

[44] Article IV. [45] Article II.

Bragança.[46] As soon as the court was established in Brazil negotiations were to be started at once for a treaty of assistance and commerce between Great Britain and the Portuguese government.[47] An additional article[48] stipulated that in case Portuguese ports were closed to British ships, there would be established on the island of Santa Catharina or some other point on the coast of Brazil, a port where British merchandise could be imported in English ships on payment of the same duties as those charged on such articles in the ports of Portugal. The prince regent ratified the convention, November 8, with certain important reservations, chief among which was the rejection of the Additional Article regarding the port on the island of Santa Catharina.[49] This matter, he said, could be taken up when and if the court arrived in Brazil.

Despite the departure of the French and Spanish ministers, the Portuguese court was tranquil, convinced that Napoleon's warnings were only threats.[50] The departure of the eldest son of the prince regent was delayed from day to day to the extreme annoyance of Strangford, and the entire Portuguese fleet was assembled in the Tagus where it would fall prey to the French if Lisbon should be taken.[51] The ports were closed to the British by the edict of October 22, and Strangford failed to make any headway with the petulant prince regent despite two long interviews.[52]

This assurance, which the Portuguese felt, of Napoleon's peaceful intentions was shortlived. On November 1, D. Lourenço de Lima, Portuguese minister at Paris, reached Lisbon with a message from the emperor. If, said Napoleon, the prince regent acceded to all of the demands as delivered by the French

---

[46] Article VI.

[47] Article VII.

[48] Additional Article I.

[49] F. O., 63/58, Domestic, *Letters and Papers from Chev. de Souza*, Dispatch of November 28, 1807. Also Borges de Castro, *Collecção*, IV, 254-262.

[50] F. O., 63/55, Strangford to Canning, Nos. 68, 71, 72.

[51] *Ibid.*, Nos. 70, 71, 75; F. O. 63/56, Strangford to Canning, No. 80. Canning was extremely anxious over the possibility that the fleet might fall into the hands of the French (F. O., 63/56, Canning to Strangford, Nos. 10, 11, 14).

[52] F. O., 63/56, Strangford to Canning, Nos. 79, 80.

minister, Portugal would be saved. No half measures would serve; war against England must be declared at once. Success in his mission, Napoleon advised D. Lourenço, meant the salvation of his country, while failure meant ruin.[53] Consequently the Portuguese court now faced a serious dilemma as the choice had to be made at last between the demands of France and those of England. By yielding to the emperor's demands, Portugal might be saved, but at the price of losing the colonies for the British fleet could easily sever the arteries binding the Portuguese possessions to the mother country. On the other hand, by yielding to England's demands, the colonies might be saved, but at the price of losing Portugal, as resistance to the Napoleonic armies was hopeless.

The vivid picture of French wrath which Lourenço painted at the council meeting stampeded the ministers.[54] On November 6, Araujo suggested that it would be advantageous to Portugal's interests if Strangford and the consul general, James Gambier, should leave Lisbon. The viscount replied that it would be better if the Portuguese ministry would cease its disgraceful subterfuges, and that he could not leave just at present. Strangford explained to Canning that his departure would be proof of Portugal's compliance with Napoleon's demands, and hence he refused to go.[55] Two days later the order to sequestrate all English property and detain English residents in the country was issued, and Strangford was forced to ask for conveyance for his departure.[56] Since the prince regent was unaware of the Treaty of Fontainebleau concluded between Spain and France, October 27, by which Portugal was divided between Napoleon, the Prince of Peace, the royal family of Spain, and the queen of Etruria,[57] he hoped that by these

[53] F. O., 63/56, Strangford to Canning, No. 84.

[54] Pereira da Silva, *Historia do Imperio*, I, 111.

[55] F. O., 63/56, Strangford to Canning, No. 89.

[56] *Ibid.*, No. 91. Comparatively little damage was done to the English at Lisbon by the decree as most of their property had been removed under the emergency permission secured by Strangford late in September and a majority of the English residents had already left the country.

[57] Pereira da Silva, *Historia do Imperio*, I, 104-105; Thiers, *Histoire du Consulat*, VIII, 258.

measures against the English, he would avoid the invasion of Portugal by the French. In case General Junot should cross the frontier with his troops, however, the flight to Brazil would be undertaken at once.[58]

Viscount Strangford lingered in Lisbon for ten days after he had asked for his passports, to the great uneasiness of the Portuguese ministry. A spirited note from Araujo drove him out on the eighteenth[59] to the British fleet which then blockaded Lisbon. But on the twenty-seventh, he was back in the Tagus to force the surrender of the Portuguese fleet or the immediate departure of the royal family to Brazil.[60]

When he landed in Lisbon on the night of November 28, 1807, he learned that the greater part of the nobility had already embarked on the fleet which was destined to sail for Brazil.[61] Six days before he returned, news had reached Lisbon that Junot had crossed the Portuguese frontier with twenty-three thousand troops. Two days later, the arrival in Lisbon of *Le Moniteur*, the official gazette of the French Empire, announcing Napoleon's decision to dethrone the house of Bragança,[62] proved to the prince regent that he could no longer hope to remain on his throne in case of the absorption of his kingdom by the French. On the other hand, he had alienated his old ally by the recent measures against the English, and the British fleet was blockading Lisbon. The embarkation had been ordered for the twenty-seventh, but as yet no command to sail had been issued.

On his arrival, Strangford learned that the prince regent wished urgently to see him. As soon as he discovered from Antonio d'Araujo that D. João still vacillated, nourishing the

---

[58] F. O., 63/56, Strangford to Canning, No. 93.

[59] *Ibid.*, Strangford to Canning, Nos. 96 and 99. Strangford argued that it would be unbefitting the dignity of an English minister to leave on a Portuguese frigate and insisted on waiting until the English fleet arrived. On the eighteenth he left on a fishing boat and reached the fleet after two very uncomfortable days of rough seas.

[60] *Ibid.*, Dispatch of November 29, Separate.

[61] *Ibid.*, No. 103.

[62] Thiers, *Histoire du Consulat*, VIII, 339-341; Sorel, *L'Europe et la Révolution française*, VII, 219.

hope that matters might yet be arranged with France, Strangford exerted his best talents to secure an immediate departure for Brazil. He wrote to the prince regent, pledging forgiveness for the acts of hostility shown by Portugal against England and help for the future, on condition of a departure for Brazil within two hours. Another note was dispatched to Sir Sidney Smith, who commanded the blockading fleet, advising him to help and not attack the Portuguese when they sailed.[63] The minister's next move, as he reported to George Canning,

> was to see the Prince Regent, and to follow up the effect of my letter. I saw that not a moment was to be lost, and that my duty was to destroy in H. R. H.'s mind all hopes of accomodating matters with the Invaders of his Country, to terrify him with dark and gloomy descriptions of the state of the Capital, which I had just left, and then to dazzle him suddenly with the brilliant prospects before him, to direct all his fears to a French army and all his hopes to an English fleet; not to permit him to doubt an instant of the reception which he would meet from the latter and finally by teaching him to expect everything from the Friendship and Magnanimity of the best and most generous of Sovereigns, to put him at peace with himself and to remove from his mind the humiliating recollections of having done amiss, and the fear of the consequences.[64]

Strangford was sure that the magnitude of the benefits accruing to England from securing such action by the prince regent would outweigh any transgression of his instructions. Successful in his appeal, the minister was

> convinced that by calling them [feelings of gratitude and respect toward the king of England for services rendered to Portugal] forth

[63] By orders from Canning dated November 7, and received after Strangford left Lisbon, the English fleet was to capture the Portuguese fleet and blockade Lisbon in case all of the terms of the Convention of October 22 were not made operative immediately by the Portuguese. The utmost that Canning would grant the Portuguese ministry was to close the ports; any further measures would mean instant war. Canning "rejected with contempt" the project of the "simulated state of war." In case the prince regent failed to go to Brazil, Strangford and Smith were empowered to repeat the Copenhagen affair in Lisbon (F. O., 63/56, Canning to Strangford, Nos. 11, 13, 14).

[64] F. O., 63/56, Strangford to Canning, No. 103.

upon this occasion, I have entitled England to establish with the Brazils the Relation of Sovereign and Subject and to require Obedience to be paid as the Price of Protection.[65]

The order was given to sail at daybreak. From eight to fifteen thousand persons[66] and half of the money in circulation in the kingdom were on board thirty-six ships, with as much furniture as could be managed. Eighty millions of cruzados of treasure accompanied the fleet.[67] In the city day and night armed bands roamed aimlessly and ominous crowds packed the quays, watching the ignominious flight of the royal family, nobles, domestics, and hangers-on. Fourteen royal personages were on board the fleet, among them being D. Pedro Carlos, Infante of Spain. Early in the morning of November 29, the fleet sailed out through the narrows and then lay to with an adverse wind. A delay of two hours in weighing anchor would have resulted in the detention of the fleet within the harbor as the wind shifted immediately after the narrows had been passed.[68]

Meanwhile Junot, obeying Napoleon's emphatic commands to hurry, pushed on over the mountains to Alcántara on the Spanish-Portuguese border and down the Tagus to Lisbon. On the thirtieth, he left Saccavem with his vanguard reduced to fourteen men and his army to twelve hundred, all that the mountains and swollen streams had left of the twenty-three thousand who had set out from Bayonne. Without cavalry, artillery, cartridges, shoes, or food, stumbling with fatigue, the troop resembled "the evacuation of a hospital more than an army triumphantly marching to the conquest of a kingdom."[69] He entered Lisbon without opposition from the sullen and dis-

---

[65] *Ibid.*

[66] Thiers gives 8,000 (*Histoire du Consulat*, VIII, 340); Monteiro gives 15,000 (*Historia do Imperio*, p. 59); Pereira da Silva agrees with Monteiro (*Historia do Imperio*, I, 121).

[67] Pereira da Silva, *op. cit.*, I, 121. A cruzado was worth about three shillings (*New English Dictionary*).

[68] Pereira da Silva, *op. cit.*, I, 122, 123; F. O., 63/56, Strangford to Canning, No. 103.

[69] Sorel, *L'Europe et la Révolution française*, VII, 231.

gusted townspeople, in time to see the sails of the Portuguese fleet, lying to beyond the narrows.[70] His prize had escaped him.

Sir Sidney Smith shared what supplies he could spare and detached four ships of the line to escort the Portuguese fleet to Brazil. Viscount Strangford returned to England for further instructions; Sir Sidney Smith blockaded Lisbon; Junot held Portugal with a handful of survivors; and the Portuguese stood off on the course followed by Cabral three hundred years before. The prince regent had been forced to the great decision; he had delivered himself and his dominions into the hands of England under circumstances which the representative of the British nation deemed such as to entitle England to establish with Brazil the relation of sovereign and subject.

---

[70] Monteiro, *Historia do Imperio*, p. 51, and footnote 1; Pereira da Silva, *Historia do Imperio*, I, 123-124; F. O., 63/56, Strangford to Canning, No. 103.

CHAPTER IV

ENGLAND SECURES PREFERENTIAL RIGHTS IN BRAZIL

ON BOARD the Portuguese fleet, conditions were deplorable. D. João's ship, the *Principe Real*, carried the incredible number of sixteen hundred people. The water supply was insufficient, food ran short, and plague beset the *émigrés* in the crowded and unhygienic quarters. Monteiro adds the interesting detail that the fleas became so bad that the ladies, including the royal princess, were forced to cut their hair in order to eliminate the pests with the usual treatment.[1] On the ninth day out the misery was increased by a storm which separated the fleet. But on January 19, 1808, the *Principe Real* with one English convoy ship and a part of the thirty-six vessels which had left the Tagus on the morning of November 29, sighted the captaincy of Bahia, and two days later, amid extraordinary manifestations of joy by the people, the prince regent landed on Brazilian territory.[2]

After a short period of rest, D. João instituted public audiences and sought advice as to what measures were necessary in view of the peculiar situation which had developed in the Portuguese empire. Taking advantage of the opportunity thus offered, a colonial, José da Silva Lisbôa,[3] urged that the ports

---

[1] Monteiro, *Historia do Imperio*, p. 59. When the court reached Rio de Janeiro, the colonials took the new style hair-dressing as the latest mode and cut their own. Monteiro cites the number on board the *Principe Real* from the figures of an English officer.

[2] Pereira da Silva, *Historia do Imperio*, II, 5-8.

[3] Later Visconde de Cayrú. He was born in Bahia, July 16, 1756, graduated from the University of Coimbra, and taught Greek, Hebrew, and Philosophy in Lisbon and the colony. He had published books on commercial law and political economy which had made him famous in Lisbon. He was secretary of the Commission of Agricultural and Commercial Inspection of the Captaincy of Bahia

of Brazil be opened to the trade of the world, a measure that at one stroke would abolish the restrictions of colonial commerce. The idea was one of common sense, he argued, for it was impossible to continue to close the ports of Brazil to world commerce and limit trade exclusively to Portugal when the French were in control of the mother country. In addition, the question of revenue was staring the Portuguese government in the face. The supply of gold had ceased, leaving industry and foreign commerce as the only resource available to the Portuguese court for a much needed income; yet no commerce was possible unless the ports were opened to vessels of foreign nations.

Bento Lisbôa, José's son, maintained[4] that his father found it difficult to carry his point. The prince regent was loath to take such an important step, within a week after arriving in his new home and without the greater part of his councillors present to render an opinion on a measure which would destroy the old principle of colonial monopoly. But "such was the force of Lisbôa's arguments," asserted the son, "that Fernando Portugal[5] yielded to his persuasions and obliged the prince regent to publish the *Carta Regia* of January 28."

By the letter patent[6] direct commerce between Brazil and nations friendly to the Portuguese crown was permitted, subject to importation duties of twenty-four per cent. ad valorem on drygoods (*mercadorias seccas*) and double the current duty on certain provisions (*generos molhados*[7]), irrespective of the

---

when D. João landed (Pereira da Silva, *Historia do Imperio*, II, 8-9, and footnotes).

[4] *Revista do Instituto Historico e Geographico Brazileiro*, 1856, Tomo I, 240. Monteiro, *Historia do Imperio*, p. 65, Varnhagem, *Historia Geral do Brazil*, II, 1081, and Pereira da Silva, *op. cit.*, II, 9, give Lisbôa great credit for securing the measure. Rocha Pombo, *Historia do Brazil*, VII, 138, footnote 2, says it was inevitable and Lisbôa had little to do with it. The Brazilian does deserve credit for getting D. João to make up his mind, however, and for suggesting a measure so liberal that all the ports were opened to all friendly nations.

[5] Fernando José de Portugal, later Conde de Aguiar, had been captain general of Bahia, from 1788 to 1792, and viceroy at Rio de Janeiro from 1801 to 1806. He became minister of the interior (which included all internal administration except war and navy) in the new cabinet. He accompanied D. João.

[6] It is given *verbatim* in Rocha Pombo, *Historia do Brazil*, VII, 137, footnote 1.

[7] Such as wines, vinegars, olive oil, etc. *Mercadorias seccas* includes, besides dry-

place of production or manufacture or the nationality of the ship bringing in such goods. Exportation duties remained the same as those charged previously. An exception to these regulations was made of the royal monopolies of Brazil-wood, diamonds, or what by law or contract were considered as monopolies.

Canning had tried to secure such an open port for British goods on the coast of Brazil at the time of the secret convention of October 22, but the prince regent had refused to ratify the additional article which conceded that privilege to the English. Now by the decree of January 28, D. João opened all of the ports of Brazil to the trade of all nations friendly to Portugal whereas Great Britain had urged one port open to England alone. Later when the prince regent, after reaching Rio de Janeiro, asked Mr. Hill, *chargé* in the absence of minister Strangford, if England was satisfied with the decree of January 28, he received the reply that "it could not fail to produce a good effect in England, but that had it authorized the admittance of British vessels, and of British manufactures upon terms more advantageous than those granted to the Ships and Merchandize of other Foreign Nations, it would necessarily have afforded greater satisfaction."[8]

The opening of the ports of Brazil to the commerce of the world meant, in reality, that, as far as Europe was concerned, they were opened only to the commerce of England as long as the war lasted on the Continent. From the English point of view, some provision had to be made for the time when the blockade of Europe would end and other nations would compete with Great Britain in Brazil. Two years were to pass, however, before Strangford framed a treaty to the satisfaction of the British Foreign Office, granting England preferential rights in Portuguese America.

The effect of the decree, although it was only provisional

---

goods, groceries such as flour, sugar, cheese, etc. *Generos molhados* includes "wet provisions." The terms are translated "drygoods" and "provisions" in this chapter.

[8] F. O., 63/63, Hill to Canning, No. 3. Dated March 30, 1808.

and exacted a higher rate of duties than those of the previous régime, was far-reaching in the development of national consciousness in Brazil.[9] Contact with the outside world awakened the torpid colony; new people, new capital, and ideas entered. As a consequence of the new importance of the colony, the Brazilians felt their destiny to be larger and more important, a factor of potent influence among this Latin people. A national self-consciousness appeared; customs, habits, dress, social contacts, business methods were changed. As a matter of fact, the political and social consequences set in motion by this provisional decree of January 28, 1808, were to lead finally to an independent Brazil. The doors shut for three hundred years were thrown open, and the colony passed beyond the control of the mother country.[10]

After a delay of nearly a month at Bahia, made more memorable by the efforts of the inhabitants of that captaincy to persuade the prince regent to establish his court there instead of at Rio de Janeiro, D. João sailed for the capital of the colony. There the rest of the fleet with the three English convoy ships anxiously were awaiting his arrival. On March 8, the prince regent landed in Rio de Janeiro amid the delirious ovations of the colonials, who cherished only respect and veneration for the Portuguese monarchy. All of the blame for past misrule was laid at the door of the ministers and favorites who, so the people thought, had failed to acquaint the prince with the just complaints sent to the court. The monarchical sentiment still dominated the colonials so profoundly that the royal person was equivalent to a kind of divinity, and the love of the

---

[9] Rocha Pombo, *Historia do Brazil,* VII, 140.

[10] In an article by Vicente d'Eça called "Abertura dos Portos do Brazil," written for the Sociedade de Geographia de Lisbôa, 1908, a version of the affair between France and Portugal from 1800 to 1808 with the part played by England, is given by a pro-English Portuguese. England is ennobled, France is an archvillain with Spain at its beck and call. The article is given *verbatim* in Rocha Pombo, *Historia do Brazil,* VII, 217-225, footnotes. On the other hand, Martins concludes his version with the statement that "We were the instrument, the servant, the beast of burden for England . . . our English allies did us greater harm than our enemies, the Spanish and the French" (*Historia de Portugal,* II, 246-247).

subject for the sovereign formed a second religion, not less respected than that of the church.[11]

As soon as the days of festival were concluded, the Portuguese court set to work with an activity unusual in that ordinarily stagnant body. The pro-French ministry had been dismissed when the flight was ordered, and the pro-English group installed. Fernando Portugal, a man of industry and experience, but of limited, mediocre intelligence, became minister of the interior. The jovial courtier, the Visconde de Anadia,[12] became minister of the navy and colonies. Rodrigo de Souza Coutinho—with the exception of Araujo now fallen from power, the most intelligent Portuguese of the court group—received the post of minister of war and foreign relations. Energetic, vivacious, impulsive, a lover of the novel and grandiose, he was an absolute monarchist with an intense aversion for the principles of the French Revolution. Nearly all of the measures proposed by the government during the next six years were products of his initiative regardless of whether they fell within his department. Decidedly pro-English in his sympathies, he was on intimate terms with Viscount Strangford.[13]

None of these ministers were colonials, nor was a single Brazilian chosen to serve on the council of state, which was nominated along with the ministers. A bureaucracy, modeled on the institutions of Lisbon without regard for the changed situation of the government, was set up with an almost infinite number of posts to care for the swarm of Portuguese nobles who had accompanied the prince regent. Colonials were excluded from participation in these offices also.[14]

[11] Pereira da Silva, *Historia do Imperio*, II, 19-20.

[12] A Portuguese who had held the post of minister of the navy in Lisbon. He died soon after his arrival in Rio de Janeiro.

[13] He was born in Lisbon, 1755. He later became Conde de Linhares. His father had been minister to Spain and his brother was then minister to London (Pereira da Silva, *Historia do Imperio*, II, 30-32).

[14] The various departments created by the ministry are given by Pereira da Silva, *Historia do Imperio*, II, 37-47. The editor of the *Correio Braziliense* pointed out that no heed was paid to the necessities of the new country. Nothing like a department of mines, of roads, maps, navigation, etc., was set up. The council of state, he affirmed, was made up of men who thought it dishonor to study. Every

Considerable economic progress was made during the two years following the proclamation of the *Carta Regia* of January 28. Cotton was planted in larger quantities; factories for sugar and salt multiplied; cultivation of wheat and hemp was begun on an extensive scale in the southern provinces of Santa Catharina and Rio Grande do Sul.[15] By the decree of April 1, 1808, permission was given to the colonials and to foreigners of any nation to establish manufacturing plants of all kinds.[16] Raw materials were exempted from import duties and drawbacks on re-exported articles were conceded. To favor Portuguese shipping, coast-wise trade was closed to foreign vessels, and foreign commerce was restricted to the ports of Rio, Bahia, Pernambuco, Maranhão, and Pará. By decree of June 11, 1808, the import duties of twenty-four per cent. ad valorem on dry-goods were lowered to sixteen per cent. and the duty on provisions was reduced by a third for goods belonging to the Portuguese and imported in Portuguese vessels.[17]

In October a bank of emission was founded.[18] Before this date there had been no commerce on credit nor any kind of bank in Brazil despite the example of England and Holland.[19] The bank, founded by the initiative of Souza Coutinho, passed through many vicissitudes in the first quarter of a century of its existence; the king used it for his "private purse" and on his return to Portugal in 1821 almost sacked it; the directors got rich and

official adviser to the prince regent was a stranger to Brazil (*Correio Braziliense*, V, 567). The editor overlooked the fact that Fernando Portugal had had experience in the colony.

[15] Dunshee Abranches, *Tratados de Commercio e Navigação do Brazil*, p. 2.

[16] The decree is given *verbatim* by Pereira da Silva, *Historia do Imperio*, II, Appendix, Document 3, pp. 308-309. By decree of January 5, 1785, all manufacturing in the colony had been prohibited.

[17] Pereira da Silva, *op. cit.*, II, 48-51.

[18] Decrees of October 8 and 12. The decree and the statutes governing the bank are given by Pereira da Silva, *op. cit.*, II, Appendix, Document 4, See also F. O., 63/68, Strangford to Canning, No. 4. By decree of May 10, 1808, the Superior Court of Rio was made the Supreme Court of Brazil (*Correio Braziliense*, I, 423). On September 10 following, the first number of the official gazette was issued from the Royal Press (Rocha Pombo, *Historia do Brazil*, VII, 83).

[19] Rocha Pombo, *Historia do Brazil*, VII, 180, footnote 2.

the bank poorer; but it weathered the storm, and after 1855 it became firmly established.[20]

In November of the same year the prince regent issued a decree conceding to any foreigner irrespective of religion who would establish himself in Brazil land grants (*dotes de terra por sesmarias*) on the same terms as such grants were made to Portuguese and Brazilians. The immigration from England, stimulated by this decree, underwent many difficulties, largely due, in the opinion of an English traveller of the times,[21] to the hatred of the Portuguese for the English. They had chosen the British in 1807 not because they loved the English, but because they feared what England could do to their colonial empire. When the effects of the treaties of 1810 became evident, the Brazilians also developed an antipathy for the British. Despite numerous attempts throughout the century on the part of the Brazilian Government and of societies in London, English immigration was a failure, except in the case of such immigrants as trained mechanics, bankers, shopkeepers and traders, engineers, ranch owners, public utilities experts, and professional men. The agricultural colonist or unskilled laborer met misery and death or begged for a free return to England.[22]

Although English immigration failed to materialize in Brazil, English commerce with the country took on new life after 1808. An order[23] published in the London papers by the Portuguese minister called upon all merchants of that city who intended to do business with Brazil to meet on June 25 to consider ways of improving their interests. One hundred thirteen London merchants joined the association which was organized at the meeting of that date. Later a permanent committee of the

[20] *Ibid.*, VII, 180, footnote 2 and 181, footnote 1; Pereira da Silva, *Historia do Imperio*, II, 55-62.

[21] Rev. R. Welsh, *Notices of Brazil in 1828-1829*, I, 320. The question of English immigration in Brazil throughout the century is interesting. Due to the climate, low standards of living, and slave labor, the English common laborer never gained a foothold in Brazil.

[22] Great Britain, *Commercial Reports, Consular*, 1870, pp. 234-235; 1874 (1-2), pp. 37-49; 1875 (4-6), pp. 1424-1426; 1876 (4-6), pp. 760-781, etc.

[23] June 1, 1808.

Association of English Merchants Trading to Brazil was elected, composed of sixteen members, two of whom were members of Parliament.[24] The association met at intervals to hear reports from the committee as to the state of trade with Brazil and to frame suggestions and demands to be presented to the Foreign Office. The permanent president kept in touch with the legation and merchants in Rio de Janeiro and with representatives in Bahia, Pernambuco, Maranhão, and Pará, and communicated with the Board of Trade and the British foreign secretary.[25] This group of merchants with their effective organization became an important factor in Anglo-Brazilian trade relations.

In 1808 ninety ships flying a foreign flag entered Rio, while two years later 422 (foreign and Portuguese) entered that port. By 1811 there were in the capital 207 Portuguese and 75 English commercial establishments besides those of other nations friendly to Portugal.[26] Bahia increased its importation by fifty and its exportation by fifteen per cent. between 1807 and 1810. The government income from the customs houses at the five ports where foreign commerce was permitted increased twenty per cent. over the amount of the years previous to 1808, despite the glaring corruption of treasury officials.[27] In the port of Rio alone, during the five months previous to December 31, 1808, merchandise brought from England in British ships mounted to nearly £674,000 while exports from the same port to England totalled over £203,000.[28]

These two years of unusual progress after the emancipation from the colonial régime are noteworthy for the impartiality shown all foreign nations at peace with the Portuguese crown.

---

[24] *Correio Braziliense*, I, 115-116.

[25] *Ibid.*, II, 129; Pereira da Silva, *Historia da Imperio*, II, 77-78; Rocha Pombo, *Historia do Brazil*, VII, 205-206; F. O., 63/61, Strangford to Canning, Nos. 33 and 35.

[26] The French, German, Italian, Spanish, and Dutch were excluded as being enemies of the crown. The United States and Sweden followed England into the new commercial field.

[27] The statistics are from Pereira da Silva, *Historia do Imperio*, II, 79-84.

[28] F. O., 63/68, Strangford to Canning, No. 10.

Although at that time, due to the European situation, England was profiting almost exclusively from the new economic freedom of the colony, world peace would bring serious competition in the Brazilian markets. Consequently from 1808 to 1810 England exerted strong pressure on the Portuguese court to secure the preferential rights in Portuguese America which it had enjoyed in European Portugal for centuries. The agent chosen for the task was the man[29] who believed that on the night of November 28, 1807, he had established the relationship of sovereign and subject between England and the Portuguese government in Brazil. Although his task was a difficult one, he succeeded beyond the expectations of the British Foreign Office.

Viscount Strangford's credentials as envoy extraordinary and minister plenipotentiary to the Portuguese court at Rio were dated April 17, 1808.[30] At the same time, he was given full powers to negotiate a treaty of friendship and alliance, which Canning considered important enough to merit special and very detailed instructions.[31]

Strangford was informed, in the first place, that "the general and political relations of the British and Portuguese monarchies" were "not altered by the removal of the seat of the Portuguese Government from Portugal to the Brazils. The ancient treaties subsisting between the two Crowns sufficiently" defined "the nature of this connection. Those treaties must be considered in force, until they" should "have been abrogated by some ulterior arrangement." But such an arrangement could be deferred until the Portuguese government had taken root in the new situation and the fate of Portugal had been decided.

The minister was authorized in the meantime to conclude formally any part of the secret convention of October 22 which D. João was willing to accept, but he was to take care to insert

[29] Viscount Strangford.

[30] F. O., 63/59, Canning to Strangford, No. 1.

[31] *Ibid.*, Nos. 2-10. These instructions occupy the major part of a volume of dispatches. They reveal clearly Canning's attitude as regards the Portuguese South American situation and merit special study. For clearness of thought and conciseness of expression, these dispatches are superb.

that all old treaties were to be renewed until further negotiations took place. The prince regent, Canning thought, would wish to have the clauses of the old treaties relating to Portugal continue, while England wished to retain those referring to Brazil. In addition, the minister was to secure permission at once for the British squadron to continue off the coast of Brazil and for the admission of all British ships—war or merchant vessels—without regard to numbers, into the ports of Portuguese America.[32]

In a secret dispatch Canning urged that Strangford press upon the prince regent the necessity of attending to his Brazilian domains and of relinquishing any hope of a quick return to Lisbon. D. João was to concentrate on internal improvements of Portuguese America and leave Portugal in England's hands.[33]

As to the commercial relations between the two countries, Canning insisted that it was not expedient to conclude a definite agreement at once, as the Brazilian court was too new. For the present, the minister was to seek to open the commerce of Brazil to England and to make secure the life and property of Englishmen engaged in that commerce. He was to obtain for them the right of free residence and exemption from molestation on account of religion and to secure the liberty of reciprocal importation of all articles of the produce or manufacture of each country, subject to regular duties. "With respect to the amount of duties," Canning added, it did "not seem necessary that any precise scale should be fixed at present. Although it would undoubtedly be advantageous to obtain for British manufactures a distinct preference over those of any other country." Brazil would profit immensely if Anglo-Brazilian commercial relations were placed on such a footing as "to induce the British merchant to make the Brazils an Emporium for British Manufactures destined for the consumption of the whole of South America."[34]

---

[32] F. O., 63/59, Canning to Strangford, No. 2.

[33] *Ibid.*, No. 3, Secret.

[34] *Ibid.*, No. 4.

The main difficulty in the way of such universal importation was the admission into Brazil of goods from the British East Indies and into England of the Brazilian staples, coffee and sugar, which would compete with the products of the British West Indies. Such merchandise could be admitted for reëxportation, however, and England would absorb great quantities of Brazilian hides, timber, tobacco, drugs, dyeing woods, hemp, and other articles. Raw cotton would find an unlimited market, and England would reduce the tax on the raw article, which had been collected when cotton had entered England in a Portuguese ship. The differential duties imposed on other Brazilian produce when brought in by Portuguese ships could be reduced also, if the reciprocal favor were granted by the Portuguese government.[35]

In case the minister secured these privileges, he was not to press the right to set up the factory association in Brazil, as the Portuguese government opposed those establishments. Such organizations were unnecessary, provided the privileges and immunities so long enjoyed by the British subject in Portugal were guaranteed to him in Brazil. These privileges were known to Strangford, but special attention was to be paid to obtaining the special court of the English judge conservator, to the security of the property of persons dying intestate, and to the exemption of the English from the jurisdiction of the Inquisition. In return, the Brazilians in England were guaranteed reciprocal privileges "by the acknowledged excellence of the British Jurisprudence, especially such as relate to matters of trade and the important administration of Justice between Foreigners and natives." There was to be no equivalent in England for the judge conservator, but Strangford was to press the point as compensation for relinquishing the factory privilege. This was "a point which must on no account be abandoned."[36]

---

[35] *Ibid.*

[36] *Ibid.*, No. 4. Consuls were to be appointed at Rio, São Sebastião (capital of São Paulo), São Salvador (capital of Bahia), Olinda (capital of Pernambuco), São Luiz (capital of Maranhão), and Belem (capital of Pará), São Salvador was another name for the city of Bahia, São Luiz for Maranhão, and Belem for Pará.

With the two most important phases of Anglo-Brazilian relations—political and commercial—cared for, Canning concluded his instructions to Strangford by suggesting certain desirable privileges which he could bear in mind. If possible, he was to secure a free port on the island of Santa Catharina, where goods might be transferred to Spanish and Portuguese ships for transportation to Spanish colonies with the connivance of the Spanish colonial governors.[37] The minister was to inform the Portuguese court that in any treaty which should embody the final arrangement of the relations between the two countries, an article dealing with the slave trade must be included,[38] and he was to do his utmost to prevent the granting of monopolies by the prince regent to private individuals or companies.[39] Finally, the last of the instructions included a project for establishing a line of packetboats between England and Brazil for carrying correspondence.[40]

Laden with these precise instructions, Strangford landed in Rio de Janeiro on July 22, 1808.[41] He found that one part of his instructions had already been decreed by the prince regent, as the jurisdiction of the British judge conservator had been recognized, and courts had been established in Rio and Bahia.[42] Souza Coutinho himself hinted at the advisability of immediately concluding a definite commercial agreement and treaties of friendship and alliance[43] and informed Strangford that the prince regent had authorized the Chevalier de Souza in London to borrow six hundred thousand pounds.[44] By September 14, the convention establishing the packetboat line was concluded, securing every point contained in Canning's instruc-

[37] F. O., 63/59, Canning to Strangford, No. 5.

[38] *Ibid.*, No. 6.

[39] *Ibid.*, No. 8.

[40] *Ibid.*, No. 10.

[41] *Ibid.*, Strangford to Canning, No. 1.

[42] *Ibid.*, No. 5.

[43] *Ibid.*, No. 8.

[44] *Ibid.*, No. 9. The loan was secured, April 21, 1809. The revenue from the commerce of Madeira Island and, if necessary, the revenue resulting from the sale of the crown monopoly of Brazil-wood were pledged as guaranty (F. O., 93/37/5, Protocol, Portugal).

tions in regard to that matter.[45] On the last day of the same month full powers were exchanged between Souza Coutinho and Strangford to negotiate the treaties of commerce and alliance.[46]

In the meantime news of the June 11 decree which had reduced the rates on goods brought in by Portuguese ships from twenty-four to sixteen per cent. reached England. Instead of gaining perferential rates in Portuguese America, England was being discriminated against in favor of Portuguese shipping. Strangford was ordered to "make the most forcible Representations upon this subject to the Brazilian government" and to inform Souza Coutinho that England expected the decree to be revoked immediately. The minister was severely reprimanded for not having effected the repeal as soon as he had arrived in Rio.[47] England, by the Order-in-Council of December 21, 1808, had removed the last of the duties on reëxported articles, which had not been included in the order of November, 1808, allowing Brazilian produce free market-passage to all European countries by way of England.[48] The British Government, expecting the prince regent to reciprocate the friendly attitude of England, was extremely disappointed in this discrimination against British commerce.

Spurred by the reprimand, Strangford labored to conclude a commercial agreement with Souza Coutinho. The two ministers soon reached an understanding, but opposition arose in the Portuguese court against the proposed treaty, while the Papal Nuncio was using all his influence[49] on the superstitious prince regent to prevent his approval of the clause granting religious toleration to the Protestants. The merchants in Rio

---

[45] F. O., 63/59, Strangford to Canning, No. 13.

[46] F. O., 63/60. Strangford to Canning, No. 15.

[47] F. O., 63/61, Canning to Strangford, No. 38. Pressure was brought to bear on Canning by the Board of Trade which insisted on the serious disadvantages under which British commerce would labor as a result of the decree. See also F. O., 63/60, Canning to Strangford, No. 28.

[48] F. O., 63/61, Canning to Strangford, No. 40.

[49] Strangford reported, F. O., 63/68, No. 5, that the Nuncio had written four memorials to D. João that were "strong and menacing . . . containing sentiments worthy of the darkest ages of persecuting Superstition."

who had been ordered by the committee of the London Association to "watch the several Regulations which" were "now under discussion at the Court of the Prince Regent," and to report to London their opinion of the negotiations, were "obtruding into the business, making things more difficult."[50] The consul general, Sir James Gambier, was creating yet more trouble for Strangford by his efforts to participate in the social life of Rio despite the strict etiquette of the Portuguese court.[51]

Nevertheless, despite these handicaps, a treaty of alliance and commerce was signed, February 28, 1809. Strangford feared that he had exceeded his instructions by making a permanent instead of a temporary agreement, but the moment was, in his opinion, too favorable to let slip. The anxiety of the prince regent over Portugal had led him to sign a treaty eminently favorable to England, since it contained a clause which guaranteed to him his possession of the mother country. Instead of "most favored nation" treatment for English commerce in Brazil, the minister had striven for "much greater concessions" as a remuneration to his country for the preservation of Portugal. He had entered on the negotiations, therefore, determined to concede no more than his instructions stated but to obtain more than they stipulated. The results were embodied in the treaty which he now sent to London.[52] In the negotiations he had been governed by the principle that "England had contented Herself with the Advantages which She must ever derive from the Magnitude of Her Capitals, from the more practiced Industry of Her Manufactures, and from the Great Extent of Her Navigation." In his opinion England by this treaty had used its "undoubted Superiority" only to "acquire a still stronger claim to the Title of Protector and Friend of Brazil."[53]

Although the treaty had been signed and a copy sent to England, Strangford and Souza Coutinho still faced serious trouble

---

[50] F. O., 63/61, Strangford to Canning, No. 33.

[51] *Ibid.*, No. 41.

[52] F. O., 63/68, Strangford to Canning, No. 8 (Duplicate).

[53] *Ibid.*

in Rio. The Nuncio threatened D. João with the "most terrible exertions of . . . the vengence of" the Holy See, and even the ministers joined the opposition in the effort to pull Souza Coutinho from power by using this treaty as a bludgeon. The viscount, to save the friend of England and the "only man of talents and judgment in the Empire," was forced to "make some strong effort" to protect Souza Coutinho from his enemies. Hence he proposed to the prince regent to drop out the clauses dealing with the Inquisition, and to add a secret article guaranteeing Englishmen against any jurisdiction of that institution. D. João acquiesced, and the additional article was signed by the minister, *sub spe rati*, and sent to England to be appended to the original agreement.[54]

When the treaty reached London, it was handed over to the "Lords of the Privy Council for Trade" for the opinion of that body on its stipulations.[55] On the whole Canning approved of the terms negotiated by his minister and praised his zeal, but the document would have to be signed anew. Two points had to be changed. In the first place, the clause which guaranteed the reciprocal right to purchase, inherit, possess, or occupy land, houses, and property of every sort would have to be modified, as in England no one except a native born or a naturalized subject could purchase or possess real property, and no one could become naturalized who was not a Protestant. The point could be remedied easily, said Canning, as this privilege could not be of importance to the Portuguese, whereas the right of the Englishman to own real property in Brazil was necessary.[56]

In the second place, the agreement reaffirmed all old trea-

---

[54] *Ibid.*, No. 11.

[55] F. O., 63/69, Canning to Strangford, No. 11. See 63/73, *Papers on the Proposed Treaty of Commerce, July-Sept.*, 1809, for the action of the council on the treaty and the exchange of letters between Canning and the council and Canning and the solicitor general. Canning opposed successfully some of the demands of the Council for Trade while he embodied others in his instructions to Strangford for the revision of the treaty. The new draft passed through the hands of the council for change and approval.

[56] F. O., 63/70, Canning to Strangford, No. 13. Dated August 1, 1809.

ties. Now by Article 23 of the treaty of 1654 "all goods and merchandise of the Enemies of either on board the ship of either, or their People or subjects," should remain "untouched," a stipulation which would confirm the Portuguese contention of "free bottoms, free goods."[57] Canning explained to Strangford that the "question of free bottoms making free goods" was "of such incalculable importance in the present state of the world, that no consideration would induce His Majesty to concede that Principle, or even to admit any modification of it at the present moment."[58]

Hence Strangford's treaty was returned to him, with a few corrections and a new arrangement of the articles which separated the political clauses from the commercial stipulations. The minister was to explain the necessity of a new signature on the grounds that the extraordinary step of changing the treaty after it had been signed and sent to England nullified the entire document.[59] Full powers to sign any treaty during his stay in Brazil were sent to Strangford in order to allow him to use his initiative in regard to such negotiations.[60]

Although the new draft of the treaty was essentially the same as Strangford's first effort, there were some changes in addition to the two points mentioned by Canning in his first criticism. The definition of what constituted a British or a Portuguese vessel was added; the religious article, so vehemently opposed by the Nuncio, was to stand in its original form; the clause stipulating the return of military and naval deserters was dropped, as no satisfactory working of such a stipulation was possible;[61] and some doubtful wording was modified.[62]

---

[57] F. O., 63/70, Canning to Strangford, No. 13.

[58] *Ibid.*, No. 14. The principle to which Canning referred was the contention supported by Brazil that a neutral flag covered all goods except contraband of war on that vessel regardless of the fact that such goods might belong to a belligerent.

[59] *Ibid.*, No. 13.

[60] *Ibid.*, No. 16. Dispatch No. 19 under date of October .., 1809, was signed by Bathurst.

[61] The present difficulty with the United States taught that lesson to England, Canning explained.

[62] *Ibid.*, No. 14. Dated September 23, 1809.

When the revised treaty reached Strangford in Rio, he found little difficulty in obtaining the consent of the prince regent to the changes desired by the British Government. The difficulty which he now encountered was the refusal of D. João to ratify for a second time some of the unaltered articles. The Nuncio was again vehement in protest against the provision concerning the religious question, and Fernando Portugal, minister of the interior, fought the stipulations concerning the slave trade. The whole court was united against the viscount and Souza Coutinho in an effort to block the ratification.[63] Strangford was forced to exert all of his magnetic influence on the prince regent, who was never "in the same mind during two Successive Days." At last, learning that the "frittering away of time" had reached the point of transferring the treaty negotiations to London, the minister felt himself obliged "to assume a tone which had the effect of instantly determining the Prince Regent to accede to all" of his proposals.[64]

The opposition to the treaty had been centered around several points. The stipulation which required that the master and three-fourths of the crew be natural subjects of the prince regent before the vessel could enter English waters as a Portuguese ship was won by the minister only after an obstinate fight, as the Portuguese merchantmen were manned largely by Spaniards and other foreigners. This clause would practically destroy the Portuguese carrying trade resulting from the Oporto wine business, as the crews of the vessels engaged in that trade were Gallician or Biscayan seamen.

It was the religious clause, however, which gave Strangford his greatest difficulty. The Nuncio declared that the phrase of the treaty stating that British subjects might perform public

[63] F. O., 63/83, Strangford to Bathurst, No. 2.

[64] *Ibid.*, No. 12; Strangford to Wellesley, No. 17. Strangford sent D. João an ultimatum demanding immediate signature; failure to sign would cause the minister to "give this court a demonstration which would prove very clearly that it was easier to lose confidence and friendship than to regain them." His conduct and success rendered him obnoxious to the ministers opposing the treaty and an effort was made to force D. João to complain to London of Strangford's "pressing and urgent manner" of carrying on the affair.

worship to the "Honour of Almighty God" seemed to him to be a scandalous abuse of language. The prayers of heretics were regarded by the Almighty as an insult, and it did not become the prince regent as a Catholic sovereign to establish a contrary principle. In support of his opinion he continued to threaten D. João with severest penalties from Rome if he signed such a clause. A favorite in the court[65] maintained that "an entire toleration of the Protestant Religion was all that was wanting to render Brazil an English colony." The best means to secure a distinction, which he deemed necessary, between foreigners and natives in Brazil was to establish severe restrictions in matters of religion. Despite the formidable opposition to the clauses, however, Strangford carried his point.

The minister even succeeded in obtaining concessions which had not been included in the first treaty. The English were now given the right, specifically stated, to sell by retail as well as wholesale; goods might be consigned to either English or Portuguese subjects on the same terms; the Portuguese crown was made responsible for loss or damage in case of goods deposited in the royal customs houses; the right to pay customs duties by three, six, or nine months notes instead of specie payment on withdrawal of goods was secured; and the formal abrogation of Article 23 of the treaty of 1654 was made by the Portuguese government, whereas all other articles, *alvarás*, and decrees of the past which granted privileges to Englishmen were specifically reaffirmed.[66]

The final stipulations, which were divided into three treaties and some secret articles, were signed February 19, 1810, and ratified by D. João seven days later.[67] The preamble of the first of these, the Treaty of Commerce and Navigation,[68] main-

---

[65] The Conde das Galveas, formerly Chevalier d'Almeida.

[66] F. O., 63/83, Strangford to Wellesley, No. 16.

[67] *Ibid.*, No. 19. The letter patent of D. João, explaining the terms of the treaties of 1810 and ordering the execution of the same, was issued March 7, 1810 (*Os Privilegios da Naçaõ Britannica*, pp. 15-20).

[68] F. O., 93/37/7, Portugal, Treaty of Commerce and Navigation, signed at Rio de Janeiro, February 19, 1810. It is given in English and Portuguese in parallel columns and contains thirty-four articles. The signatures are those of Strangford and Linhares (Souza Coutinho).

tained that the sole purpose of the agreement was to consolidate and strengthen "the ancient friendship and good understanding which so happily subsist, and have during so many ages subsisted between the two Crowns" and to improve and extend "the beneficial effects thereof to the mutual advantage of their respective subjects."

The first nine articles were devoted to establishing the reciprocal rights of the two contracting parties under the system of opendoor commerce and navigation. The right of a subject of one nation to sojourn or travel or trade in any port, town, or province of the other country was guaranteed[69]; most favored nation rights were set up as to payment of taxes and imports[70]; reciprocity in drawbacks and bounties of exported goods was instituted[71]; mutual commerce and navigation of both countries on the basis of the most favored nation was expressly permitted in the ports and seas of Asia[72]; the sanctity of the home of the subject of one nation dwelling in the territory of the other was assured[73]; Portugal reserved the crown monopolies of ivory, brazil-wood, urzela, diamonds, gold-dust, gunpowder, and tobacco in the form of snuff[74]; and the reciprocal right to appoint and maintain consuls was ceded.[75] A clause, which later became irritating to Brazil when it wished to develop its own merchant marine, stipulated that British vessels should not pay any higher port duties within Portuguese dominions than the Portuguese ships paid in English ports.[76]

The lofty purpose enunciated in the preamble, of "liberal commerce and reciprocal benefits" was strikingly illustrated in the famous article ten. The prince regent by this clause granted to England the privilege of nominating special magistrates to act as judges conservators in those ports and cities of his dominions in which national tribunals and courts of justice were or might hereafter be established. The judges were to try all cases involving British subjects according to the laws established in Portugal for such jurisdiction since the 1654 treaty. Eng-

[69] Article II.
[70] Article III.
[71] Article V.
[72] Article VI.
[73] Article VII.
[74] Article VIII.
[75] Article IX.
[76] Article IV.

lish subjects residing in the port or city where the tribunal was to be set up should choose the magistrate by a plurality vote, subject to the ratification of D. João or his successors. Removal of judges by Portugal was possible only by appeal through the British ambassador or minister. In return for this concession by Portugal, his Britannic Majesty engaged to guarantee the "most strict and scrupulous observance of the laws, by which the persons and property of Portuguese subjects residing within His Dominions are secured and protected, and of which they (in common with all foreigners) enjoy the benefit, through the acknowledged equity of British jurisprudence and the singular excellence of the British Constitution."[77]

Article XII granted to the English religious toleration and the right to worship in their homes or in the churches and chapels to be built by them, provided such chapels and churches should resemble private dwelling houses and no bells should be rung to announce public worship. No one should be persecuted for his belief unless he declaimed against the Catholic religion or endeavored to gain converts to his own faith. Offenders, however, should be amenable to the civil police and not to religious tribunals and should be punished by fines or confinement to their dwellings.

The "liberal system of commerce founded upon the basis of reciprocity and mutual convenience," announced as the purpose of the treaty in the preamble, was exemplified by the clause which set the duties to be paid on British goods whether consigned to English or Portuguese subjects, at fifteen per cent. ad valorem. The tariff table by which this duty was to be assessed was to be drawn up by an equal number of British and Portuguese merchants, aided by the English consul general and the Portuguese administrator general of the customs. On the other hand, Portuguese goods entering England were to pay

[77] This tactless vaunting of British superiority following the implied reasons for the establishment of the special magistrates in Brazil was bitterly resented by the Brazilians. The "acknowledged equity . . . " phrase became to Brazilian writers a pass word for British pretensions and effrontery. The phrase is usually attributed to Strangford, but the idea and part of the phrasing were taken from Canning's instructions of April 17, 1808 (F. O., 63/59, Canning to Strangford, No. 4).

the duties demanded of the most favored nation.[78] An attempt was made to render these terms iron-clad by the clause which prohibited the extension to any other nation whatsoever of the special privileges in import duties, granted exclusively to England by Portugal or to Portugal by England.[79] As the import tariff for all nations was twenty-four per cent. established by the *Carta Regia* of January 28, 1808, with the special rate of sixteen per cent. conceded to Portuguese vessels by the decree of June 11 of the same year, England gained a lower rate than even the colony or the mother country.[80]

Brazilian sugar, coffee, and other articles similar to the produce of the English colonies were denied entrance to British markets, although the right was granted to Portugal to send such produce to England for reëxportation, exempt from the higher duties imposed on such articles destined for consumption within the British Dominions,[81] a stipulation which insured British vessels of cargoes and English merchants of business. Likewise, the prince regent could set up prohibitory duties on English articles known by the name of British East Indies goods and on West Indies produce, such as sugar and coffee.[82]

To facilitate communications, a packet line was to be established between England and Rio de Janeiro.[83] All former treaties and agreements existing between the two crowns not contrary to the new treaty were declared in force, while special mention was made of the continuance of the articles of the Methuen Treaty of 1703, in regard to Portuguese wines and

[78] Article XIX. [79] *Ibid.*

[80] By decree of October 18, 1810, the duties on merchandise brought in by Portuguese ships was lowered from sixteen to fifteen per cent. (Pereira da Silva, *Historia do Imperio,* II, 138, footnote 2).

[81] Article XX. [82] Article XXI.

[83] Article XIII. The convention, which constituted the third of the treaties signed February 19, 1810, set up a monthly service between Falmouth and Rio touching at Madeira on the way. Regulations as to sailing dates, port privileges, management, postal rates, etc., were specified. The convention is given by L. Herstlet, *Commercial Treaties,* V, 406-411. The convention was included in these treaties although it was practically the same as the earlier agreement made by Strangford soon after his arrival in Rio.

English woolens.[84] Stipulations as to contraband of war, shipwrecks, pirates, and rights of subjects residing in the dominions of the other country at the time of the outbreak of war occupied several articles.[85]

To conserve the advantages gained for England by the agreement, Strangford added to the above the final articles[86] that "it is agreed and stipulated by the high contracting Parties, that the Present Treaty shall be unlimited in point of duration, that the obligations and conditions expressed or implied in it shall be perpetual and immutable; and they shall not be changed or affected in any manner in case His Royal Highness the Prince Regent of Portugal, His Heirs or Successors, should again establish the seat of the Portuguese Monarchy within the European Dominions of the Crown." At the end of fifteen years from the date of ratification,[87] the articles of the treaty might be revised, with the stipulation, however, that no modification could become effective until both parties agreed to the change.[88]

The second[89] of these treaties dealt with political questions. Perpetual union between the two countries was guaranteed[90] and the obligation to preserve peace was accepted by both.[91] Great Britain promised never to recognize as sovereign of Portugal any prince who was not the legitimate heir of the house of Bragança; while the additional articles of the secret convention of October 22, 1806, relative to Madeira Island, were reaffirmed.[92] Portugal was to indemnify British subjects who had suffered losses during the crisis of 1807, while England reciprocated in regard to Portuguese losses caused by the seizure of Gôa by the British.[93] In grateful remembrance of the assistance rendered him by the English fleet, D. João conceded the privi-

[84] Article XXVI.

[85] Articles XXVII-XXXI.

[86] Articles XXXII-XXXIII.

[87] June 18, 1810.

[88] Article XXXIII. This last stipulation was added at the insistence of Galveas and Aguiar (F. O., 63/83, Strangford to Wellesley, No. 16).

[89] F. O., 93/37/8, Portugal, Treaty of Friendship and Alliance.

[90] Article I.

[91] Article II.

[92] Article III.

[93] Articles IV and V. The English seized Gôa when the order of sequestration of English property in Portugal was issued.

lege to the British of cutting timber from Brazilian forests for the construction of war vessels,[94] and pledged supplies of fresh meat, vegetables, and wood in case English war ships again came to his aid.[95] British war ships without limit as to the number might enter any port in the Portuguese Dominions, even in time of peace, a privilege which was expressly prohibited to the ships of any other nation.[96] Finally, the prince regent declared that the Inquisition should never be established in his American possessions,[87] and forbade his subjects to carry on the slave traffic from any place in Africa except from the actual possessions of the Portuguese crown in that continent.[98]

By two secret articles[99] England pledged its good offices with the Ottoman Porte and the Barbary States in order to secure peace between these states and Portugal and promised to work for the restoration of Olivença (seized by Spain by the Treaty of Badajoz) and for the settlement of the boundary dispute over the French Guiana region according to the Portuguese interpretation since the Treaty of Utrecht. In return D. João promised to prohibit the slave trade at Bissao and Cacheo on the West African coast, and to cede these places to England for fifty years, provided Great Britain secured Olivença and the desired solution to the Guiana boundary.

Thus an astute English minister, ably directed by the British Foreign Office, secured preferential rights for his country in Brazil. In negotiating the treaties, the Portuguese court had in mind almost exclusively the necessities of Portugal itself. No Brazilian was in the ministry or in the prince regent's council of state to fight for the welfare of the colony and point out the stipulations which would be detrimental to its interests. The

---

[94] Article VI.

[95] Article VII. This article was reciprocal; if Portuguese war vessels should come to the aid of England, Great Britain was to furnish similar supplies.

[96] Article VIII.

[97] Article IX. This article was severely criticized by the Portuguese and Brazilians as being a humiliating declaration. D. João should have decreed the closing of America to the Inquisition, as the declaration in a treaty had the appearance of having been forced by England.

[98] Article X.

[99] F. O., 93/37/9, Portugal.

Portuguese minister, pro-English in his sympathies, ignorant of conditions in Brazil, and precipitate in his manner of conducting public business, was guided by his preoccupation with the situation of Portugal, whereas England's attention was directed principally to Brazil. Although the treaties were concluded in Rio de Janeiro, they were negotiated by a Portuguese court on the basis of past Anglo-Portuguese relations, with the European situation of the mother country uppermost in the minds of the small clique which controlled Portuguese foreign policy. In addition, strong pressure was exerted by the representative of the other party to the compact, under circumstances which forced on the Portuguese court a well-nigh hopeless handicap. In the words of Oliveira Martins, "once more the dynasty sold the kingdom as Esau had sold his birthright; once more, the House of Bragança, to preserve its throne, sacrificed the nation."[100]

Brazilian historians are quite unanimous in condemning the treaties, maintaining that England had cornered the unheroic prince regent in such a way that he could do nothing but sign when the masterful Strangford presented his terms.[101] While the negotiations were still in progress, the editor of the *Correio Braziliense* warned his readers from London that a treaty of commerce between Brazil and England was a most delicate task, as the agreements existing between England and Portugal could not serve as precedents. The two principal bonds of union between those two countries, mutual interests of exportation and protection against enemies, did not apply to Brazil, for the colony was self-sustaining in produce and, being isolated, feared no invasion. In addition it was impossible to foresee what path either the cultivator or the manufacturer would take in Brazil, or whether the United States would not offer articles at less price than would England. In view of these facts, the present negotiations were very dangerous for Brazil, in the opinion of

[100] *Historia de Portugal*, II, 248.

[101] Pereira Pinto, *Apontamentos para o Direito Internacional*, I, 29 ff., is especially bitter; Abranches, *Tratados de Commercio e Navigação do Brazil*, pp. 2-5, condemns the treaty unsparingly; Rocha Pombo, *Historia do Brazil*, VII, 173 ff., restrains himself to stating that the treaty "was an error" and gives proof for his assertion; Pereira da Silva, *Historia do Imperio*, II, 137, calls the treaty "defective and fatal."

the editor, especially since the Portuguese court possessed little knowledge or experience of conditions in the colony.[102]

In November of 1809, the *Correio* was warning Brazilian merchants that English traders were bringing influence to bear on the British negotiator and was calling on them to awaken and send in suggestions and demands of their own to serve as weapons with which the Portuguese court could refute the English demands.[103] Early in the succeeding year the editor gave as his opinion that Brazil under the present circumstances could not close an equitable treaty with England and preached the Manchester doctrine of *laissez faire*.[104] Realizing the handicaps under which the Portuguese negotiator was laboring, the editor throughout the negotiations was determined to defend him when the terms of the agreement should become known; but the complete "capitulation" of Brazil to English demands which the publication of the treaties revealed, deprived him of any possible grounds on which he could support the minister.[105]

The Portuguese version of the treaty, the editor pointed out, demonstrated clearly that the agreement was a translation from the English original and that the English negotiator had taken the initiative throughout,[106] while the terms themselves demonstrated the truth of that assertion. There was no real reciprocity in the stipulations, although such an assertion was repeatedly made in the treaty; the English were to enjoy privileges in Brazil denied even to the natives living in the colony; the effects of

[102] *Correio Braziliense*, II, 129-130. The editor was Hipolyto José Soares da Costa. He was born in Colonia de Sacramento, 1774. While in Portugal, he had suffered torture by the Inquisition, and had fled to London. He started the *Correio Braziliense* in 1808 and continued the paper until 1822. He died 1825 (Pereira da Silva, *Historia do Imperio*, II, 84-85). The British Museum has the set of twenty-nine volumes. The September, 1811, and March, 1820, numbers are missing, however. For the influence of the journal on Brazilian questions see F. O., 63/204, Chamberlain to Castlereagh, September 6, 1817, Separate.

[103] *Correio Braziliense*, III, 526-527.

[104] *Ibid.*, IV, 188.

[105] *Ibid.*, V, 189.

[106] Snuff (*tabacco em pó*) was translated "*tabacco manufacturado*," which included cigarettes, cigars, etc., in Portuguese. Thus England recognized only the monopoly of snuff whereas Portugal recognized as a monopoly all articles manufactured of tobacco. The editor pointed out several such inaccuracies (*Correio Braziliense*, V, 189).

the treaty would retard the growing prosperity of the colony; and the dignity and honor of the Portuguese nation was humiliated before the world by the confessions and admissions contained in the agreement.[107]

If the treaty had frankly stated what everybody knew to be the truth, that England was the only support of the Portuguese government, which was maintaining itself exclusively by means of British troops, loans, munitions, arms, and ships; that these benefits were so great and essential that in the actual state of affairs, without them, the Portuguese would cease to be even nominally a nation; that the Portuguese government, being devoid of any other means of repaying such favors, had granted preferential commercial privileges to the English nation, then the lack of reciprocity in the treaty would have appeared to be the result of facts which were evident to all the world.[108] The Portuguese government had now paid in full for the support received from Great Britain.

The editor, however, did not censure England for securing such a treaty, for that power was simply behaving in accordance with a national ambition which resulted in prosperity, greatness, and power. The blame for the fatal agreement of 1810 lay at the door of the Portuguese ministry and court. By inefficiency, ignorance, and selfish ambition to maintain themselves and their patron in power, the ministers of the prince regent had betrayed the nation.[109]

While these criticisms, made by a man who was a fervent Brazilian and an acute observer, have grounds of truth, it must be admitted that the colony received some benefits from the transaction. The influx of British capital and enterprise stimu-

---

[107] *Correio Braziliense*, V, 189.

[108] *Ibid.*, V, 302. He points out Articles 7, 10, 15, 16, and 19 as demonstrating a lack of reciprocity in the treaty.

[109] *Ibid.*, XI, 218-219. Pereira da Silva, *Historia do Imperio*, II, 131, lays the responsibility entirely on Souza Coutinho who dominated the councils of the price regent "by the superiority of talents" which he displayed in advocating the treaty terms. There were good reasons for concluding such a treaty from the point of view of Portugal, a fact which influenced Souza Coutinho far more profoundly than the necessities, largely unknown to him, of the colony of Brazil.

lated the economic growth of Brazil, even though it crushed the budding industries which had sprung up since 1808. Professional men, artisans, trained mechanics, capitalists, and traders, invited by the special privileges announced in the treaties, flocked to Brazil. In 1808 the colony was emancipated, economically, from the decadent mother country; in 1810 it acquired a rich step-mother. Whether the emancipation of 1808 would have been sufficient, or whether the legal recognition of England's special position was necessary, is a question difficult to decide. The economic superiority enjoyed by Great Britain over its world competitors would have enabled it to baffle competition, but it is doubtful whether the economic resources of that country would have been attracted to Brazil without the legal recognition of special privileges and personal security. Moreover, under the system of government promotion of trade practised by the powers of Europe, it was incumbent upon England to guarantee itself against action by its rivals. Strangford's treaty forestalled any possible discrimination against Great Britain in favor of any other country. In any case, the treaties of 1810 were vital factors in Anglo-Brazilian relations until the middle of the century.

The English trade set in motion by the *Carta Regia* of 1808 received a powerful stimulus from the new treaty of commerce. There was an influx of British merchants at Rio de Janeiro, and speculation ran rife in England. So great was the volume of goods sent out that the distracted customs service was unable to clear its warehouses. Goods were left in the open, and the natives, amazed at such a quantity of merchandise and listening to golden rumors of Britain's kindness to their sovereign, thanked the "generous English" and "helped themselves to what their own countrymen had hitherto charged a good price for."[110] The supplies sent out of cut glass, brilliant chandeliers, superfine woolen cloths, high priced English saddles, whips, and bridles found no market; and ice skates, shipped to sub-

[110] John Mawe, *Travels*, pp. 450-471. He pictures trade conditions on or before 1816. The following pages of description of conditions in Rio are taken from information given in his book of travels.

tropical Rio, were left to rust themselves into junk. Crates of prospectors' hatchets with the sharp edge on one end and the hammer on the other, destined for the use of those who wished to go to the nearest mountain, break the rocks, and cut out the precious golden metal, testified to the sanguine and ignorant hopes of English exporters.

The gullible representatives of these exporters exchanged their goods, or money, for turmalines bought for emeralds or for fake diamonds. They accepted at face value gold dust largely mixed with powdered brass. The young agents, recently arrived from England, had "grand ideas" as to the manner of conducting their business. They took big stores at outrageous rentals, set aside their hours for riding in the morning, visited their country-seats in the afternoons, and attended gay parties at night. Shopkeeping being considered manual labor, they were forced to sell their goods by auction at ruinous prices. Brazilians and some levelheaded Englishmen who were less concerned with their social position bought marketable merchandise, sold at these auctions at prices below the wholesale quotations from Europe, and set up firmly established businesses catering to the real necessities of the population. Eventually the crash came; bankruptcy notices filled the London *Gazette;* judges conservators and the Brazilian authorities coöperated in clearing away the débris; and trade between England and Brazil was established on a firm basis.

By 1816 England was exporting to Brazil a steady stream of goods, half of which went to Rio alone. The study of the articles included in this stream gives a curious side light on the life of Brazilian colonials with a European court in their midst. Stout, fine cloth, particularly blue or black, sold quickly. There was a steady demand for dress hats, boots, and shoes; earthenware and glass; bottled porter, cheshire cheese, and butter; mirrors, silk and cotton hosiery, and fashionable dresses for women. Hams, tongues, and pork; oil, wine and brandy; cotton goods of all kinds, linens, and common woolens brought good prices. Although the smiths preferred Swedish iron, there was a good market for iron and steel articles. Salt, some hardware, glass, and some plated goods found ready sales. Tinplate, matches, brass, lead, shot, gunpowder, and drugs sold well. Flour, turpentine, tar, staves household furniture, and other items from North America prevented any great sale of such articles of British manufacture.

In return for these articles shipped to Brazil, British merchants carried back to England from Rio de Janeiro gold, diamonds, and precious stones; sugar, raw cotton, hides, and tobacco; rum, wax, indigo, and certain highly prized woods. The port of Bahia led in the raw cotton shipments, sending eight-ninths of its cotton export to Liverpool. Much molasses and rum left this port for England also. Britain took three-fourths of the cotton exported from Pernambuco and half the sugar. From tropical Pará, English vessels carried back cocoa, coffee, rice, sarsaparilla, gums, drugs, sugar, hides, molasses, and woods.

A comparison of British exports to various foreign markets demonstrates the importance of this Brazilian trade to English foreign commerce. In 1812 Portuguese America took twenty-five per cent. more English merchandise than did all of Asia, half as much as did the United States or the British West Indies, and more than four-fifths of the total sent to South America.[111] Over three-fourths of the value of articles exported to Brazil were cottons, with woolens ranking a poor second.[112] World peace in 1815, with thirsty markets thrown open to British exporters, reduced the importance of Portuguese America, for Asia during that year surpassed Brazil by a million pounds sterling, the British West Indies did the same by nearly five millions, and the United States by ten millions. Yet the prince regent's American possessions still took two-thirds of the total

---

[111] Customs 8/1, *Exportation from Great Britain by Countries, 1812*. Exports to Asia were £1,648,067 plus New Holland (Asia) £15,210; to the United States £4,032,-445; to West Indies £4,109,096; to Foreign Colonies of South America (including Pensacola) £2,470,006; to Brazil £2,003,253. There is little reason to believe that smuggling thrived during this period, as the low rate of fifteen per cent. discouraged that sort of trade.

[112] The value of cottons exported to Brazil was £1,557,455; of woolens £199,945 (*ibid.*).

amount sold to continental American foreign colonies.[113] By 1820 Brazil had regained the importance of the earlier period, however, for in that year it purchased of British exporters more than half as much as did all Asia or the British West Indies and very nearly two-thirds as much as did the United States, while it still absorbed three-fourths of the total amount shipped officially to the Spanish and Portuguese colonies of America.[114]

The fact that the principal interest of the Englishman in the Brazilian trade has always been in selling rather than in buying was demonstrated in this early period. In 1812 Brazil sold to the Britisher less than £700,000 worth of goods[115]; while three years later the value had advanced only to a little over £829,000.[116] Five years later England took nearly £1,300,000 of Brazilian goods, the most important item being raw cotton.[117] These figures ranked Brazil far down the scale among the foreign suppliers to England, and left a big balance of trade in favor of Great Britain. Thus, soon after the opening of the ports of Portuguese America to foreign trade, a permanent characteristic of Anglo-Brazilian commercial relations was determined. Brazil was henceforth an important market for English manufactures, but a secondary source of British importation.

Strangford's success united the Portuguese court in a campaign to oust both the viscount and the foreign minister from power, but the effort was hopeless as long as Souza Coutinho lived. At the marriage of D. Maria Thereza, eldest daughter of the prince regent, to D. Pedro Carlos, Infante of Spain,

[113] Customs 8/3. Exports to Asia were £2,930,412; to British West Indies £6,587,999; to the United States, £12,746,913; to Continental Foreign Colonies of America, £2,547,368 (East Florida £231,103, Buenos Aires, £399,025), and to Brazil, £1,896,064. These figures are according to the official value in conformity with the rates of 1696.

[114] Customs 8/12. Exports to Asia £3,809,246; to the United States, £3,691,365; to British West Indies, £3,860,260; to Spanish colonies £820,271; to Brazil, £2,099,396. Figures are by real or declared value.

[115] Customs 4/8. Principal items were: raw cotton, £473,067; woods, £55,676; hides, £34,661; sugar, £19,091; coffee, £15,393.

[116] Customs 4/10. Official value according to the rates of 1696.

[117] Customs 4/15. Total imports from Brazil, £1,294,025, of which raw cotton amounted to £942,857; coffee to £182,998; sugar to £110,351; hides to £8,390; and woods to £5,655. Figures are by real or declared value.

Strangford was placed at D. João's right hand over the vehement protests of the Nuncio and of the Spanish minister.[118] Yet despite such marks of favor shown to the British representative, by the end of 1810 the relations between England and the Portuguese court were not so promising, due to court intrigues at Rio and to the unpopularity of Englishmen in the American possessions of the prince regent. "The Brazilians," Strangford reported,[119] were "in general jealous and discontented; they" looked "upon the English as usurpers of their commerce; they" were "offended with the haughty language and proceedings of our Consuls, and with the heavy charges which" were "levied in their Departments; and they" complained "(certainly not without reason) of the insults daily offered to their Prejudices, Customs, and Religion, by the English Settlers of this country." The commerce of the Brazilian merchants, the minister admitted, had "in truth fallen into utter decay."[120] In addition, the main support of the popularity of England among the Portuguese was not valid in the minds of the Brazilians, as the maintenance of the Bragança family on the throne was not of the least importance to the colonials after four years of experience with the court.

As had happened in the case of past treaties between England and Portugal, trouble arose over the execution of the terms of the agreements of 1810. The most serious complaint made by England was in regard to the Oporto Wine Company. In August, 1811, Wellesley sent a fourteen page[121] letter to Strangford demanding that the monopoly enjoyed by that company be abolished as contrary to the eighth and twenty-fifth articles of the commercial treaty. Two months later the chairman of the committee of merchants trading to Brazil reiterated the same complaint.[122] The Board of Trade added its voice to the chorus, denouncing the "unwarrantable and unaccountable de-

[118] Casa Irujo. The wedding took place May 13, 1810. F. O., 63/84, Strangford to Wellesley, No. 42.

[119] F. O., 63/86, Strangford to Wellesley, No. 86.

[120] F. O., 63/103, Strangford to Wellesley, Nos. 58 and 63.

[121] F. O., 63/101, Wellesley to Strangford, No. 14.

[122] *Ibid.*, No. 18.

lay" of D. João in executing several of the leading articles of the treaty.[123] Castlereagh also insisted on the same point immediately after entering office.[124]

In obedience to the commands accompanying these complaints, Strangford informed Souza Coutinho[125] in strong and explicit language that either the monopoly at Oporto would have to be abolished in accordance with the stipulations of the treaty or confidence between England and Portugal would be suspended. He learned in reply that the Portuguese government did not intend to abolish the wine company as the result of the treaty, but simply to refuse to renew the charter which would expire at an early date. Strangford suggested to Lord Wellesley that he could frighten D. João into obedience by absenting himself from court, or the Foreign Office could withdraw the British squadron from the Brazilian coast. Either method would be effective. The minister reported regretfully that he had not succeeded thus far in his efforts to abolish the wine company, due to the waning power of Souza Coutinho caused by his illness, to the growth of the opposition in the court to English influence, and to D. João's growing antipathy to England for interference in other things than the defense of Portugal itself.[126]

The influence of Souza Coutinho abruptly terminated at his death on January 26, 1811. Only Strangford stood now as a bulwark between the prince regent and the wave of anti-English sentiment in the court.[127] From that date Strangford's path was beset with increasing difficulties. He was exasperated almost beyond endurance by the passive, inert opposition which resulted in no action by the Portuguese ministry, favorable or otherwise, on the complaints which he presented in regard to the non-execution of the terms of the treaty of 1810.[128] Eventu-

[123] F. O., 63/101, Wellesley to Strangford, November 14, 1811.

[124] F. O., 63/103, Castlereagh to Strangford, Nos. 2 and 38.

[125] Now Conde de Linhares.

[126] F. O., 63/122, Strangford to Wellesley, No. 3. Dated January 24, 1812.

[127] *Ibid.*, No. 10.

[128] F. O., 63/148, Strangford to Castlereagh, No. 132. F. O., 63/144, Castlereagh to Strangford, No. 8, dated March 11, 1813, gives a résumé of the complaints.

ally the matter was transferred to London by the Rio court to be threshed out between Castlereagh and the Chevalier de Souza.[129] The British foreign minister refused to take the matter out of Strangford's hands, however, and at the end of 1812, he demanded of the prince regent a categorical decision on the disputed points of the treaty of 1810, with special reference to the two main points at issue: the Oporto Wine Company monopoly and the suppression of the slave traffic. Strangford was to conclude a signed agreement on these points, and any reference of the matter involved to the court at London by the Portuguese minister would be considered as a rejection of the negotiations.[130]

On the last day of 1813 Strangford gloomily reported that nothing now was "to be expected from the Justice or Good Faith of the present Brazilian Ministers," and the time had come to show the Rio court that its reluctance to fill its engagements would no longer be tolerated, and that the "change of System which it" had "adopted since the Death of the Conde de Linhares [Souza Coutinho]" was "not unnoticed by an Ally to whom so much" was due and "whose Exertions have hitherto met such inadequate returns of Gratitude."[131]

Two months later the prince regent was forced to call Antonio d'Araujo to enter the ministry. He could not do otherwise after the death of Souza Coutinho,[132] for it was "an absolute fact," in the opinion of Strangford, "that the Ignorance of the Individuals composing this court" was "such that scarcely one among them" was "capable of writing an ordinary letter." There was no one to appoint to the office except Araujo, unless D. João called on a colonial. There were men of undoubted talent among that element, but such promotion would be contrary to the customs of the Portuguese court and inimical to

[129] Now Conde de Funchal. *Ibid.*, No. 30. Dated October 11, 1813.

[130] F. O., 63/144, Castlereagh to Strangford, October 11, 1813, Secret and Separate.

[131] F. O., 63/148, Strangford to Castlereagh, No. 157.

[132] Souza Coutinho's brother, the minister in London, was ordered to return to Rio to take his brother's place, but he refused to obey. Nor did he lose his post for his disobedience.

the interests of England, as there existed "not a class of men under the government less friendly disposed towards Great Britain than the members of the Brazilian Magistracy." Strangford prevented the appointment of Araujo to the foreign office, but he was certain that the Conde de Aguiar, who became foreign secretary, would be a pliable instrument in the hands of the new minister. The appointment of Araujo pleased the Rio public, and illuminations on three successive nights after the announcement took place as a demonstration of joy over the rise to power of the anti-English faction.[133]

England's influence in Portuguese affairs, which had reached the crest in 1810, now began to decline sharply. The struggle resolved itself into a conflict between Strangford on the one hand and the ministers and court group on the other, for possession of the prince regent. The viscount, deprived of the support of Souza Coutinho, strove to get D. João to return to Lisbon, where once more he would be under traditional English influence, while Araujo endeavored to keep the prince regent in Brazil, where the "hatred of the natives . . . towards England" was "more violent than" Strangford could describe, and where London was on the other side of the globe. In addition, Araujo counted on the support of Lord Holland in England in his opposition to the English envoy and Castlereagh.[134] At first D. João inclined to Strangford's point of view and publicly and privately signified his willingness to return to Lisbon if an English squadron should appear in Rio to take him back. Consequently, during the latter part of September, two ships of the line and one frigate were dispatched from England under Sir John Beresford to conduct the prince regent to Lisbon.[135]

The categorical answer demanded by Castlereagh in the dispatch of October 11, 1813, in regard to the Oporto Wine monopoly and the slave trade regulations, was given to Strangford by the Conde de Aguiar at the end of November, 1814. News

---

[133] F. O., 63/167, Strangford to Castlereagh, No. 7. Dated February 20, 1814.

[134] *Ibid.*, Nos. 8, 9, 23.

[135] *Ibid.*, No. 53. Dated June 21, 1814. F. O., 63/166, Bathurst to Strangford, No. 21.

of Napoleon's defeat had relieved the anxiety of the Portuguese court over the mother country and the reply was totally unacceptable.[136] When, in order to influence public opinion in favor of the suppression of the slave traffic, the viscount requested permission from the Portuguese Foreign Office to publish the recent messages of the British House of Commons and Lords in regard to the slave trade, the Conde de Aguiar accused Strangford of willfully desiring to incite the Negro slaves of Brazil to rebellion under the protection of Great Britain and warned him that the utmost rigors of the law would be imposed on anyone, native or foreigner, who disturbed the public tranquillity. When Strangford indignantly complained to D. João of such outrageous language used to a foreign diplomat, he received a note from the Conde de Aguiar saying that he had transgressed the respect due the prince regent and would be debarred from further private interviews with the sovereign.[137] Thus Araujo through Aguiar closed the avenue so long open between Strangford and D. João, and the wire to London was cut.

On December 28, 1814, Sir John Beresford with the fleet arrived in Rio,[138] and the play had reached the climax. Beresford and Strangford used every effort to get the prince regent to return, but Araujo triumphed, for the hapless D. João, through the mouth of the Conde de Aguiar, affirmed that he had never requested the ships, that the English minister had presumed by sending for the squadron, and that he intended to remain in Brazil. Strangford, who had foreseen the trend of events, had written to Castlereagh before the arrival of the ships that his word could not stand in the face of the word of a sovereign, "although all the world knew that the sovereign's word was false," and had petitioned for leave to return to London.[139] On January 3, 1815, Bathurst signed his recall at the request of the prince

[136] F. O., 63/169, Strangford to Castlereagh, No. 110. Dated December 1, 1814. The Portuguese court offered to submit the points in dispute to the Congress of the Allies. "Preposterous," Strangford said.

[137] *Ibid.*, No. 114.

[138] *Ibid.*, No. 126.

[139] *Ibid.*, December 17, 1814, Separate.

regent,[140] and on April 8, the minister turned the files over to Chamberlain as *chargé* and sailed for home.[141] Before he left, however, the decree was issued which extended the charter of the Oporto Wine Company for fifteen years, from January 1, 1817. The proclamation was totally unnecessary as the company still had twenty-two months to run before the old charter expired.[142] It was Araujo's parting shot at his old enemy.

British influence at the Portuguese court in Rio and among the Brazilians and Portuguese living in Brazil was at low ebb during the succeeding six years. Chamberlain noted in 1816 that the extreme unpopularity of England among the Brazilians and Portuguese was getting worse. No story, however extravagant, of unjust pretensions on the part of England against Brazil failed to receive implicit confidence.[143] An attempt was made to restrict the commercial freedom of the British within Brazil, for in December of the same year, the transport of English-owned goods from one Brazilian port to another even in Portuguese ships was forbidden.[144] In June, 1817, however, Araujo died, and his virulent anti-English policy was softened by his successors.[145] In November, 1819, Edward Thornton, the new minister to Rio de Janeiro, took over the office from Chamberlain, who had remained *chargé* since Strangford's recall.[146]

On his arrival, Thornton, who had been ordered to secure an arrangement in regard to the disputed points of the treaty of 1810, a settlement of the slave traffic question, and the return of the king to Lisbon,[147] found that he himself was caught

---

[140] F. O., 63/181, Bathurst to Strangford, No. 1.

[141] *Ibid.*, Strangford to Castlereagh, No. 22.

[142] *Ibid.*, No. 7. The question of the slave traffic regulation which embittered Anglo-Portuguese relations during this period will be discussed in a separate chapter.

[143] F. O., 63/193, Chamberlain to Castlereagh, April 27. Separate.

[144] Decree of December 16, 1816. F. O., 63/202, Chamberlain to Castlereagh, No. 2.

[145] F. O., 63/203, Chamberlain to Castlereagh, No. 61.

[146] F. O., 63/221, Chamberlain to Castlereagh, No. 74.

[147] The insane queen mother died March 16, 1816, and D. João was acclaimed king, February 6, 1818, after almost two years of delay.

in the stream of events which were leading to the critical days of 1820. Portugal, abandoned by the prince regent in 1807 and governed by a *junta* which had been controlled partly by Marshal Beresford,[148] now begged for the return of the king, while the colonials, surfeited with the sycophantic court, urged his departure for Lisbon. In Europe Beresford shared the unpopularity of D. João among the Portuguese, who had been thoroughly angered by the loss of the Brazilian commercial monopoly, transferred to England by the opening of the ports and by the treaty of 1810. The decree of December 16, 1815, raising Brazil to the status of co-kingdom with Portugal,[149] increased this irritation, while it freed the Brazilians from fear of a return to the status of the colonial régime.

The news of the Spanish uprising of 1820 set off the spark in Portugal; a revolution broke out in August, and the *junta* ordered the king to return. Afraid of losing his Portuguese kingdom if he did not return and yet dreading what the *Côrtes* might do to him after his arrival, divining that his eldest son would be difficult to check if he were left alone in Brazil as governor in the absence of the king, D. João vacillated between two opinions until, during the stormy April events in Rio de Janeiro, he was bustled on board a ship and dispatched to Europe.[150] The *émigré* of 1807 returned, leaving his son, D. Pedro, as regent of Brazil.[151]

---

[148] For the history of Portugal during the absence of D. João, see Oliveira Martins, *Historia de Portugal*, II, 240-257, for a brief account, and Pereira da Silva, *Historia do Imperio*, II-V, various books, for an extended study.

[149] Borges de Castro, *Collecção de Tratados*, V, 248.

[150] For the story of these days in Rio, see: Oliveira Martins, *O Brazil*, pp. 104-112; Pereira da Silva, *Historia do Imperio*, V, 55-109. The dispatches from Thornton and Chamberlain from 1819 to 1821 give excellent contemporary accounts by witnesses, of the events leading up to the return of the king to Lisbon (F. O., 63/210 to 63/237).

[151] Pereira da Silva, *op. cit.*, V, Documents, p. 315, decree of April 22, 1821. Beresford had gone to Rio early in 1820 to obtain decisive action by D. João in regard to the regency in Portugal and had returned with complete control to find that the revolution had broken out during his absence (F. O., 63/228, Thornton to Castlereagh, No. 23; *ibid.*, May 31, Separate; August 12, Separate. Secret and Confidential). When news of the revolution reached Rio, Thornton advised the king to grant moderate constitutions to both Brazil and Portugal and to send his

Thornton, an experienced and able official, exerted what pressure he could to secure the departure of D. João. Late in 1820, after the outbreak of the revolution in Lisbon, he was instructed by the Foreign Office to emphasize with the king two important points. In the first place, D. João could not count on the Holy Alliance to reconquer Portugal for him if he lost it on account of the revolution. Castlereagh had always endeavored to awaken the Portuguese king's ministers "to a just estimate of the illusory character of that league as a resource."[152] In the second place, England by its guaranty of Portuguese integrity under the old treaties was not bound to sustain the authority of the sovereign over his subjects, an authority which the revolution had now put in jeopardy. Nor, if a third power, Spain for instance, should interfere, would England undertake the whole burden of maintaining the king's interests both against his own people and against the Spaniards. Castlereagh emphasized these two points in order to show D. João the indispensability of "accepting what He" could "save out of the wreck of His own Power, which by bad management and unfounded jealousy of and indifference to" England's "councils, His Majesty" had "exposed to an entire dissolution." The Portuguese court had given evidence that it considered England would combat not only the threatening movements of Spain toward Portugal,[153] but also the revolutionary move-

eldest son, D. Pedro, to Portugal (F. O., 63/229, Thornton to Castlereagh, August 12, Separate; October 12; and No. 60). Distrustful of Pedro's fidelity, D. João refused to act until a revolution in Rio expelled him from his South American capital.

[152] The Portuguese ministers at St. Petersburg and Berlin, alarmed at the events in Spain, with which Portugal was in bitter controversy in South America over the River Plate region, had asked for the guaranty of the Holy Alliance from Russia and Prussia. Their request was made before the Madrid revolution of 1820 (C. K. Webster, *The Foreign Policy of Castlereagh, 1815-1822*, p. 228). Castlereagh, however, secured from the great powers of the Alliance recognition of the fact that England's guaranty of Portuguese territory, while it did not include internal peace, would become operative by the armed invasion of another power. Hence the Portuguese were freed from the danger, which faced Spain, of a foreign invasion (*ibid.*, pp. 277 ff).

[153] England fulfilled its pledge to protect Portuguese territory from violation by a foreign power by opposing actively the designs of Spain (Webster, *Foreign Policy of Castlereagh*, pp. 233-249).

ments within the latter kingdom. That opinion was erroneous, for Great Britain had no intention of interfering with the internal politics of its ally and would not guarantee the house of Bragança against its own people.[154]

In the turmoil of the months preceding the return of the king to Lisbon, Thornton's efforts to obtain a revision of the commercial treaty of 1810 and the final abolition of the slave traffic were fruitless. But from January 8, 1821, to the departure of the king in April of the same year, the minister coöperated intimately with the Conde de Palmella, who had just arrived from England to take over the Foreign Office, in the effort to force D. João to go back to Portugal.[155] When the king sailed for Lisbon April 25, 1821,[156] the foreign envoys followed close on his heels. The Baron de Maréchal remained in a rather undefined character of Austrian agent, due to the close connections between the ruling houses of Austria and Portugal,[157] but all other official representatives returned home. Thornton sailed June 19,[158] and Rio de Janeiro became once more a provincial capital.

Although the court had returned to Portugal, the commercial treaty of 1810 remained intact with its stipulations still applicable to the colony. The thread of continuity had been woven and the privileges enjoyed by England in Portugal for centuries had been transferred to Brazil. The impartial economic tendency manifested by the court during the first two years of its residence at Rio was checked by the treaties negotiated by Strangford, and England secured for itself a special position in the colony. From the first, Portuguese and Brazilians protested against the terms of the agreement of 1810 while England accused its ally of bad faith in carrying out the stipula-

---

[154] F. O., 63/227, Draft to Thornton, No. 17. Dated November 15, 1820.

[155] F. O., 63/228, Thornton to Castlereagh, No. 1; No. 5 (Most secret and confidential); No. 6; No. 7 (Most secret).

[156] F. O., 63/237, Thornton to Castlereagh, No. 29. The most authoritative work on Brazilian history between 1808 and 1821 is Oliveira Lima's *Dom João VI no Brazil, 1808-1821*. 2 volumes.

[157] F. O., 63/237, Thornton to Castlereagh, No. 35. D. Pedro's wife was an Austrian princess.

[158] *Ibid.*, No. 40.

tions specified in the treaty; yet at the time of the departure of D. João, England still retained its privileged position in Brazil. When D. Pedro sought recognition by England of Brazilian Independence, a part of the price exacted by Great Britain was the ratification by the new state of the commercial stipulations which were negotiated by the Portuguese element of the court at Rio with the situation of Europe as the dominating factor. The commercial relations of England and Portugal from 1808 to 1821 constituted the intermediate step in the transfer of England's century-old preëminence in Portuguese economic life to the independent state of Brazil.

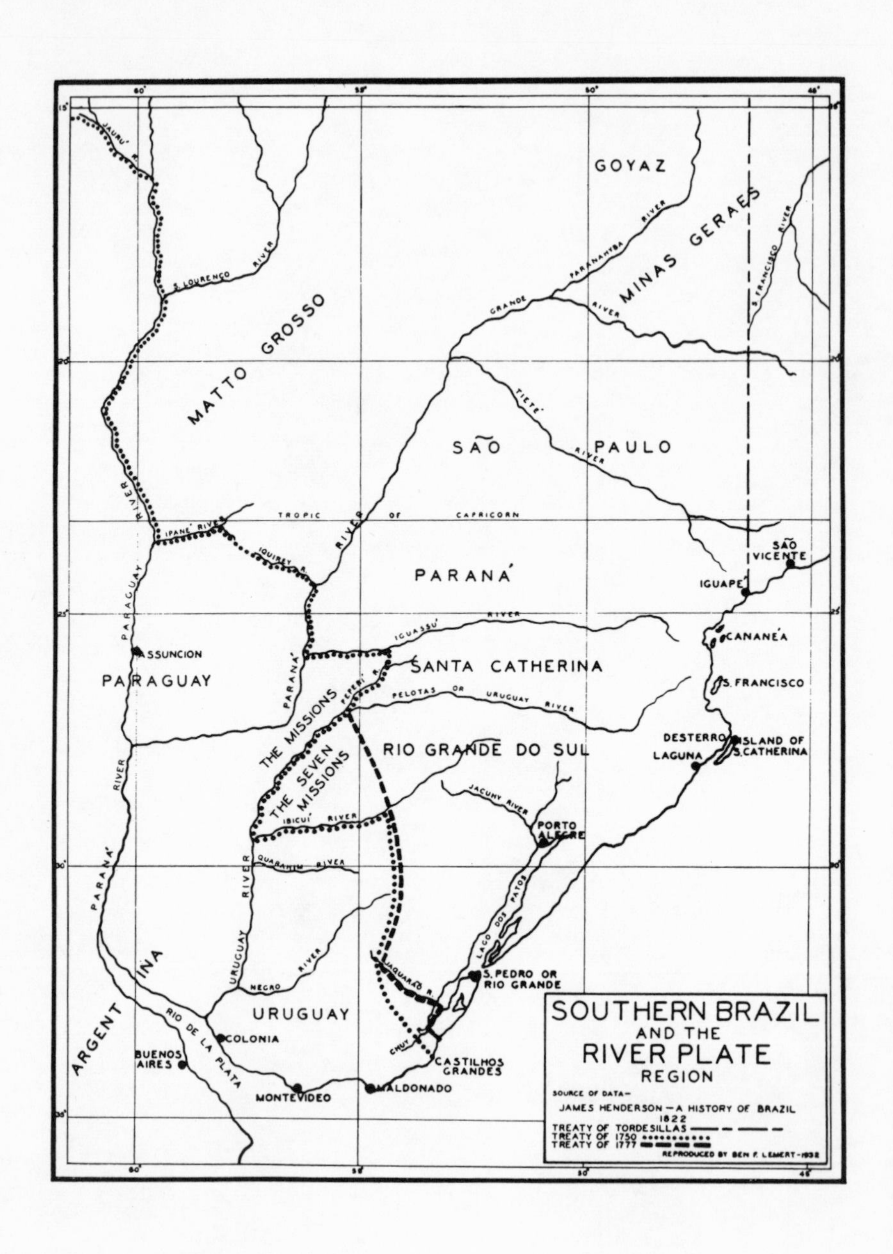

GOYAZ
MINAS GERAES
MATTO GROSSO
SÃO PAULO
PARANÁ
SANTA CATHERINA
PARAGUAY
RIO GRANDE DO SUL
THE MISSIONS
THE SEVEN MISSIONS
URUGUAY
ARGENTINA
ASSUNCION
SÃO VICENTE
IGUAPE
CANANEA
S. FRANCISCO
DESTERRO
ISLAND OF S. CATHERINA
LAGUNA
PORTO ALEGRE
S. PEDRO OR RIO GRANDE
COLONIA
BUENOS AIRES
MONTEVIDEO
MALDONADO
CASTILHOS GRANDES
RIO DE LA PLATA
LAGO DOS PATOS
TROPIC OF CAPRICORN
SOUTHERN BRAZIL
AND THE
RIVER PLATE
REGION
SOURCE OF DATA–
JAMES HENDERSON – A HISTORY OF BRAZIL
1822
TREATY OF TORDESILLAS
TREATY OF 1750
TREATY OF 1777
REPRODUCED BY BEN F. LEMERT–1932

CHAPTER V

LORD STRANGFORD AND THE PORTUGUESE DESIGNS ON THE BANDA ORIENTAL

A GLANCE at the map of South America demonstrates the economic and strategic importance to Brazil of the north bank of the River Plate basin. The three great tributaries which form the river have their origin in Brazilian territory and drain all of the rich central and southern part of that country. The Paraguay starts southward from the watershed of Matto Grosso. The Paraná flows for nearly twelve hundred miles, separating the states of Goyaz and Matto Grosso from those of São Paulo and Paraná, before it becomes the dividing line between Paraguay and Argentina. By a magnificent system of tributaries it serves the interior of two of the most progressive states of the union, São Paulo and Minas Geraes, and drains the promising state of Paraná. One of these tributaries, the Tiete, crosses the coffee state from east to west with a course of six hundred miles, for its source is almost within sight of the Atlantic Ocean between the coast towns of Santos and Rio de Janeiro. The Uruguay, the third of the rivers which unite to form La Plata, serves the two southernmost states of Santa Catharina and Rio Grande do Sul and forms the dividing line between Brazil and Argentina and, in continuation, between Argentina and Uruguay.[1]

Thus, due to the abrupt mountain range which follows the coast from the shoulder of Brazil to the southernmost state of the union, the rivers of the region which since 1700 has been the most important part of the country, drain westward into three great streams which unite to form the River Plate. Com-

---

[1] Delgado de Carvalho, *Geographia do Brasil*, pp. 104-107; 377-381; Varnhagem, *Historia Geral do Brasil*, I, Secção I.

mercial strategy, ever since early colonial times, has demanded that the Portuguese control the mouth of the system, while military strategy has required that the broad La Plata and the Paraná-Paraguay rivers, or at least the Uruguay, divide Portuguese America from its Spanish neighbors. But such a position would enable the Portuguese at will to choke the only available outlet eastward open to that part of Spanish America which lies south of the Amazon and east of the Andes. The inevitable clash between these two conflicting interests centered in a struggle for control of the eastern bank of the Uruguay river, generally known as the Banda Oriental.

The simplicity of the conflict which began in 1580 was complicated by two factors of importance. In the first place, the legal grounds on which each side rested its claim for possession were confused by a universal doubt as to the location of the famous Line of Demarcation set by Pope Alexander VI[2] and by the Treaty of Tordesillas.[3] Both the Portuguese and Spanish officials on occasion showed authenticated maps which placed the Banda Oriental within the territory allotted to each nation.[4]

[2] The Bull *Inter caetera*, May 4, 1493, assigned to the present and future sovereigns of Castile the lands discovered or to be discovered by their subjects to the west of a line drawn from pole to pole at a distance of one hundred leagues to the west of the Azores (Francis Davenport, *European Treaties Bearing on the History of the United States and its Dependencies to 1648*, p. 56, document 7).

[3] Portugal, protesting vigorously against the Papal bull, forced Spain to sign the Treaty of Tordesillas, June 7, 1494, which moved the line of demarcation 270 leagues farther west, and stipulated that a commission should be set up to determine the boundary (Davenport, *op. cit.*, p. 84, document 9). This extension of the line made possible the claims of Portugal to Brazil.

[4] Spain asserted that the line ran from Pará in the north to Iguapé, just south of São Vicente; while the Portuguese located the line from Pará to a point close to the Paraná river, west of Buenos Aires. Although Spain's contention very closely approximated the line as measured to-day, Portugal's claims seem to have been accepted by a large number of Continental authorities throughout the period of dissension. For the Spanish claims, see L. Domínguez, "Conquest of the River Plate," *Hakluyt Society Publications*. For the Portuguese side see Clovis Bevilaqua, "As Capitanias Hereditarias perante o Tratado de Tordesillas," *Revista do Instituto Historico e Geographico Brasileiro*, tomo especial, part II. For the history of the dispute over the line of demarcation, see Davenport, *European Treaties Bearing on the History of the United States*, Bevilaqua, *op. cit.*, L. Domínguez, *op. cit.*, E. G. Bourne, "The History and Determination of the Line of Demarcation Established by Pope Alexander VI," Amer. Hist. Asso., *Reports*, XXII; Rocha Pombo, *His-*

It was not until the middle of the eighteenth century that a definite treaty settled further doubt in the matter by superseding the old line of demarcation.[5]

In the second place, the commercial interests of the great powers drew the question into the maelstrom of European politics. Whereas Portugal granted other nations a share in its colonial commerce on condition that the stream pass through the ports of the mother country, Spain endeavored to maintain a strict colonial monopoly to the exclusion of all foreigners and for a century even closed La Plata itself to any trans-oceanic commerce. Under Portuguese control, therefore, the mouth of the river would serve as a base for European contraband trade with the southern Spanish colonies and even with the viceroyalty of Perú. In the course of events, although France and Holland maintained an active interest in the question, England, due to its close relations with Portugal, became the umpire in the struggle between the Spanish and the Portuguese for control of the Banda Oriental.

The importance of Colonia do Sacramento, which was returned to Portugal by the Treaty of Utrecht,[6] finally penetrated to Madrid. When in 1723 Philip V cut Colonia off from the sea by ordering Montevideo to be fortified, the Portuguese under João V's instructions seized the place, but were forced to relinquish it to the Spanish governor of Buenos Aires.[7] The governor then attempted to strengthen the town against the wave of Portuguese settlers from the north and decided to stop the "barefaced contraband" trade carried on through Colonia by destroying that town,[8] but England, Holland, and France again united to prevent the expulsion of the Portuguese from the River Plate region.[9]

---

toria do Brazil, I, *passim;* Calvo, *Collección completa de los tratados*, I, 190-262, 263-302.

[5] Treaty of 1750. [6] See *supra*, pp. 27-28.

[7] *Revista del Archivo, General Administrativo; Colección de Documentos*, collected by Dr. Pedro Mascaró, pp. 5, 21, 52, 53.

[8] Robert Southey, *History of Brazil*, III, 287; Grimaldi, "Respuesta del Marqués de Grimaldi, Ministro de España, a la memoria . . . de Portugal de D. Francisco Ignacio de Souza Coutinho," Calvo, *Colección de los tratados*, III, 5.

[9] Altamira, *Historia de España*, IV, 110; B. Moses, *Spain's Declining Power in South*

After the 1735 incident, the contraband trade of Colonia grew until Spain felt that "the necessity of cutting out that sore spot of commercial corruption" was urgent.[10] In 1750 Ferdinand VI, under the influence of his mother, D. Barbara de Bragança of the reigning house of Portugal, attempted to reach an amicable settlement with João V by taking Colonia for Spain and relinquishing the Seven Missions territory to Portugal,[11] but neither José, who succeeded João, nor Charles III of Spain approved of the agreement. An accord in 1761 between Portugal and Spain therefore annulled the 1750 arrangement, and England saw to it that the possession of Colonia by Portugal was firmly reëstablished by the Treaty of Paris in 1763.[12]

After 1763 Governor Cunha at Rio de Janeiro, by ordering an advance south and west from the captaincy of Santa Catharina, secured for the Portuguese the territory which extended from the village of S. Pedro westward to the Ibicuí and Pepirí rivers.[13] Moreover, Portuguese depredations continued, one expedition alone taking half a million head of cattle and seven thousand Indian families.[14] Charles III, losing patience in 1777, sent a strong expedition to America which seized the island of Santa Catharina and the village of S. Pedro in Brazil and Colonia on the River Plate.[15] Portugal was thereupon forced to sign an agreement which ceded Colonia with all its claims on the north bank of La Plata and acknowledged the exclusive

---

America, 1730-1806, pp. 31-32. In 1735 Portugal and Spain were on the verge of war, but were quieted by the intervention of England, France, and Holland. Walpole sent a fleet of twenty-eight ships and 12,840 men to Lisbon as a gesture of warning to Spain (*Historical Register*, 1735, pp. 192-203; *London Magazine*, 1735, p. 333; Innes, *Britain and Her Rivals*, p. 44; *Newcastle Papers*, CX, Add. Ms., 32,795, Trawley to Keene, Lisbon, May 5 and 15, 1737; S. P. Foreign, Portugal, 89/36, 38, and 39; S. P. Foreign, Spain, 94/122, 123, 125, 126, and 127).

[10] Altamira, *Historia de España*, IV, 110.

[11] Martens, *Recueil des Traités, Supple.*, I, 328-374; Southey, *History of Brazil*, III, 443.

[12] Altamira, *op. cit.*, IV, 61; Calvo, *Colección de los tratados*, II, 148, 359, 384; S. P. For., Port., 89/54, 55, 56, 57, 58.

[13] M. Lastarria, "Memoria sobre la línea divisoria de los dominios de S. M. Cathólica y del Rey de Portugal en la América Meridional," Calvo, *Colección de los tratados*, IV, 364.

[14] Altamira, *Historia de España*, IV, 61.

[15] Calvo, *op. cit.*, VI 258, 266.

right of Spain to the estuary and to the Uruguay river as far up as the Pepirí-Guazú. The line of demarcation between the Banda Oriental and Portuguese territory was fixed approximately as it exists to-day, except for the region of the Seven Missions, which was regained by the treaty of Badajoz in 1801.[16] By Article VII of the treaty of Amiens England guaranteed the *status quo*.[17]

Thus when D. João fled to Brazil in 1807, Portugual had been forced to relinquish all claims to the north bank of La Plata basin. Yet during the next twenty years the Portuguese court was to make its most determined effort to obtain possession of the Banda Oriental by taking advantage of Ferdinand VII's imprisonment by Napoleon, and, later, of the revolt of the Spanish colonies. England's intervention and final mediation were the determining factors in the outcome of this last attempt by the Portuguese to secure control of the mouth of the River Plate.

The Portuguese, hatching their plans for the conquest of the Banda Oriental on the high seas between Lisbon and Rio, were ready to put them into execution as soon as the court disembarked. By chance a Spanish agent, Antonio López, on his way from Buenos Aires to Spain, was waiting in Rio to continue his journey when Souza Coutinho arrived. The Portuguese minister induced him to return with a message for the *cabildo* which proposed a commercial union of Brazil and Buenos Aires and the protection of the Spanish colony by the Portuguese monarchy now established in America. This protection presupposed liberty of commerce and cessation of all hostilities between the two peoples, so that its refusal by La Plata authorities would force D. João to yield to the necessity of making common cause with his powerful ally, England.[18] The message was dated

[16] The 1777 treaty is found in Martens, *Recueil*, II, 545-558. The 1801 treaty is found in Martens, *op. cit.*, *Supple.*, II, 340. England guaranteed the 1801 agreement.

[17] Martens, *Recueil*, *Supple.*, II, 542.

[18] Diego Luis Molinari, *Antecedentes de la Revolución de Mayo*, I, 5-6, and appendix xvii, xv. The threat involved in the last sentence was intended to call to mind the English occupation of Buenos Aires of two years previous.

March 13, 1808, five days after the arrival of the prince regent in Rio de Janeiro. At the same time a Portuguese agent, Brigadeiro Curado, was dispatched to Buenos Aires with private instructions.[19]

Coincident with these events came the arrival of Count Luiz Enrique Liniers, brother of Santiago Liniers of Buenos Aires, who under an assumed name touched at Rio on his way from Europe. He was recognized and taken to Souza Coutinho, who proposed that the count undertake the task of completing the negotiations suggested in his message of March 13 to the *cabildo*. The minister informed the count that his purpose was to work out commercial security and personal safety for the subjects of each power trading to or residing in the territory of the other, and to prevent the Spaniards of Buenos Aires from being molested by the English, since an attack by that nation on La Plata would be very harmful to commerce between the two parties involved. As a pledge of good faith on the part of Buenos Aires, Portuguese troops were to be admitted into certain strategic places in the viceroyalty.[20] The count refused to consider the guaranty of security, but communicated the proposals to his brother, Santiago de Liniers, in Buenos Aires.

Chargé Hill was unaware of this activity until the first week in April, when Souza Coutinho expressed to him with great earnestness his preoccupation over the possibility of inducing the Spanish-American colonies "to declare in favour of the Prince Regent, who would by that means become the sole Sovereign of this immense Continent." The Portuguese government would attempt to gain this object by fair means; but if the effort failed, the assistance of England would be asked in order to take the Spanish colonies by force. Hill expressed neither approval nor objection to this surprising communication.[21]

---

[19] Molinari, *Antecedentes*, I, 7, footnote 4.

[20] *Ibid.*, I, 7 and documents in appendix, xii-xv. Reports sent by the count to his brother in Buenos Aires are dated March 26 and April 12.

[21] F. O., 63/63, Hill to Canning, No. 4. Although Hill did not discourage the project, he did not encourage it; or if he did, he failed to report the action to Canning.

Having acquainted his ally with his plans, Souza Coutinho continued his operations. On May 1, the manifesto declaring war between Portugal and France[22] ended with such a menacing tone toward Spain that Luiz Liniers realized the true intent of the prince regent toward La Plata.[23] He remained two weeks longer, however, until Sir Sidney Smith reached Rio with the English fleet and forced his departure by expelling all subjects of the Bourbons.[24]

In the meantime the Portuguese agent, Brigadeiro Curado, having presented in writing his friendly overtures in regard to a commercial convention and peaceful relations between the two countries, obtained permission to enter Buenos Aires over the protest of the *cabildo*.[25] About the same time, however, Souza Coutinho's note of March 13 with the veiled threat was delivered to that body, which rejected the Portuguese offer of protection and passed the note on to Liniers in the hope that the menacing tone adopted by Souza Coutinho would induce him to refuse Curado entrance. The viceroy suspected the *cabildo* and Elío, the governor of Montevideo, of setting a trap for him, and Curado was allowed to enter, but secret instructions were sent to Elío by Liniers to detain him at Montevideo until further orders. Active preparations to attack the province of Rio Grande were begun by the *cabildo*, only to be stopped by the news of Sir Sidney Smith's arrival in Rio, for that body believed that England was behind the moves initiated at the Portuguese capital and perceived that Buenos Aires was power-

---

[22] *Correio Braziliense*, I, 255.

[23] The *cabildo* of Buenos Aires was so concerned over Liniers' safety that it sent a spy to Rio to effect his escape from prison in case he had been seized. Luiz Liniers was a Frenchman.

[24] Hill had been worried about Liniers' long stay at Rio, certain that the latter was collecting information to be used against Portugal. Liniers, Hill said, was an enemy of England, being French by birth and sympathies (F. O., 63/63, Hill to Canning, No. 13). The count reached Buenos Aires August 17 (Molinari, *Antecedentes*, I, 10).

[25] Molinari, *op. cit.*, documents in appendix, xvii, xxii, xxiii, lv. The *audiencia* opposed Curado's entrance but the viceroy argued that it was better to let him in peacefully than to refuse him entrance and have him come in anyway. Oliveira Lima in *D. João VI no Brazil*, I, 289, sets Curado's mission in 1809, a mistake, Molinari says, *op. cit.*, p. 13.

less to attack Brazil backed by the English fleet and army.[26]

When Santiago Liniers[27] was informed by his brother of the warlike preparations also begun by Souza Coutinho, he notified the *cabildo* that the Portuguese minister would never embark on such a path were he not being instigated by the English minister.[28] Yet *Chargé* Hill, by June 2, still had no more to communicate to Canning than that the Spaniards feared a combined English and Portuguese attack but could offer little resistance to such a move. Perhaps Hill inclined to the proposed plan in view of the fact that during the preceding three months alone the value of the commercial intercourse between Rio and Buenos Aires had amounted to £120,000.[29]

The reply of the *cabildo* of Buenos Aires refusing Souza Coutinho's offer of protection against France provoked orders from the Portuguese court addressed to Curado, which instructed him to inform the viceroy that unless the *cabildo* were forced to accept the Portuguese proposals, he would be obliged to withdraw to the frontier of the Rio Grande. Consequently, Curado prepared a letter to Liniers in which he peremptorily demanded the delivery to the prince regent of the north bank of La Plata under the pretext of the menace of an occupation by the French.[30] He presented his ultimatum to the *audiencia* at the

[26] Molinari, *Antecedentes*, I, 13-21 and documents in appendix, xxvii, xxviii, lii, liii.

[27] By orders from Godoy which reached Buenos Aires May 13, 1808, Liniers was given supreme political command of the colony. Hitherto he had had supreme command of the army (Molinari, *op. cit.*, I, 21 and footnote 2). But his position was very precarious, with the *cabildo* of Buenos Aires, led by Alzaga, and the governor of Montevideo intriguing against him. The merchants turned against him when he attempted to raise much needed money by imposing import duties, June 1. The tariff was modified, July 13, giving the viceroy the power to grant special privileges to traders with foreign countries by exempting them from the tariff, but this modification increased the opposition among the native merchants who had to pay the tariff (Molinari, *op. cit.*, II, 12-18).

[28] Molinari, *op. cit.*, II, 5-6.

[29] F. O., 63/63, Hill to Canning, No. 13. June 2. It is probable that Hill lent some support to the Portuguese plan as D. João praised Hill highly to Strangford later (F. O., 63/59, Strangford to Canning, No. 1).

[30] "Oficio del Mariscal de Campo, Joaquín Xavier Curado a Santiago Liniers, en que le hace saber que el Príncipe Regente exige que le entregue la guarda de la margen septentrional del Río de la Plata, antes la amenaza de una occupación

same meeting in which Elío and the *cabildo* of Montevideo demanded the resignation of the viceroy. Liniers in reply told Curado to leave Spanish territory at once.[31] The general retreated to Rio Grande, fearing an immediate invasion by the troops of Buenos Aires,[32] but conscious also that he had contributed to the breach between Liniers and Elío which eventually was to enable Souza Coutinho to interfere between the conflicting elements of La Plata.[33]

Up to this point England's participation in the affair had been limited to tacit acquiescence by the *chargé d'affaires* at Rio and the active coöperation of the English admiral in command of the fleet in South American waters. But on July 22 the masterful Strangford landed in Rio, and Souza Coutinho hastened to acquaint him with what had been done and to ask his help in carrying out the Portuguese plans in La Plata. D. João, the minister reported, was afraid of French designs in that region[34] and was determined to take possession of both sides of the river. As peaceful methods had failed, more violent measures were necessary. Therefore it had been planned that the *Paulistas* who first were to take Asunción, Corrientes, and the Missions regions, were to join the forces from Santa Catharina and Rio Grande in an attack on Montevideo, while Sir Sidney Smith with the English fleet, after landing two thousand troops from Rio in La Plata, was to prevent communications between Montevideo and Buenos Aires. To this proposal Strangford murmured a non-committal reply and suggested to Canning that

francesa." Dated September 2, 1808. The document is given by Molinari, *Antecedentes*, III, appendix, i.

[31] Molinari, *op. cit.*, III, 5. The Portuguese court later attempted to disallow Curado's action but Molinari does not believe he was acting contrary to instructions.

[32] *Revista do Instituto Historico e Geographico Bras.*, XLI, 302.

[33] The *cabildo* of Buenos Aires accused Elío of being in communication with Curado after the withdrawal of the latter (Molinari, *op. cit.*, III, 6, footnote 3).

[34] Liniers was accused of being pro-French and D. João's fears were grounded on the opinion held by a large group in La Plata itself. Bernardo de Sassenay, agent of Napoleon sent to Buenos Aires in 1808, asserted that Liniers would have acted favorably to the French view had he been able to ignore public opinion (Carlos A. Villanueva, *Napoleón y la Independencia de América*, pp. 205-214).

England should retain either Montevideo or Buenos Aires in case the plan succeeded.[35]

In less than a month this grandiose scheme grew in Souza Coutinho's mind until on August 20, he proposed to the English minister a joint Portuguese-British expedition to take the Philippines and to attack the west coast of South America. The viscount, waiting for news as to Britain's relations with Spain, continued to be non-committal in his attitude.[36]

But quite suddenly those plans were cast aside and an entirely different policy was inaugurated, for news arrived from Europe of the abdication of Charles IV, the mutiny at Aranjuez, the captivity of Ferdinand, and the proclamation of the Napoleonic dynasty at Bayonne. The plans for the joint attack were replaced by a scheme to establish the wife of D. João as regent of the Spanish-American colonies. The prince regent's wife, D. Carlota Joaquina, being the sister of Ferdinand (later VII), now became in her opinion the representative of the royal house of Spain, since the legitimate king was incapable of ruling.[37] Four manifestoes were published in which D. Carlota and the Infante D. Carlos as members of the royal family of Spain protested against the forced abdication of the Spanish Bourbons and required the recognition by all Spanish-American colonies of their rights *ad interim* as representatives of their dynasty. One of the manifestoes was addressed to D. João, requesting that he approach Sir Sidney Smith in order to obtain

[35] F. O., 63/59, Strangford to Canning, No. 2. Dated July 25, 1808.

[36] *Ibid.*, No. 11, August 24, 1808.

[37] Alfredo Varela in *Duas Grandes Intrigas*, I, 71-72 and 628, note (2), maintains that the change in policy was due to Carlota's efforts exerted on Coutinho. The minister drew up the minute of the manifesto asserting her claims, on August 11, and Sir Sidney Smith corrected it before it was translated into Spanish. Molinari, *Antecedentes*, III, 7 and footnote (4), believes that Coutinho changed suddenly due to the extraordinary successes won in the Spanish Peninsula and to the influence of the English cabinet. Strangford's correspondence does not show any influence of the sort however. Strangford said the manifesto was drawn up by Sir Sidney Smith (F. O., 63/59, Strangford to Canning, No. 12). The legal basis of D. Carlota's claims to succession to the throne in case of failure by her brothers and their legitimate descendants is given by J. M. Rubio, *La Infanta Carlota Joaquina y la Política de España en América*, pp. 42-45.

from that officer the means of defending Spanish America against the designs of France. The prince regent, in his reply, which was also one of the manifestoes, promised to support the claims of the princess and the infante.[38]

Strangford prophesied that these documents, which were to be broadcast throughout Spanish America, would only intensify the hatred of the Spanish for the Portuguese. João's real purpose was to extend "the Portuguese American Empire as far as the River of Plate," and to recover the territories which had been ceded by treaty either to France or to Spain. The prince, so the minister thought, hoped that the reception of these proclamations by the colonials would warrant him in commencing hostilities. Strangford, until he should receive definite information as to the relations of England with Spain, would continue to be careful not to "check the Energy and Spirit" which João had developed on the subject, but personally he was opposed to such a project, which was far beyond the strength of the prince regent.[39]

The viscount received his desired information in short order, for on September 2, Canning wrote that it was "scarcely necessary to inform your Lordship, that in the present state of His Majesty's relations with Spain, He cannot countenance any design hostile to the Peace and Independence of the Spanish Dominions in South America." Strangford was ordered, therefore, earnestly to urge the Portuguese minister to suspend all further operations undertaken with this in view, and to respect in the South American colonies those ties of common interest

[38] The manifestoes are dated August 19 and 20, 1808. They are given in facsimile by Molinari, *Antecedentes*, III, appendix, documents 2, 3, 4, 5. Strangford enclosed copies in F. O., 63/59, Strangford to Canning, No. 12. The first manifesto was the complaint against Napoleon's action made by D. Carlota and the Infante Don Carlos to D. João, requesting his aid and that of the admiral of the British squadron in support of the two petitioners. The second was the reply of D. João promising to support these claims. The third was directed to the faithful vassals of Spain by D. Carlota, in which she declared null the forced abdication of her father and brothers, asserted that she was the nearest representative of her house, and called on all Spaniards to acknowledge her claims during the imprisonment of Charles and Ferdinand. The fourth was a similar document signed by the Infante Don Carlos.

[39] F. O., 63/59, Strangford to Canning, No. 12. August 24, 1808.

and friendship by which Spain and Portugal were now united in Europe.[40] Two months later Canning added to those instructions that "nothing could be more futile than the attempt" made by João to extend his empire to Spanish America, "except the manner of conducting it." Strangford was to continue to oppose any such moves and to express England's "entire disapprobation of them." Especially was Britain opposed to any pretensions of João through his wife to the regency of Spain.[41]

These instructions left no doubt as to the course which Strangford was to pursue. Henceforth he was to employ all of his subtlety and masterfulness in checkmating the Portuguese designs on the River Plate basin. To execute his instructions he needed every bit of finesse of which he was capable, for his position was a delicate one. D. João, with his faction, had acceded to the publication of the manifestoes in the hopes that they would result in a situation which would enable Portugal to take the Banda Oriental by force under the cloak of a legitimate defense of Spanish rights in America. The ambitious D. Carlota, who was living separated from her husband, hoped to make herself queen over all of Spanish America. Sir Sidney Smith, in command of England's fleet in South American waters, used all of his social and naval power to support D. Carlota's aspirations in opposition to the policies of D. João and Lord Strangford. Spain added a further element of difficulty by sending the firebrand, Casa Irujo, as minister to Rio after his withdrawal from Washington, while revolutionary and royalist agents from La Plata swarmed to the Portuguese capital in the hope of securing aid.[42]

---

[40] F. O., 63/59, Canning to Strangford, No. 18.

[41] F. O., 63/60, Canning to Strangford, No. 30. November 26, 1808. D. Carlota sent letters to important political leaders in Spain such as D. Melchior Gaspar, Dr. Francisco Saavedra (member of the *Junta Central*), the Conde de Floridablanca, and the Bishop of Orense (who became the president of the regency). Letters were sent also to military leaders such as José Palafoy, Francisco Xavier Castanos, Gregorio de la Cuesta. Local and sectional *juntas* also received communications from her, and she wrote to her father, mother, and brother recommending changes in America (Rubio, *La Infanta Carlota Joaquina*, pp. 65-73).

[42] José Presas, *Memorias secretas de la Princesa del Brasil, por su antiguo secretario*, pp.

In addition to the manifestoes, D. Carlota began an extensive private correspondence in support of her pretensions. Personal letters copied in her own hand were sent by means of an English agent under Smith's orders to Viceroy Liniers, to the *audiencia* of Buenos Aires, to Juan Almagro (*assessor* of the viceroyalty), to the dean of the Cathedral of Córdova del Tucumán, and to others in the viceroyalty of La Plata. Letters were sent also to the governor, to the *ayuntamiento*, and to private individuals of Montevideo; to the viceroy of Perú and to Goyeneche, who commanded the troops in that region; and to the *audiencia* of Chile.[43] Communications were addressed also to the Marquis de Someruelos, governor of Havana, and to the authorities of Guatemala. Most of the letters to the west coast were carried by an Englishman who was supercargo on a British ship, D. Carlota having secured him a commission as a royal agent of the Portuguese monarchy in order to clothe him with the proper authority.

The manifestoes reached Buenos Aires on the day following the receipt of Curado's ultimatum.[44] Such a sudden change of front led Liniers to believe the manifestoes were either spurious or a trap for his fall. Consequently, he denied the right of D. Carlota to assume the regency over the Spanish colonies. Since Buenos Aires had sworn to support Ferdinand VII and the *Junta* of Seville had proclaimed him king, the viceroy could not acquiesce in the assertion that Carlota and the Infante Carlos were the titular heads of the Spanish House. The *audiencia* adopted the same attitude in its reply to the private letter which Souza Coutinho directed to that body, while the *cabildo* called the documents "*tumultuarios*" and the governor of Montevideo politely declined to support Carlota's claims. The *audencia* of Chile was equally unenthusiastic over the plan.[46]

27, 36, 39, 55-64, 84-99, 132-133. Casa Irujo insisted that João allow Carlota to go to Madeira Island in order to be near Spain in case the Spanish government should invite her to occupy the throne in the absence of Charles and Ferdinand (F. O., 63/83, Strangford to Bathurst, No. 11. February 6, 1810).

[43] Presas, *op. cit.*, pp. 27-34; Rubio, *La Infanta Carlota Joaquina*, p. 49, footnote 2.

[44] They arrived September 11 (Molinari, *Antecedentes*, III, 6-7).

[45] *Ibid.*, III, 9-14.

[46] Presas, *Memorias*, pp. 33-34. The *Junta Central* of Spain also refused to ac-

In general, therefore, the manifestoes met a cold reception. Yet a powerful group in Buenos Aires did accept the idea as a means of opposing the *Junta* of Seville, whose authority many in the colony denied. A secret society counting such illustrious names as Manuel Belgrano, Martín Pueyrredón, and Mariano Moreno, was formed to watch the movements of the new viceroy, Hidalgo de Cisneros, who had taken the place of Liniers by orders of the *Junta*, to call the people to arms when the time was ripe for action, and to proclaim D. Carlota Joaquina regent of all Spain. General Pueyrredón was sent by the committee to Rio to hasten the arrival of the princess in Buenos Aires.[47]

In the meantime, D. Carlota was fishing in very troubled waters at the Portuguese capital. While Sir Sidney Smith and Viscount Strangford were spending a few days at D. João's place at Santa Cruz outside of Rio, letters came from the princess addressed to the prince and to Smith. D. João was informed —his permission was not asked; he was merely informed—that the princess intended to go at once to Buenos Aires, taking with her D. Miguel, their second son, and all of the princesses. Smith was nominated plenipotentiary for D. Carlota who now considered herself an independent sovereign with jurisdiction over Spanish America. He was given powers by the princess to cede to D. João La Plata territory desired by Portugal on condition that the Amazon river be opened to her subjects, the Spaniards. The English admiral was to take the princess to La Plata; or, in case he could not go, D. Carlota was to go alone, for go she would regardless of what might arise to frustrate her plans.[48]

Although the letters were in D. Carlota's handwriting, it was evident, at least to the prince, that Smith himself had composed them. D. João was exceedingly angry and requested Strangford to make representations to London against the ad-

---

quiesce in the pretensions announced in the manifestoes. D. Carlota then sought the consent of the regency and the *Cortes* to her claims and succeeded eventually, but too late (Rubio, *La Infanta Carlota Joaquina*, pp. 50-51).

[47] Pereira da Silva, *Historia do Imperio*, II, 108-111.

[48] F. O., 63/60, Strangford to Canning, No. 20. Most Secret and Confidential. October 9.

miral. When the party returned to Rio and the prince regent discovered that D. Carlota had already taken her jewels from the palace preparatory to leaving, he was shaken from his placid taciturnity and complained violently to Strangford of the admiral's instigation of D. Carlota's outrageous conduct. The minister, in reporting the affair to Canning, lamented that such an able officer as Smith should have been led astray by a "Service replete with circumstances of a new and romantic Nature."[49]

On October 15, D. João called Smith and Strangford together for a conference on D. Carlota's pretensions in Buenos Aires, but the admiral cut short any conversation by stating laconically that his recently arrived instructions gave him all he needed to know and that they were so secret that even Strangford was not to be informed of their contents. "The fate of South America," he asserted, "was in his hands." This declaration checkmated Strangford until he could write home, while it stimulated Souza Coutinho to urge Smith to go to La Plata to calm the dissensions reigning in that region. D. Carlota, belligerently encouraged by Smith's stand, was determined to accompany the admiral, "even though the batteries of Rio de Janeiro should fire upon her at her departure." The admiral went so far as to promise England's support of Carlota's claims to the throne of Spain in case of the failure of the reigning branch, thus putting the entire Peninsula wholly under the Bragança family.[50]

In the face of these developments, D. João once again halted between two opinions. Quite willing to have the English admiral capture La Plata for a member of the house of Bragança, he acquiesced at first in Souza Coutinho's insistence that Smith be allowed to sail for Buenos Aires. But Strangford sowed seeds of distrust in his mind by insinuating that, once queen of Spanish America, D. Carlota might swallow Brazil with Smith's aid with as much facility as D. João could absorb the Spanish colonies. The prince regent, perceiving clearly the imperious am-

---

[49] *Ibid.*

[50] *Ibid.*, Nos. 23 and 25.

bition of his wife and realizing what that energetic princess thought of her fat, irresolute, unheroic husband, wavered between the advice of his own minister and that of the viscount.[51]

Strangford's pressure soon began to bear fruit, however. On October 24, he protested formally and energetically to the Foreign Office against Smith's interference in affairs of state, and three days later a protest from D. João was added. The next day Souza Coutinho, by authority of the prince regent, asked that the admiral be recalled; and a few days later D. João flatly ordered his wife not to leave for Buenos Aires until he had secured the official concurrence of England in that move.[53]

Although the Carlota faction was balked temporarily, the princess and the admiral continued to agitate D. João, driving him at times to the verge of his endurance.[54] In April, 1809, D. Carlota visited Smith at his country home, presented him with a jeweled sword in recognition of his services,[55] and promised him the title of Duke of Montevideo as soon as they should arrive in Buenos Aires. That happy event was never consummated, however, for on March 1, 1809, Canning wrote to Strangford that England would never "countenance any measure which" had "for its object any interference in the political state" of Spanish dominions in America. The viscount was praised for his moderation and steadiness during the interfer-

[51] Rocha Pombo, *Historia do Brazil*, VII, 251-254. The Portuguese ministers were not averse to Carlota's pretensions (F. O., 63/70, Strangford to Canning, No. 65). Smith maintained that D. João actually gave his consent to Carlota's expedition (F. O., 63/61, Strangford to Canning, No. 39). Rubio, *La Infanta Carlota Joaquina*, appendix, document VIII, gives a letter dated November 22, 1808, in which D. João formally gave permission for D. Carlota to go to Buenos Aires. The permission was revoked by a letter dated November 28, 1808, on the grounds that the British minister called the project "Absolutely inadmissable" (*ibid.*, appendix, document IX).

[52] F. O., 63/60, Strangford to Canning, Nos. 25, 26, 28.

[53] F. O., 63/61, Strangford to Canning, No. 39. Presas lays the chief blame for this refusal to the activity of Strangford (*Memorias*, p. 38). Brazilian authorities concur in asserting that Strangford was the chief element in frustrating D. Carlota's plan (Rocha Pombo, *Historia do Brazii*, VII, 240-258; Pereira da Silva, *Historia do Imperio*, II, 112-113). Calvo also lays the responsibility at the minister's door (*Anales de ia Revolución de la América Latina*, I, 80).

[54] F. O., 63/61, Strangford to Canning, No. 39.

[55] Presas, *Memorias*, pp. 55-62.

ence in his business which had resulted in such confusion in the Rio court, and Sir Sidney Smith was recalled.[56]

This dispatch cleared the air when it arrived at Rio. Strangford at once wrote to the governors of Montevideo and Buenos Aires, assuring them that England "would not countenance any attempt to effect a change in the established authorities of the Spanish colonies" as long as they persevered in their allegiance to Ferdinand VII.[57] As D. Carlota herself had long foreseen, without the admiral's help, hers was a lost cause.[58] The plan had received very chilly reception in Buenos Aires in the first place; now her inability to appear in person to be acclaimed regent frustrated the efforts of the secret committee, and Pueyrredón, disgusted, returned to La Plata. The conspirators lost interest in part also because they learned that D. Carlota absolutely refused to consider a constitutional monarchy. Thus failed the second attempt of the Portuguese court to win the Banda Oriental by peaceful means.

Although they had been balked twice in their efforts to secure control of the River Plate basin, both D. João and Souza Coutinho, with characteristic Portuguese tenacity, continued to work for the annexation of the north bank of the river. This time they were aided by events in La Plata itself, which set them on the path which eventually led them to success.

Late in 1809 the viceroy at Buenos Aires lifted the ban on foreign merchandise and induced great quantities of British goods to enter the city, assuring the merchants that sufficient time would be given them for the sale of these imports. Yet on

---

[56] F. O., 63/68, Canning to Strangford, No. 2.

[57] F. O., 63/69, Strangford to Canning, No. 40. June 7, 1809. Both Montevideo and Buenos Aires were convinced by Smith's action that England was encouraging a total change in the colonial government of Spain. Strangford prophesied a serious danger to the friendly relations of England and Spain unless something were done at once (F. O., 63/70. Strangford to Canning, No. 59, July 2, 1809). The minister therefore in addition to his first note, assured the governors and *juntas* of La Plata that England would not interfere to aid either side in the dissensions which were rapidly developing between Montevideo and Buenos Aires (*ibid.*, No. 63, August, 16).

[58] "Yo voy viendo el caso perdido si sir Sidney Smith afloja," Carlota wrote to Presas (Presas, *Memorias*, p. 39).

December 25, the *alcaldes* notified British subjects in Buenos Aires by order of the viceroy to leave within eight days regardless of the vast amount of goods which had been landed but still remained unsold. The committee of British merchants, appealing to Strangford for aid, estimated the British property involved to be "a million and a half" pounds sterling.[59] The Portuguese were ordered to leave also.[60]

Such acts on the part of Cisneros inclined Strangford to favor the revolutionary group in La Plata although he perceived clearly that the colonies were very near to an assertion of independence. D. João, fearing quite naturally to have the independence wave break against his own dominions, would be satisfied, in Strangford's opinion, by the cession of the north bank of the River Plate, which was half-Portuguese anyway. Moreover, the prince's liberal commercial policy, contrasted with Spain's narrow restrictions, inclined the inhabitants of that region to union with Brazil. Perhaps it might be wise to let the prince have that region, the viscount hinted to Wellesley. Unless England took the lead in some way and at once, in regard to the situation created by the independence party of La Plata, the United States would step in ahead of Britain. Why not give the Banda Oriental to D. João and let the insurrectionary element in Buenos Aires feel that England was sympathetic with the aspirations of autonomy and liberal commercial policies, provided of course the allegiance to the Spanish royal house was preserved? In great perplexity, Strangford urgently requested instructions in regard to the proper attitude to be assumed with reference to the revolutionary movement.[61]

Scarcely had the minister written this dispatch when news of the May revolution in Buenos Aires reached Rio. Simultaneously with the news of the uprising, there arrived a special letter from the *cabildo* beseeching Strangford to represent the

[59] F. O., 63/83, Strangford to Wellesley, No. 26.

[60] *Ibid.*, Strangford to Bathurst, No. 10. June 10, 1810.

[61] F. O., 63/84, Strangford to Wellesley, No. 48. June 10, 1810. The minister was worried over Sumter's mission. A plenipotentiary with full powers from the United States must have important business, Strangford thought. Thomas Sumter was United States minister to the Portuguese court in Brazil from 1810 to 1819.

new government in a favorable light to the London court and to secure from Brazil a pacific policy toward Spanish America. An agent, following close on the heels of the letter, explained that the *junta* at Buenos Aires wanted England, first, to protect the new government from the *Junta* of Seville as well as from D. Carlota's faction until the Federal Government could be formed; second, to protect the new government after its formation with a just recompense granted to England by Buenos Aires for that protection; third, to furnish arms and ammunition; and fourth, through Strangford, to prevent Brazil from embarking on any military action on the frontier. In reply Strangford promised to forward these requests to London and to endeavor to induce D. João to refrain from using his army beyond the southern boundary of his dominions.[62]

At an interview granted the minister at the palace, the prince regent assured Strangford that he would be guided in his attitude toward the American Spaniards by that of England. Souza Coutinho, however, bombarded the viscount with letters which pointed out the urgency to England as well as to Brazil of having a natural southern boundary to Portuguese America. The minister, Strangford reported, was only too glad of the outbreak of revolutionary spirit in La Plata, since it offered an opportunity of extending Brazil to the river. The minister assured Wellesley, however, that he would prevent any measures in that direction until orders from England should arrive.[63]

Once more the claims of D. Carlota to the government of the Spanish colonies was pressed. The movement now was backed by Carlota's ambitions, by the Portuguese government, which again hoped to obtain the north bank under the cloak of her pretensions, and by the Spanish officials at Montevideo, who conceived this plan to be the only way left to them of perpetuating their power. In Strangford's opinion, however, it was "scarcely possible to devise any project more entirely and universally contrary to the wishes of the Spanish Americans than that of establishing the Princess of Brazil as their Regent."[64]

[62] *Ibid.*, No. 49. June 20, 1810.

[63] *Ibid.*, No. 49.

[64] *Ibid.*, No. 56.

On July 23, 1810, the viscount learned that Cisneros had been expelled from Buenos Aires and had been sent back to Europe. At the same time he was informed that Portuguese troops had crossed the borders into the Banda Oriental between the Ibicuí and Quarahim rivers, and Casa Irujo communicated to him officially that he had protested to the Portuguese government against such a step. Strangford thereupon presented a note to Souza Coutinho which, he hoped, would put "a complete stop" to such designs of the Portuguese court.[65] Souza Coutinho in reply denied any knowledge of an advance by the troops—a diplomatic subterfuge, snorted Strangford,[66] who immediately warned the minister that nothing could endanger the relations between Portugal and England more quickly than a premature move on the part of Portugal to occupy territory on the north bank of La Plata.[67]

In a dispatch written toward the end of September, the viscount revealed the motives which impelled him to oppose both the Portuguese and the Montevideo governments in their efforts to crush the Buenos Aires revolutionists. "Unless some assurance of future protection and countenance on the part of Great Britain" should be given right speedily to the *junta*, there was "great reason" to fear that it would "throw off its allegiance to its legitimate Sovereign" and thus be forced to a "premature declaration of independence, too probably under the guarantee of France." As only some action by England could now prevent the Spanish colonies from becoming French, the minister urged that his country recognize immediately the new *junta*, which upheld the sovereignty of Ferdinand VII, before complete independence should be declared. He warned Wellesley that to force the revolutionists to submit to the colonial restrictions imposed by the *Junta* of Seville would result in the total independence of Buenos Aires.[68]

The delicacy of the minister's position was increased by the failure of the Foreign Office to reply to his plea of June 10 for

---

[65] F. O., 63/85, Strangford to Wellesley, Nos. 57, 58, 60.

[66] *Ibid.*, No. 61.

[67] *Ibid.*, No. 63.

[68] *Ibid.*, No. 72. September 28, 1810.

instructions as to the attitude of his government toward the revolutionists. Montevideo, the stronghold of the adherents of the Seville *Junta*, blockaded Buenos Aires, with Captain Elliott, commander of the British squadron in that region, acquiescing.[69] Carlota fomented discord between the two capitals of La Plata, going so far as to send her jewels to Elío, the governor of Montevideo, when she could not send arms or money. She even managed to obtain a printing press and type for him for propaganda purposes.[70] In October the Portuguese government advised Strangford that if the Buenos Aires forces crossed the Paraguay or Paraná rivers to attack Montevideo, Portuguese troops would cross the frontier. As Montevideo controlled the naval forces of the region, the revolutionists were thus forced either to acquiesce in the blockade or to face both the Spanish troops of Montevideo and the Portuguese troops from the province of Rio Grande. The English minister, however, by great exertions succeeded in obtaining a promise from D. João not to allow his troops to move until news of England's attitude could be ascertained.[71]

By the middle of November D. João became tired of waiting on England's pleasure. Several vessels had returned from Britain without a reply since the urgent request for instructions, sent on June 10. The increasing body of Buenos Aires troops which were being massed near the Brazilian border necessitated action on the part of the Portuguese,[72] although through de

[69] *Ibid.* The blockade was illegal, Strangford asserted, since it was the local government at Montevideo and not the sovereign power which had declared it.

[70] F. O., 63/86, Strangford to Wellesley, No. 87. D. João was highly incensed at the jewel episode (Presas, *Memorias*, pp. 127-128). The printing press was obtained by Presas for Carlota from the Royal Printing shop with the permission of Souza Coutinho. Strangford protested vigorously and obtained an order to withhold the press and type; but he was too late, as the boat which was taking it to Montevideo left two hours before the order was delivered to Presas (*Memorias*, pp. 120-122). Rubio, *La Infanta Carlota Joaquina*, chapter XII, gives the story of the jewels in detail. The value of the jewels sent was 40,030 pesos.

[71] F. O. 63/85, Strangford to Wellesley, No. 76. October 13.

[72] F. O., 63/86, Strangford to Wellesley, No. 90. November 15. No reply from the English government as to its opinion on the political events in La Plata had been received by December 5, although Strangford's urgent request had been sent June 10 (*ibid.*, No. 97).

Courcy's intervention, the blockade in La Plata had been lifted in so far as British commerce was affected.[73]

Early in 1811 Portuguese troops crossed into Paraguay at the request, Souza Coutinho maintained, of a Spanish commander who was attempting to cut off General Belgrano's revolutionary troops.[74] Strangford protested and then showed the letter from Souza Coutinho, which announced the movement of the troops, to Casa Irujo, who immediately exploded to D. João, demanding that the Portuguese stay out of Spanish territory.[75] The situation in La Plata had at last reached such a critical stage that Strangford judged he should not only throw off passive resistance to Portuguese aggression, but should also stop the fight between the two Spanish parties in the south. He therefore offered to Elío and to Buenos Aires the good services of England as mediator, a proposition to which João acceded on condition that he be co-mediator with his ally. Even Casa Irujo agreed to coöperate in the effort. But when a violent insurrection in favor of the revolutionists broke out in the Banda Oriental, Souza Coutinho ordered Portuguese troops to advance, regardless of the effect on the plan of mediation,[76] security, not

---

[73] *Ibid.*, No. 95. December 1. De Courcy had succeeded Sir Sidney Smith. British property worth seven millions had been tied up in Montevideo by the blockade. De Courcy was having trouble with his subordinate, Elliott, who supported the Montevideo party in opposition to the interests of British commerce. Elío's party planned to reinstitute a rigorous colonial policy very detrimental to English interests. Rubio, *La Infanta Carlota Joaquina*, pp. 120-124, maintains that the raising of the blockade at the demand of the English assured the revolutionists of Buenos Aires of eventually winning their independence as by the loss of the weapon of blockade, the reactionary forces of Montevideo fell an easy prey to Buenos Aires. Thus, he maintains, England was responsible for the loss by Spain of the River Plate region.

[74] The Portuguese commander, Diogo de Souza, carried secret orders from the minister which show that the plan was to get D. Carlota declared regent. She was then to settle the limits question with Portugal in a manner favorable to Brazil's interests (Rocha Pombo, *Historia do Brazil*, VII, 262-263 and footnote (2), p. 262).

[75] F. O., 63/102, Strangford to Wellesley, No. 18. April 7, 1811.

[76] *Ibid.*, No. 30. April 12, 1811; F. O., 63/103, Strangford to Wellesley, No. 37, June 17. Buenos Aires was still loyal to Ferdinand but only on condition that Buenos Aires be made an integral part of the monarchy with equal privileges with the rest of the empire.

conquest, being the real motive in this case. Nevertheless Strangford's intervention bore fruit, for on October 20, 1811, the first armistice was signed at Montevideo by which the troops of Buenos Aires were to retire beyond the river, leaving Elío in command of the Banda Oriental, while the Portuguese were to withdraw at once.[77]

A new menace now arose to threaten Montevideo, for Artigas appeared in the Banda Oriental in favor of revolution. As his only means of safety, Elío, now viceroy by order of the Cádiz *junta*, requested the Portuguese troops to remain. Diogo de Souza, the Portuguese commander, gladly complied and hovered within striking distance of the viceroy's capital.[78] Buenos Aires, in retaliation, confiscated all Portuguese property and declared its exceeding embitterment against England, due largely to the activities of an American, Joel R. Poinsett, or so Strangford thought.[79]

At this critical juncture the longed-for instructions from England arrived. The British minister was informed by Castlereagh that an English commission of mediation between Spain and its colonies had left London (April 7) for the purpose of reconciling the colonies with the regency of Spain, of assuring Ferdinand of recognition, and of obtaining for the colonies an integral part in the Spanish monarchy. It was not expedient, the instructions read, for the Portuguese to share the mediation of a dispute in which they had such a deep interest; and furthermore, they should keep out of the Banda Oriental until the English mediators could do their work.[80]

It was fortunate for Strangford that he could act now with the full authority of England to back his words. The armistice of October 20, 1811, was strained to the breaking point, while

---

[77] Pinto da Rocha, "A Politica Brasileira do Prata até A Guerra contra Rosas," *Revista do Instituto Hist. e Geogr. Bras.*, 1917, tomo especial, V, 573; F. O., 63/103, Strangford to Wellesley, No. 73; Rocha Pombo, *Historia do Brazil*, VII, 263-264. The events from January to October 20, 1811, are given in detail by Rubio, *La Infanta Carlota Joaquina*, Chapters XIV, XV.

[78] Pinto da Rocha, "A Politica Brasileira do Prata," p. 573.

[79] F. O., 63/123, Strangford to Wellesley, No. 16. March 16, 1812.

[80] F. O., 63/122, Castlereagh to Strangford, Nos. 2 and 13. April 10 and May 29.

Galveas[81] was demanding vehemently that England comply with the guaranty of Portuguese territory stipulated under Article I of the treaty of alliance and friendship of 1810. Brazilian forces, he argued, were totally unable to cope with the danger which arose from the threat of the insurgents against Portuguese territory in the south. The minister had reason on his side, for Strangford, after reviewing the resources at the disposal of the Portuguese government, confessed himself convinced that only total ruin could result from a war with Buenos Aires.[82]

Therefore, he proposed, instead of military aid from England, that another armistice be signed. Over the vehement but ineffectual protests of the Portuguese secretary of state, Strangford dispatched his confidential agent, Lieut.-Col. John Rademaker, of the British army, to La Plata with instructions from the Portuguese court, which had been approved by the viscount, to mediate between Montevideo, Buenos Aires, and the Portuguese commander. In addition, the minister sent to the Buenos Aires *junta* a personal letter of assurance that Rademaker had the support of England in his present mission and of guaranty that the terms agreed upon would be carried out by Brazil.[83]

On the night of the day of his arrival at Buenos Aires, Rademaker signed the agreement which again stopped hostilities in La Plata.[84] An armistice, which could be broken only after three month's notice by either side, was agreed upon, and both the Buenos Aires and Portuguese troops were to retire within the limits of their respective countries as understood before the Brazilian troops began their march. Montevideo was not included in the negotiations despite Rademaker's instructions to

[81] Galveas, it will be remembered, had succeeded Souza Coutinho as secretary of state and war at the death of the latter in January, 1811.

[82] F. O., 63/123, Strangford to Castlereagh, No. 30. May 2, 1812.

[83] *Ibid.*

[84] Calvo, *Anales*, II, 53-54. The armistice was dated May 27, 1812, although it was concluded on the twenty-sixth. It was signed by Nicolás Herrera for Buenos Aires and John Rademaker for Portugal (Quesada, *Historia Diplomática Latino-Americana*, II, 32-35; Rocha Pombo, *Historia do Brazil*, VII, 265-267).

do so. On May 27 orders were sent to both commanders to withdraw.[85]

When the stipulations of the armistice reached Strangford, he was exceedingly annoyed, as he had instructed Rademaker to state specifically that the Buenos Aires troops hereafter should not cross the Paraná River. The territorial limits of the two parties to the armistice as "understood before the Brazilian troops began their march" included Montevideo within Buenos Aires jurisdiction, according to the claims of the insurgents. Thus the revolutionists of La Plata could again advance on Montevideo and threaten the Brazilian frontiers, apparently without violating the terms of the armistice. The viscount forced Galveas to hasten new instructions to Rademaker in an effort to rescind the first agreement and to rectify the mistake by signing a second document, but the agent had left before the orders to that effect reached him. The first agreement had to stand, therefore, although it took the utmost pressure by Strangford on Galveas to obtain the ratification of the armistice by Portugal.[86] Nevertheless, the Portuguese troops withdrew within their own frontiers, despite the angered remonstrance of the Portuguese commander of the forces in the south and the urgent request from Montevideo begging them to stay.[87]

The armistice stood as long as Strangford remained in Rio de Janeiro, due almost entirely to his efforts. Although his earlier regard for the insurgents was fast breaking down, as the radical tendency of the revolutionists became evident, he stuck by his attitude of neutrality in favor of the *status quo* in La Plata. Before the end of 1812 the minister warned Castlereagh that Buenos Aires was showing unmistakable signs of desiring a com-

---

[85] F. O., 63/123, Strangford to Castlereagh, No. 37.

[86] F. O., 63/124, Strangford to Castlereagh, Nos. 52, 66. D. João's ratification was dated September 13, 1812 (Calvo, *Anales*, II, 54-55). Later Rademaker explained his haste in concluding the armistice and returning to Rio as quickly as possible. He had learned of a plot participated in by Carlota and Diogo de Souza, Portuguese commander, to assassinate the members of the government of Buenos Aires in order to secure control in that city. Vigodet, the governor of Montevideo, was involved also (F. O., 63/124, Strangford to Castlereagh, No. 68).

[87] F. O., 63/123, Strangford to Castlereagh, Nos. 52, 66, 67, 79.

plete separation from its European connections.[88] In August of the next year he reported that the Spanish colonies were forever lost, with no hope of the reëstablishment by Spain of the old order of things, and that the new government of Buenos Aires was reviving the "wretched and Vulgar Cant of the Jacobins."[89]

Yet the minister was forced to make one more effort to pacify La Plata before his recall early in 1815. The liberation of Spain in 1813 impressed the insurgents with the necessity of obtaining England's backing, while the constant refusal of the Portuguese court to accede to Governor Vigodet's requests for troops to aid him in the defense of Montevideo impelled that government to seek security also under England's protection. Therefore in December, 1813, Strangford and the Spanish minister, Castillo, were working at Rio on an armistice between Buenos Aires and Montevideo which was to enable England to mediate between the two factions.[90] It appeared as though the last months of Strangford's stay in Rio were to be undisturbed by further troubles in La Plata.

Yet the clouds began to gather once more before his recall. In March, 1814, news arrived in Rio that Artigas had broken with the Buenos Aires government and in his activity in the Banda Oriental was threatening the Portuguese frontier. Consequently troops were again assembled on the Rio Grande front just in time to receive the news of the surrender of Montevideo to the revolutionists of Buenos Aires. Although the viscount gloomily predicted that the armistice so strenuously negotiated two years earlier would soon be broken, he still exerted all his ingenuity to restrain D. João from ordering his forces to cross the frontier.[91] He succeeded in his efforts, frustrating to the last any move of Portugal to acquire control of the River Plate region. Yet when news came that Artigas had taken Montevideo

---

[88] F. O., 63/125, Strangford to Castlereagh, No. 102. December 24, 1812.

[89] F. O., 63/147, Strangford to Castlereagh, No. 103. August 1, 1813.

[90] F. O., 63/148, Strangford to Castlereagh, No. 150. December 18, 1813.

[91] F. O., 63/167, Strangford to Castlereagh, Nos. 15, 21; F. O., 63/168, Strangford to Castlereagh, Nos. 67, 71.

and had agreed to unite with Buenos Aires in case Spain attempted to reconquer La Plata basin,[92] he realized that the affairs of that region were fast approaching another crisis. Perhaps if he had remained in Rio, he might have controlled events as he had done in 1812, but on April 8, 1815, he sailed for London, leaving the Portuguese court free from English domination for the next six years.

High praise is due the minister for the part which he played in La Plata troubles during the seven years of his stay at Rio. He had received definite instructions to keep Portugal out of Spanish affairs in the colonies and in the Peninsula as regards both military and political intrigues. Moreover, he had conceived on his own account that whereas he should sustain the insurgents of Buenos Aires as long as they adhered to their loyalty to Ferdinand, he should not allow them to meddle in Montevideo. His efforts, therefore, had been directed toward restraining each group from executing a political or military offensive against the others. In carrying out his plan, he faced the opposition of the prince regent, the Portuguese ministry, D. Carlota Joaquina, the admiral of the English squadron, the revolutionists of Buenos Aires, and the Spanish authorities at Montevideo. Single-handed, by virtue of the authority of England with which he was clothed as minister plenipotentiary and by his own forcefulness and finesse, he maintained peace in the River Plate basin until the end of the Napoleonic wars and frustrated Portuguese efforts to extend their territory to the river. It was a remarkable exploit.

---

[92] F. O., 63/181, Strangford to Castlereagh, No. 17. March 29, 1815.

CHAPTER VI

SUCCESS AND FAILURE IN THE BANDA ORIENTAL —1815-1828

EVEN AS STRANGFORD was relinquishing his task in Rio de Janeiro, other hands were picking up the question of the River Plate Basin. From 1808 until the fall of Napoleon, the conflicting interests involved in the struggle for control of the Banda Oriental were concentrated at Rio de Janeiro. Now the lines of influence were extended across the waters, where the powers of Europe were to play a decisive rôle in the final outcome.

The events which transpired in the Spanish Peninsula were of the utmost importance in determining the action of the Portuguese court at Rio and of the European powers in regard to the River Plate affair. Until 1815 Spain was incapable of paying anything more than the scantiest attention to her colonies. After the forced abdication of the Spanish Bourbons and the proclamation of Joseph as king of Spain, a *Junta Central* of twenty-four members (later thirty-five) was set up at Aranjuez as the supreme body over the many local *juntas* which had arisen in protest against Napoleon's action. Later this *Junta* fled to Seville, where it remained for a year before it finally established itself at Cádiz. In January, 1810, it set up the Regency of Five with instructions for that body to call the *Córtes*. The assembly met late in 1810 to pass its liberal measures and eventually to adopt the Constitution of 1812. When Ferdinand returned two years later, however, he declared null and void the constitution and the liberal decrees of the *Córtes*, and instituted a rigorous reactionary policy, which was blind, unscrupulous, and rancorous in its severity.[1] The liberal régime adopted by the *juntas* with regard to the colonies was doomed.

[1] Charles E. Chapman, *A History of Spain*, pp. 492-496.

In the larger field of Europe as a whole, the unity which had existed during the common effort to defeat Napoleon was succeeded now by a spirit of intrigue and suspicion. The rivalry among diplomats and ministers for predominant influence was especially violent at Madrid, where, due to the conflict between the reactionary policy of Ferdinand and the liberal measures demanded by the colonies, the dominance of the great powers over the liberties of the small found a fruitful field for action. The Quadruple Alliance had been formed with obligations which only the great powers could undertake. In it the smaller powers had no rights, but it was precisely the complications raised by these lesser powers, such as Spain and Portugal, which were to prove difficult to overcome. The temptation was great for the powers of Europe to treat the smaller states peremptorily; yet the necessary concerted action among the members of the Alliance in reference to the lesser powers, and particularly to Spain, was to prove increasingly difficult of attainment.[2]

From the very first England through Castlereagh protested against dragooning the rest of Europe to force the acceptance of the decisions of the great powers. Although he agreed to have the dangerous dispute between Spain and Portugal over differences in Europe and South America brought up before the conference of ambassadors at Paris, he vetoed the proposal of the Russian, Pozzo de Borgo, to have the entire question of the independence of the Spanish colonies discussed by the conference and refused point blank to accede to Metternich's suggestion that the conference should become the organ of the great powers in putting down intrigues of revolutionists all over Europe. He would not allow the use of the ambassadorial committee sitting at Paris as a means of arrogating to the great powers a directing authority over the internal affairs of the other states of Europe.[3]

Thus early[4] in the restoration period following the fall of Napoleon did Castlereagh demonstrate his divergence from the

[2] C. K. Webster, *Foreign Policy of Castlereagh*, pp. 63-69. [3] *Ibid.*, pp. 70-73.

[4] The documents cited by Webster in support of these statements are dated from 1815 to 1817.

plans of the Quadruple Alliance. The various congresses which met during the years from 1815 to 1822 carried this deviation to a final break between England and Eastern Europe; but before that time came, Portugal was to feel the conflicting currents of intrigue which were fomented by the various great powers in their efforts to attain their ends. It was into this maelstrom of European politics that the question of La Plata was drawn. The problem was particularly difficult, as it concerned not only the relations of two of the smaller European powers, Spain and Portugal, but also the critical question of the status of the South American colonies themselves, which were directly involved in this dispute.

In the River Plate region the situation was critical. Artigas with his band of revolutionists held Montevideo and the Banda Oriental, having forced the withdrawal of the Buenos Aires troops which had held the capital since capturing it from the Spanish governor, Gaspar de Vigodet. Artigas had an agreement to unite with Buenos Aires if Spain should make an attempt to regain the colonies; otherwise he intended to keep on fighting the troops from across La Plata.[5] The control of the Banda Oriental by Artigas and the prevalence of what the Rio government called revolutionary excesses aroused an uneasy feeling in the autocratic Portuguese court and lent an aroma of righteousness to its dreams of territorial expansion.

The desire of the Rio court to conquer the north bank of La Plata had been frustrated thus far by two principal factors: the opposition of Strangford and the lack of adequate military forces. In 1815, however, simultaneously with the withdrawal of the English minister, came the demobilization of troops in Europe, which freed Portuguese forces for use in South America and provided an army of adventurers who preferred to fight under any banner rather than return home to postwar readjustment. By November 25, more than twelve hundred Portuguese troops had reached Rio from Europe and more were expected daily.[6] Preparations for war at the Brazilian capital

[5] F. O., 97/76, *Memorandum-Montevideo—1811-1824* (February, 1826), extracts from dispatches of July 9, 1814, to March 29, 1815.

[6] F. O., 63/183, Chamberlain to Castlereagh, No. 61.

became so pronounced that the foreign minister, Aguiar, was forced to confess to *Chargé* Chamberlain that the Portuguese court planned an aggressive campaign against Artigas in the Banda Oriental. The expedition, he added, was almost ready to sail.[7] On June 12, 1816, the fleet with about three thousand five hundred men left for La Plata.[8] Chamberlain's protests, made in conformity with the instructions sent to Strangford by the Foreign Office, proved entirely unavailing. His efforts merely elicited the reply that since Artigas was a very undesirable neighbor for Brazil and a disturbing enemy to Spain and Buenos Aires, the only thing to do was to suppress him by force. Buenos Aires had tried and failed; Spain was in no condition to bring about his subjugation; therefore, Brazil must do it in behalf of Ferdinand VII.[9]

This laudable declaration, Chamberlain reported, was serving as a camouflage for the real purpose of the Portuguese court. The plan was to acquire the Banda Oriental and perhaps to annex the entire viceroyalty of Buenos Aires to Portuguese territory, thereby establishing the "Empire of South America." This dream was only in part chimerical, for a secret understanding existed between certain leaders in La Plata and the Portuguese court. Manuel García, secretary of state for foreign affairs of the Buenos Aires government (1816), after several trips to Rio on secret business, had proposed that Buenos Aires and its dependent provinces should acknowledge for their sovereign the prince regent of Portugal. D. João refused to sign a treaty to this effect, but he intended to take advantage of the offer to secure the northern bank of La Plata.[10] The plan to form the "Empire of South America" was wildly impracticable, but there was every possibility of D. João's securing the coveted Banda Oriental.[11]

---

[7] *Ibid.*, No. 47. [8] *Ibid.*, No. 51.

[9] F. O., 97/76, *Memorandum*, extracts from dispatches November 25, 1815, to June, 1816.

[10] F. O., 63/194, Chamberlain to Castlereagh, July 20, 1816, and August 2, Secret. The *chargé* enclosed numerous secret documents, which he obtained, as proof of this intrigue (F. O., 97/76, *Memorandum*, extracts from dispatches, July 20-August 2, 1816).

[11] When news of the Portuguese expedition reached Buenos Aires, Balcarce, the

In August the Portuguese forces entered Spanish territory,[12] and in November the Spanish minister at Rio formally protested, hinting that the continuation of the project of aggrandizement would result in a break between Spain and Portugal. In reply the Rio court informed Minister Villalba that Portugal had taken the River Plate region once before in behalf of Spain to prevent the spread of the revolutionary propaganda emanating from Buenos Aires and had been forced to withdraw; that the revolutionary movements still continued, with Spain incapable of suppressing them; that Portugal in self-defense was forced to take drastic steps; and that the nearness of Artigas to Brazil compelled Portuguese troops to enter Spanish territory. Villalba in his counter-reply asserted that the proposed action by Portugal was illegal unless approved by the Spanish court, and such approval had not been given, nor had it even been asked.[13]

Chamberlain reported that the Spanish minister was wanting in energy, and the Portuguese court felt that nothing was to be feared from Spain. The minister's protests would be unavailing, therefore, unless England stepped in to back Spanish demands.[14] Moreover, the position maintained in the Portuguese reply that their action was based on self-defense against the spread of revolutionary propaganda was strengthened when news reached Rio that the United Provinces of Rio de La Plata had declared their independence at Tucumán, July 9, 1816, and had hurled defiance at Ferdinand and his successors or any other foreign power which should try to subjugate them.[15]

As Chamberlain had foreseen, the Portuguese were deter-

---

acting director, made no preparations to oppose it. The *junta* turned him out, put in two of themselves until Pueyrredón, named supreme director by the Congress at Córdoba, could arrive, and prepared to defend themselves against the Portuguese. Thus the Portuguese party in La Plata was turned out (F. O., 63/195, Chamberlain to Castlereagh, No. 82).

[12] F. O., 63/195, Chamberlain to Castlereagh, No. 84. See also Carlos A. Villanueva, *Bolívar y et General San Martín*, pp. 30-33, 51-57.

[13] *Ibid.*, Nos. 102, 105.

[14] *Ibid.*

[15] *Ibid.*, No. 89. October 8, 1816.

mined to carry the thing through to completion. On January 20, 1817, General Lecor with the Portuguese troops entered Montevideo, proclaimed himself captain-general of the province, and appointed his second-in-command, Sebastião Pinto, governor of Montevideo. In reply to a demand from Buenos Aires that the Banda Oriental be turned over to the United Provinces, Lecor announced that Buenos Aires had nothing to do with the question, that the Portuguese troops had rid both the United Provinces and Brazil of a common enemy, that the territory was entirely independent of the authorities across the river, and that the whole question was one which had to be taken up in Rio de Janeiro.[16] Buenos Aires thereupon declared Portugal to have violated the armistice of 1812, and announced the beginning of hostilities between them and the Rio government.[17]

The dream of centuries had come true for Portugal; for at last its boundaries extended to La Plata, and the Banda Oriental was under Portuguese control. The triumph resulted when Antonio d'Araujo, after his return to power, took the bit between his teeth and proceeded to the conquest of La Plata over the protests of the English and the Spanish representatives at the court of D. João. Favored by the release of Portuguese troops from the European battlefields and by a large number of foreign volunteers, he was able to defeat Artigas and his band of *gauchos*. The question which now arose was whether Portugal would be able to retain the River Plate region after having conquered it.

Unfortunately for Portuguese aspirations, when General Lecor's forces crossed the frontier and entered Spanish territory, Portugal thereby was plunged into the maelstrom of European politics. The first warning came from Castlereagh, who wrote to Chamberlain, December 19, 1816,[18] that Spain had appealed to Austria, France, Russia, and England to mediate in the face

[16] F. O., 63/202, Chamberlain to Castlereagh, No. 19.

[17] F. O., 63/203, Chamberlain to Castlereagh, No. 26. General Lecor informed his government, however, that he had an understanding with the supreme director that the latter would not execute the order to begin hostilities.

[18] F. O., 63/195, Castlereagh to Chamberlain, No. 11.

of the Portuguese aggressions against Spanish dominions in South America. Unless the Portuguese court could give a satisfactory explanation for its conduct, England would consider that Portugal had forfeited all claim to the fulfillment by England of the guaranty of Portuguese dominions made by Article 3 of the treaty of January 22, 1815.[19] If the breach between Spain and Portugal over the South American question should lead to war, Spain would attack Portugal in Europe, and England would not defend its ally unless D. João could convince Chamberlain as to the correctness of its action in La Plata. But Chamberlain was to use this threat only as a last resort.

Furthermore England and the other powers appealed to by Spain had accepted the proposal to mediate and had agreed to settle the question by their envoys assembled at Paris. Accordingly, the Portuguese court, said Castlereagh,[20] was to give full powers to a minister in Europe to complete a settlement of the Plate affair without further reference to Brazil.

Chamberlain, in accordance with his instructions, interviewed Antonio d'Araujo. The minister informed the *chargé* that the Banda Oriental belonged to Spain, but that Portugal would not give it up even if a sufficiently large Spanish force should be sent over to insure the security of the Brazilian frontier. His court, however, was willing to negotiate the question. Much voluminous correspondence then ensued between the two agents, Chamberlain endeavoring to get Portugal to withdraw from the Banda Oriental and Araujo attempting to justify its seizure. Finally the *chargé* informed the minister that his explanations were not satisfactory and therefore, by orders from the Foreign Office, he declared England's guaranty of Portuguese territory no longer valid.[21]

This declaration failed to frighten the Portuguese, for at the court levee given by D. João to receive the congratulations of

---

[19] This article annulled the treaty of alliance and friendship of 1810, but it guaranteed Portuguese territory from attack by any foreign power, in conformity with the old treaties since 1642 (Martens, *Recueil*, *Supplement*, VI, 100).

[20] F. O., 63/201, Castlereagh to Chamberlain, No. 5. April 9, 1817.

[21] F. O., 63/203, Chamberlain to Castlereagh, No. 27. April 5, 1817.

the diplomatic body on the marriage of his eldest son, D. Pedro, the deputies from Montevideo were received by the royal family in the same manner as the subjects of Brazil.[22] But Araujo showed himself greatly vexed when Chamberlain delivered the threat ordered by Castlereagh that Britain would withdraw all English officers from the Portuguese army unless Rio submitted to the demands of England in regard to La Plata. The loss of such officers in that region and in Portugal would be a serious blow, especially as it would mean the retirement of Marshal Beresford, who was holding Portugal for D. João during his absence at Rio.[23] Yet, when the *chargé* delivered the message sent in Castlereagh's dispatch of April 9, in regard to the mediation of the great powers, Araujo still refused to change his plans in La Plata, although D. João did promise to send a full explanation to the conference.[24]

The Spanish envoy had no better success when by specific instructions from his court, he demanded that the Portuguese troops withdraw at once from the Banda Oriental, for Araujo flatly refused[25] and, instead of withdrawing troops, sent reinforcements. Alarmed by this move, Chamberlain called the ministers of the mediating powers at Rio together and presented a joint note to the Portuguese government, offering to transmit to the respective courts represented by the note any explanation which the Portuguese minister wished to give.[26] This united pressure exerted in the name of the great powers and presented after the manner of the Quadruple Alliance, elicited a dictatorial reply from the new minister, Bezerra,[27] who refused to recognize the right of the envoys at Rio to meddle in the matter. Apparently, Chamberlain reported, Portugal was determined to hold the Banda Oriental.[28]

[22] *Ibid.*, No .50.

[23] *Ibid.*, No. 51.

[24] *Ibid.*, No. 55.

[25] F. O., 63/204, Chamberlain to Castlereagh, No. 77.

[26] *Ibid.*, No. 89. September 6, 1817.

[27] Araujo died June, 1817. Conde de Palmella, minister at London, was made minister of foreign affairs and war; Conde de Arcos, captain-general of Bahia, was appointed minister of navy and colonies; but João Paulo Bezerra was to occupy both posts until the new ministers should arrive.

[28] F. O., 63/204, Chamberlain to Castlereagh, Nos. 89, 92. Castlereagh did not

Chamberlain was traveling too fast to suit Castlereagh, however, for early in January, 1818, the foreign minister informed his *chargé* that he had misunderstood his instructions in regard to the withdrawal of England's guaranty of Portuguese territory. By the dispatch of December 19, 1816, Chamberlain had been told to declare that if the explanations of the Portuguese government in regard to the Plate expedition did not satisfy the prince regent of England, then the guaranty would be withdrawn. No such declaration by the British government had been made as yet, although trouble had arisen in Paris and Madrid, where the belief was current that Chamberlain had declared in an official manner, the abrogation of the guaranty.[29]

Castlereagh's motive was clear in restricting to a threat the annulment of England's guaranty of Portuguese dominions. If Great Britain should relinquish the pledge to preserve the frontiers of Portugal in Europe, the minister would lose one of the most effective weapons available to him against the growing policy of intervention which the powers of Europe were announcing with increasing insistence. By the loss of the right to protect Portugal, a right which was based on the sacred obligations of treaties of nearly three centuries' standing, Castlereagh would place himself on the same footing as the Eastern European powers in regard to Portugal. In the face of the impending conference at Paris, which was to settle the difficulties between the two most troublesome of the lesser powers, Portugal and Spain, the minister could not afford to relinquish the advantage accruing to him through the special guaranty of Portugal, which Europe had long accepted as an established fact.

That Castlereagh would have need of every available weapon in the impending settlement of the Portuguese-Spanish question was made evident by the manner in which the intervention

approve of the method adopted by Chamberlain in the protest against sending reinforcements. He had meant for the *chargé* to coöperate with the other ministers, but he was to protest individually, not in a joint note (F. O., 63/201, Castlereagh to Chamberlain, No. 20. December 2, 1817).

[29] F. O., 63/210, Castlereagh to Chamberlain, No. 1. January 6, 1818.

was suggested. The Russian minister first brought the question before the conference of ambassadors at Paris in consequence of a representation to the Czar from the Spanish minister at St. Petersburg, in which the interference of the Russian government was requested in order to prevent the rupture which must ensue between Spain and Portugal should their differences not be settled speedily. The ambassador was to propose that Russia and the three governments included in the appeal should demand an explanation from Rio of the occupation of Spanish territory in South America. Unless a satisfactory reply was received, the Russian ambassador was to declare that his emperor could not view with indifference the unprovoked aggression which had taken place and that in conjunction with his allies he would omit no effort to enable the court of Spain to support its rights and to compel the Portuguese government to return to that state of affairs which the interests of both parties required. Austria agreed to this proposal, but France demurred on the grounds that the territory occupied was not governed by persons acknowledging the authority of Spain. France, therefore, could not admit that Portugal's occupation was an act of hostility.[30]

The Austrian ambassador was then instructed by his government to propose an amicable mediation as a substitute for the menacing one made by the Russian minister. Consequently in March the five powers agreed to a joint note to both Spain and Portugal in which they took upon themselves the mediation of the dispute and called upon Portugal for an explanation of the invasion. Castlereagh authorized Sir Charles Stuart to sign the note and agreed to transmit it to D. João through the English representative at Rio, with the understanding clearly expressed, however, that Great Britain was not thereby pledged beyond the employment of its good offices.[31] The note was transmitted in Castlereagh's dispatch to Chamberlain of

[30] F. O., 97/76, *Proceedings of the Ministers of the Mediating Powers at Paris and of the Congress of Aix-la-Chapelle, on the subject of the differences between Spain and Portugal, January, 1817 to January, 1820*, pp. 109-111.

[31] *Ibid.*, pp. 112-113.

April 9, 1817,[32] while the Spanish ambassador at Paris was appealing vehemently to the conference on the necessity of immediate use of arms against the Portuguese.

In May, 1818, Sir Charles Stuart, at the request of the other ministers, presented a project to settle the differences between Spain and Portugal. The plan was submitted to both the Spanish and Portuguese representatives, each of whom returned proposals for a settlement. The mediating ministers on receipt of these counter-proposals, drew up the project which was to serve as the basis of the settlement suggested by the powers. By it Montevideo was to be delivered to Spanish troops equal in number to the Portuguese forces then holding that city with the express declaration that the surrender of the place was due to the mediating powers; Spain was to indemnify Portugal by the payment of seven million five hundred thousand francs at the time of the delivery of Montevideo; a negotiation was to be initiated under the mediating powers to settle all territorial disputes between the two lesser powers in Europe[33] and in America; the Spanish expedition to Montevideo was to number at least eight thousand troops; and if the expedition did not arrive within six months, Spain was to pay Portugal an indemnity of three hundred thousand francs a month until the city was delivered to Spanish troops.[34]

A few modifications were made at the insistence of both the Spanish and Portuguese envoys, and the document was delivered to Spain with the statement by the mediating ministers that Portugal had agreed to every concession which could reasonably be expected. The mediating powers therefore hoped that Spain would accept and end the trouble.[35]

There the matter stuck, for no satisfactory reply could be obtained from Spain. Early in October the Portuguese plenipoten-

---

[32] See *supra*, p. 142, footnote 20.

[33] Spain still held Olivença on the Spanish-Portuguese frontier in Europe, contrary to treaty stipulations. Portugal affirmed that the seizure of the Banda Oriental was no more violation of Spanish territorial rights than this retention by Spain of Portuguese territory.

[34] F. O., 97/76, *Proceedings*, pp. 124-127.

[35] *Ibid.*, pp. 127-134.

tiaries gave their ultimatum, stating that since they had accepted the mediation of the powers and the settlement proposed by them, Portugal was absolved from further responsibility to the conference.[36] At Aix-la-Chapelle nothing was done except to authorize the ambassadorial conference at Paris to receive Spain's reply,[37] if one should ever be forthcoming. In December, 1818, Sir Charles Stuart reported to his government that the delay by Spain in replying was intentional. Montevideo, in the power of the Portuguese, was safe from the danger with which the remainder of Spanish America was threatened as a result of insurrectionary movements; the indemnity per month had not begun; and the expedition being prepared at Cádiz could be sent to other parts of Spanish America.[38]

Six months later, June, 1819, the English ambassador at Paris was instructed to enquire confidentially of the Portuguese representative what his government would do in case the mediation failed. He was to inform the Portuguese agent also that from the moment when Portugal had accepted unconditionally the project of the mediating powers, the "King of Portugal was considered to have satisfied the claims of justice, and thereby to have entitled Himself to the full measure of His Rights, under Treaty with Great Britain."[39]

In August, 1819, the Spanish representative suddenly retracted certain promises made on behalf of his government in regard to the mediation and left Paris on a special mission.[40] The Portuguese envoy[41] thereupon declared the negotiations at an end and returned to London. The Spanish minister on his return to Paris issued a long note justifying Spain's action during the mediation; the Portuguese representative replied from London; and no further proceedings took place.[42] Spain's dila-

[36] *Ibid.*, pp. 137-138.

[37] *Ibid.*, pp. 138-142.

[38] *Ibid.*, p. 147.

[39] *Ibid.*, pp. 155-156. The dispatch to Stuart was dated June 29, 1819.

[40] The minister went to Strassburg to compliment the Spanish queen.

[41] Palmella, nominated foreign minister at the death of Araujo, was still ambassador at London. He had been named plenipotentiary to Paris for the mediation.

[42] F. O., 97/76, *Proceedings*, pp. 157-161. For a Portuguese version of the mediation, see Pereira da Silva, *Historia do Imperio*, IV, 41-75.

tory tactics and characteristic refusal to make the slightest concessions had spiked the guns of the mediators.

The Portuguese emerged victorious from this intervention of the European powers in the River Plate question for the Rio court still retained the guaranty of England for its European territory despite the fact that it now enjoyed complete possession of the Banda Oriental. When Montevideo was occupied in 1817, the Portuguese maintained that their forces would withdraw when the necessity for their presence should cease. But, tired of bloodshed and anarchy, the local body at Montevideo intervened in the struggle still going on out on the plains and the Banda Oriental became pacified[43] at about the same time that the mediation of the powers was coming to a standstill. Artigas was forced to flee to Paraguay, and Portuguese domination over the Banda Oriental was complete.

But there still remained the task of convincing the British government that the Portuguese should retain the north bank of La Plata. In his instructions to the new minister to Rio, Castlereagh ordered Thornton to inform D. João that England expected Portugal so to conduct itself in South America that the continued mediation of the great powers would be furthered. Unless such a conciliatory attitude were shown, the British government would be forced "even to hesitate as to the propriety . . . of giving effect" to its guaranty. D. João, Castlereagh warned, was to observe "a scrupulous delicacy towards Spanish Rights and Interests."[44]

Thornton, however, soon after his arrival in Rio, recommended that his government favor the *status quo* in La Plata. Although the Buenos Aires government had declared war on the Portuguese as far back as March, 1819, no active operations had followed. Now, with the failure of the Cádiz expedition, there was every likelihood of a renewed activity on the part of the insurrectionists. If Portugal withdrew from Montevideo, the envoy said, that district would be irrevocably lost to Spain.

---

[43] *Río de la Plata*, written by Ignacio Núñez at the request of Woodbine Parish, 1824, pp. 295-296; Pereira da Silva, *Historia do Imperio*, IV, 271-276.

[44] F. O., 63/227, Castlereagh to Thornton, No. 6. May 25, 1820.

Let the Portuguese retain their coveted prize, therefore.[45]

The stream of events began to move rapidly toward the end of 1820. The Portuguese government disclaimed any knowledge of the plan to place the Duke of Lucca, a Bourbon prince, on the throne of Buenos Aires, thus clearing its skirts of complicity in the French intrigue which so aroused the ire of Castlereagh.[46] On April 26, 1821, D. João sailed for Lisbon, leaving Brazil in care of D. Pedro, and the diplomatic body, including Thornton, soon followed. In July, the congress of the province of Montevideo declared its incorporation with Brazil under the title of the Cisplatine Province. On September 7 of the following year D. Pedro raised the cry of "Independence or Death," and the Baron de Laguna, captain-general of the Cisplatine Province, declared in favor of the Brazilian cause. The Portuguese troops in Montevideo returned to Europe in March, 1824, and the Brazilian army, which took the place of the Portuguese force, requested D. Pedro to allow the Cisplatine Province to continue as an integral part of the Brazilian Empire.[47]

During the four turbulent years from 1821 to 1825, when Brazil was striving for independence, tranquillity reigned in Buenos Aires. The provincial administration of the United Provinces fostered trade and established commercial intercourse with the rest of the world upon the most liberal principles, with the result that foreign trade was brisk.[48] The proportion of British merchandise in this trade was significant in view of later events in the struggle for control of La Plata. In 1822 England's exports to Buenos Aires constituted over half of the total of all foreign goods entering that city. Compared with the figures of the most liberal period of the Spanish colonial

[45] F. O., 63/228, Thornton to Castlereagh, No. 9. February 19, 1820. Rocha Pombo, *Historia do Brazil*, VII, 300-310.

[46] F. O., 63/229, Thornton to Castlereagh, No. 48. September 29. For the intrigue, see F. O., 63/227, Castlereagh to Thornton, No. 10, and July 13, Most Secret and Confidential; Thornton to Castlereagh, No. 18; F. O., 63/229, Thornton to Castlereagh, No. 48; Webster, *Foreign Policy of Castlereagh*, pp. 423-425.

[47] F. O., 97/76, Extracts from dispatches dated from September, 1820, to the end of 1824.

[48] Woodbine Parish, *Buenos Aires and the Provinces of the Rio de la Plata*, edition of 1839, p. 335.

system, British imports alone were now more than double the average value of the whole yearly importation into the viceroyalty for the supply of Upper Perú and Paraguay in addition to Buenos Aires.[49] In 1824 England sent over a million Spanish dollars worth of produce and manufactures (exclusive of foreign and colonial produce) to the United Provinces of La Plata,[50] while over three thousand British residents were living in Buenos Aires.[51] In addition, Brazil ranked second, after Great Britain, as a supplier to the United Provinces, and a large proportion of that trade was in English hands.[52] There was, therefore, an important economic aspect involving Great Britain in the question of the peace and security of the River Plate basin.

Coincident with this increasing prosperity, there developed among the people of Buenos Aires a determination to reconquer the lost province of the Banda Oriental. The United Provinces could not permit any foreign nation, and especially their Portuguese rival, to possess the key to their ports and the control of their trade. When D. João, on leaving Brazil, sent an agent to La Plata to promise recognition of their independence by Portugal on condition of the acknowledgment by Buenos Aires of Portuguese possession of Montevideo, the offer was refused. An envoy sent by D. Pedro a year later asking for the recognition of Brazilian independence by the United Provinces met the same reply, for Buenos Aires refused to treat with Brazil as long as the troops of D. Pedro remained in the Banda Oriental.[53]

Taking the aggressive in response to a universal demand

[49] Parish, *Buenos Aires*, pp. 336-338. Value of total British exports of Buenos Aires in 1822 was 5,730,952 Spanish dollars; total imports at Buenos Aires were 11,267,622 Spanish dollars. Official valuation of average imports from 1792 to 1796 was 2,606,754 dollars. Parish obtained his figures from the custom house at Buenos Aires.

[50] *Ibid.*, p. 340.

[51] J. Fred Rippy, *Rivalry of the United States and Great Britain over Latin America*, p. 140.

[52] In 1822 Brazil exported to Buenos Aires goods worth 1,418,768 Spanish dollars. The United States came third with 1,368,277 dollars (Parish, *Buenos Aires*, p. 337).

[53] Núñez, *Río de la Plata*, pp. 299-304.

which arose throughout the province, the government at Buenos Aires then sent an agent to Rio to negotiate the return of the disputed territory. This special commission, the English *chargé* at Rio reported, was to be the last effort to negotiate by peaceful means; if D. Pedro should refuse to give up the Cisplatine Province, Buenos Aires would be forced to resort to arms. The Brazilian government formally declined to cede the territory, and Gómez, the agent from Buenos Aires, left, threatening war.[54]

Nothing happened for over a year, but early in 1825 the flag of insurrection was raised by Lavalleja and harsh decrees were issued against the "rebellion" by the Brazilian authorities in the capital of the province. Letters from Consul Parish in Buenos Aires indicated the certainty of a rupture between the United Provinces and Brazil, although D. Pedro insisted that he would avoid a break by all means within his power.[55] Chamberlain in great distress informed the Brazilian emperor that England's "interests, and indeed those of all Commercial Nations in these countries, were essentially connected with a State of Peace and Tranquility." He warned D. Pedro "that it would become all parties in South America to ponder well before they adopted any line of conduct by which those Interests might be effected; or that, besides endangering their own Comfort and prosperity, might also perhaps compromise their very existence."[56]

The question of the Montevideo territory had again reached an acute stage, and unless it were settled soon, the *chargé* warned Canning, it would cause trouble for England. Whatever might be said by the Brazilian authorities, the *chargé* had no doubt that with the exception of a few rich and respectable persons within the city of Montevideo, the whole of the population of the Cisplatine Province was absolutely opposed to remaining Brazilian. It was equally as opposed to becoming subject to

---

[54] F. O., 63/261, Chamberlain to Canning, No. 125. October 17, 1823; F. O., 63/276, Chamberlain to Canning, No. 18. February 10, 1824.

[55] F. O., 13/9, Chamberlain to Canning, Nos. 54 (May 21, 1825), 59, 85.

[56] *Ibid.*, No. 85.

Buenos Aires, however—independence was the real object in view in the Banda Oriental itself. But the United Provinces would be forced to enter the question, since as long as Brazil held Montevideo, Maldonado, and Colonia, it controlled the commerce of Buenos Aires and La Plata basin.[57] The *chargé* might have added also that the situation was complicated seriously by the fact that England's stake in that region would not let the British stand by with folded hands while the two principals were fighting it out between themselves.

Chamberlain predicted the final solution of the question when he insisted to Canning, in August, 1825, that there was no hope of reaching a settlement between Brazil and Buenos Aires as long as the two protagonists were left alone, as the passions of both were too violent. A third party to mediate was necessary.[58] Eventually England was to take upon itself the task, but only after the two principal actors had fought to a draw before they would accept the proffered aid.

War started when the Buenos Aires Congress on October 25, 1825, incorporated the Banda Oriental into the United Provinces of Rio de la Plata. Brazil considered the act a declaration of war and retaliated with a formal declaration dated December 10.[59] Seven days later, the blockade of the Provinces of La Plata was announced by the Brazilian authorities at Montevideo.[60] D. Pedro determined to settle the matter by arms.[61]

The blockade of the River Plate began to produce results, although on land the armies of D. Pedro suffered reverses. British imports into Buenos Aires dropped from over a million Spanish dollars in value in 1824 to less than 155,000 in 1826.[62] Canning was overwhelmed with applications for interference in the enforcement of the blockade, but he steadfastly refused to demand of Brazil that it relinquish belligerent rights which Great Britain had always insisted upon when at war. Provided

---

[57] F. O., 13/9, Chamberlain to Canning, Nos. 59, 85.

[58] *Ibid.*, No. 85.

[59] F. O., 13/11, Chamberlain to Canning, Nos. 145, 155.

[60] F. O., 13/22, Chamberlain to Canning, No. 13.

[61] F. O., 13/23, Chamberlain to Canning, No. 37.

[62] Parish, *Buenos Aires*, p. 340.

the blockade were effective, England would not interfere on the score of injuries suffered by its commerce in consequence of the naval policy of Brazil.[63]

Although Canning refused to interfere on account of the blockade, he did not refrain from taking active steps to stop the conflict between Brazil and Buenos Aires. Before the war broke out, Brazil had requested the mediation of Great Britain in the settlement of the Montevideo question,[64] in the hopes that its old ally would aid in the retention of the Cisplatine Province by the Brazilians.[65] Lord Ponsonby, appointed minister plenipotentiary to Buenos Aires after the recognition by England of the independence of the United Provinces, had been instructed by Canning to pass through Brazil to see if he could avert war.

In various instructions to Ponsonby, Canning suggested that Buenos Aires had the strongest claim to Montevideo and had the force necessary to back it. He was anxious that D. João should not antagonize the rest of Spanish America by his action in La Plata and warned that Bolívar was being incited to undertake a war against Brazil to overthrow the only monarchy which existed on the continent of America. Ponsonby was not to take sides under any circumstances in the struggle going on, but to demonstrate that despite the large stake which England possessed in La Plata, its action was impersonal. Later, after his own failure, the minister was instructed to coöperate with Gordon at Rio in the efforts of the latter to bring about a settlement.[66]

Ponsonby reached Rio too late to stop hostilities and sailed for La Plata to take up his duties there.[67] Sir Charles Stuart was instructed not to go into the question when he came to negotiate the recognition of the independence of Brazil,[68] but

[63] F. O., 13/25, Canning to Gordon, Nos. 11, 14. September 16 and November 20, 1826.

[64] F. O., 13/11, Chamberlain to Canning, December 7, 1825, Secret.

[65] F. O., 13/22, Chamberlain to Canning, No. 10.

[66] Harold Temperly, *Foreign Policy of Canning*, pp. 182-184.

[67] F. O., 13/24, Chamberlain to Canning, August 13, 1826, Secret and Confidential, No. 86.

[68] F. O., 13/2, Canning to Stuart, No. 23.

the irrepressible minister could not refrain from suggesting as a solution to the problem that an independent state of Montevideo should be set up in case Buenos Aires and Rio could not be brought to agree. Canning received the idea coldly, saying that in such a case England would be accused of self interest.[69] As a matter of fact, at the time, General Sarratea from Buenos Aires was in London, where a proposal of mediation was then being discussed.[70]

The war was disastrous to the Brazilians. Twice in the closing months of 1825 the imperial forces were defeated by the troops from Buenos Aires. When D. Pedro took the field himself in November, 1826, in order to incite his men to valor, he was forced by the illness of the empress to return to Rio without having gained a victory. Early in 1827 his forces on land suffered a serious defeat; one fleet was captured by Admiral Brown, commander of the Buenos Aires squadron; another fleet was lost off the coast of Patagonia;[71] and an agent from La Plata appeared in Rio to negotiate terms.[72]

But by the first article of the preliminary treaty of peace which was signed by the agent, Manuel García, and the Brazilian government, the Republic of the United Provinces recognized the independence of Brazil and renounced all of its rights to the Cisplatine Province. Thus by diplomacy did Brazil recoup what its army and navy had lost.[73] Although this preliminary convention was rejected by the Buenos Aires government, the Brazilians were aroused to a new enthusiasm by their elation over the terms obtained from García[74] and new impetus was given to the war. While Gordon at Rio was counselling moderation to D. Pedro, the Brazilian navy under Admiral Norton defeated the Buenos Aires squadron under Admiral Brown, and the commander of the land forces of the republic confessed to his government that he could not end the war. An attempt

[69] F. O., 13/2, Canning to Stuart, No. 39. December 5, 1825.

[70] *Ibid.*, No. 40.

[71] Pinto da Rocha, "A Politica Brasileira no Prata," p. 583.

[72] F. O., 13/37, Gordon to Canning, No. 39. May 10, 1827.

[73] Pinto da Rocha, *op. cit.*, p. 584; F. O., 13/37, Gordon to Canning, No. 45.

[74] F. O., 13/38, Gordon to Dudley, No. 6.

to draw Bolívar into a concerted attack on the Brazilian Empire failed, and internal anarchy threatened to disrupt the United Provinces. D. Pedro at Rio maintained an obstinate refusal to any solution which would separate the Banda Oriental from the empire, until the news that the *Caudilho* Rivera had invaded the Missions territory induced a more conciliatory mood.[75]

Minister Gordon, since his arrival on October 13, 1826, had striven fruitlessly to bring about a settlement of the Montevideo question. Now in the following October, he advised his government firmly, and somewhat grimly, that the war between Buenos Aires and Brazil called for the direct interference of Great Britain. The reasons for such action by England were sufficiently weighty, in the opinion of the minister. The struggle waged on the sea was a war between Englishmen, for twelve hundred English seamen were in the Brazilian navy alone, and the commanders of both sides were English. Every British vessel which entered Brazilian ports lost a large quota of its crew, for considerable numbers of seamen deserted from each ship to join their countrymen in the service of Brazil. That the conflict had long since escaped from the control of Buenos Aires was demonstrated by the fact that the many privateers commissioned by that government were largely English and American and acted like pirates in their disrespect of neutral property. If the war continued, both the Buenos Aires and Rio governments would be shattered, since the United Provinces were already shaken by internal anarchy, while the avowed purpose of the Buenos Aires government in the war was to cause the dismemberment of the Brazilian Empire. A proclamation calling on Pernambuco, Bahia, and other centers of disaffection within the empire to secede from their allegiance to the Braganças had been published by the government of La Plata. Such a state of affairs, the minister maintained, warranted the intervention of England, just as the three powers had intervened between Greece and the Ottoman Porte. It was now up to

[75] Pinto da Rocha, "A Politica Brasileira no Prata," pp. 584-585; Hildegarde Angell, *Simón Bolívar, South American Liberator*, pp. 203-204.

England to decide independently what interference was advisable in order to end this war, "than which none was ever waged more iniquitous or more disastrous to all parties concerned."[76]

Gordon, turning from eloquence to action before a reply to his statement of the case came from London, presented a project to the Brazilian secretary of state for foreign affairs, which should serve as a basis of pacification. The project, which the minister received favorably, raised the Banda Oriental to a free and independent state through the mediation of the British Government.[77] The Brazilian court at the earnest insistence of Gordon accepted the proposal with slight modifications and agreed to an armistice on the basis of the *status quo;*[78] and Buenos Aires signified its concurrence and promised to send agents to Rio to conclude the formal preliminary convention.[79] Gordon had high hopes of ending the dispute quickly.

But the minister was not permitted to finish the task so well begun, for he was promoted to a European post, leaving Rio August, 1828, before the envoys from La Plata arrived. Lord Ponsonby, who was shifted from Buenos Aires to Rio, assisted at the birth of the new nation by witnessing the signature of the preliminary convention of August 27, 1828. By the agreement both parties concurred in the establishment of an independent Banda Oriental and bound themselves to defend the new state for the length of time to be set in the final treaty of peace which was to be negotiated on the basis of the present convention. Certain articles provided for a temporary government to rule the new state until the permanent organization could be set up, while others specified the machinery for the prospective elections and for the framing of a constitution, granted amnesty to all concerned, and provided for the evacuation of the territory by the troops of the contending armies.[80]

---

[76] F. O., 13/39, Gordon to Dudley, No. 26 (October 1, 1827) and No. 30 (November 10).

[77] F. O., 13/47, Gordon to Dudley, No. 9. January 17, 1828.

[78] *Ibid.*, No. 14. February 13.

[79] *Ibid.*, No. 18. February 17.

[80] F. O., 13/50, Ponsonby to Aberdeen, No. 5. August 29, 1828.

Ponsonby then notified the agent from Buenos Aires that "any retreat on his part from the engagements to me as a minister of the Mediating Sovereign, must originate the most serious question between His Majesty's government and the Argentine republic." Then, turning to the other party in the dispute, he later repeated the same threat "in pretty strong terms" to the Brazilian minister.[81] His ponderous bombast was unnecessary, however, as both parties were agreed on the necessity of calling the dispute a drawn battle. On October 4, 1828, ratifications were exchanged at Montevideo[82]; the constitution of the new state was accepted by Brazil and Buenos Aires two years later; and the troops of the contending parties were withdrawn.[83]

Thus from 1680 to 1826 the wave of Portuguese control receded and advanced incessantly; Colonia changed hands five times; the Brazilian frontier advanced to La Plata and the Uruguay rivers only to fall back in the darkest days of the eighteenth century far northward into the province of Santa Catharina; while by the agreements of 1777 and 1801 the Portuguese were penned up behind the legal barriers of what, approximately, are the limits of to-day. When the Portuguese court was transferred to Rio, however, D. João seized the golden opportunity created by the Napoleonic wars in Europe and the independence movement of the Spanish colonies, to extend his boundaries to La Plata and the Uruguay rivers. Strangford

---

[81] *Ibid.* [82] *Ibid.*, No. 21.

[83] W. S. Robertson, *History of the Latin American Nations*, p. 256. The preliminary convention of peace between Brazil and Buenos Aires is given in Parish, *Buenos Aires and the Provinces of the Rio de la Plata*, 2nd edition, Appendix V. Article 7 called for commissioners to be appointed by Buenos Aires and Rio to approve the constitution which was to be drawn up by the Constitutional Assembly of the proposed state of Uruguay before it should be sworn to by the new state. Article 17 called for commissioners to be appointed after the ratification of the present preliminary treaty to draw up a definitive treaty of peace. The convention was ratified by Buenos Aires September 29, 1828, and by Brazil August 30, 1828. An additional article assured free navigation of La Plata river for fifteen years. No definite treaty was negotiated, but on May 25-27, 1830, the commissioners from Brazil and Buenos Aires, meeting at Rio, approved the proposed constitution of Uruguay (*República Argentina, Tratados, Protocolos, Actos y Acuerdos Internacionales*, II, 411-425).

postponed the realization of the project until Europe had settled down in 1815; but at his withdrawal, the Portuguese court pushed on to victory in spite of the intervention of the great powers. Yet the movement for independence among the Spanish colonies, which enabled D. João to succeed, foreshadowed the very forces which caused the eventual failure of the aspirations of the Rio court. For Buenos Aires, once convinced that it could not hold the province for itself, yielded to the yearnings for independence manifested among the inhabitants of the Banda Oriental, and Brazil was not strong enough to hold the north bank of La Plata against the insurrectionary forces. Through the mediation of Great Britain, the new state of Uruguay emerged and the Portuguese aspiration of nearly two centuries was realized in 1817 only to be irrevocably lost in 1828.[84]

[84] A recent discussion of the war between Brazil and Buenos Aires is Juan Beverina's, *La Guerra contra el Imperio del Brasil.* 2 volumes.

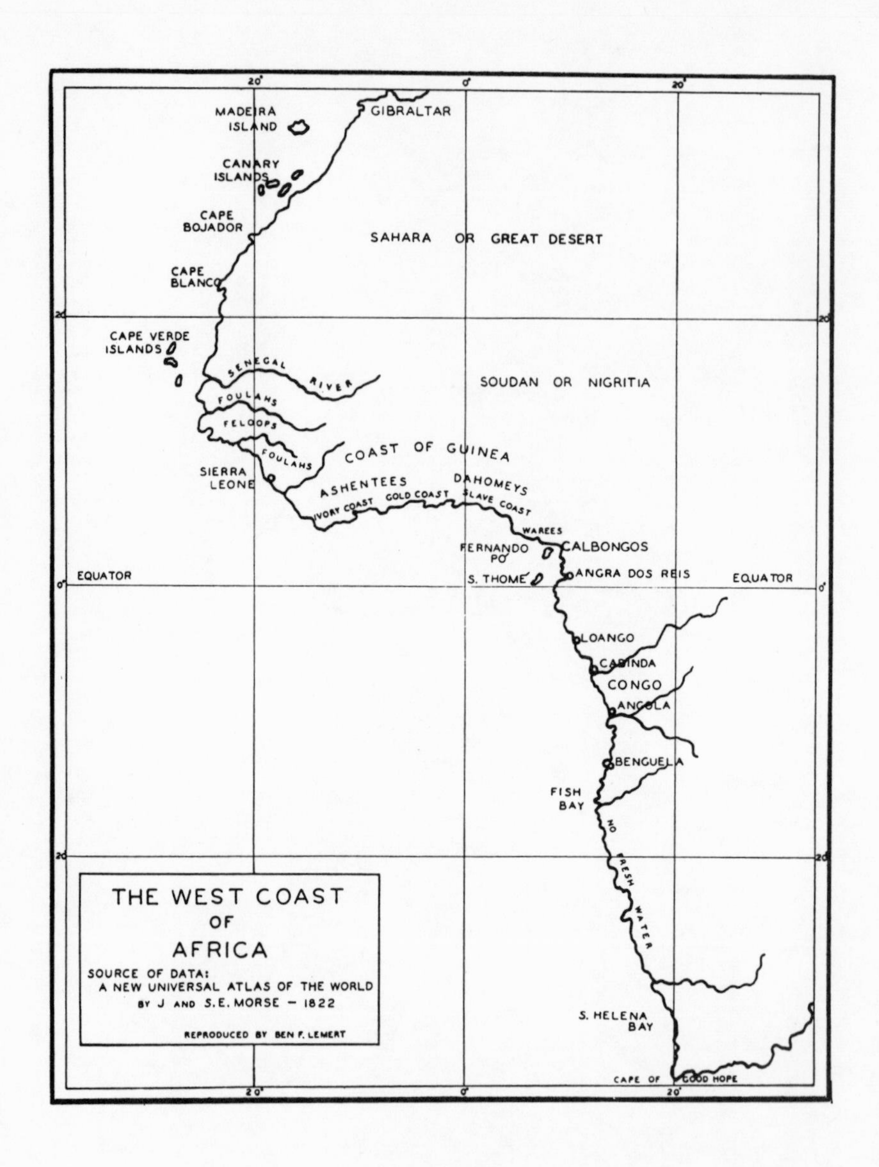
MADEIRA ISLAND
GIBRALTAR
CANARY ISLANDS
CAPE BOJADOR
SAHARA OR GREAT DESERT
CAPE BLANCO
CAPE VERDE ISLANDS
SENEGAL RIVER
SOUDAN OR NIGRITIA
FOULAHS
FELOOPS
FOULAHS
COAST OF GUINEA
SIERRA LEONE
ASHENTEES
DAHOMEYS
IVORY COAST
GOLD COAST
SLAVE COAST
WAREES
FERNANDO PO
CALBONGOS
EQUATOR
S. THOME
ANGRA DOS REIS
EQUATOR
LOANGO
CABINDA
CONGO
ANGOLA
BENGUELA
FISH BAY
NO FRESH WATER
S. HELENA BAY
CAPE OF GOOD HOPE
THE WEST COAST OF AFRICA
SOURCE OF DATA:
A NEW UNIVERSAL ATLAS OF THE WORLD
BY J AND S.E. MORSE – 1822
REPRODUCED BY BEN F. LEMERT

CHAPTER VII

ENGLAND'S ATTEMPTS TO ABOLISH THE PORTUGUESE SLAVE TRADE, 1808-1822

THE MOST SERIOUS friction which has ever arisen between England and Portuguese America resulted from the attempts of the British government to suppress the slave trade. From 1808 through the century until slavery was abolished in Brazil (1888), the constantly increasing pressure which the London Foreign Office brought to bear in its efforts to abolish the traffic caused such an intense feeling of resentment on the part of the Brazilians that the friendly relations of the two countries were seriously menaced. The question disturbed Anglo-Portuguese relations during D. João's sojourn in Rio and contributed to the growth of the separatist, republican sentiment in the provinces of Pernambuco and Bahia; it became a *sine qua non* of recognition by England of Brazilian independence; and it injected itself so forcibly into the relations of the two countries between 1827 and 1842 that it frustrated every effort of England to renew the commercial treaty negotiated as the price of the recognition of Brazilian independence. The climax came in the two decades between 1845 and 1863, which terminated in the severance by Brazil of diplomatic relations with the British government.[1]

[1] *The Cambridge History of British Foreign Policy*, II, 238, states that in "1826 Brazil entered into a Convention with Great Britain promising to abolish the trade in three years; and in 1830 this promise was carried out." Yet in 1842 the House of Commons complained to the cabinet that "at no period had the Brazilian Slave Trade been so intensively carried on as it is at the present moment in Rio de Janeiro itself" (F. O., 84/583, Aberdeen to Hamilton, No. 10, June 4, 1845). Oliveira Martins estimates the average importation into Brazil from 1819 to 1847 at 40,000, not counting the loss during the voyage by death or capture. Before England's attempt to suppress the traffic, fifteen per cent. of the slaves died during

The special economic privileges which the English had enjoyed in Portugal for centuries were transferred to Portuguese America with the removal of the Lisbon court to Rio and were eventually fastened on the independent empire of Brazil as a part of the price of the recognition of its independence by Great Britain. There was a continuity, therefore, in the commercial relations of the English and the Portuguese from the formation of the independent state of Portugal in the twelfth century to the Brazil of the nineteenth century. In like manner, England imposed on the new empire of Brazil the agreements concluded with Portugal in regard to the suppression of the slave trade at a time when the latter state was virtually a vassal of the British Empire. The agreements under which England acted, and against which Brazil protested so vehemently after 1827, were negotiated between the British and Portuguese governments before D. Pedro raised the cry of independence. As in the case of the special economic privileges, the ratification by Brazil of the stipulations concerning the slave trade, together with a promise of total abolition in 1830, was demanded and obtained as a part of the price of the recognition of its independence by England. Thus there were foisted on Brazil, as the only way out of an impossible situation, restrictions of which neither the government nor the people approved, with the result that the enforcement of these stipulations by Great Britain aroused bitter resentment among the Brazilians after 1830.

The future course of Great Britain in regard to the international suppression of the slave trade was forecast even before the final bill for the abolition of the traffic passed the houses of Parliament. On March 31, 1806, the importation of slaves into those American colonies which had been conquered by the British in the course of the war was prohibited; English subjects were forbidden to import slaves into the colonies of any foreign country whether neutral or hostile; and all British capital and subjects were denied the privilege of engaging in the traffic in

---

passage, while after the attempt began, the loss rose to twenty-five per cent. British cruisers captured only four per cent. of the total shipped from Africa (Oliveira Martins, *O Brazil e as Colonias Portuguesas*, p. 58, footnote 1).

foreign ships. The outfitting of slavers of any nationality in English ports was prohibited also.[2] The following June, realizing that the complete abolition of the trade by England was merely a question of time, Wilberforce moved to address the king "praying that he would be graciously pleased to direct a negotiation to be entered into, by which foreign powers should be invited to coöperate with his majesty, in measures to be adopted for the abolition of the African Slave-trade." His resolution passed both the Commons and the Lords without a division.[3]

These measures were forerunners of the acts of 1807, which abolished the traffic entirely as far as the subjects of England were concerned. Early in that year the bill was passed declaring illegal any participation by a British subject in the purchase, sale, or transfer of slaves on or from the African coast after May 1. No slave was to be admitted into any British colony after March 1, 1808, and any vessel fitting out in the United Kingdom for the traffic was to be confiscated.[4]

England thus decreed the end of the slave trade in so far as its own subjects were concerned. With the cruisers at its command and the determination to enforce the laws enacted, the British government was abundantly able to make its prohibition effective. Yet the battle was only half won, since Holland, France, Spain, the United States,[5] and Portugal still carried

[2] Thomas Clarkson, *History of the Abolition of the African Slave-Trade by the British Parliament*, p. 334; *Abstract of the Laws of Jamaica relating to Slaves*—"An Abstract of the Acts of Parliament Relating to the Abolition of the Slave-Trade," pp. 149-165. The bill passed the Lords, May 7.

[3] Clarkson, *op. cit.*, pp. 337-341.

[4] *Ibid.*, pp. 344-347; *Abstract*, pp. 165-174. The bill was passed in the Commons despite the vigorous opposition of the West India interests which were supported by the Duke of Clarence (later William IV). "The victory . . . was a crushing defeat for the planter-merchant group . . . a triumph . . . over the power of vested interest and property" (Lowell Joseph Ragatz, *The Fall of the Planter Class in the British Caribbean, 1763-1833*, p. 276).

[5] W. E. B. DuBois points out that despite the Act of March 2, 1807, which prohibited the importation of slaves after January 1, 1808, and the Treaty of Ghent by which the United States bound itself to suppress the trade, the traffic continued briskly until the Civil War. He estimates the annual importation between 1807 and 1862 to have been from 1,000 to 15,000 (American Historical Asso., *Reports*, 1891, "The Enforcement of the Slave-Trade Laws," pp. 161-174).

on a thriving trade in slaves. Under the formidable pressure exerted by public opinion ably directed by enthusiastic reformers and under the powerful influence brought to bear by those financially interested in the British West Indies, the English government, in conformity with the resolution of Wilberforce of June, 1806, now turned to securing the complete abolition of the trade. "The subject was one in which almost the whole nation had become interested. It could not be ignored. To the leaders of the movement no sacrifice appeared too great to secure the complete cessation of the abominable traffic. They insisted that it should be put in the forefront of every diplomatic transaction. The relations between Britain and every other Power were thus affected, particularly relations with other maritime Powers, with whom, naturally, there was always the most friction."[6]

Chief among the nations[7] on whom England exerted its influence to obtain the abolition of the traffic was Portugal, since that country was the traditional sinner and, on account of the peculiar relations existing between the two governments, offered special opportunities for action by Britain. Yet the Portuguese were to prove, perhaps, the most recalcitrant of all in their determination not to renounce the trade. The reforming public of England quite naturally failed to understand Portugal's reluctance to follow Britain's example and laid the persistence of the Portuguese slave traffic to the natural perversity of that race. Yet there were fundamental reasons which impelled the subjects of the Braganças to cling to the trade in slaves, which long since had been restricted to an exchange between Africa and the colonies, principally between the west coast of Africa and the east coast of South America.

Negro slavery was deeply rooted in Brazil, far more so than in Spanish America. The Indians, fleeing, disappearing, or dying, failed to supply the needed labor, as they did in the Spanish

[6] Webster, *Foreign Policy of Castlereagh*, p. 454.

[7] The diplomacy of the abolition of the slave trade has never been investigated. Such a study is much needed (Webster, *op. cit.*, p. 454, footnote). The nearest approach to an investigation along this line is the work of William Law Mathieson, *British Slavery and Its Abolition* and *Great Britain and the Slave Trade, 1839-1865*.

possessions, while even the Jesuits themselves favored the African slave trade in an effort to save the Indians from the hands of the Portuguese *mameluco*. Between the founding of Rio (1567) immediately following the defeat of the French and the expulsion of the Dutch from Pernambuco (1662), came the golden age of the Jesuits with their monopoly of Indian labor in the missions of Bahia and the Amazon valley. Consequently the Brazilian settler in those regions was forced to abandon his plantation or to import Negro slaves,[8] with the result that the Portuguese became the first to develop the modern slave trade extensively. Without Negro labor Brazil could never have been developed, nor would Portuguese America exist to-day.[9] From 1575 to 1591 from Angola alone fifty thousand Negroes were exported to Portugal, Brazil, and the Spanish Indies, while during the first half of the seventeenth century the number reached fifteen thousand annually. After the expulsion of the Dutch in 1662, a new impetus was given to the trade; but the Marquez de Pombal, by his abolition of Indian slavery and the emphasis which he placed on plantations instead of mines, caused a striking increase in the traffic. During the first years of the Company of Grão-Pará more than one hundred thousand Negroes were carried to Brazil annually. From 1759 to 1803 the colonial registers state that between fourteen and fif-

---

[8] Oliveira Martins, *O Brazil*, pp. 24-30. The need for slave labor in Bahia was acute since that region was the center of the sugar production of Brazil. From the middle of the sixteenth century to the beginning of the seventeenth, the Brazilian output was large, the Brazilian product being the only sugar consumed in Europe during that half century (Pereira da Silva, *Historia da Fundação do Imperio*, I, 233). Since the Indians of Brazil had an unconquerable aversion to agriculture, Negro labor was necessary for the sugar plantations (Azeredo Coutinho, *An Essay on the Commerce and Products of the Portuguese Colonies in South America*, p. 53).

[9] Oliveira Martins, *O Brazil*, pp. 52-53. The same was true of the development of the British West Indies sugar plantations. F. W. Pitman in *The Development of the British West Indies, 1700-1763*, says that "it is very probable that the production of sugar would not have developed as soon as it did if slavery had not existed to furnish a sufficiently large and continuous body of labor." He adds (pp. 62-63) that "there is little doubt that" the decline in the annual average of sugar exported from the British sugar colonies after 1805 "was owing to the abolition of the slave trade and slavery itself." The Portuguese sugar growers in Brazil had pointed the way to such a solution of the labor problem (p. 61).

teen thousand yearly left Angola.[10] In 1803 in the city of Rio de Janeiro there were over fourteen thousand Negro slaves and nearly ten thousand free Negroes out of a total population of almost forty-seven thousand.[11]

By 1807 slave labor in Brazil had become an economic god with the slave trade as its strong right arm. To attempt to suppress the traffic, which was an essential adjunct to slavery itself, by simply passing statutes and signing treaties was a futile performance. In England a long and intensive education of public opinion preceded the final abolition of the trade, but now the British Foreign Office was being compelled to force the same measure on a country which believed fervently in the necessity of slave labor and relied on the African trade for the needed supply of fresh Negroes. The religious appeal which exercised such a deep impression in Britain[12] did not influence either the Portuguese government or the subjects of the Braganças, whereas the economic influences in England which demanded universal abolition served only to strengthen the financial and agricultural interests of the Portuguese in their determination to hold fast to the traffic. Faced by this opposition,

---

[10] Oliveira Martins, *O Brazil*, pp. 54-56 and 56 footnote (1). Not all came to Brazil. There was a market for Brazilian sugar in Europe throughout the century for England did not preëmpt the European sugar trade. Although the import of raw sugar into Great Britain from the British plantations grew from 500,000 cwt. in 1700 to close to 2,000,000 in 1770, the export of raw sugar to Europe remained practically stationary around 200,000 cwt. annually (Pitman, *British West Indies*, p. 168). Brazilian sugar found ready markets in Italy and the eastern Mediterranean country (*ibid.*, pp. 163-164). The export of English refined sugar was killed by 1693 and very little of the refined article was exported thereafter (*ibid.*, p. 157). Brazilian sugar in 1760 constituted one-third of the total world production. By 1776, however, the percentage had fallen to less than six per cent. of the world total, but toward the end of the century the production revived. By 1800 there were over 1000 *engenhos* in Brazil (Pereira da Silva, *Historia da Fundação do Imperio*, I, 232-233). With the European market open to the Brazilian product and with the principal agricultural emphasis of the colony being placed on sugar, the need for slaves in Brazil continued to be pressing and the slave trade flourished.

[11] F. O., 63/84, Strangford to Wellesley, No. 35.

[12] Webster, *Foreign Policy of Castlereagh*, p. 455. A discussion of the propaganda in favor of the slave-trade suppression is given by Ragatz, *Fall of the Planter Class*, pp. 237-276.

both Canning and Castlereagh, nevertheless, honestly exerted every effort to bring about the complete abolition of the trade by Portugal.

Canning, who made the first attempt before D. João fled to Rio, was rebuffed in unmistakable terms by Araujo, then foreign minister. Araujo assured Strangford, in reply to the enquiries of the latter as to the attitude of the Portuguese government relative to the suppression of the slave traffic, that it was impracticable to expect Portugal either to annihilate or to discourage the trade. He explained that public opinion was entirely opposed to such a step, and although he himself admired the philosophy which impelled Great Britain to abolish the traffic, he would be very sorry to imitate it in his own country. Moreover, he added, the Portuguese colonists would never consent to such a measure.[13]

The London Foreign Office was not allowed to accept such an answer, for both the reformers and certain financial interests were determined to check the Portuguese slave trade. A sample[14] of the propaganda which was carried on about 1808 demonstrated the part played by economic influences in the humanitarian mania which demanded the cessation of the so-called "inhuman traffic." The author of this document states unequivocally that "the establishment of an independent metropolitan Government in Brazil" would be "ruinous to our Sugar Colonies and to the commercial interests dependent upon them, and" would prove also "a heavy political incumbrance, instead of an advantage to Great Britain, unless the renunciation of the African Slave Trade" were made an "article of any Treaty of Commerce and Alliance into which we may now en-

---

[13] F. O., 63/54, Strangford to Canning, No. 31. June 4, 1807.

[14] The sample referred to is an unsigned, undated paper found among the Miscellaneous Papers of Lord Bexley, 1796-1844, Add. Ms., 31, 237, pp. 182-191. The paper was written between 1808 and 1810, however. Nicholas Vansittart, first Baron Bexley, was secretary to the treasury in Grenville's administration to 1809 (March). He was very active in the Commons during 1809 in regard to financial measures. He refused the chancellorship of the Exchequer in October, 1809, but accepted in 1812. He was chancellor during Castlereagh's period in office (*Dictionary of National Biography*, LVIII).

ter with that power." In order to prove such a statement to the public, pamphlets should be prepared and scattered abroad in England, for the fate of the British West Indies was at stake.

The danger which threatened the sugar colonies, that of overproduction, would be remedied by the cessation of the slave traffic within the British dominions, since such a measure would prevent the extension of sugar growing through lack of labor. But that remedy was now imperiled by the threat of a new and enormous increase of sugar planting in Brazil. "In that vast and fertile territory, an influx of British Capital and British enterprise alone" was "wanting to compleat the ruin of all our Islands in the Antilles . . . ." Land was ninety per cent. cheaper in Brazil than in Jamaica while most of the supplies for a sugar plantation were raised within the country. Hence the Brazilian planter could sell with profit in Europe at a price which would mean ruin to the West Indian plantation owner, and the European market was essential to the British sugar trade, since England no longer absorbed anything like the total output of the sugar colonies.

The only solution to the difficulties confronting the West Indies, therefore, was either to abolish the Portuguese slave trade which supplied cheap labor to Brazilian plantations, or to prohibit any commercial intercourse between Great Britain and Brazil; for the latter measure would prevent the influx of British capital and enterprise into the Portuguese colony. Since commercial relations with England were fundamentally necessary to Brazil, the Portuguese government should be made to pay the price of attaining that advantage by a renunciation of its traffic in slaves. By the influx of British capital into the colony and by the pledge of alliance and protection by the British government, Great Britain would acquire a right to prescribe the terms of the partnership between the two countries. Therefore let England "refuse to form any conventional relations, commercial or political, with Brazil, of which the cessation of its Slave Trade" was not a fundamental article.

The group which was represented by this propaganda was an important element in British economic life. Since the West

Indies were largely one-crop colonies, whatever affected the sugar interests became at once the vital concern not only of the plantation owners themselves, but also of the shippers and London middlemen. More indirectly but no less seriously, a group of English exporters also was linked to the rise or fall of the sugar business, for the merchandise shipped to the British West Indies constituted one of the principal items of English trade. If the sugar industry should decline, the manufacturers of West Indies necessities, the exporters, and shipping interests would suffer in proportion. Therefore these economic groups of England joined those of the islands in the demand for the universal abolition of the slave trade, once that traffic had been forbidden to the sugar colonies. Together these interests wielded an important influence.[15]

The propaganda was only in part successful, for although the treaty of alliance of 1810 did include a clause dealing with the slave traffic, D. João merely prohibited the trade from any part of Africa not belonging to Portugal, while within the Portuguese dominions full license was allowed to the traders. He promised, however, to coöperate with England in an effort to

[15] In 1830 sugar constituted in value two-thirds of the total exports of the island of Demerara, over one-half of the exports of Jamaica, ten-elevenths of those of Barbadoes, and more than eight-ninths of those of St. Vincent. Sugar alone accounted for over sixty-one per cent. of the total exports of the British West Indies in that year (Customs, 4/25, British Imports by Countries). Diagrams opposite pp. 98 and 108 of *The Development of the British West Indies* by Pitman demonstrate the one-crop agricultural system of the Barbadoes and Jamaica through the eighteenth century as far as 1770. The same characteristics were true for Antigua, Montserrat, Nevis, and St. Christopher. The exports to the West Indies in 1812 were greater than those to the United States and double the value of exports to Brazil. In 1815, an unusual year, exports to the islands equaled half the value of merchandise shipped to the United States and over three times the amount sent to Brazil. In 1820 the British West Indies absorbed more English exports than did the United States or Brazil. In 1825 the islands took over half as much as did the United States and more than half as much as all of the South American States. In 1830 and 1835 the United States forged ahead but the British West Indies maintained their position in regard to the South and Central American states. In 1835 the value of exports from Great Britain to the British West Indies was nearly £3,200,000, while all of the South American states took less than £4,900,-000. Brazil in that year received over £2,600,000 of English exports (Customs, 8/1, 3, 12, 21, 32, 42).

bring about the gradual abolition of the traffic throughout the world.[16]

Even this mild concession was gained with difficulty, and England from the first accused Portuguese slave ships of violation of the prohibition imposed by the treaty.[17] Subjects of other powers changed their flag to the Portuguese banner and plied the trade unhampered by the international agreements of their countries,[18] while in Brazil immediate complaints arose against the seizure of slavers off the coast of Africa by British cruisers.

The city of Bahia especially grew very bitter over the subject, for out of thirty-two vessels which had been fitted out for the slave trade at that place in 1811, seventeen were known to have been seized by British cruisers, while others were conjectured to have suffered the same fate. Five principal commercial houses failed by the early part of 1812 and the indignation of Bahia against England reached a high pitch. This attitude was extended to include the Portuguese government at Rio, which by its supineness in the face of Britain's action was considered by the inhabitants of that region no longer to merit the support of Brazilians. Strangford warned his government that a very real danger of rebellion in that province threatened the unity of the colony as a result of the action of the British cruisers. The envoy advised that the English authorities relax a bit in their efforts to suppress the trade, for the abolition would have to be very gradual as far as Brazil was concerned. Later over half a dispatch book of documents was submitted by the Rio government in proof of its contention that the aggressions of the English cruisers were illegal and arbitrary.[19]

---

[16] Article 10 of the treaty of friendship and alliance, 1810. F. O., 93/37/8, Portugal.

[17] The minister of the interior, Fernando Portugal, opposed it bitterly (see *supra*, p. 85. F. O., 63/122, Draft to Lord Strangford, No. 1. January 7, 1812).

[18] The British government repeatedly demanded of Portugal an act of renunciation of its rights to be the carrier of slaves for other states and the positive prohibition of the use of the Portuguese flag in the slave trade not permitted by Article 10 of the treaty of 1810 (F. O., 63/122, Draft to Strangford, No. 1).

[19] F. O., 63/123, Strangford to Castlereagh, No. 32. May 20, 1812. F. O., 63/125, Strangford to Castlereagh, No. 78. November 10, 1812.

In reply to these complaints, Castlereagh preached the Rio court a sermon. "It is high time," he wrote,[20] "that the Prince Regent of Portugal should seriously set about redeeming his Pledges for the abolition of this traffic in human blood," for it was only under the Portuguese flag that such a traffic was now possible to any great extent.[21] In a later note, the foreign minister dryly advised Strangford that the cruisers would continue to bring in Portuguese slave ships off the Gold Coast and north Africa for adjudication. If the commanders erred, the *Bahianos* would receive indemnity; but if the courts of admiralty upheld the seizures, there would be no remedy for the inhabitants of that city. It was unfortunate if the *Bahianos* did not approve, but their complaints were useless. The best solution was for them to trade within the territory specified in Article 10 of the treaty of alliance of 1810.[22]

The net result thus far of the attempt to suppress the Portuguese slave trade forced on the British Foreign Office by home influence was to drive D. João into the opposite camp. Early in 1814, Strangford reported that there was no hope of any further steps being taken by the Portuguese court toward abolishing the traffic, for any inclination which the prince regent had had in the past had now disappeared in consequence of the "universal clamour and discontent which the indiscriminate captures made by the British cruizers on the coast of Africa" had excited. This was the only point, the viscount remarked, on which he had seen such a general national feeling exhibited by the Brazilians and Portuguese. The sentiment was most powerful and very extensive throughout the kingdom.[23] Despite the action of the cruisers, nearly twenty-four thousand slaves were imported into Bahia alone between May, 1811,

[20] F. O., 63/144, Castlereagh to Strangford, No. 19. May 12, 1813.

[21] This statement was true, in view of the European situation in 1812 and 1813.

[22] F. O., 63/144, Castlereagh to Strangford, No. 30. October 11, 1813. As later events showed, the *Bahianos* had grounds for their complaints, as the indemnity of 1815 and the London Mixed Commission confessed that many seizures had been illegal (see *infra* pp. 170, 179). England needed vessels between 1810 and 1815.

[23] F. O., 63/167, Strangford to Castlereagh, No. 40. April 20, 1814.

and June, 1814, by far the greater number of vessels giving the Gold Coast (*Costa da Mina*) as the origin of their Negroes.[24] Into Rio during the same four years (but including all of 1811 and 1814 to November) there were imported over sixty-three thousand.[25]

In the face of this activity and the attitude of the Portuguese government, Strangford despaired of concluding any negotiations relative to the traffic and intended merely to issue a declaration "defining the limits beyond which Great Britain" would "*not suffer* the Portuguese Flag to be used in the Slave Trade, and 2° the Circumstances which would render a Ship under Portuguese colours liable to capture within these Limits." Castlereagh could back this declaration and enforce it, regardless of the Portuguese position in the matter. This, so Strangford asserted, was the only way left to England in its efforts to restrict the Portuguese slave traffic.[26]

Castlereagh succeeded where his minister failed, however, for early in 1815, he concluded two treaties with the Portuguese plenipotentiaries who acted for their court at the Congress of Vienna. By the first,[27] signed January 21, England gave three hundred thousand pounds in full payment of all claims of the Portuguese arising from seizures made by British cruisers before June 1, 1814.[28] By the second,[29] signed the following day, the Portuguese prohibited all trade in slaves north of the equator; the traffic was expressly permitted between Portuguese Af-

---

[24] F. O., 63/168, Strangford to Castlereagh, No. 74.

[25] F. O., 63/169, Strangford to Castlereagh, No. 109. Neither the figures for Bahia nor those for Rio included those dying during the passage. Nearly 5,000 of the importations to Rio died on the way.

[26] F. O., 63/169, Strangford to Castlereagh, No. 88. October 1, 1814.

[27] F. O., 93/37/10, Portugal.

[28] This was not a bribe to win Portugal's consent to the treaty which was signed the next day, but just compensation for damages done to Portuguese shippers. D. João, however, being in need of money, stipulated that the distribution of the sum to the various claimants should be made by his government at Rio, an arrangement to which the *Bahianos* objected strenuously, as the "probity of England" was recognized as more just than that of the Rio court. They feared that they would never receive payment from their sovereign (F. O., 63/182, Chamberlain to Castlereagh, No. 34).

[29] F. O., 93/37/11, Portugal.

rica to the south of the line and Brazil; the prince regent bound himself to negotiate a separate treaty later which should set a definite time for the complete abolition of the traffic;[30] and the Portuguese were forbidden to carry slaves to any country or possession not under the dominion of the house of Bragança. The treaty of friendship and alliance of 1810 was declared annulled, with the express understanding, however, that all the ancient treaties between the two powers should continue in force, while England remitted the unpaid balance due on the loan of six hundred thousand pounds made to D. João in 1809. Ratifications were to be exchanged at Rio within five months.

Bathurst sent the treaties to Chamberlain with instructions to present two explanations for the acceptance of D. João before the *chargé* should exchange ratifications. The prince regent was to agree that the purpose of England in signing the treaties was to remove misunderstandings and misinterpretations from Anglo-Portuguese relations and to promise that he intended thoroughly to coöperate with other nations in their methods of prohibiting the slave trade within the limits set down in these treaties.[31]

Armed with these pious declarations, Chamberlain presented the treaties to D. João for ratification. The prince regent accepted the explanations without comment and exchanged ratifications on June 16, 1815.[32] But Chamberlain prophesied an unfavorable reaction in Bahia to the agreements when they should become known, since the trade to the Gold Coast, the principal source for the Bahia slave traffic, was prohibited (the

[30] Webster in his *Foreign Policy of Castlereagh*, pp. 459-460, states that Portugal promised to abolish the trade altogether within eight years. No such time limit appears in the copy of the treaty preserved at the Record Office, however. The convention of 1817 also failed to set a definite date for the final abolition. Webster likewise states that in return for this promise by Portugal the treaty of commerce of 1810 was altered in its favor. The treaty of commerce remained intact; it was the treaty of friendship and alliance dealing with political matters of a temporary nature that was abolished entirely (see Article 3 of the treaty of January 22, 1815). The treaty of commerce and the treaty of friendship and alliance were separate and distinct treaties (see *supra*, pp. 86 ff.).

[31] F. O., 63/181, Bathurst to Strangford, No. 3. February 28, 1815.

[32] F. O., 63/182, Chamberlain to Castlereagh, Nos. 30, 31.

Gold Coast lay north of the equator), and the inhabitants of that province would not approve the arrangement in regard to the indemnity for the seizures by the British cruisers.[33] Later the *chargé* informed[34] Castlereagh that Pernambuco also refused to acquiesce in the stipulations, the inhabitants of that city going so far as to fit out fast sailing ships for illicit trade to the north of the equator with the tacit approval of the Rio court. Moreover, large Portuguese vessels entered African ports nearest to the line and were there supplied with Negroes from north of the equator by small boats. In 1815 nearly fifteen thousand slaves entered Rio from Africa, despite the restrictions imposed on the traffic by the agreements.

In the face of such activity it was evident that the Portuguese were quite out of sympathy with England's efforts to suppress the slave traffic, yet the British policy of abolishing the trade on paper was pushed industriously by the Foreign Office. Basing his demands on the clause in the treaty of January 22, 1815, in which D. João promised to negotiate the complete abolition of the trade, Castlereagh forced the signature in London of the famous agreement of 1817.[35] By the additional convention (ad-

---

[33] F. O., 63/182, Chamberlain to Castlereagh, No. 34. July 18, 1815; F. O., 63/194, Chamberlain to Castlereagh, No. 71, July 30, 1816.

[34] F. O., 63/192, Chamberlain to Castlereagh, No. 5. February 10, 1816.

[35] F. O., 93/38/15, Portugal. The additional convention was signed July 28, 1817, and the separate article, September 11, 1817, by Castlereagh and the Conde de Palmella. Webster in his *Foreign Policy of Castlereagh*, p. 460, says that Castlereagh obtained from Portugal a further convention dated September 28, 1817, to carry out the terms agreed upon at Vienna, that this convention granted a limited right of visit and search, and that the slave trade south of the equator should be legal under the Portuguese flag for another five years. The convention was signed July 28, however, with the separate article dated September 11. No time limit as to the Portuguese trade south of the equator appears in the copy of the convention preserved at the Record Office and signed by Castlereagh and the Conde de Palmella. Since England signed an agreement with the Portuguese government in 1823 which was termed "additional" to the 1817 convention with the purpose of regulating seizures by British cruisers of Portuguese slavers south of the equator, it would seem that the five years limit mentioned by Webster did not exist. No mention is made in this 1823 additional convention of a promise to abolish the trade entirely (see F. O., 93/38/16, Portugal). The trade south of the equator was allowed in conformity with the terms of the Vienna agreement, which placed no time limit to that traffic.

ditional to the Vienna agreement) and the separate article signed less than two months later, the English foreign minister laid the foundation on which Great Britain based its action in enforcing the abolition of the Brazilian slave trade until the disturbing question was finally settled. When all other means failed, England recurred to certain provisions contained in the convention and the separate article and acted on them regardless of the Brazilian interpretation of those documents.

The convention of July, 1817, declared the object of the agreement was to prevent the subjects of the respective powers signatory to the documents from carrying on any illicit slave trade. Such traffic was declared illicit if prosecuted by British ships, under British flag, or by British capital; by Portuguese vessels engaged in any other manner than that specified by the Vienna agreement of January 22, 1815, or bound for any port not in the dominions of the Portuguese king. The territories in which the traffic was permitted to the subjects of D. João were specified by name.[36] Within two months from the date of the ratification, the Portuguese king was to publish the penalties prescribed for violations of the existing agreement and to prohibit by decree the importation of slaves into Brazil under any other flag than that of his country, assimilating "as much as possible the legislation of Portugal on this subject to that of Great Britain." All Portuguese vessels engaged in illicit slave traffic were to carry royal passports, drawn up in conformity with the model annexed to the convention.[37]

Thus far the stipulations did not differ much from former agreements on the subject, but the next article furnished the weapon so long desired by England in the fight to suppress the trade universally. In order to carry out the purpose of the convention the two signatory powers agreed that the ships of war of each could visit any merchant vessel of the two nations that might be suspected upon reasonable grounds of having slaves

[36] All of them lay to the south of the equator in Africa, on the east and west coasts.

[37] Articles I-IV inclusive. The decree publishing the penalties to be inflicted upon the offenders in the slave trade was dated January 26, but printed in May, 1818 (F. O., 63/212, Chamberlain to Castlereagh, No. 85. August 23, 1818).

on board. Guilty slavers should be detained and brought for adjudication before special tribunals which were to be established. Ships empowered to make such seizures were to carry specially prepared instructions drawn up in conformity with the model annexed to the convention, while any losses incurred by the subjects of either party by virtue of unlawful detention were to be paid by the respective country implicated.[38] Thus did Great Britain obtain the right from Portugal of visit and search applicable to merchant vessels in time of peace.

The next article[39] was a costly mistake on the part of Castlereagh, for it stipulated that no seizure was lawful unless slaves were actually found on board. Evidence of the recent presence of illicit slaves was not sufficient to condemn the vessel—a stipulation which resulted in the wholesale dumping overboard of Negroes by slave-traders when they were in danger of capture by British cruisers.[40] Two mixed commissions were to be appointed within a year of the ratification of the convention to adjudicate captured ships, one in English and one in Portuguese territory,[41] in Africa and in Brazil, while regulations were annexed to the convention for the guidance of those tribunals. A third commission sitting at London was to settle Portuguese claims arising from illegal detention by British cruisers between June 1, 1814, and the setting up of the mixed commissions mentioned above.[42]

The three hundred thousand pounds indemnity promised by the treaty of January 21, 1815, had never been paid by England, but now the promise was renewed and the manner of payment guaranteed, such payment to be effected only after D. João had ratified the present convention.[43] The first annex gave the passport which the Portuguese merchant vessel was to carry, and the second the instructions[44] for the ships of war of each

[38] Article V. [39] Article VI.

[40] Peter Leonard, *The Western Coast of Africa, Journal of an Officer, 1830-1832*, pp. 92-96, gives an instance witnessed by him of such action by a slaver off the coast of Africa.

[41] Article VIII. [42] Article IX. [43] Article XI.

[44] No slave ship or merchantman could be searched in a port or roadsted belonging to either crown. Every Portuguese vessel engaged in legal traffic had to

nation destined to prevent the illicit traffic in slaves. In the third annex, it was stipulated that the mixed commissions were to render judgment on detained vessels within twenty days after such ships were brought in, and the decisions were to be absolutely without appeal. The commissions were to have a commissioner judge and a commissioner of arbitration from each nation. In case the two judges could not agree, one of the commissioners of arbitration should be chosen by lot, and the majority decision would be final. The Negroes found on those ships which the commissioners judged to have been guilty of illicit traffic were to be freed, and each country bound itself to guarantee the liberty of those slaves consigned to it.[45]

To this detailed and complete plan for the restriction of the Portuguese slave traffic was added on September 11 of the same year a very significant separate article, which stated simply that "as soon as the total abolition of the Slave Trade for the subjects of the Crown of Portugal" would have taken place, "the Two High Contracting Parties" should agree to "adapt to that State of circumstances, the stipulations of the Additional Convention concluded at London" on July 26 previous. "But in default of such alterations the additional convention of that date" should remain in force "until the Expiration of fifteen years, from the day on which the General Abolition of the Slave Trade" should take place on the part of the Portuguese government.[46]

At last Castlereagh had obtained from the worst sinner[47] en-

---

have a Portuguese skipper and the crew had to be at least three-fourths Portuguese. No conveyance of slaves from one port of Brazil to another or from the continent or islands of Africa to possessions of Portugal outside of America was to be permitted except by vessels carrying a special passport from the Portuguese government.

[45] This stipulation was to give rise to a peculiar form of slavery in Brazil. The Negroes nominally freed by the commissioners sitting in Brazil were re-enslaved by various schemes, so that there arose in the '40's and '50's the problem of the emancipation of slaves legally held and of Negroes already emancipated but still slaves.

[46] F. O., 93/38/15, Portugal.

[47] Denmark abolished the trade to take effect in 1804 and forbade its citizens to engage in the traffic in 1814. Sweden prohibited its subjects from participating in the trade in 1814; Holland in 1815. Spain prohibited the trade by its subjects

gaged in the slave trade definite restrictions on that traffic. The trade was limited to Africa south of the equator and to Portuguese America, with the right of visit and seizure granted to British war vessels. Detained slavers were to be tried by mixed commissions from whose decisions there was to be no appeal. If Portugal should ever consent to abolish the trade entirely, these stipulations were to be modified by common consent; but in case the Portuguese could not be brought to agree to the terms that England deemed best, the present regulations—including the right of visit and search—were to continue for fifteen years from the date of the abolition of the traffic. There was only one serious slip to be found in the provisions of the convention and separate article; namely, the stipulation which required the actual presence of illicit slaves on board to justify seizure.[48] By the convention the traffic was severely restricted on paper; the problem was to obtain from D. João the complete abolition of the trade within his dominions and to effect the enforcement of the restrictions already agreed upon.

The first of these two tasks proved impossible, for the Portuguese king stubbornly refused to advance another step on the road toward the complete suppression of the traffic despite the pressure exerted by his dominating ally. At first Castlereagh attempted to obtain his end by calling in the great powers, but he had made little headway by 1817. After the Vienna declaration signed by all of the European powers, which unanimously

to foreign colonies in 1814, granted England the right of visit in 1817, and abolished the trade to its colonies in 1820. France refused to allow the slave trade to be called piracy or to permit mutual visit and search until 1831 and 1833 when the reciprocal right of search was granted England. The United States remained recalcitrant until the Civil War (*Cambridge History of British Foreign Policy, 1783-1919*, II, 235-238; DuBois, "Enforcement of the Slave-Trade Laws," pp. 167-174).

[48] This error was partially remedied as far as Portugal was concerned by the additional article signed March 15, 1823, at Lisbon, which legalized the seizure of Portuguese slavers provided evidence was found that illicit slaves had been on board in the particular voyage in question (F. O., 93/38/16, Portugal). But by that date Brazil had declared its independence, and the stipulations therefore did not apply to the Brazilian trade, which soon came to overshadow the traffic of the mother country. The new empire refused to grant this right to England and held fast to the original stipulation.

condemned the slave trade, he instituted formal and permanent conferences at London where he hoped to create a center of information and action for the complete suppression of the traffic. Fourteen meetings were held prior to the conference at Aix-la-Chapelle, but the minister accomplished nothing, beyond the collection of material, toward the suppression of the trade[49] either by the European powers or by his ally at Rio. After the Portuguese Convention of 1817, he was driven on by the reformers to make another attempt at the conference soon to meet at Aix-la-Chapelle to persuade the powers to support a universal condemnation of the trade. The abolitionists sent Clarkson to the conference as an "unofficial observer" in behalf of the African Association, while Wilberforce exerted pressure on the British Foreign Office; but the net result was merely a pious joint note signed by all the powers and addressed to the king of Portugal, which urged the complete abolition of the traffic carried on by that country.[50] Under date of January 12, 1819, Chamberlain transmitted his copy of the note to the Portuguese Foreign Office and a month later obtained from Villanova Portugal an acknowledgment of the receipt of the note and its contents with no comment whatsoever.[51]

Any observation by the Portuguese court was unnecessary in the face of the lists of slave importations which the *chargé* was sending in to his government. Despite the fact that his every move was closely watched by the authorities and statistics were hard to get, Chamberlain succeeded in reporting over twenty thousand slaves brought into Rio in 1816 with over five thousand taken to Bahia from Africa.[52] In September, 1817, twenty-one slave ships left Rio alone with the certainty that this fleet would bring in half as much as the total number brought in during the previous year.[53] Not all of these vessels returned to Rio but, even so, over twenty-two thousand Negroes were embarked in Africa for the Brazilian capital,[54] while Bahia con-

[49] Webster, *Foreign Policy of Castlereagh*, pp. 455-458. [50] *Ibid.*, p. 463.

[51] F. O., 63/220, Chamberlain to Castlereagh, No. 17. February 20, 1819.

[52] F. O., 63/202, Chamberlain to Castlereagh, Nos. 7, 24.

[53] F. O., 63/204, Chamberlain to Castlereagh, No. 97.

[54] F. O. 63/220, Chamberlain to Castlereagh, No. 7, January 22, 1819.

tinued to trade north of the equator despite the convention of 1817.[55] From 1811 through 1818 nearly one hundred forty thousand slaves were actually landed in Rio de Janeiro, while very incomplete returns from Bahia give close to thirty thousand as entering that port in spite of the activity of the British cruisers, which disrupted that traffic so disastrously.[56] No figures are available for Pernambuco, Maranhão, or Pará during this period owing to local disturbances which prevented the proper supervision of the affairs of those provinces by the central government at Rio. It is likely, however, that this northern section participated to some extent in the astonishing increase which occurred in the slave traffic after the removal of the Portuguese court to Rio and the opening of the colony to foreign trade and enterprise. In the face of this activity, it would have meant disaster for D. João to decree the total suppression of the traffic, for his throne was none too secure toward the end of the second decade of the century. Even had he so desired, he could not have abolished the trade.

Yet Castlereagh continued to the end in his efforts to satisfy the abolitionists of England. Once more before he tossed aside the burden which had become intolerably heavy, he preached a sermon to the Portuguese court. Early in March, 1821, he called Thornton's attention to "the subject which the King's Government and the Country" had "anxiously at heart, to witness by a general prohibition of the Slave Trade throughout the Portuguese Dominions, a prospect of a complete abolition of that inhuman Traffick in every part of the world and forever." The time set by Spain for the final abolition had arrived, leaving Portugal as the only nation represented at Vienna which still legalized the traffic. The subject of the dispatch was "one of the most anxious solicitude to His Majesty" and Thornton was to press it upon the attention of the Portuguese government.[57] This persistence in the face of the impossible was

[55] F. O., 63/246, Chamberlain to Londonderry, No. 20. July 3, 1822.

[56] These figures were obtained from consular reports sent in by the consul general at Rio. F. O., 63, 1811 to 1818, various volumes.

[57] F. O., 63/237, Castlereagh to Thornton, No. 3. March 5, 1821. Overproduction brought on by the increase of British possessions in the British West and East

worthy of better success, but the minister died without having attained his object. Yet his efforts were not entirely in vain, for he restricted the Portuguese trade to the region south of the equator and he obtained the signature of the king of Portugal to the convention and separate clause of 1817.

The first task, therefore, which confronted the British Foreign Office after the negotiation of the agreements of 1817—the complete abolition of the traffic— was not accomplished before D. Pedro raised the cry of independence. In his efforts to effect the enforcement of the restrictions imposed by the convention, the English government was only partially successful. Portugal signed on the dotted line, obedient as always to its powerful ally; but the government lacked both the ability and the will to carry out the terms agreed upon. The work of the mixed commission set up by the convention demonstrated clearly this attitude on the part of the Rio court.

The London commission, which was to settle claims arising from illegal detention of slavers by British cruisers between June 1, 1814, and the setting up of the permanent mixed commissions, carried on its work with some minor friction and was dismissed after successfully accomplishing its task.[58] The commission sitting at Sierra Leone on the coast of Africa likewise dispatched its business quickly, after it had declared itself ready, and continued to function efficiently during the years of revolt and the independence period which followed.[59] Since

---

Indies was glutting the English market and causing the ruin of the planter class of the West Indies. "Of far greater moment, however, was the fact that continental consumers were increasingly turning to new tropical areas where produce might be obtained more cheaply. The development of Cuba and Brazil, begun during the period of high prices ushered in by the French Revolution, was carried on at an astonishing rate" (Ragatz, *Fall of the Planter Class*, pp. 332-337).

[58] The commission opened for business on November 4, 1819. A difficulty arose in August, 1821, over the death of one of the commissioners of arbitration, but it was settled favorably to the Portuguese contention. The detention by British cruisers was proved illegal in many cases and indemnities were imposed on England (F. O., 84/5, November 4, 1821; 84/12, August 18 to October 25, 1821; 84/17, March 8, 1822; and 84/12, London Commission, *passim*).

[59] The British commissioners, Thomas Gregory and Edward Fitzgerald, were sent to Sierra Leone early in 1820 (F. O., 63/219, Castlereagh to Chamberlain, No. 3). Portugal could not obtain anyone of ability to go to such a place to serve

it was advantageous to Portugal to support the London Commission and the African court was beyond the reach of its influence, these two tribunals succeeded in carrying out the task assigned to them.

But the special tribunal at Rio de Janeiro was hampered from the beginning. After a vexatious delay arising from an excess of formality and procrastination in the Rio court, the commission held its first session on December 23, 1819.[60] It took a year for the commission to work out a set of regulations by which it was to be governed, while another half year passed before the Portuguese government furnished a place in which the tribunal should hold its sessions.[61] When the first case arose, two years after the arrival of the British commissioners, the tribunal was still unable to operate, as the Portuguese government had not yet ratified the regulations submitted for its approval. But the arrival of the captured slave ship, the *Emilia*, with three hundred slaves aboard at last forced the Rio court to take action in regard to the commission.[62]

The principal point of disagreement between the English commissioners and the Portuguese court was over the manner in which the captured ship and the emancipated slaves were to be disposed of. The decree issued by D. João on January 26, 1818, which regulated the execution of the convention of 1817, took out of the hands of the commissioners both the sale of the condemned vessel and the registering and disposal

and was obliged to authorize the minister in London to secure two Portuguese subjects resident there to go (F. O., 63/220, Chamberlain to Castlereagh, No. 32 and 63/221, Chamberlain to Castlereagh, No. 65). From February, 1820, to September, 1821, the commission condemned six vessels flying the Portuguese flag, for illicit slave trade (F. O., 84/17, April 10, 1822. London Commission). Later after Brazilian independence had been declared, the Anglo-Brazilian commission adjudicated 109 Brazilian ships (F. O., 315, Bundles 41-45). The Sierra Leone commission was effective.

[60] F. O., 84/5, Rio Commission, August 21, October 13, December 22, 1819.

[61] F. O., 84/12, Rio Commission, March 20, 1821. Copy of the proceedings from November 2, 1819, to date.

[62] F. O., 84/12, Rio Commission, July 22, 1821, from Henry Hayne. The captor delivered the papers seized on board the slaver and turned over the three hundred slaves and the vessel for adjudication on July 10.

of the liberated Negroes. The judge of contraband was to supervise the auction of the ship, the proceeds to go to the expenses of the commission, while the slaves were to be handed over to the district judge (*Juiz da Ouvidoria da Camarca*), to be employed in the public service at sea, in forts, in agriculture, or to be hired to individuals for fourteen years as free blacks under prescribed conditions. The British commissioner wished to place the disposal of both the ship and the slaves directly under the commission, and, with the approval of his Portuguese colleague, so recommended to the Rio court. The request elicited a flat refusal and a reprimand for the Portuguese commissioner.[63]

The *Emilia* was condemned August 10, and the schooner was turned over to the judge of contraband to be sold at auction and the slaves to the district judge to be hired out[64]; but the sentence of condemnation, which was identical in form to those issued at Sierra Leone, was rejected by the Portuguese authorities on the grounds that due legal procedure had not been followed. The British commissioner contended, but in vain, that the decision, being without appeal, was not subject to the regular Court of Chancery, and that the commission was a special tribunal independent of all other judicial procedure in the Portuguese government and exempt from all fees usually paid to the courts.[65]

The Negroes eventually were auctioned off to the highest bidder at the door of the district judge after each had received a certificate of emancipation from the mixed commission. A bond was given by the successful bidder for each Negro, guaranteeing proper clothing, maintenance, and instruction in the Christian religion, with the added obligation of teaching the emancipated slave some mode of livelihood. A sum was agreed upon in advance, which the bidder was to pay annually; and in addition certain fees to the judge, his clerk, and the curator

---

[63] *Ibid.*

[64] A review of the case is given in F. O., 84/12, Rio Commission, August 27, 1821.

[65] *Ibid.*, September 7, 1821.

were due at the time of the signature of the bond. Competition was great and Negroes were hired at the rate of 9$000 to 34$000 per year.[66] An account was to be opened in the name of each Negro and "the money received on [his] account" was "to be placed in a coffer which" was "to have three keys, to be in the possession of the judge, [the] Curator, and a treasurer." Whatever might be due each was to be paid at the expiration of their servitude,"[67] which by law was to last fourteen years.

When six months after the condemnation of the *Emilia*, the Portuguese commissioner joined in a complaint to the Rio court insisting on the immediate sale of the ship, he was severely reprimanded by his government for even listening to a proposal which criticized the manner in which his government was conducting the case.[68] Meanwhile, over twenty thousand slaves from Angola, Cabinda, and Mozambique, entered Rio during 1821[69]; nearly fifteen thousand entered during the first six months of the following year[70]; and in February, 1822, the judge of contraband presented voluminous documents explain-

[66] 1$000 was equal to 54d on July 25, 1820 (*Correio Braziliense*, XXV, 37). The current price of slaves in Rio varied. A Negress house servant eighteen years old was offered for sale at 300$000. A monthly rental of 30 patacas (about 60 shillings, F. O., 63/123, Strangford to Castlereagh, No. 84. November 21, 1812) was offered for two slaves fit for general service. Other house servants (female) were offered at prices from 192$000 to 260$000 (*O Diario do Rio*, May 19, 1825). Exchange was quoted in this same edition as 54d to the 1$000.

[67] F. O., 84/12, Rio Commission, October 24, 1821. In 1830 at Sierra Leone, after adjudication, the emancipated slaves were taken to a spot assigned to them in the colony and under a superintendent were set to work cutting wood and building and thatching huts. Sometimes they were distributed throughout the colony. For six months they were supported by the government, 2d a day being given to males. Clothing, necessary tools, and seeds were furnished by England also. After six months they were left to their own devices. Some labored on public works, picking up money enough to start small farms. The articles furnished were valued at £1,10s. With the six month's subsidy, the cost per male to the British government was £3. Women received 2d for three months and the children were apprenticed out (Leonard, *The Western Coast of Africa*, pp. 59-60).

[68] F. O., 84/17, Rio Commission, No. 25.

[69] *Ibid.*

[70] *Ibid.*, March-June, *passim*. The importation for 1822 was 31,240 embarked in Africa and 27,784 landed at Rio (F. O., 84/23, Rio Commission, February 13, 1823).

ing why the *Emilia*, rotting in the Rio harbor, still remained unsold.[71]

It is evident therefore from the attitude assumed by the Portuguese government toward the mixed commission that the Rio court lacked both the ability and the will to carry out the stipulations of the convention of 1817. The English commissioners attributed this attitude to the perversity of the ministers of the king, yet the advisers of D. Pedro were not altogether free agents in the matter. As the editor of the *Correio Braziliense* pointed out in 1815, the difficulty which would confront the government in any attempt to restrict the slave trade was a serious one. Such measures, he maintained, would mean an increase in the price of slaves in Brazil with a resultant rise in the cost of labor; every person in the colony who enjoyed the service of slaves or the profits derived from the institution, would be affected; and, consequently, the opposition of the mass of the population of Brazil would be aroused.[72] In addition the slave traders, who imported around thirty thousand Negroes yearly into Rio alone, were powerful interests and used

[71] F. O., 84/17, Rio Commission, February 16, 1822. The *Emilia* was sold finally and the money used to pay the expenses incurred by the maintenance of the slaves during the extended period before their auction took place (F. O., 84/23, Rio Commission, February 20, 1823). When D. Pedro definitely broke with the mother country late in 1822, the English commissioners remained at their posts to transact business as usual, thereby winning the approval of Canning, who had succeeded to the direction of the Foreign Office (F. O., 84/23, Rio Commission, from Canning, January 10, 1823). The *Emilia* was the only case decided by the commission before Brazilian independence.

[72] *Correio Braziliense*, XV, 735-739. In 1822 there were 1,136,669 slaves, 800,000 Indians, and 2,543,839 free out of a total population of 4,480,508 (*Correio Braziliense*, XXIX, 332). The figures were taken from the *Amigo do Rey e da Nação*, a periodical of Rio, the calculations having been made by M. Pizarro. The provinces of Rio Grande and Cisplatina were lacking, and no figures were included as to the proportion of whites and blacks in the free population statistics given, although there must have been a considerable number of free Negroes in Brazil in that year. Strangford gave the number of slaves in Brazil in 1810 as 754,626, with no figures for Ceará, Maranhão, Pará, upper Amazon, and Matto Grosso (F. O., 63/84, Strangford to Wellesley, No. 35). If the two estimates are correct, the death rate of slaves in Brazil was quite high in view of the large number imported between 1810 and 1822.

every influence to balk the operation of the restrictions set up by the convention and to prevent any further steps along the road toward the total abolition of the traffic. Had D. João been secure on his throne between 1817 and 1822, the enforcement of the restrictions imposed by the convention of 1817 would have been beyond his strength; but his authority in Portugal was actually maintained by Marshal Beresford, an English army officer, while in Brazil, the colonists were moving toward the revolt of 1822. The English nation, which, as the editor of the *Correio Braziliense* maintained, was ready to go to war against any country rather than to allow the continuation of the traffic,[73] was attempting to impose upon its ally a measure of which neither the government nor the people approved. The failure of the Portuguese court to enforce the stipulations of the convention of 1817 was the natural outcome of these circumstances.

Both Canning and Castlereagh did their best to carry out the wishes of the reformers and the financial interests of England for the suppression of the Portuguese slave trade. Canning took the first step in the mild provisions of the treaty of 1810, which limited the traffic to the Portuguese dominions. Castlereagh gained another advance in 1815 when he restricted the trade to the region south of the equator and exacted a promise from D. João to abolish the traffic entirely at some date in the future. But the greatest contribution was obtained in 1817, when the British minister set up the mixed commissions whose judgments were to be swift and without appeal and gained the right of visit and search of Portuguese merchantmen by British cruisers in time of peace, with the understanding that the right was to last fifteen years beyond the date of the total abolition, if the Portuguese government should ever decree such a measure. But every effort to force the Rio court to take the final step of total abolition, or even to enforce the restrictions imposed by the convention of 1817, met failure, as neither the ministry nor the people of Brazil were willing to dethrone the economic god, slavery, or to interrupt the source by which

[73] *Correio Braziliense*, XV, 735 (1815).

that god was fed. Between 1808 and 1822 the British Foreign Office restricted the Portuguese slave trade on paper, but to carry those restrictions on to the total abolition of the traffic, or even to make them effective, was beyond its power. More slaves entered Brazil in 1821 than in 1808.[74]

---

[74] Andrew Grant, writing about 1808, stated that around 5000 slaves were sold annually in Rio de Janeiro, this number representing about one-fourth of the number imported into Brazil (*History of Brazil*, p. 153). In 1821 a total of 20,854 arrived at Rio alone. The first six months of 1822 saw 14,827 actually landed in the Brazilian capital (F. O., 84/17, Rio Commission, Nos. 23, 24). These figures do not include the slaves brought to other ports.

CHAPTER VIII

THE PRICE OF RECOGNITION, 1822-1827

England's concern in its relations with Brazil during the residence of the Portuguese court at Rio were centered on three principal currents of interest. One of these was the attitude which the Portuguese monarchy adopted in regard to the Banda Oriental; another was commercial; and the third was involved in the suppression of the slave-trade. The first of these points was carefully detached by the British Foreign Office[1] and eventually was settled apart,[2] while the other two were more or less closely associated. The commercial and slave traffic questions converged in 1822 when they became the price exacted by Great Britain for its recognition of Brazilian independence. The new state was forced to ratify the special economic privileges obtained by England in the treaty of 1810 and to accede to the continuation of the African-trade stipulations of Castlereagh's conventions of 1815 and 1817. In addition, the total abolition of the traffic within a specified number of years was required by the London court.

The payment of the price demanded involved the new state in serious difficulties which arose from the manner in which the independence movement had developed in the colony. Hence to understand the attitude which the Rio court assumed toward the terms exacted by England, some knowledge of the situation in Brazil itself is necessary.

[1] Sir Charles Stuart who negotiated the treaties of recognition of Brazilian independence by Portugal and England was instructed by Canning not to enter into the question of the Banda Oriental, which was finally settled in 1828 (F. O., 13/2, Canning to Stuart, No. 23).

[2] Consequently this point was treated as a separate topic in this work in chapters V and VI. Chapter VIII thus continues the two themes presented in chapter IV and chapter VII.

Events in the revolting colony are associated with the name of the young prince, D. Pedro, eldest son of the king of Portugal. Despised by his mother who preferred her second son, D. Miguel, and feared and distrusted by his father, who favored D. Pedro Carlos, a son-in-law and nephew, Pedro grew up in the stables of the palace at Rio. Uncultured, inexperienced in the business of government, untrained in the court etiquette of Europe, and uneducated beyond the rudimentary stage, he was more of a colonial than a European. A superb horseman, impulsive, vivacious, handsome, and vigorously self-willed, his immorality has become proverbial, his bonhommie a tradition, and his personal bravery the subject of many ballads. He was a very democratic-mannered son of a divine-right father.[3]

His appointment as prince regent of Brazil after the Portuguese court sailed for Lisbon in April, 1821, forced him into the field of action when he was twenty-three years old. Almost coincident with the departure of D. João, the *Côrtes* in Lisbon began to manifest its purpose of limiting the powers of D. Pedro and of restricting the liberties of the co-kingdom. In consequence of an order issued in April, which detached all provincial governments from Rio and made them subject directly to Portugal, petty provincial and municipal *juntas* sprang up throughout the colony but especially in the north, each corresponding with Lisbon and refusing to pay revenue to Rio. Thus though nominally regent of all Brazil, Pedro really became merely governor of Rio and the southern provinces. The bank, looted by the king and robbed by the directors, failed in July, and the treasury of the prince was empty.[4] In September the downfall of the co-kingdom was completed when the *Côrtes* by decree[5] abolished the chancery court, the treasury, the *junta* of commerce, and the various tribunals and establishments set

[3] For different pictures of the prince, see Oliveira Martins, *O Brazil*, pp. 108-109; Oliveira Lima, *O Reconhecimento da Independencia*, pp. 65-67; John Armitage, *The History of Brazil*, I, 37-38.

[4] Armitage, *History of Brazil*, I, 41-49; Pereira da Silva, *Historia da Fundação do Imperio*, V, 143-177; *Cartas de D. Pedro a Seu Pae, 1821-1822*, letter of September 21, 1821.

[5] Decree of September 29, 1821.

up during the reign of D. João; at the same time D. Pedro was peremptorily ordered home. Two days later another decree appointed governors-at-arms for each of the provinces. It was clear that the *Côrtes* intended to reëstablish the colonial status of Brazil which had been abolished when the colony was raised to the rank of a kingdom in 1815.[6]

The issue divided the inhabitants of the colony into two camps; one approving the action of the *Côrtes* and favoring the return to the colonial status, the other insisting on the equality of the two kingdoms under one ruler. To the first belonged those Portuguese who had immigrated during the residence of the court at Rio or those who still looked on the mother country as the center of their interests although they had resided in Brazil before 1808. These Portuguese constituted that part of the commercial class which hoped to reëstablish its ancient privileges and immunities. Every foreigner was an interloper in their eyes and the treaty of commerce of 1810 with England was the special object of their detestation.[7] They formed the element which, with the soldiers and functionaries who looked to Lisbon for their positions, remained loyal and forced a civil war during the struggle for independence.

To the other class belonged the Brazilians and those Portuguese who, by marriage or interest, had become attached to the colony. Both of these elements looked to D. Pedro as their leader, yet between them there existed a traditional hostility. During colonial times the descendants of the first conquerors or of those who had occupied colonial governmental positions, refused to accept the new arrivals as equals. Consequently the latter were forced into commercial or mechanical pursuits, leaving farming to the Brazilian colonial aristocracy. These landowners with their relatives who lived in the cities as colonial office holders created a nobility native to the colony, and forced the new arrivals to join the commercial and industrial

---

[6] Armitage, *History*, I, 50-54; Pereira da Silva, *Historia*, V, 211-243.

[7] Armitage, *op. cit.*, I, 41-42. In the northern provinces of Bahia and Pernambuco this element constituted a very large part of the commercial class. In Rio there were more Portuguese of Brazilian sympathies (*ibid.*, I, 42).

class of the cities which reciprocated the antagonism of the Brazilians.[8] The traditional cleavage still existed at the time of the independence movement.

This Portuguese element among the colonists which had become firmly rooted in Brazil by financial or social ties and had severed connections with the mother country, was faced with ruin[9] when the *Côrtes* threatened to restore the exclusive, monopolistic system of colonial commerce. The Brazilians, for their part, found it impossible to relinquish the gains which had been obtained since the *Carta Regia* of 1808 had taken the first step toward releasing the colony from its subjection to the mother country. Both parties looked to D. Pedro to lead their resistance to the decrees of the *Côrtes* and, if necessary, to save them by proclaiming the independence of Brazil from Portugal.[10] Both elements, uniting to bring every influence to bear which might lead the young prince to disobey the orders dispatched from Lisbon, coöperated in inducing D. Pedro to defy the *Côrtes* and to raise the cry of "Independence or Death."[11]

During the early part of the revolt, the two parties continued to coöperate in supporting D. Pedro in his struggle against the loyalists and the feeble efforts made by Lisbon to subjugate the colony. Yet, as the loyalists were expelled or silenced, a

---

[8] Pereira da Silva, *Historia*, I, 209-211.

[9] The old system of Portugal as the *entrepôt* for the commerce of the colony was to be reëstablished by stringent legislation proposed in the *Côrtes* (Pereira da Silva, *op. cit.*, VI, Documento 14, *Parecer da Commissão Especial das Côrtes sobre as Relações Commerciaes entre Portugal e Brazil*).

[10] Pereira da Silva, *op. cit.*, V, 215, 232-234, 236-237; Oliveira Lima, *O Imperio Brazileiro*, pp. 41-42.

[11] The province of São Paulo was the most active in its influence; it was the first to protest against the decrees of the *Côrtes;* it furnished the principal leaders of the independence movement, such as the Andrada brothers, João Carlos Oyenhausen, José Costa Carvalho, and others; and the cry of independence was raised on the outskirts of the city of São Paulo. The province was the center of traditional colonial disobedience and the birthplace of the slave-hunting *Bandeira* expeditions. With Minas Geraes this province was the center of the Brazilian party. For the history of the manner in which the two parties influenced D. Pedro to proclaim independence, see: Pereira da Silva, *op. cit.*, V, 235-277, VI, 3-41, 69-151, 197-233; Rocha Pombo, *Historia do Brazil*, VII, 622-757; *Cartas de D. Pedro a Seu Pae, 1821-1822,* entire, but with special reference to letters of December 10, 1821, and June 19, 1822.

distinct cleavage began to appear between the two groups which supported the prince. The Portuguese party on the one hand favored an absolute monarchy under D. Pedro, with a government entirely independent of the Lisbon court, but with the two crowns united by family ties. To these Absolutists belonged the Portuguese office holders who had been thrown out by the suppression of the Brazilian courts and governmental departments, the Portuguese commercial class and wealthy families, and some Brazilians who, while they admitted the advantages of constitutional government, yet denied the policy of applying it to the ignorant and heterogeneous population of the new empire. The Brazilian party, or the Patriots, favored a constitutional monarchy totally independent of Lisbon, while a large element in the group leaned toward republican ideas. In numbers the Patriots were stronger; but in experience in government, in negotiable wealth, and in strategic location in the cities, the Absolutists had the advantage. The divergence between the two parties grew more acute as the success of the independence movement became evident, while the struggle for control of the prince grew more bitter. His adherence to either party meant the dominance of that group.[12]

It is evident therefore that the final success or failure of the movement for independence in Brazil depended on the support which both the Absolutists and the Patriots gave D. Pedro. It is evident also that the two elements were so antagonistic that the prince eventually would be forced to choose one side or the other. His own arbitrary nature and the anarchy which the

[12] Armitage, *History*, I, 198-200; Pereira da Silva, *Historia*, VI, 126-149, VII, 107-191. The division between Brazilians and Portuguese was shown clearly by the dissolution of the Constituent Assembly. Two "Patriot" papers, the *Sentinella* and *Tamoyo* attacked all Portuguese born who were in the service of Brazil; two Portuguese army officers chastised the supposed author, and the troops, largely Portuguese, demanded the punishment of the Brazilian deputies of the Constituent Assembly who were responsible for the two newspapers. The Assembly took up the matter; Pedro moved the troops to a site near his palace and ordered the Assembly to dissolve. The first experiment in constitutional government failed, due in part to a conflict between the Portuguese and Brazilian elements (*Annaes do Parlamento Brazileiro, Assemblêa Constituinte, 1823*, tomo VI, 229-247; Oliveira Lima, *O Imperio Brazileiro*, pp. 13-15).

disintegrating factors of republicanism had sown in Spanish America and which constantly threatened to disrupt the new empire, inclined D. Pedro toward absolutism,[13] although that policy, as the year 1831 later demonstrated, was to lead to his expulsion from Brazil. On the other hand, he was a liberal at heart[14]; his regard for the colonials was sincere[15]; and the constitution which he conceded after the dissolution of the Constituent Assembly remained the fundamental law of the nation until 1889[16]. Between 1821 and 1824 by relying on the Brazilians, or Patriots, for support, he succeeded in establishing his authority throughout the empire. Separatist movements were suppressed, the new constitution was in force, and no foreign soldier or functionary was in Brazil.[17] Thus by the aid of the Constitutionalists, the prince made himself supreme.

But the price demanded by England as payment for recognition entailed the alienation of the support of these very patriots and of a large part of the absolutist party. The strength of the Constitutionalists rested in the support of the Brazilian landowners, who clung to slavery and the slave trade as the only possible solution to their labor problem, while the commercial element of the Absolutists had long cherished a particular grievance against the preëmption of Brazilian trade and commerce by English agents who were acting under the special privileges obtained in 1810 by the treaty of commerce. This situation furnishes a key to the response which the Rio court made to the action of Great Britain throughout the drama of 1822 and 1827.

---

[13] Pereira da Silva, *Historia*, VII, 191-307.

[14] Oliveira Martins, *O Brazil*, 108-109.

[15] Armitage, *History*, I, 39-40.

[16] Pereira da Silva, *op. cit.*, VII, 245-246. For a detailed comparison of the two constitutions, see Oliveira Lima, *O Imperio Brazileiro*, pp. 68-78. The constitution was amended by the additional act of 1834. The project presented by the Assembly is given in Pereira da Silva, *op. cit.*, VII, Appendix, pp. 372-412. The constitution granted by D. Pedro is given by H. G. James, *The Constitutional System of Brazil*, pp. 237-252.

[17] Pereira da Silva, *op. cit.*, VII, 305-306. The letters of Consul Chamberlain at Rio to the Foreign Office give an excellent description of the events in Brazil from 1822 to 1824 (F. O., 63/246, 258-261, 276-279).

The immediate recognition of the new state by England was a vital necessity, for "in quite a peculiar way Brazil's destiny was bound up with those of Portugal, of Europe, and above all, of England."[18] The special relations which had existed for centuries between Great Britain and Portugal enabled the latter to claim by treaty rights assistance against foreign aggression, which was held to include help against the revolting colony[19]. The Continental powers refused to acknowledge the independence of the new empire until the Lisbon court had done so[20]; yet relying on the obligation which it considered England owed to Portugal, that court resolutely refused to consider the recognition of the new state. The powers of the Holy Alliance through their ministers urged the Lisbon government to delay any action with reference to Brazil[21], and although in reality he did not differ with Canning in his views in regard to Portuguese America, Metternich was obliged to support the theory that the prior consent of the king of Portugal was necessary to establish the independence of Brazil.[22] Alexander of Russia called D. Pedro "a rebel and a Parricide" and exerted his influence with Austria to prevent the recognition of the new state,[23] while Hyde de Neuville, French minister at Lisbon, used his dominant influence to uphold D. João in his obstinate course.[24]

Under these circumstances, Brazil was forced to turn to Eng-

---

[18] H. Temperly, *Foreign Policy of Canning*, p. 212.

[19] The Portuguese court asserted that this protection extended to internal danger arising from revolting colonies. Both Castlereagh and Canning denied that England was obligated by treaty to maintain Portugal's control over the colonies, but Canning did admit that Lisbon had a general moral claim on England in reference to internal questions with its possessions (Temperly, *Foreign Policy of Canning*, pp. 194, 212; F. O., 13/7, Canning to Chamberlain, No. 1). The Portuguese court cited the treaties of 1642, 1654 (Articles 1 and 16), and 1661 (secret article) as the basis of its demand for protection by England against Brazil (Oliveira Lima, *O Reconhecimento*, p. 57).

[20] A. A. de Aguiar, *Vida do Marquez de Barbacena*, p. 98.

[21] F. O., 13/7, Canning to Chamberlain, No. 1.

[22] Temperly, *op. cit.*, p. 215; *Archivo Diplomatico da Independencia*, IV (Austria), Telles da Silva to Carvalho e Mello, July 10, 1824.

[23] Temperly, *op. cit.*, p. 215 and footnote (1).

[24] *Ibid.*, pp. 201-208.

land.[25] Unless Great Britain could be induced to recognize the new state, complete independence would be delayed indefinitely, with disastrous results to the empire. For, as long as Portugal refused to grant recognition, anarchy and the division of Brazil into smaller republics after the manner of the rest of South America threatened the huge colony. A big, united, homogeneous republic like the United States, a form of government repugnant to the dominant faction and yet the only satisfactory alternative to an empire, would have been the first and only example of that sort of thing among Latin races.[26] Consequently D. Pedro was forced to stake the existence of the new state on England's action.

Great Britain was not free to act as it wished, however, for in the opinion of Canning, Portugal appeared "to be the chosen ground on which the Continental Alliance" had "resolved to fight England hand to hand," and Great Britain had to be "prepared to meet and defeat them, under every imaginable form of intrigue or intimidation, or to be driven from the field."[27] In addition Canning was faced with the delicate question of the succession to the Portuguese crown. If by the recognition of the independence of Brazil, its emperor should lose his right to succeed his father as king of Portugal, D. Miguel, the absolutist son of the autocratic D. Carlota and the tool of Metternich and France, would inherit the crown with unfavorable results to British influence in the "chosen ground of battle."[28] Therefore in order to preserve English influence in the traditional strategic position in Europe, Canning was forced to secure some arrangement regarding the succession and to

[25] On July 23, 1823, Brant Pontes, Brazilian agent in London, wrote to José Bonifacio, foreign minister of D. Pedro, that "with England's friendship, we can snap our fingers at the rest of the world . . . it will not be necessary to go begging for recognition from any other power, for all will wish our friendship in order to participate in the advantages of commerce, which will be exclusively for our friends" (*Archivo Diplomatico*, I, 278).

[26] Aguiar, *Barbacena*, pp. 98-99.

[27] A. G. Stapleton, *George Canning and His Times*, p. 501. The conflict between England and the Continental powers which took Portugal as the field of battle is given in detail by Temperly, *Canning*, pp. 189-225.

[28] *Archivo Diplomatico*, I, lxxxv-lxxxvii.

obtain the consent of the Portuguese monarch to the recognition of the independence of the colony before Great Britain itself could act.

A second difficulty prevented England from yielding to the insistence of the Brazilians for recognition. Although, in the opinion of Canning, there were no specific stipulations which required England to maintain the control of the Lisbon court over its possessions as long as Brazil remained a colony, the mere recognition of its independence would turn the new empire into a foreign country, thus obligating the London court to fulfill against Brazil every guaranty which had been made to Portugal since 1640. Unless Portugal acquiesced in the independence of the colony, a state of war between the two kingdoms would continue despite the recognition by England, and Great Britain *ipso facto* would be forced into war against Brazil.[29] In addition, Canning considered that since his father still reigned over Portugal and his father-in-law was emperor of Austria, D. Pedro was too intimately connected with Europe to detach himself from the ties which linked his new kingdom to the old world.[30] It was clear therefore that England did not possess as much independence of action in regard to Brazil as it enjoyed in relation to the Spanish American republics.

By 1824 Canning believed the attainment of Brazilian independence was assured. The question was, how best to conciliate the establishment and recognition of that independence with the powers of the Old World.[31] Hence the subsequent negotiations which took place in London, Lisbon, and Rio de Janeiro were centered around this point. On September 23, 1823, the Portuguese minister in London, Villa Real, applied for British mediation, but insisted on conditions which Canning could not accept. The appeal was renewed in December and Canning, still not acquiescing in the grounds specified by Portugal, ac-

---

[29] F. O., 13/7, Canning to Chamberlain, No. 1.

[30] *Ibid.* Canning throughout this long dispatch emphasized the difference between England's relations with the Spanish American republics and its obligations to Spain on the one hand and its connection with Brazil and its duties to Portugal on the other. The cases were entirely different, he argued.

[31] *Ibid.*; F. O., 63/257, Canning to Chamberlain, No. 17. December 8, 1823.

cepted the task of mediator and asked Brazil to send agents. In April Felisberto Caldeira Brant Pontes returned from Rio to unite with Manuel Rodrigues Gameiro Pessôa as the Brazilian commissioners nominated to negotiate the recognition of independence by Portugal. The conference, held under the mediation of England and Austria,[32] lasted from July 12, 1824, to February 18, 1825, when the Brazilian commissioners formally rejected the ultimatum of Portugal and declared their negotiation ended. They could not accept the demand made by the Lisbon commissioner that the basis of any agreement should be the reëstablishment of the sovereignty of Portugal over Brazil.[33] Canning likewise lost patience and, politely ignoring Austria, despatched Sir Charles Stuart on a special mission to Lisbon and Rio to negotiate with D. Pedro a final settlement of the question, preferably with, but if necessary, without, the previous agreement of Portugal.[34]

There were several reasons why Canning changed his policy

---

[32] Baron Neumann, and later Prince Esterhazy, represented Austria during the negotiations. Brant (later Marquez de Barbacena) had been in London in 1821-1822, as the agent of D. Pedro to checkmate any move of Lisbon in London and to win Canning to support the Brazilian cause. He had purchased supplies and recruited soldiers and sailors for the Brazilian service. Portugal proposed to treat with Brazil on the basis of four conditions: cessation of hostilities, restitution of Portuguese property seized by Brazil, obligation of Brazil not to seize any colony faithful to Portugal, and dismissal of all English subjects in the Brazilian service (Rocha Pombo, *Historia do Brazil*, VII, 903). Portugal called on the treaties closed with England since 1640 to substantiate the demand for protection against the colony. To this and to the fourth condition Canning disagreed (Oliveira Lima, *O Reconhecimento*, pp. 57-58).

[33] Portugal's persistence in maintaining its sovereignty was based on more than obstinacy. The Lisbon court feared that, since Pedro refused to state formally the renunciation of his rights to succeed to the throne of Portugal, the mother country eventually would become subordinate to the colony when D. João should die. The danger lay in the fact that the rich, powerful colony would exchange places with the weakened and decrepit mother country. The tail would wag the dog (Aguiar, *Barbacena*, p. 56, letter from Palmella to Brant, Lisbon, August 7, 1824).

[34] The story of the London negotiations has been worked out in detail by Temperly, *Canning*, pp. 213-220, and Oliveira Lima, *O Reconhecimento*, pp. 73-166. The minutes of the conferences are given in the appendix to this work. For original sources on the negotiations, see *Archivo Diplomatico*, I, 39-155, II, 1-543; Canning's letters to Chamberlain, F. O., 63/275, Nos. 4, 5, and 13/7, Nos. 1, Confidential, 2, 6; Aguiar, *Barbacena*, various letters.

of waiting until Portugal could be induced to recognize the empire before England took action. In the first place, while the conference of allies at Paris was urging D. João to sustain the conditions which he had laid down as the basis of any recognition, France[35] and Spain signed the agreement of December 10, 1824, which continued the French penetration in Spain.[36] To counteract the evident wish of the allies to aid Portugal to reconquer the lost colony, Canning felt himself obliged to act. Consequently he forced the pro-French minister, Subserra, from power in Lisbon,[37] achieved the recall of the obnoxious de Neuville as French minister to the Portuguese Court,[38] and dispatched Stuart on his mission.

In the second place, the commercial treaty of 1810 would be subject to revision in the middle of 1825 and the commercial elements of England were pressing him to reach an agreement as to their standing in Brazil.[39] On February 7, therefore, Canning informed Brant that he had warned Portugal of his intention not to delay direct negotiations between England and Brazil beyond the date when the commercial treaty should have to be renewed. Unless Portugal yielded before that time, Stuart would treat independently with Brazil to obtain a commercial agreement which would mean the recognition by England of the independence of the other contracting party.[40]

[35] Temperly, *Canning*, p. 219.

[36] *Archivo Diplomatico*, I, ciii.

[37] Rocha Pombo, *Historia*, VII, 906-908; Temperly, *Canning*, pp. 206-208; *Archivo Diplomatico*, I, cv-cvi. The Lisbon court tried twice to enter into direct negotiations with D. Pedro, but on the basis of the sovereignty of D. João over Brazil. The Conde do Rio Maior was sent officially and reached Rio on September 17, 1823. He was unsuccessful (Pereira da Silva, *Historia*, VII, 175-186). In June, 1824, during the London mediation, a tool of Subserra's, one Leal, was sent secretly to Rio where he was thrown into prison (Temperly, *op. cit.*, pp. 218-219). Brant advised his government that the Holy Alliance was behind the obstinate refusal of Portugal to grant independence to Brazil (*Archivo Diplomatico*, II, Brant to Carvalho e Mello, December 15, 1824).

[38] Temperly, *op. cit.*, pp. 205-206.

[39] Stapleton, *George Canning and His Times*, pp. 501-503, Canning to Liverpool, October 25, 1824.

[40] *Archivo Diplomatico*, II, 201-204, Brant to Carvalho e Mello, February 10, 1825. Rio threatened to increase the import tax on British goods from fifteen per cent. as stipulated by the treaty of 1810 to twenty-four per cent., the rate charged all

A third reason impelled England to recognize the new state regardless of Portugal's attitude. Canning feared that the one nation of the new world which promised to establish a stable monarchy would set up a species of Monroe Doctrine of its own and would join definitely the New World in opposition to the Old. Brazil, he advised Rio, would profit greatly if its new rank "should be not merely arrogated by Herself but confirmed to Her by the Consent of Portugal with the sanction of the other Powers."[41] He had tried to obtain the consent of Lisbon and the other powers and had failed: now he was desirous of introducing into the family of European nations a monarchy established in the continent of republics, with the new member under the protection of England, since it would owe its existence to that power.[42]

A final reason inclined Canning to recognize the new empire before Austria or France could take matters into their own hands and reconcile the two branches of the family of Bragança. If England should permit the house of Austria to come to the aid of its son-in-law or France to win special favors in Brazil[43] on the basis of a defense of the slave traffic, the opportunity to

---

other foreign merchandise, the increase to go into effect at once after June 19, 1825 (F. O., 13/8, Chamberlain to Canning, No. 61). The foreign minister of Brazil informed Chamberlain in November, 1822, that the "Emperor had resolved not to mix in the politics of Europe and would not allow Europe to interfere in those of Brazil, or of South America" (F. O., 63/247, Chamberlain to Bathurst, No. 9).

[41] F. O., 63/275, Canning to Chamberlain, No. 1.

[42] *Ibid.* January 9, 1823, Secret and Confidential; Stapleton, *George Canning and His Times*, pp. 394-395. The United States had recognized Brazil in 1824 (May 26). The United States was the first to recognize the new state, and Brazil was the first government to adhere to the Monroe Doctrine (Rocha Pombo, *Historia*, VII, 909, footnote 1).

[43] The Comte de Gestas de Roquefeuille, French minister at Rio, by orders from Chateaubriand, offered the Brazilian Government the coöperation of the French squadron then in the harbor of Rio in putting down disaffection and maintaining the authority of the emperor (F. O., 63/276, Chamberlain to Canning, No. 29. March 3, 1824). In June, 1825, Gestas offered D. Pedro recognition of the complete independence of Brazil in return for a treaty of commerce (F. O., 13/8, Chamberlain to Canning, No. 64. Confidential). This was before Stuart arrived in Rio. Pedro's wife, Princess Leopoldina, constantly urged her father, the emperor of Austria, to recognize her husband's position as emperor (Rocha Pombo, *Historia*, VII, 897).

strike at the root of that trade would be lost.[44] Unless Great Britain by its mediation or independent action should guarantee the independence of the new state, the bill for services rendered could not be presented. On the other hand, if the obstructive tactics of Austria and France were to delay recognition so long that the disintegrating factors in the new empire caused its fall, the advantages which would accrue to England from the commercial concessions demanded of the new empire would be seriously lessened.

Brazil, therefore, succeeded in winning England to support its declaration of independence. If possible, Portugal was to be forced to concede the validity of the separation; but if the Lisbon court remained obstinate, then Great Britain would negotiate separately with the new empire.

By Canning's instructions to Stuart, dated March 14, 1825, the envoy was to seek to preserve in both hemispheres, the interests of the family of Bragança; yet, since the treaty under which the trade with Brazil was carried on was now threatened with revision at the option of the new state, England could not delay longer. As it was only by entering into new stipulations that Great Britain could continue to enjoy a special footing in Brazilian commerce, the Lisbon court was to be informed clearly that Stuart could not "in any case leave Brazil, without some arrangement with the Brazilian Government respecting the treaty of 1810." D. João by his own act, Canning argued, had abolished the colonial character of Brazil, had given it an independent judicature, had raised it to a separate kingdom, had established a national representation, and had provided for the case in which it might be necessary for the safety of that separate kingdom to pronounce its independence of Portugal.[45] Pedro for his part had preserved the Portuguese monarchy in America despite the unwise action of the Lisbon *Côrtes*. Nothing now remained but to complete the work.

---

[44] *Archivo Diplomatico*, I, xlv-xlvi.

[45] On leaving Rio, D. João told Pedro to seize the crown for himself in case some adventurer threatened to grasp the throne (*Cartas de D. Pedro a Seu Pae*, 1821-1822, D. Pedro to D. João, June 19, 1822).

Therefore D. João should command, not merely consent, that Brazil be independent, that Pedro hold the royal authority under whatever titles the representative assembly of Brazil might confer upon him, and that the connection between the two crowns should be continued. This union between the two crowns was to be signified by the use of the title "Heir Apparent of Portugal" when reference was made to the prince in the royal letter. Brazil had already consented to a commission to settle claims as to property losses, most favored nation commercial privileges, and similar questions. Nothing short of independence would now serve, nor should Portugal attempt to retain any rights of sovereignty over Brazil.[46] Stuart was authorized to be the bearer of the royal decree commanding the independence of Brazil, or he could serve as plenipotentiary for the Lisbon court if Portugal chose to negotiate a treaty. If D. João preferred to send an agent of his own, however, he could do so, but Stuart was forbidden to accept the collaboration of a Portuguese envoy, or even to accompany one to Brazil. In case the Lisbon court refused to yield, he was to proceed to Rio at once to treat independently on the part of Great Britain.[47]

Stuart was not to negotiate the revision of the 1810 treaty. On the contrary, he was authorized merely to continue that agreement for two years from the date of its expiration in order to allow for proper provision without undue haste, to waive

---

[46] Portugal offered to acknowledge Pedro as emperor provided D. João should share the same title and all future legislation, acts of grace, titles, and appointments should be submitted to João for approval. Later Portugal proposed that the right to negotiate treaties for Brazil be reserved to Lisbon, while both countries were to have one diplomatic service and one army (F. O., 13/3, Stuart to Canning, No. 6). Such stipulations were vicious, Canning said (F. O., 13/1, Canning to Stuart, No. 1). Canning's fears as to the fate of Portugal after the death of D. João were realized when the reactionary revolution under D. Miguel broke out soon after the recognition of Brazilian independence (Temperly, *Canning*, pp. 208-210; Armitage, *History*, I, 230-236, 293-308; Oliveira Martins, *Historia de Portugal*, II, 263-284).

[47] F. O., 13/1, Canning to Stuart, No. 1. Canning also suggested to Stuart the possibility of securing reparations for losses by obtaining from Brazil the pledge to pay some debt or to deliver property values to the mother country (*ibid.*, No. 3).

any objection by England to the admission of Portuguese commerce with Brazil to a more favored footing than that of the British, and to stipulate that in the revised treaty there should be introduced an article for the immediate and effectual abolition of the Brazilian slave trade.[48]

The envoy encountered an exasperating obstinacy in Lisbon when he arrived to carry out his instructions. The trouble arose over the question of the manner by which D. João should style himself in granting the independence. He consented to acknowledge an emperor of Brazil by himself either as emperor of Brazil and king of Portugal and the Algarves, or as emperor of Portugal, Brazil, and the Algarves; or to acknowledge a king of Brazil by himself as king of Portugal, Brazil, and the Algarves. Canning remarked, dryly, that these three royal letters included every variety "except the one which would have ensured a speedy as well as a fortunate end to the negotiations." But D. João would not concede a royal letter which acknowledged an emperor of Brazil by the king of Portugal, Brazil, and the Algarves.[49] Every other point was arranged easily enough, but Stuart could not force D. João from his position in regard to the employment of the titles. Canning therefore instructed him to do his best to secure the approval of the Rio court to one of the three forms proposed by the Portuguese king.[50]

Stuart eventually obtained verbal permission from the Lisbon court to modify one of the three royal letters after his arrival in Rio in case of absolute necessity, provided the entire outcome of the negotiations hung on such a revision.[51] His full powers as plenipotentiary of the Portuguese Government were drawn up in due form and a bill of Portuguese claims against Brazil amounting to around three million sterling was handed to him before he left Lisbon in May, 1825.[52] In ad-

[48] F. O., 13/1, Canning to Stuart, No. 19. May 12, 1825. Later Canning instructed Stuart to extend the treaty for three years to give the London Office time to negotiate a commercial treaty with Portugal first (F. O., 13/2, Canning to Stuart, No. 31. October 10, 1825).

[49] F. O., 13/2, Canning to Stuart, No. 22.

[50] *Ibid.*

[51] Oliveira Lima, *O Reconhecimento*, p. 201.

[52] F. O., 13/3, Stuart to Canning, Nos. 6, 20, 27, 43.

dition D. João specified as the conditions under which the royal letter conceding independence could be delivered that Brazil should consent to the cessation of hostilities, the restitution of prizes, the return of sequestered property, the assumption by the new state of a part of the public debt, the payment of the sums due by the Lisbon treasury to the holders of original donations in the colony, and the basic stipulations for a commercial treaty favorable to Portuguese interests.[53]

Stuart arrived in Rio de Janeiro on July 18, 1825, and entered into immediate negotiations with three Brazilian plenipotentiaries.[54] Trouble arose at once over the question of the titles, since any of the three forms advocated by the Lisbon court connoted that independence had resulted, not from any efforts of the colony but from the gracious condescension of the king of Portugal. Brant Pontes suggested that D. João first grant independence, acknowledge D. Pedro as emperor, and then assume the title for himself, a formula which would acknowledge the part played by the colonials without granting to their emperor a title which D. João did not himself enjoy.[55] The Brazilians flatly refused to consider any other form of recognition.

Stuart finally consented to a fourth royal letter which adopted the suggestion of Brant Pontes. D. João acknowledged the independence of the colony and D. Pedro as emperor, then assumed the same title for himself and transferred, freely and of his own volition, his rightful sovereignty over the empire to his son. The reciprocal question of the right of D. Pedro to the throne of Portugal was carefully avoided, nothing appearing in the treaty on that point. Stuart signed a reciprocal note which

[53] Oliveira Lima, *O Reconhecimento*, p. 201. Metternich favored the negotiations and persuaded France and Russia to instruct their ministers at Lisbon to render any aid possible (*ibid.*, pp. 180-181, 195-196; *Archivo Diplomatico*, II, Brant and Gameiro to Carvalho e Mello, April 28, 1825).

[54] They were Carvalho e Mello, minister of foreign affairs, Villela Barbosa, later Marquez de Paranaguá, then minister of the navy, and the Visconde de Santo Amaro, who later succeeded Carvalho e Mello as foreign minister.

[55] Oliveira Lima, *op. cit.*, pp. 223-224. Any formula which failed to emphasize the part played by the colonials connoted to their mind the hidden purpose of the house of Bragança to reunite the two kingdoms when an opportune moment should arrive. The Absolutists favored such a policy, but the Patriots were vigorous in their denunciation. This was why the formula became so important.

prohibited the publication by Portugal of any of the royal letters formulated in Lisbon, although D. João might issue a *diploma regio* (royal declaration) modeled after the preamble of the treaty, antedating the document to precede the time of the negotiations.[56]

Brazil acceded to the six conditions which constituted the price which the colony was required to pay the mother country. In addition, D. Pedro pledged himself not to accept the union of any other Portuguese colony to the new empire, even though such possessions should so petition.[57] Hostilities were declared at an end; a mixed commission with the collaboration of England was to determine the indemnity for prizes, confiscated or sequestered property; Portugal was to receive compensation for the loss of public property in Brazil; mutual most favored nation clauses and fifteen per cent. importation tax were granted and five months were given for ratification.[58]

By an additional article, which was kept secret until the Brazilian Assembly met in 1826, Brazil agreed to pay two millions sterling to compensate Portugal for all losses sustained by the independence of the colony. In liquidation of that sum, the Rio treasury took over the debt of one million four hundred thousand pounds which had been contracted by the Lisbon court in London (1823[59]), and pledged itself to pay the

---

[56] Oliveira Lima, *O Reconhecimento*, pp. 132-141. D. João violated this agreement, as the royal letter of May 13 with all the objectionable features including the assertion that Pedro was to inherit the Portuguese throne was issued at the time of the publication of the terms of the treaty in Lisbon. The incident aroused bitter feeling in Brazil against Portugal and created distrust of Pedro among the Patriots.

[57] England linked great importance to this provision, for if Benguela, Angola, or the other African colonies which furnished Negroes for the slave trade should unite with Brazil, there would be even greater difficulty in stopping the traffic. The matter would be purely a domestic one and would cease to be a question of international trade (Oliveira Lima, *op. cit.*, p. 241).

[58] The treaty is given in Oliveira Lima, *op. cit.*, Appendix, pp. 352-360. It is dated August 29, 1825. It was ratified by D. Pedro the next day and by D. João November 15, 1825. Copies were enclosed by Stuart in F. O., 13/4, Stuart to Canning, No. 67.

[59] The purpose of the loan had been to acquire funds to prosecute the war against the Brazilians. The original debt had been £1,500,000, but £100,000 had been paid by Portugal.

remaining six hundred thousand within one year of the ratification of the treaty.[60]

Such was the price demanded of the new state by the mother country in payment for the recognition of independence, a price which had been negotiated under the direct intervention of England. Less than three years had passed since D. Pedro had declared himself emperor of Brazil, and yet independence was an accomplished fact. Gameiro Pessôa was received as minister from Brazil by the king of England, January 30, 1826. Austria recognized the new state in December, 1825, and France followed its example the next month. Recognition by the Vatican[61] (January 23), Sweden (January 5), Switzerland (January 30), the Hanseatic States (February 14), Holland (February 15), Hanover (February 18), and Prussia (March 6) followed rapidly.[62] England had turned the key and opened the door to the new nation, and the powers welcomed the empire at once.

By its own efforts and alone, Great Britain thus secured recognition for Brazil; Sir Charles Stuart now presented England's bill for the service rendered. After divesting himself of his powers as Portuguese envoy, he declared himself a minister from England and began negotiations for an extended treaty of commerce which was to take the place of the agreement of 1810. To the surprise of the court of Brazil, instead of the simple two-year prolongation of the 1810 treaty, he asked for the immediate conclusion of a permanent agreement, which should contain the special privileges specified by the earlier treaty. Carvalho e Mello, foreign minister, wrote to Gameiro Pessôa in London, bitterly commenting that although such a proposal

---

[60] Oliveira Lima, *op. cit.*, Appendix, pp. 363-365. The negotiations between Stuart and the three Brazilians are given in *Archivo Diplomatico*, VI, Portugal, pp. 36-142.

[61] The right of patronage was granted D. Pedro by the Pope, May 15, 1827. The Chamber of Deputies refused to approve the Bull and declared that D. Pedro possessed the right of patronage by virtue of the Imperial Constitution, Article 102 (Oliveira Lima, *ibid.*, p. 297).

[62] Oliveira Lima, *op. cit.*, pp. 287-305; *Archivo Diplomatico*, II, Itabayana (Gameiro Pessôa) to Rezende, January 31, 1826. Russia recognized the empire in 1827 and Spain in 1834 (Rocha Pombo, *Historia*, VII, 916, footnote 1).

was repugnant to the Rio court in view of the fact that England was not treating with Brazil on the same basis as that which had been employed for the negotiations with the Spanish republics, he could not refuse the demand for special privileges in consequence of the part which the London government had taken in the question of the recognition of independence. Sir Charles Stuart, said Carvalho e Mello, was demanding disproportionate commercial advantages and the immediate abolition of the slave traffic without adequate compensation as payment for the intervention of his government, but Brazil could not refuse.[63]

Stuart, however, was exceeding his instructions.[64] When Canning learned of the negotiations, he was biting in his criticism and ordered the envoy, in case he had signed such a treaty as the project which he had remitted to London, to inform the Rio court that he had done so without instructions.[65] But before Canning's dispatch reached Brazil, Stuart had signed two permanent treaties, one of commerce and the other for the abolition of the slave trade, and had secured the ratification of D. Pedro to both documents.[66] When they reached Canning's hands, he found it was impossible to approve of either, although he had anticipated that at least the slave trade treaty would be in the correct form. His rejection of the commercial agreement was due to three principal defects; first, the right of visit and search in time of war had been relinquished; second, the so-called reciprocity clause in commerce guaranteed nothing to England since no one knew as yet what privileges the "most favored nation" in Brazilian trade would enjoy, whereas all the world knew what favors the Rio court would secure

[63] *Archivo Diplomatico*, I, Carvalho e Mello to Gameiro, September 28, 1825.

[64] Canning had hinted to Stuart that he would send detailed instructions for the negotiation of a new treaty (F. O., 13/2, Canning to Stuart, No. 22) but later he forbade the minister to close a definite treaty in revised form. He was merely to obtain the simple prolongation of the 1810 agreement (F. O., 13/2, Canning to Stuart, No. 31). Stuart began negotiations without waiting for the detailed instructions (F. O., 13/3, Stuart to Canning, No. 48, 64).

[65] F. O., 13/2, Canning to Stuart, Nos. 33, 35. The project was sent to London on September 30, F. O., 13/5, Stuart to Canning, No. 81.

[66] F. O., 13/6, Stuart to Canning, No. 86. The treaties were dated October 18.

from England; and third, the office of judge conservator was abolished.[67] As for the slave trade treaty, it would have been sufficient merely to state that the new empire accepted the obligations incurred by Portugal under the convention of July 28, 1817, and that it pledged the abolition within a stated number of years.[68]

Fortunately the ratification by Brazil enabled England to accept or reject the agreements as a whole, so that one point of disagreement would suffice as grounds by which Canning could reopen negotiations. But before the London Office could take action, news arrived that the terms of both treaties had been published in the *Diario Fluminense*[69] at Rio in the edition of November 14, 1825. Apparently, thought Canning, the Brazilian government was attempting to force his hand.[70] In fact he was placed in a very embarrassing position by the publication of the terms of the agreements, for enquiries were made immediately on the floor of Parliament and Russia demanded the extradition of a political refugee.[71] The treaty with Mexico had been rejected on the grounds that it included the abolition of the right of visit and search, and just the year before Canning had refused to define that right despite the fact that the United States had been very insistent. By the present treaty closed by Stuart, right of visit and search was relinquished. In addition although the minister had persistently demanded the continuation of the office of judge conservator in Portugal during the negotiations with that country concerning the renewal of the treaty of 1810, his efforts were rendered futile by the publication of Stuart's document, for the Portuguese agent, immediately after having read the *Diario Fluminense*, presented a project in which that privilege was omitted. In view of these embarrassments, therefore, Canning was forced to send a gen-

---

[67] F. O., 13/17, Canning to Stuart, Nos. 1, 2.

[68] *Archivo Diplomatico*, I, cxxix; F. O., 84/56, Slave Trade, Draft 1.

[69] *Archivo Diplomatico*, I, cxxix and II, Gameiro to Carvalho e Mello, January 9, 1826.

[70] The Rio ministry denied any share in the publication of the terms (*ibid.*, Inhambupe [Pereira da Cunha] to Itabayana, May 6, 1826).

[71] Stuart's treaty had granted the right of extradition of political refugees.

eral disavowal of the work of his envoy to all British ambassadors and agents with instructions that it be communicated to all foreign governments.[72]

The first bill presented by Great Britain to the new empire failed, therefore, to receive the sanction of the Foreign Office. To rectify the errors of Stuart's attempt, Charles Gordon was nominated by Canning as minister plenipotentiary to the court of Brazil, with full powers to negotiate treaties of commerce and the suppression of the slave trade.[73] He was given projects for both agreements which had been carefully worked out with the collaboration of the Brazilian minister at London, and Canning expected Gordon would have little difficulty in securing the acceptance of D. Pedro to both treaties. The minister was authorized to conclude the negotiations in Rio provided no substantial alterations were made by Brazil in the terms demanded by England. The correspondence which Gordon would find in the Rio legation would suffice for his instructions, but under no condition was he to yield to the Brazilian demand for the abolition of the judge conservatorship. Also he was not to sign the slave traffic agreement until the commercial treaty had been agreed upon.[74]

Gordon reached Rio on October 13 and began negotiations at once on the two-fold task assigned to him. The commercial problem which faced the minister was less complicated than the slave trade question, since the economic preëminence of England in Brazil was a fact of long standing to which the Brazilians had become more or less reconciled. From the English point of view, the empire had usurped the old place occupied for centuries by Portugal. Canning, in addressing Palmella during the Anglo-Portuguese negotiations for the renewal of the treaty of 1810, was forced to admit to him that "the English merchants considered the treaty with Brazil as an object of greater importance, far superior, without comparison, to the treaties with Portugal."[75] In the interests of those mer-

[72] F. O., 13/17, Canning to Stuart, April 19, 1826. Separate.

[73] F. O., 13/25, Canning to Gordon, No. 1. August 1, 1826.

[74] *Ibid.*, No. 3.

[75] *Archivo Diplomatico*, I, cxxi.

chants, the British minister had maintained resolutely through the period of revolt that the terms of the treaty of 1810 still held for the colony, although the authority of the government which had negotiated this agreement had been renounced.[76] He maintained his attitude in view of the importance of the Brazilian trade to the British merchants. In 1825 the exports to Portuguese America equalled almost half of the value of the merchandise shipped to the United States and was a little less than the total amount sent to the British West Indies. In that year Brazil alone absorbed almost half of the entire value of goods exported to all South America and Mexico combined,[77] while England, on the other hand, purchased very little from the empire.[78]

In addition, the shipping interests were deeply concerned over their economic relations with the new state. The number of British ships which entered the harbor of Rio grew steadily after 1815, the fleet engaged in that trade having more than doubled by 1821. Although England itself did not absorb any great amount of the exports carried on the return trip, the British ships enjoyed the profits accruing from the steadily increasing value of goods which Brazil sold abroad. That carrying trade was becoming constantly more profitable, for between 1815 and 1821, merchandise which left Rio for foreign ports multiplied five times in value.[79]

Gordon's mission therefore was an important one. He was chosen for his known ability and his negotiation proved his

---

[76] F. O., 63/275, Canning to Chamberlain, No. 17; 63/261, Chamberlain to Canning, No. 123, Confidential. For a time the Rio court threatened to declare the treaty at an end and did announce that it had expired *de jure* and only existed *de facto* by virtue of the good will of Brazil (F. O., 63/260, Chamberlain to Canning, No. 101). This attitude was temporary, however (*ibid.*, No. 122; F. O., 13/8, Chamberlain to Canning, February 22, 1825. Separate. Secret; 13/11, Chamberlain to Canning, December 5, 1825).

[77] Customs, 8/21, Comparative Tables. The same ratio held for 1830 (Customs 8/32). In 1835 the same ratio held in reference to the United States and the British West Indies, but in that year Brazil took close to a million sterling more merchandise than did all of South America and Mexico combined (Customs 8/42).

[78] Customs, 4/20. The same was true in 1830 (Customs 4/25) and 1835 (Customs 4/30). Raw cotton always constituted by far the largest item.

[79] F. O., 63/247, Chamberlain to Londonderry, No. 59.

worth. He acted with an efficiency which resembled that displayed by Strangford in 1810. Although he took up the commercial question only after having concluded the vexing problem of the suppression of the slave trade and although he had met "most strange reverses," he was able to send the treaty, ratified by the Rio court, to the Foreign Office with provisions which were "precisely according to the terms" which he had been "instructed to require" of the Brazilian government.[80] On November 10, 1827, ratifications of the commercial treaty of 1827 were exchanged in London and the agreement became effective.[81]

The document[82] was an adaptation of the 1810 treaty to the empire, with all of the old privileges of the earlier agreements retained by England. Some of the articles were unobjectionable in the eyes of Brazil. Peace and friendship were to exist between the two countries; consuls were to be appointed with their powers clearly specified by the treaty; perfect liberty of conscience in matters of religion was guaranteed; the inviolability of domicile was assured; deserters were to be delivered up on demand; mutual liberty of commerce in all ports of both parties was granted, although coastwise trade was restricted to national ships; port duties were specified; the packet service was to continue; piracy was outlawed; shipwrecked or distressed vessels were to be protected; mutual right of warehousing and reëxportation without payment of consumption tax were conceded; drawbacks or bounties on reëxported articles were declared to be independent of the nationality of the vessels receiving such reëxported articles; Brazil abolished all monopolies or exclusive commercial companies, except existing crown monopolies; and the English merchants obtained the privilege of making payments to the customs house on the same footing as the subjects of Brazil.[83]

[80] F. O., 13/18, Gordon to Dudley, No. 17. Dated August 18, 1827. In contrast to Stuart's verbose reports, Gordon merely stated that it was unnecessary to tell of his difficulties. His mission had been successful and that would suffice.

[81] F. O., 13/35, Dudley to Gordon, No. 31.

[82] Martens, *Recueil*, *Supplement*, XI, Seconde Partie, 479-491.

[83] Articles I-V, VII-XI; XIII-XIV, XVI-XVIII, XXII-XXIII, XXV-XXVII respectively.

There were other stipulations, however, to which the Brazilians objected strenuously. Article VI conceded that since "the Constitution of the Empire of Brazil" had "abolished all special jurisdictions," the "office of Judge Conservator for the British Nation," should "subsist only until some satisfactory substitute for that jurisdiction" should "be established, capable of providing, in an equal degree, for the protection of the persons and property of His Majesty's Subjects." That time never arrived, however, and the extra-territorial jurisdiction of Great Britain in Brazil continued until the Rio court declared the treaty void and refused to negotiate another agreement.

Another source of friction arose from Article XII, which specified that the nationality of a vessel, whether British or Brazilian, was to be determined by the ownership, place of construction, and nationality of the master and three fourths of the crew, except such ships as should be lawfully captured in war or as pirates. By such a stipulation the number of vessels sailing under the Brazilian flag which could enter British ports and enjoy the fruits of the present treaty was greatly diminished, since Brazil purchased from abroad a large part of its merchant fleet and manned its vessels principally with foreigners.

Despite the efforts of the Rio court to limit the number of articles declared to be contraband of war, Gordon secured a long list favorable to England's traditional viewpoint (Article XV). The low import duty of fifteen per cent. on British imports was to continue,[84] also, with the additional pledge by Brazil that no other country, Portugal excepted, should be conceded a lower rate than that granted to England.[85] By virtue of most favored nation stipulations, the empire was forced to grant to the other powers the same low rate,[86] which Brazilian

[84] England had enjoyed exclusively the low rate of fifteen per cent. since 1810, whereas all other foreign countries had paid twenty-four per cent. (Oliveira Lima, *O Imperio Brazileiro*, p. 199). Brazil had threatened to raise the rate of Portuguese imports to twenty-four per cent. also during the revolt since Portugal became a foreign nation in the eyes of Brazil.

[85] Article XX.

[86] Austria, June 30, 1826; Prussia, July 9, 1827; the Hanseatic Cities, November 17, 1827; Denmark, April 26, 1828; the United States, December 12, 1828; Hol-

ministers of finance continually assailed as the underlying cause of the poverty of the national treasury. The empire might have found compensation for the loss if its sugar and other tropical produce could have gained entrance to the market in England, but the preferential rates in favor of the British West Indies, recognized by Article XXII, prevented this importation for English consumption.

The duration of the treaty[87] was for the same period as the 1810 agreement; namely, for fifteen years from the date of ratification, with the understanding that its stipulations should remain in force thereafter until one of the contracting parties should give notice of its termination. In case of such notification the treaty was to expire only at the end of two years from the date of the notice.[88]

The transfer of the special privileges which England had enjoyed for centuries in Portuguese commerce was completed and the continuation of Great Britain's preëminence in the economic life of its old European ally was assured in Portuguese America despite the severance of the colony from the mother country. The thread of continuity is remarkably clear, running back through the transition years of 1810-1827 to the Anglo-Portuguese relations of the seventeenth and eighteenth centuries. In a very real sense, the triple complementary treaties of 1642-'54-'61 may be considered as the basis of the Anglo-Brazilian commercial agreement of 1827.

One item of the bill due England had been paid, but there

---

land, December 20, 1828. France was the first to obtain the privilege of fifteen per cent. duties by reason of the most favored nation clause. The treaty was signed on January 8, 1826, with slight modifications effected June 7, 1826 (Oliveira Lima, *O Reconhecimento*, pp. 287-292). By decree of September 24, 1828, all nations with or without treaty were granted the fifteen per cent. rate. In 1844 the tax was raised to thirty per cent. The fifteen per cent. rate deprived Brazil of the easiest tax for revenue and in 1836 the ministry was forced to impose an eight per cent. export tax (Oliveira Lima, *O Imperio Brazileiro*, pp. 199-200).

[87] Article XXVIII.

[88] The treaty actually expired in November, 1844, despite vigorous efforts by England to renew it or to negotiate a new agreement (see F. O., 131/12, 15, *Proposed Treaty of Commerce—1842-1845* and Hamilton's dispatches, February, 1844, to December, 1845, F. O., 13/211-215, 221-227).

still remained the far more difficult question of the suppression of the slave trade. By a long tradition inherited from previous centuries, the colonials had become reconciled to British dominance in their economic life, but no such preparations had paved the way for the suppression of the slave traffic. On the contrary, the history of England's attempts to suppress the trade between 1810 and 1822 demonstrated the obstinate opposition of the Brazilians to any measure which threatened to cut off what they felt to be their only effective supply of labor.

So impossible was it for D. Pedro to curb the trade that he was forced to refuse a direct offer of recognition of independence which England made as early as November, 1822, on the condition that Brazil abolish the traffic.[89] Although Brant Pontes warned his government that Great Britain was so determined to give the death blow to the trade that Brazil would be compelled to yield by force unless it should conform of its own free will,[90] the Rio court merely expressed its determination to abolish the trade as soon as it could do so without endangering the very existence of the government itself.[91] Canning demonstrated the sincerity of his offer by sending Lord Amherst by Rio on his way to India, with an offer of immediate recognition in payment for abolition; but José Bonifacio, minister of foreign affairs, was forced to confess that as necessary as recognition was to the harassed empire, he could not stop the traffic at once. He was willing to take measures to effect the gradual cessation of the trade, but Canning could not be content with half-measures.[92] Abolition of the Brazilian slave traffic was so desirable in the eyes of England that it outweighed the difficulties which instant recognition of the new state would raise for Great Britain in Europe, but the cessation had to be absolute and immediate.

---

[89] F. O., 63/257, Canning to Chamberlain, No. 5. Secret; *Archivo Diplomatico*, I, Brant to Bonifacio, November 16, 17, 20, 1822 and May 6, 1823.

[90] *Archivo Diplomatico*, I, Brant to Bonifacio, June 1, 1823.

[91] *Ibid.*, I, Brant to Bonifacio, June 29, 1823; Carvalho e Mello to Brant and Gameiro, January 3, 1824.

[92] Rocha Pombo, *Historia*, VII, 899; *Archivo Diplomatico*, I, Brant to Bonifacio, May 10, 1823; F. O., 63/259, Chamberlain to Canning, No. 20.

José Bonifacio, intimate friend of D. Pedro in the first months of the revolt, assured Consul Chamberlain in April, 1823, that he heartily detested the traffic and desired total abolition. But it could not "be done immediately, the people" were "not prepared for it and until this" had "been brought about, it would endanger the existence of the Government if attempted suddenly." The minister insisted that it was impossible for him to undertake an international promise which he was unable to fulfill. Yet he ardently wished that English "cruisers would take every Slave Ship they" encountered at sea, for, he said, "I want to see no more of them, they are the gangrene of our Prosperity. The population we want is a White one."[93]

The minister was sincere in his personal desire to see the trade exterminated, but two reasons forced him to withhold his hand. In the first place, Negroes were an absolute necessity for the cultivation of the land until white immigration should set in to take their places. As this immigration increased, Bonifacio promised, the incoming supply of Negroes would be lessened until final abolition was secured. In the second place, the actual precarious stability or even the very existence of the government itself would have been destroyed by any measure which precipitously abolished the traffic. The interests engaged in the trade, powerful as they were, might possibly be faced successfully, but there was no hope of a victorious conflict with the owners of the great plantations of the interior, the element which formed the backbone of the Patriot Party. The government, Bonifacio asserted, did not share in the opinion firmly held by the agricultural people of Brazil, but that class was the powerful element of the country. Manifestly, D. Pedro could not abolish the trade at once, although the Brazilian government was willing to enter into negotiations for the gradual extinction of the traffic.[94] Chamberlain added to his report of the interview the interesting detail that the government in-

[93] F. O., 63/259, Chamberlain to Canning, April 2, Secret.

[94] *Ibid.*, No. 55. Secret, April 26, 1823. The consul was reporting an interview with Bonifacio in which the latter gave him the result of a cabinet meeting at which D. Pedro himself was present.

come from the tax on Negroes imported into the country was close to two hundred thousand pounds a year. It was his opinion that "a gradual abolition" was "the only one this new government dared agree to."[95]

Brazil was forced, therefore, to refuse the enticing bait of an early recognition by Canning, who offered to act irrespective of the attitude of Portugal if the new state would grant him one condition. The Rio court was obliged to follow the longer path of negotiations at London and Lisbon, and to await the result of the interplay of European politics before England turned the magic key. Then Stuart came with his instructions to secure the abolition of the traffic, not on the basis of an unconditional concession by Brazil to a positive demand by England, but merely as the continuation of engagements made by the Rio government in 1815 and 1817.[96] To the preamble of the proposed treaty, which stated that "the separation of Brazil from Portugal entitles England to claim from Brazil the observance of the Treaties concluded between England and Portugal before the separation." Canning added four simple articles. The trade should be prohibited entirely within a specified number of years, with the penalty of piracy to be inflicted on violators thereafter; until the abolition should take place, the treaties, conventions, and additional articles of January 22, 1815, and of July 28, 1817, should continue; the instructions, powers, forms, and regulations annexed to the 1817 agreement should be applied to the present understanding[97]; and the mixed commissions should continue.[98]

---

[95] *Ibid.* The British agents reported "scandalous frauds" practiced by the Brazilians in the question of the slave trade. Freed slaves serving their fourteen years were fraudulently declared dead; Negroes were secretly taken from seized slavers, declared dead, and sold into slavery; and the traffic was carried on openly in an illegal manner in Maranhão despite the protests of the British agent (F. O., 84/56, Canning to Gordon, Nos. 2, 3, 4). Stuart wrote from Bahia that 18,000 Negroes were imported annually into that province, by far the greater number coming from the part of Africa north of the equator (F. O., 84/56, Stuart to Canning, March 14, 1826).

[96] F. O., 84/56, Canning to Stuart, No. 1.

[97] This provision guaranteed the right of visit and search of Brazilian merchantmen by British cruisers to ascertain the illegal presence of slaves.

[98] F. O., 84/56, Canning to Stuart, No. 1. January 12, 1826.

Stuart failed,[99] but Gordon took over the task and on October 30, 1826, held his first conference with two Brazilian commissioners. The first obstacle which he encountered was the fact that the Assembly itself during its last session had proposed a bill to abolish the traffic within six years, and the Brazilian agents considered themselves unable to negotiate until the representative body had taken action. Gordon countered by pointing out that since Brazil no longer constituted a part of the Portuguese dominions, the trade was automatically prohibited by virtue of the conventions of 1815 and 1817 between England and Portugal, as those agreements abolished the traffic between Portuguese Africa and any foreign country. England was merely insisting upon a free will expression by which the Rio government should acquiesce in a fact that had already been accomplished.[100] The Brazilians were reminded also that Great Britain had treaty rights with Portugal which would enable it to enforce the prohibition of the slave trade between its old ally and foreign powers. Any resistance, therefore, which the Rio court could make to the proposed total abolition of its traffic, would be futile.[101]

At the second conference, the Brazilians notified Gordon that D. Pedro himself preferred to wait until the Assembly could meet and take action. But again the envoy refused, suggesting as a solution to the difficulty that the negotiation and the treaty should be kept secret until the Chamber met.[102] At the next meeting, Gordon brusquely refused to consider a four-year time limit for the traffic and stated laconically that the indemnity demanded by D. Pedro for loss of revenue to his government could not be granted by England. He likewise refused to change the preamble required by Canning, by which the empire acknowledged the validity of the conventions of 1815 and 1817.[103] On November 22, the Brazilians finally gave

[99] F. O., 84/56, Canning to Stuart, No. 1. In this dispatch Canning gives in detail the reasons why the treaty negotiated by the envoy was unsatisfactory.

[100] F. O., 84/56, Gordon to Canning, No. 1. Protocol of First Conference.

[101] F. O., 13/38, Gordon to Dudley, No. 10. Gordon denied making this threat but the situation was quite clear to the Brazilian commissioners (*ibid.*).

[102] F. O., 84/56, Gordon to Canning, No. 1. Protocol of Second Conference.

[103] *Ibid.*, Protocol to the Conferences of November 21 and 22.

their consent to a three year time limit to count from the date of ratification, and the next day the treaty was signed.[104]

Gordon, by obeying orders, thus obtained the treaty in the exact terms set down by Canning,[105] but he was dubious as to the outcome of the affair. Writing to the foreign minister, he admitted that it could not "be denied that the measure of abolishing the Traffic in Slaves" was "to the highest degree unpopular in this country. . . ." From the first he had been convinced "that so far from its being advisable" to yield to the emperor's desire to wait until the meeting of the Assembly, D. Pedro would not have been able to grant the abolition at all if the decision had been left to that body. Moreover, the trade, as Gordon foresaw, would be carried on ten-fold during the next three years and afterwards it would continue by a system of contraband with the connivance of the Rio government. When the final abolition should take place, therefore, "the task of sweeping the seas" would be thrown "entirely upon the hands of Great Britain."[106]

The minister was a true prophet, for when the convention was transmitted to the Assembly at the next regular session, the storm raged for days.[107] By a document[108] dated May 22,

[104] *Ibid.*, Protocol to the Conferences of November 22 and 23. A "reversal note" was presented by the Brazilians which required the English government to enter into negotiations in London for a reasonable prolongation of the time limit with the sole view of fulfilling the obligations of the ministry toward the pending law in the Assembly (*ibid.*). Gordon transmitted the note to his government without guaranteeing its ratification.

[105] Ratifications were exchanged in London, March 13, 1827 (F. O., 13/35, Canning to Gordon, No. 19). Hence the traffic was to cease on March 13, 1830. Some difficulty arose in Rio over the ratified document returned to Brazil, since it lacked the signature of the British secretary of state. To render such a document valid in Brazil, the foreign minister was required to sign. An attempt was made to throw out the entire convention on this pretext of improper ratification by England, but the movement failed (F. O., 13/37, Gordon to Canning, Nos. 37, 42, June 8, Separate; Gordon to Dudley, Nos. 3, 17).

[106] F. O., 84/56, Gordon to Canning, No. 2. November 27, 1826.

[107] F. O., 13/38, Gordon to Dudley, No. 3. July 14, 1827. The Assembly met May 3, 1827. It was the second time that body had held session since the dissolution of the Constitutent Assembly in 1823. The other meeting occured May 6, 1826 (Armitage, *History*, I, 281, 237).

[108] The document was enclosed in F. O., 13/38, Gordon to Dudley, No. 10. Gordon immediately protested against this letter and demanded an explanation

1827, the Marquez de Queluz, foreign minister, delivered the treaty to the Chamber with explanations as to why D. Pedro's ministers had consented to such an agreement. The progress of the negotiations was given in detail; the desire of the Brazilian commissioners to delay matters until the Assembly could act on its own project, Gordon's refusal to postpone a settlement, and his insistence that the trade actually was prohibited at the moment by treaties existing between England and Portugal were explained accurately. The marquis pointed out that the envoy had made it perfectly plain, that in case the Brazilian government refused to act, England would oblige the king of Portugal to close his African ports to Brazilian slavers or it would prevent by means of its cruisers any access to those ports by Brazilian ships. He explained that in the face of the fearful losses which would accrue to Brazilian lives and property under the threat to treat slavers as pirates, the ministers of D. Pedro had been forced to concede what would otherwise be accomplished by forceful means, and the slave trade treaty had been signed.

The letter of the foreign minister fanned the flames of indignation which consumed the deputies as they listened to the death knell of their slave traffic. Five members of the Committee on Diplomacy and Statistics reported caustically against the convention on June 16. Although the deputies had no voice in the matter, due to the provision in the Constitution which placed the treaty making power exclusively in the hands of the emperor,[109] they could express an opinion and they were vociferous in their denunciation of the accomplished fact. The convention was derogatory to the honor, interests, dignity, independence, and sovereignty of the Brazilian nation, asserted Cunha Mattos, who advanced seven arguments to prove his

from Queluz, on the grounds that the abolition had not resulted from menaces by Great Britain nor as a concession to that government, but for humanity's sake and the honor of Brazil. Queluz explained more or less satisfactorily (*ibid.*).

[109] The constitution had been formulated by the emperor and had been declared in force without the sanction of any constituent assembly. Some municipal bodies voted to accept it (Oliveira Lima, *O Imperio Brazileiro*, p. 76).

charge.[110] By virtue of this treaty, he argued, Brazilian citizens would become subject to the jurisdiction of British Admiralty courts; the only supply of labor possible to the country was checked; and the only shipping business left open to the Brazilians after the commercial treaties with England and France was prohibited.

The Bishop of Bahia favored the convention, but the Bishop of Maranhão opposed it.[111] Clemente Pereira, historic leader of the republican wing of the Patriots, in a clear, forceful speech delivered in the session of July 4, agreed entirely with Cunha Mattos in his opinion that the convention was a serious mistake. But the treaty was signed, he pointed out, and, in the face of that action taken by D. Pedro and his ministers, there was no recourse left to the Chamber but to accept it.[112] His speech was roundly cheered throughout.

On July 4, after a long debate, the Chamber merely voted not to take any action in regard to the convention but to reserve its deliberations for the proper time.[113]

The second item of the bill which Great Britain had presented for its services in securing the recognition of the independence of Brazil was thus paid in full. But the payment had entailed the desertion by D. Pedro of the Patriot, or Constitutionalist Party, for it was only by virtue of his absolute power that the demands of England could be met. Early in 1824, the prince stood hesitating between the Absolutist and the Patriot

[110] Raymundo José da Cunha Mattos, member of the Committee on Diplomacy and Statistics. He spoke during the session of July 3.

[111] Debate of July 3.

[112] Clemente Pereira demonstrated that Brazil had not a sufficient number of laborers. Yet neither would the Indians serve nor would the Europeans come. Since the Negro supply from Africa was to be cut off, the only recourse left was to propagate the Negroes already in Brazil. More than three years were necessary for that solution, however, and yet in 1830 the traffic must cease. The trade should be stopped for philanthropic reasons, if for no other, but he could not believe that England's action was based exclusively on that ground. Economic and special class motives likewise instigated its action, but Brazil also had its own economic and special class reasons for delaying abolition.

[113] Gordon enclosed copies of the speeches in F. O., 13/38, Gordon to Dudley, No. 3.

parties, with powerful influences pulling him toward both camps. He chose the way of the autocrats and surrounded himself with adulating sycophants and ignorant favorites. The liberty of the press, though nominally guaranteed, was extinguished; presidents of provinces who exercised arbitrary authority were promoted; legislative powers were arrogated by the cabinet; and members of the Absolutist Party were favored throughout the empire.[114]

Other factors than his relations with England undoubtedly influenced the prince in the adoption of his autocratic course. But it is evident that only absolute power in his hands could have enabled D. Pedro to concede the price demanded by England for its old ally Portugal and to pay in full the bill rendered by Great Britain for its services in securing the recognition of the empire by the mother country and by the European nations. To establish the empire and to repress the disintegrating tendencies of republicanism which threatened to disrupt Brazil, the prince was forced to betray the party by which he had made himself supreme. The treaty with Portugal, negotiated under the pressure of London, placed the monarchy and the cabinet in a precarious position in the eyes of the Brazilians who were becoming ever more suspicious of the reactionary tendencies of their government.[115] While it caused serious difficulties in the Absolutist Party and annoyed the Patriots, the commercial treaty with England was accepted for the time being, since the traditional dominance of Great Britain in Portuguese economic life had prepared the Brazilians for the inevitable preëminence of that nation in their own commerce. But the slave trade convention, the work of a monarch acting with absolute power and surrounded by irresponsible ministers,

[114] Armitage, *History*, I, 200-204; Oliveira Lima, *O Reconhecimento*, pp. 255-256.

[115] Oliveira Lima, *O Reconhecimento*, p. 255; Pereira da Silva, *Historia*, VII, 332-333. The payment of the £2,000,000 was especially objectionable to the Brazilians. It was not published along with the Portuguese Treaty recognizing the independence, but the article, which was secret, was reserved until its final presentation to the Assembly when that body met. It also was an accomplished fact and there was nothing that the Chamber could do about it. It served as an additional reason for distrust of Pedro's intentions in regard to the future union of the two kingdoms.

raised a storm of protest. Canning was almost violent in his denunciation of D. Pedro when he heard the rumor that the prince had offered to abolish the constitution in return for recognition by Austria[116]; and yet to satisfy the demands of that very minister the prince was forced to resort to absolute power and to ignore the will of the Assembly and the dominant party in the empire. The fiasco of the emperor's policy in the Banda Oriental and the distrust of his intentions in relation to Portugal after the death of D. João in 1826 completed the alienation of the Patriots, and on April 13, 1831, the Brazilian party expelled the absolutist prince who had established the empire of Brazil and had secured the entrance of the new state into the society of the nations of Europe.[117] England's price for its recognition of the independence of the empire was a serious contributing factor to the downfall of the founder of the Brazilian nation.

---

[116] *Archivo Diplomatico*, II, Brant and Gameiro to Carvalho e Mello, May 11, 1825.

[117] Rocha Pombo, *Historia*, VIII, 254-264; Armitage, *History*, II, 103-143; Oliveira Lima, *O Imperio Brazileiro*, pp. 21, 210. For a discussion of the manner in which D. Pedro won and lost the support of the Brazilians between 1822 and 1831 see the article by the author, "The Paradoxical Pedro, First Emperor of Brazi " *The Hisp. Amer. Hist. Review*, XII (1932), May.

CHAPTER IX

THE BEGINNINGS OF THE REVOLT AGAINST BRITISH DOMINANCE

BETWEEN 1825 and 1827 British preëminence in Brazil reached its culmination. The traditional supremacy in Portuguese economic life was transferred to the independent empire between 1808 and 1827; the virtual monopoly of Brazilian commerce enjoyed by England during the Napoleonic wars was prolonged until 1827 by means of the preferential importation tax secured in 1810; and the opening of the ports of the colony to world trade stimulated British interests. Between 1808 and 1827 Great Britain thus secured a favored position among foreign powers in Brazilian commerce, investment, and shipping, and established the Englishman as a permanent factor in the economic life of the nation. Politically, Great Britain was beginning to exercise a virtual protectorate over the empire. Under the compelling direction of the London Foreign Office, peace terms with Portugal which aroused the distrust and resentment of the Brazilian Patriot class were forced on the Rio government; due solely to English influence, acknowledgment of independence by Portugal and recognition by the European powers were achieved by D. Pedro; a commercial treaty, disliked but tolerated, solidified British economic privileges; a convention suppressing the slave trade was forced on a vehemently protesting people who were unable to prevent ratification; and extra-territorial privileges freed the Englishman from Brazilian jurisdiction. Thus in 1827 British economic and political preeminence in Portuguese America was definitely established.

The parallel between England's position in Brazil in 1827 and the Anglo-Portuguese situation after 1703 is striking. In both cases England had helped to establish the independence of a revolting nation; a profitable economic interchange promoted by special privileges which were guaranteed by treaties tightened the union between the allies; and the Englishman became the paramount factor in the economic life of the weaker power. But here the parallel ceases: whereas in the eighteenth century, England pushed these advantages until Portugal became virtually an economic and political vassal,[1] nineteenth century Brazil resisted similar efforts so strenuously that by 1845 the special favors granted England were revoked, the commercial and slave trade treaties were declared annulled, and the Rio court was frankly in revolt against the pressure exerted by the London Foreign Office.

This revolt against British preëminence revealed two phases one political and the other economic. The issue in the first phase arose from England's efforts to suppress the slave trade; in the second phase, it was forced by Brazil's determination to place Great Britain on an equal footing economically with other foreign powers. The discussion of Anglo-Brazilian relations during the hundred years following 1827 will be concentrated, therefore, upon these two principal issues.

England's attempt to abolish the traffic was the direct cause of the decline of its political preëminence in Portuguese America. From the very moment of the signature of the convention of 1826 until the late 'sixties, Anglo-Brazilian relations were embittered by the slave trade, the distrust and contempt of the British[2] being matched by the fear and hatred of the Brazilians in whose minds the suppression of the traffic and subordination to England were synonymous. Even the more moderate historians and statesmen of Portuguese America consid-

---

[1] See *supra*, pp. 39-40.

[2] The attitude of distrust in regard to the sincerity of the Rio government and of contempt for the moral degradation of the Brazilians in continuing the inhuman slave trade were evidenced in the diplomatic correspondence between the Foreign Office and the British representatives in Rio. See, as examples, F. O. 84/84, Aberdeen to Ponsonby, December 6, 1828; F. O. 84/122, Palmerston to Aston, November 1, 1831; F. O. 84/583, Aberdeen to Hamilton, June 4, and August 9, 1845; and F. O. 97/97, Scarlett to Clarendon, June 25, 1857. The most extreme expression occurs in W. D. Christie, *Notes on Brazilian Questions*.

ered Britain's actions as equivalent to an effort to maintain political control over its ally. In the opinion of one senator,[3] Great Britain wished to dominate Brazil; it desired that the weaker power should acknowledge a shameful protectorate unworthy of the Brazilian. An ambassador[4] who had served in London for many years asserted that "under the pretext of our old faults (which were numerous) the British legation assumed a tone of censure, of vigilance, of insufferable dominance." The foremost historian[5] of the founding of the empire complained that every argument with England was settled according to its own interpretation and the Brazilian nation was forced to submit to the violence and force of a stronger power. Writing in the 'sixties, the noted compiler[6] of Brazilian treaties asserted that although he admired the excellence of British institutions, rendered homage to its civic development, and valued the help of its capital in opening roads and developing national industries in Portuguese America, he could not" tolerate passively the affronts which this country" had "arrogated to itself to force" on Brazil. The drastic conduct of the English resulted, in his opinion, not in the abolition of the traffic (the Brazilians suppressed the trade by their own efforts), but in mutual resentment between the two nations.[7]

This hostile resentment of the weaker toward the stronger nation was reflected in the attitude of the Brazilian citizen as well as in that of the historian and statesman. The clearest expression of this point of view was given by Consul Pennell in his reports to Canning and Dudley[8]. In Bahia, he said, the general public seemed "to regard the Treaties with England on the Slave Trade, as the dictations of a superior authority, from

[3] Visconde de Jequitinhonha. Speech made in the Senate as quoted by Oliveira Lima, *O Imperio Brazileiro*, p. 211.

[4] Letter of Barão de Penedo to Rio Branco, May 6, 1856. Quoted by Oliveiro Lima, *op. cit.*, p. 212. Penedo was minister in London from 1855 to 1888.

[5] J. M. Pereira da Silva (author of the seven-volume *Historia da Fundação do Imperio Brasileiro*), *Memorias do Meu Tempo*, I, 101.

[6] Antonio Pereira Pinto, *Apontamentos para o Direito Internacional*, I, 386.

[7] *Ibid.*, p. 387.

[8] F. O. 84/71, Pennell to Canning, June 8, 1827; Pennell to Dudley, August 22, 1827.

which it is lawful to escape, rather than as compacts which they are bound to enforce." The opinion was current, moreover, that the Rio government had submitted to the conventions under duress, sacrificing the national dignity before the dictatorial power of England. This dictation by Great Britain was particularly odious to the public, he reported, since it was exerted over a weaker but friendly nation which, since independence, had favored English interests beyond all others. The conduct of the London court in attempting to abolish the traffic by all legitimate means was conceded to be highly honorable; but when Great Britain employed threats, it carried zeal to reprehensible lengths and violated the principles of non-intervention on which it professed to act.

These expressions indicate the deeply-rooted conviction[9] which existed in the minds of the Brazilians that England in its effort to stop the slave trade was intervening in the affairs of the empire in a manner which was not permissible under international usage and which evidenced a determination to force upon a weaker country policies favorable to the more powerful nation. An absolute emperor against the will of the elected representatives of the people[10] had undertaken obligations which the Brazilian nation was unable to renounce. The prince could be expelled from his throne, but the efforts of the Rio government to induce England to rescind or modify his engagements were entirely fruitless. The situation, therefore, resolved itself into a tale of distress in which the Brazilian government at Rio was caught between the two millstones of the inexorable pressure exerted by Great Britain to end the traffic and the dogged determination of the Brazilian public to continue it.

---

[9] Similar expressions might be multiplied. For others see article in the *Jornal do Commercio*, March 19, 1845, enclosed in Hamilton's dispatch to Aberdeen, F. O. 84/581, March 22, 1845; copies of speeches made in the Assembly of 1845, enclosed in Hamilton's dispatch to Aberdeen, F. O. 84/581, April 21, 1845; João Luiz Alvez, "A Questão do Elemento Servil. A Extincção do Traffico e a Lei de Repressão de 1850. Liberdade dos Nascituros," *Revista do Instituto Historico e Geographico Brasileiro*, Tomo Especial VI, Parte IV (1916), pp. 196-204, 206-208, 253.

[10] See *supra*, pp. 217-219.

Under these circumstances the position of the Rio court was difficult. Its first move was to try to obtain an extension of time beyond the stipulated period during which the traffic should be legal. Preliminary action in favor of an extension had been taken during negotiations of the convention itself when the two Brazilian plenipotentiaries presented a "reversal note" for the acceptance of Gordon. The note stipulated that Great Britain should enter into an understanding to be reached in London for a reasonable prolongation of the time agreed upon.[11] The British minister consented to transmit it to London although he assured the Brazilian agents in writing that he did not consider it more than an "observation" and that he could see no necessity for a prolongation of the time specified in the convention.[12]

Two years later, on the strength of this reversal note, Ambassador Itabayana in London proposed that the period of the final abolition be deferred.[13] Aberdeen not only refused[14] to encourage Itabayana in his efforts to obtain an extension,[15] but informed Ponsonby at Rio in categorical terms that "His Majesty's Government" refused "to admit any modification of that stipulation of the Convention of November 23rd 1826," which limited the slave trade to March 13, 1830.[16] When Itabayana persisted in the appeal for more time, Aberdeen was astonished at his "extraordinary misconception" of the value of the reversal note presented by the Brazilian plenipotentiaries; evidently, Brazil considered it had the right "to cancel solemn obligations of Treaty" on the strength of a "prefatory *observation* which was itself not complied with."[17]

---

[11] F. O., 84/56, Gordon to Canning, No. 1. November 27, 1826. Enclosure No. 6, conference of November 23. [12] *Ibid.*, No. 2 and enclosure No. 3.

[13] F. O., 84/84, Aberdeen to Ponsonby, No. 3. December 3, 1828.

[14] *Ibid.*, Draft, Aberdeen to Itabayana, September 15, 1828.

[15] Some consideration was given to the proposal, however, for a memorandum is included in this group of documents, advancing certain considerations which would tend to make it advisable for England to discuss Itabayana's proposal. The principal consideration was that an extension might be used to secure an equipment clause (*Ibid.*, Aberdeen to Ponsonby, No. 3, Enclosure 1).

[16] *Ibid.*, Aberdeen to Ponsonby, No. 3.

[17] *Ibid.*, Draft to Itabayana, November 29, 1828.

Despite emphatic denials by the British government[18] the report persisted in Rio that an extension of time was being arranged.[19] It was a futile hope, for beyond conceding that any slave vessel encountered at sea after March 13, 1830, would not be detained if it left the African coast before the date of expiration, Aberdeen refused to acquiesce in any modification whatever.[20] On October 1, 1829, the Rio *Gazetta* announced that after the tenth no passports to slavers would be granted,[21] and on March 13 of the following year the traffic in slaves from any part of the world to the coast of Brazil became illegal under the treaty between England and Brazil. Castlereagh's dream of securing an absolute prohibition of the slave trade to Brazil was realized.[22]

The traffic was forbidden but, instead of ceasing at the stipulated time, the importation of African Negroes grew steadily after 1830. The continuation of the trade in the face of treaty obligations was the principal source of that friction between the Rio and London courts which resulted in the decline of British political influence in Brazil; but there were certain allied questions which also contributed to the growing irritation. These may be grouped under three heads: England's desire to add an equipment clause to the convention prohibiting the trade; the disposal of captured slaves brought into Brazilian ports; and the finality of the decisions of the Sierra Leone commission. Each merits attention.

When Castlereagh secured for British cruisers the right to

[18] An official refusal to consider an extension of time was delivered to the Rio Government by the British minister early in 1829 (F. O. 84/95, Ponsonby to Aberdeen, No. 2. March 23, 1829).

[19] *Ibid.*, No. 4.

[20] *Ibid.*, Aberdeen to Ponsonby, No. 7; Aberdeen to Aston, Nos. 2 and 3; and Aberdeen to Itabayana, March 18, 1829.

[21] *Ibid.*, Aston to Aberdeen, No. 1. Issue of October 1.

[22] An effort was made to import free Negroes from Africa as colonists to supply the needed agricultural labor which was threatened by the cessation of the slave trade. Aberdeen ordered the British envoy to inform the Rio government that those Brazilians who participated in such a scheme would be treated as regular slave traders (F. O. 84/95, Aberdeen to Aston, No. 4; F. O. 84/95, Consular, No. 2, Weatherby to Bidwell, Rio, January 26, 1829; F. O. 84/111, Aston to Aberdeen, No. 2. March 27, 1830).

visit and search Brazilian ships in peace times, it was specifically stated that seizures would be permitted only in case illegal slaves were actually on board.[23] Evidence that the ship was a slaver, that it was outside the region in which legal traffic might take place, or that slaves had been on board on that particular voyage, was insufficient to warrant detention of the vessel. Consequently, Great Britain was seriously handicapped in its efforts to suppress the trade both before and after the prohibition of March 13, 1830. Slaves were assembled on the shores of Africa to be embarked only when darkness or fog made sailing comparatively safe from detection; and masters of vessels often threw slaves overboard to destroy the technical evidence of guilt when they were threatened with capture.[24] Ships fully equipped with hand and leg cuffs, chains, water casks, between decks, and food could sail unmolested to the coast of Africa, land at some secret point where a supply of slaves had been assembled, and escape to the high seas where the danger of capture was practically non-existent.[25] The evil could be remedied only by ordering the seizure of vessels equipped for the trade[26]; for armed with such a stipulation, the British cruiser could detain the Brazilian slaver on the outward as well as the inward voyage and on the coast of Africa before the swift flight after loading could be effected. To obtain

[23] See *supra*, pp. 173-174.

[24] W. L. Mathieson, *Great Britain and the Slave Trade, 1839-1865*, p. 13.

[25] Peter Leonard, *The Western Coast of Africa*, pp. 92-96.

[26] England attempted to secure an equipment clause in connection with other nations engaged in the traffic. In 1822 Spain agreed that evidence of slaves on board during that particular voyage warranted seizure, but a four year delay in ratification and difficulties of proving the presence of slaves on the voyage of the seizure rendered the provision useless. Holland (1823) and Sweden (1824) agreed to satisfactory equipment clauses. France (1833) agreed to equipment and breaking up clauses. Spain refused until 1835 when equipment and breaking up clauses were signed, but the severe penalties to be imposed by the Spanish government to make these clauses effective were delayed. Similar negotiations with Lisbon in 1835 broke down. By the Portuguese Bill of 1839 (August) the English Parliament authorized seizure of vessels flying the Portuguese flag if they were equipped for the traffic and in 1842 an agreement was reached between England and Portugal. Only Brazil and the United States resisted the pressure by Great Britain to secure equipment clauses (Mathieson, *Great Britain and the Slave Trade*, pp. 14-23).

Brazil's consent to that remedy England exerted every effort.

With the absolute prohibition of the trade set for March, 1830, an equipment clause became urgently necessary. Therefore, in obedience to instructions received from the Foreign Office, Gordon addressed a note to the Brazilian foreign minister in which he proposed that an article should be concluded which would establish "the illicit employment of ships by their *fitting up* and by general circumstances therein specified in lieu of the clause requiring proof of the *slaves having been actually embarked.*" Great Britain, he continued, considered it to be essential for the maintenance of the spirit and object of the slave trade treaty that such an article should be concluded. Furthermore, he advised the minister, the commissioners at Sierra Leone already had been given instructions to act in the spirit or principle of such an article.[27]

The proposal, which received no answer from the Rio court,[28] was revived in 1831 when Palmerston instructed *Chargé* Aston to bring the question of seizures of vessels fitted out for the trade before the Brazilian government.[29] Two years later[30] Consul General Ouseley again proposed negotiations, this time with some slight hope of success, he thought.[31] The present administration, he reported in a confidential letter,[32] was favorable to such a clause, but it was probable that "the Interest taken by the Inhabitants of this Country generally in defeating the Intentions of the Govt. and rendering negatory their efforts for an effective suppression of the illegal Traffic in question"

---

[27] F. O. 84/71, Gordon to Dudley, No. 3. December 24, 1827. British cruisers had already seized vessels equipped for the trade but without slaves on board when they were found north of the equator (since Castlereagh's convention the traffic north of the equator had been illegal). F. O. 84/71, Gordon to Dudley, No. 1; 84/84, Aberdeen to Ponsonby, No. 3.

[28] F. O. 84/84, Aberdeen to Ponsonby, No. 3, Enclosure: Draft, Aberdeen to Itabayana, December 1, 1828.

[29] F. O. 84/122, Palmerston to Aston, No. 9. October 8, 1831.

[30] Palmerston on May 7, 1833, sent authorization to Fox to conclude an additional article to the Convention of 1826, securing an equipment clause, provided he could prod the Brazilian government to action (F. O. 84/141, Palmerston to Fox, No. 2).

[31] F. O. 84/141, Ouseley to Palmerston, No. 14. July 4, 1833. [32] *Ibid.*

might succeed once more. In carrying on the negotiations, he was refraining from any mention of how effective the desired clause had proved to be in suppressing the Dutch trade, for the "Brazilian Chambers" would "be much less likely to object to any measure, however great its prospect of success, the effect of which" was "still uncertain, than to one that" had "been actually proved to be effective in suppressing the Slave Trade." Experience had shown them that despite every precaution exercised by the framers of the conventions, they had been able to evade the stipulations thereof. It was quite true, he concluded, that although the chambers did not wish to incur the odium of encouraging the trade, many representatives would be "very unwilling to adopt any measure that would in their opinion practically prevent it."

Ouseley read the situation correctly, for although the foreign minister expressed willingness to negotiate [33] and an additional convention was agreed upon, the lower chamber prevented ratification.[34] During the minority of D. Pedro II, the regency was forbidden to ratify any treaty of which the Assembly had not previously approved[35]; that body by delaying action on the proposed convention for eight months, was able, therefore, to prevent ratification.

This was not the first, nor the last, time that the lower house of the Assembly prevented action by the regency or the cabinet in the question of an equipment clause. In August of the previous year the Senate had passed a law for the better execution of the slave trade suppression only to have the lower house kill the project by adjourning the discussion and never voting on it. The famous Barbacena project of June 30, 1837, carrying

[33] F. O. 84/141, Ouseley to Palmerston, No. 18.

[34] The articles were signed by Henry S. Fox and Alves Branco, July 27, 1835. Fox presented his credentials as envoy extraordinary and minister plenipotentiary on August 25, 1833. The convention agreed that a vessel might be seized if *prima facie* evidence proved that it was destined for the traffic although no slaves were on board, condemned seizures were to be broken up before being sold, and ratifications were to be exchanged within eight months (Alves, "A Questão do Elemento Servil," p. 222).

[35] This was by the law of June 14, 1831, Art. 20. p. 1 (Alves, *op. cit.*, p. 222).

an equipment clause, was approved by the Senate but defeated in the Chamber of Deputies.[36] Two years later negotiations between the foreign offices at London and Rio were renewed, but the propositions presented by Great Britain on the basis of a memorandum drawn up by the Rio government were again declined. In 1842 the Brazilian foreign minister, in reply to further proposals by England, refused peremptorily even to enter into negotiations on the subject of the slave trade,[37] as the mere fact that the minister had entertained the possibility of conversations had aroused public opinion and disturbed the Chamber of Deputies.[38]

Aberdeen, accordingly, had recourse to force. He warned the Rio office that since Brazil declined to agree to stipulations which would enable the convention of 1826 to be executed efficiently, England intended "to take alone and by Her own Means the Steps which She" might "feel called upon to adopt for carrying into full and complete effect" the first article of that convention. Great Britain, therefore, would fall back upon that stipulation and seize all Brazilian slavers on the grounds of piracy unless the Brazilian government agreed to a convention similar to those signed by England with Spain in 1835 and with Portugal in 1842.[39]

Yet no convention including an equipment clause was ever agreed upon between the two countries[40]; for as long as the Aberdeen Bill of August 8, 1845, was in force, the Rio court refused to treat with England on any matter dealing with the means of suppressing the traffic.[41] When an equipment article sanctioned by Brazil finally came into existence, it was not the result of negotiations between the two nations; it was an act passed by the National Assembly to be effective

[36] Alves, *op. cit.*, pp. 221, 226-228.

[37] F. O. 84/583, Aberdeen to Hamilton, No. 10. June 14, 1845.

[38] Pereira da Silva, *Memorias do Meu Tempo*, I, 102-108.

[39] F. O. 84/583, Aberdeen to Hamilton, No. 10. The article referred to declared that the slave trade would be considered piracy after March 13, 1830.

[40] Renewed negotiations took place after the expiration of the convention in 1845 and the Aberdeen Bill of August 8, of the same year, but they ended in failure (F. O. 84/582, Hamilton to Aberdeen, Nos. 25, 35, 40, 42, 49, 52, and 55).

[41] Alves, *op. cit.*, p. 234.

in Brazilian territory or on the high seas when a Brazilian cruiser met a Brazilian slaver. In 1850 when the central government of the empire became firmly enough established to enforce its will in regard to the slave trade, an equipment clause was the first article of the drastic law passed to make the suppression effective.[42] England, therefore, never succeeded in obtaining from Brazil a formal acquiescence to the coveted agreement; but with the rapid extinction of the traffic after 1850, the necessity for an equipment clause ceased and that element of friction between the two governments was removed.

Thus Brazil resisted successfully the pressure exerted by England to secure an international convention containing an equipment clause. The second of the irritating questions related to the traffic, the disposal of the captured slaves, ran a similar course: continued friction arising from the enslavement of free Negroes by the Brazilians and the vigorous but unavailing protests of England from 1826 to 1850 culminated in action by the central government at Rio after it had fought its way to stability.

The case of the captured slave (*emancipado*) was presented by Consul General Ouseley in a report to Palmerston in 1833.[43] "In every instance," he asserted, "the humane Intentions of the Framers of the Convention of 1826" had been defeated as far as they related to the victims of the traffic.[44] Not one of the Africans taken from captured vessels and placed at the service of private individuals for a term of years had escaped from a more rigorous species of slavery. Every Brazilian authority from the highest to the lowest person, employed nominally to protect the Negro, was actively engaged in placing the Africans in a state of slavery beyond the reach of any remedy or interference from the British, or even from his own government. Old and worn out slaves were substituted for the *emancipado* who became a legal slave in place of the old one; Negroes

[42] Alves, "A Questão do Elemento Servil," p. 250, note 20.

[43] F. O. 84/141, Ouseley to Palmerston, No. 15. July 8.

[44] For the stipulations in regard to the disposal of captured slaves see *supra*, p. 175.

obtained by auction were sent to the interior far from the supervision of the government and beyond the investigation of the British agent; false certificates of death were produced, and, he concluded, "every device that unprincipled and unscrupulous cupidity" could "put in force, assisted by the connivance or support of those whose duty it was to prevent such proceedings" were "daily and hourly made use of in this country."[45]

Although this severe arraignment was quite accurate, the Brazilian government was not entirely to blame for the situation. It had taken steps already to remedy the evil, but they had proved abortive due to circumstances over which the Rio authorities had little control. Realizing that it would be impossible to guarantee freedom to *emancipados* as long as they remained in Brazil, the government included in the law of 1831,[46] passed to make the abolition of the trade effective, a provision that captured slaves should be exported to the coast of Africa with the greatest possible dispatch.[47] Six months later a decree of eleven articles was issued regulating the reëxportation of Africans liberated by capture in Brazilian territory.[48] But England immediately pointed out that this regulation was contrary to the convention of 1826 which provided for the emancipation of the captured slaves in Brazil itself,[49] and negotiations were begun in London and Rio to reconcile reëxporta-

---

[45] This was not the first complaint sent in by English representatives in Brazil. Consul Hesketh of Maranhão reported to Consul General Chamberlain that fake burial certificates were being used to enslave *emancipados* in the north (F. O. 84/71, Hesketh to Chamberlain, No. 2. February 27, 1827. Enclosure 1). In November, 1830, Aston reported that of 981 Africans sequestered from three vessels (sequestrations dated from September 9 and October 30) only 419 remained by November 20. Such excessive mortality was evidence of fraud, he contended (F. O. 84/111, Aston to Aberdeen, No. 15). For other complaints, see F. O. 84/122, Aston to Palmerston, No. 2; F. O. 84/129, Grigg to Palmerston, No. 7. Enclosure; Extract from the report of the minister of justice to the Assembly at the opening session of May, 1832.

[46] F. O. 84/120, Cunningham and Grigg to Palmerston, No. 18. Copies in Portuguese and in translation of the Law of November 7, 1831, are given.

[47] Article 2.

[48] F. O. 84/129, Grigg to Palmerston, No. 7. Copy of the decree of April 30, 1832, is given.

[49] F. O. 84/141, Ouseley to Palmerston, No. 1. February 13, 1833.

tion with the provisions of the 1817 and 1826 agreements.

Palmerston refusing to consider reëxportation on the ground that the fate of the Negro sent to Africa would be death on the return voyage or re-enslavement after landing, demanded that the law and decree be rescinded at once,[50] and blocked the efforts of Brazil to secure a safe destination for reëxported slaves. Various places in Africa and America were suggested; but the only one which received Palmerston's consent proved impossible of attainment,[51] economic difficulties preventing a satisfactory arrangement.[52] Until some agreement could be reached which would grant asylum for the reëxported slaves, Brazil was forced, therefore, to continue to dispose of captured Negroes by auction with the consequent abuses[53] complained of so bitterly by Ouseley.

As no agreement was ever reached, the disposal of the *emancipados* continued to be an irritating question between the two governments[54] until local legislation and the extinction of the traffic settled the problem. Article 6 of the law of 1850 stated categorically that captured slaves should not be auctioned to private individuals; in December, 1853, any *emancipado* who petitioned the proper authorities at the expiration of his fourteen years apprenticeship was declared free; and on September 24, 1864, emancipation was granted to all free Negroes in the empire.[55] Since the extinction of the traffic after 1850 had prevented the influx of additional *emancipados*, the second of the minor causes of friction between London and Rio fell from

---

[50] F. O. 84/141, Palmerston to Fox, No. 3, and No. 4, Enclosures.

[51] Sierra Leone, the West Indies, and British colonies on the northern coast of South America were refused by Palmerston. He favored negotiations with the United States in favor of exportation to Liberia (F. O. 84/141, Ouseley to Palmerston, Nos. 15 and 19; Palmerston to Ouseley, No. 7).

[52] *Correio Official*, April 24, 1835. Correspondence exchanged between Aureliano and Fox and Aureliano's report to the Assembly, dated August 9, 1834.

[53] *Ibid.*, May 20, 1835. Report of the minister of justice to the Assembly, dated May 20, 1835.

[54] The fate of the *emancipado* provoked Christie to severe criticisms of the Brazilian government in 1865 (*Notes on Brazilian Questions*, pp. 3-6, 38-39).

[55] Christie, *Notes*, pp. 38-39; Joaquim Nabuco, *Estadista do Imperio, Nabuco de Araujo, Sua Vida, Suas Opiniões, Sua Epoca*, I, 244.

sight. But as in the first case, Brazil had shown clear and unmistakable evidence of a successful revolt against the pressure exerted by Great Britain.

The third of the allied questions arising from England's attempts to suppress the traffic, the dispute over the finality of the decisions of the Sierra Leone commission, did not terminate in the same manner as the two already discussed. Since the commission existed by virtue of an international agreement, it could not be restricted by Brazil to national legislation; and instead of dropping into oblivion at its expiration in 1845, it left a heritage of claims to vex the foreign offices of both nations. The present discussion will be limited to the period during which the commission actually functioned.

By Castlereagh's convention of 1817, mixed commissions were set up, one on British territory in Africa and one on Brazilian soil in Brazil, to decide on the legality of seizures made under the terms of the convention. The Rio commission, which has been discussed in an earlier chapter,[56] never became an efficient instrument for the suppression of the slave trade. But the court at Sierra Leone, located on English territory and subject to the influence of the British Foreign Office, rendered decisions which aroused the Rio government to heated protest and left claims that remained unsettled for decades. In this case the revolt of Brazil against what its ministers termed the arbitrary and illegal proceedings of Great Britain proved ineffectual; yet the attempt was made and friction resulted.

[56] *Supra*, pp. 180-183. The inability to operate efficiently continued after the renewal of the 1817 convention was effected in 1826. It is fair to add, however, that the Rio government in the later period attempted to facilitate its operation (Brazil, Ministerio das Relaçoes Exteriores, *Relatorio da Repartição dos Negocios dos Extrangeiros apresentado a Assembléa Geral Legislativa*, 1839, pp. 4-5). Located in territory where public opinion strongly favored the traffic and severely hampered by the difficulties surrounding the disposal of the *emancipados*, the Rio commission was hopelessly handicapped. Consequently British cruisers began to take prizes seized in Brazilian waters to Cape of Good Hope or to Demerara colonies for adjudication instead of to the regular mixed commission (*Relatorio dos Negocios Extrangeiros*, 1841, p. 7, and 1844, p. 4). A list of vessels adjudicated by the Rio Commission between November 28, 1826, and September 13, 1845, is given in *Relatorio dos Negocios Extrangeiros*, 1846, pp. 17-21.

Trouble was precipitated by the case of the slave ship *Activo*, which was brought before the Sierra Leone mixed commission in May, 1826. The capture had taken place south of the equator (the traffic was permitted south of the line until 1830) and no slaves were on board at the moment of seizure; but it was fairly well established that three hundred slaves escaped to the shore and that the ship had obtained the Negroes from north of the equator. The claim for damages entered by the owners for illegal seizure was awarded by the commission, but payment of damages was to be made only if the governments should decide that such claims were "according to the true interest and meaning of the Convention." In September of the same year, another slaver, the *Perpetuo Defensor*, was brought in under similar circumstances and received the same sentence. Four months later the *Heroina* was captured north of the equator with no slaves on board but with all the equipment necessary for the transportation of Negroes.[57] All of these ships were returned to the owners by the court since the letter of the convention had not been violated, but the claims of compensation for illegal seizure were to be decided upon by the two governments.

The decision was a shrewd one in that it forced negotiations on the legality of seizure when a vessel was obviously engaged in illegal traffic although no slaves were actually on board. Minister Gordon immediately invited the Brazilian government to issue "a joint declaration which" should "set at rest the above and all the future cases of the same nature," by authorizing the seizure of vessels with or without slaves on board if they were found in places where the trade was not permitted.[58]

By the convention of 1817 authorizing visit and search, detention on such grounds was illegal if judgment was rendered

---

[57] For the detailed correspondence relating to the three cases, see: F. O. 84/84, Aberdeen to Ponsonby, No. 3 and Enclosures: drafts, Aberdeen to Itabayana, December 1 and 2, 1828; 84/84, Gordon to Dudley, No. 2; 84/95, Draft, Aberdeen to Itabayana, March 17, 1829.

[58] F. O. 84/71, Gordon to Dudley, No. 1, July 5, 1827.

according to the letter of the law; and Brazil at once demanded that a special commission be appointed to review the decisions of the Sierra Leone court.[59] But an appeal from the decisions of the mixed commissions was forbidden by the same convention, and Aberdeen laconically refused to entertain any such proposal.[60] Later, he confessed that there had been an evident breach of the treaty in the cases of the *Activo* and the *Perpetuo Defensor*, but indemnities had been awarded "provided the British and Brazilian Governments" agreed in declaring "that the said sums ought to be paid according to the said Convention and *not otherwise.*" It was not the fault of England, he continued, that the agreement in question had not been concluded, since the Brazilian government had maintained a studied silence in the face of Gordon's repeated efforts to conclude an additional clause to the convention of 1826.[61] As to the *Heroina*, Aberdeen replied somewhat scornfully that since Brazil had violated the convention in respect to the issuance of passports to slavers,[62] "England had no alternative" but to consider such action as the expression of "Brazil's determination to break the Convention" and orders had been issued to the commissioners "to use the latitude thus given to the meaning of the Convention." The *Heroina* was the result of one such capture. If Brazil did not like this point of view, it could obey the convention or sign an article containing an equipment clause.[63] He

[59] F. O. 84/84, Aberdeen to Ponsonby, No. 3, Enclosures: drafts, Aberdeen to Itabayana, September 15 and November 29, 1828.

[60] *Ibid.*

[61] *Ibid.*, No. 3, Enclosure: draft, Aberdeen to Itabayana, December 1, 1828. The negotiations referred to were those begun by Gordon in an effort to secure an equipment clause. By the shrewd manipulation of the Sierra Leone Commission the question of an equipment clause was thus forced to an issue. See *supra*, pp. 225-230.

[62] Aberdeen asserted that "the Brazilian Government themselves have departed in respect to the Passports, both from the spirit and the letter of the original Convention: not only by allowing their subjects to infringe with impunity, the stipulations of the Convention with respect to the Passports actually granted to them [the *Heroina* had no papers permitting it to land north of the equator and should not have been in waters north of the line]" but by issuing passports at variance with the terms of the convention (F. O. 84/84, Aberdeen to Ponsonby, No. 3, Enclosure; draft, Aberdeen to Itabayana, December 2).

[63] *Ibid.*

ordered Gordon to inform the Rio government, therefore, that England refused to establish a commission to revise the decisions of the Sierra Leone court, that such sentences were final and without appeal, and that British cruisers would continue to stop illicit trade by seizing slavers north of the equator under similar circumstances.[64]

Cruisers assigned to the coast of Africa continued to bring in vessels suspected of illicit traffic regardless of whether Negroes were actually on board and the commission continued to release the ships but to refuse claims of compensation for time and expense incurred by the slavers.[65] In answer to further protests by the Brazilian minister at London, Aberdeen explained that the cruisers and the court were acting "in strict accordance with the spirit of the Convention."[66]

Since Great Britain refused to consider a special commission to revise the decisions of the Sierra Leone court, Brazil's next step was to attempt to abolish the tribunal entirely. The mixed commissions, Rio maintained, had been established to decide the legality of seizures while the traffic was permitted; but when abolition came in 1830, there was "nothing for those courts to decide upon and therefore all sentences pronounced by them after the 13th of March, 1830," had to "be considered as complete nullities." Moreover, one injustice after another had been perpetrated by the commission: vessels without slaves on board had been condemned; ships that had proved they were not engaged in the trade and others that had just begun voyages and had not been near the African coast had been detained; seizures had been made by vessels other than author-

---

[64] F. O. 84/84, Aberdeen to Ponsonby, No. 3. When Itabayana protested such seizures and demanded that the cruisers be instructed not to detain vessels on which no slaves were actually found, Aberdeen refused (F. O. 84/95, Aberdeen to Ponsonby, March 24, 1829).

[65] The *Minerva*, *Cerqueira*, and *Creola* were detained by cruisers and brought before the commission (F. O. 84/95, draft, Aberdeen to Itabayana, March 10, 1829). Other seizures were: *Tres Amigos*, *Tentadora*, *Eclipse*, *Venturoso*, *Esperanza*, *Voador*, and *Vencedora* (F. O. 84/111, draft, Aberdeen to Chev. de Mattos, December 10, 1830).

[66] F. O. 84/95, draft, Aberdeen to Itabayana, March 17, 1829. The seizures continued after March 13, 1830, south as well as north of the equator.

ized ships of war; some vessels had been detained but never tried; and others that had been granted indemnities had never received payment. The commission had exceeded its authority and had adopted a code of action agreeable to its own fancy. Therefore the imperial government felt justified in attacking the proceedings at Sierra Leone.[67]

Again Britain refused to accede to the demand made by the Rio Government, for Palmerston pointed out that by the separate article annexed to the treaty of 1817, the mixed commissions were to continue until some new arrangement should be reached, or, in case such an agreement was not made, until fifteen years after the date set for the final abolition. As no arrangement had been concluded between the two governments, the commissions would continue. And furthermore, England could not acquiesce in any re-opening of cases already decided by the court at Sierra Leone.[68]

The negotiations had reached an *impasse* from which they never emerged. In 1833 the Rio government made its last futile effort to secure an appeal from the decisions of the Sierra Leone court[69]; and when Palmerston remained obdurate, the Chevalier de Mattos delivered a formal notice, dated November 30, in which he stated that his government protested most solemnly against the injustice and arbitrary decision of Great Britain and denied that the enforced silence on the subject, which

[67] F. O. 84/122, Palmerston to Mattos, August 16 and September 16, 1831; and F. O. 84/122, Palmerston to Aston, No. 3, Enclosure.

[68] F. O. 84/122, drafts, Palmerston to Mattos, August 16 and September 16, 1831. The Sierra Leone commission frequently acted without the full quota of Brazilian commissioners as the unhealthy and desolate character of the town led representatives nominated by the Rio government to delay sailing or to refuse to accept the post. This was one cause for the evident anti-Brazilian bias demonstrated by the commission (F. O. 84/141, Ouseley to Palmerston, No. 9. May 28, 1833).

[69] Brazil offered to submit the revision to the arbitration of a third power, but Palmerston could "see no reason to doubt the principle upon which" the English government "declined to submit the Sentences of the Mixed Commission Court to revision" and refused to consider the arbitration of a third power (F. O. 84/141, drafts of correspondence exchanged between Palmerston and Mattos, January 26, March 6, May 3 and May 18, November 30, and December 13, 1833). This correspondence was the culmination of the whole matter and served later as the basis for each side in the claims question.

would follow the protest, would in any way prejudice the right of his government to enter claims for damages at a later date.[70] On March 13, 1845, the convention signed in 1826 terminated; the mixed courts continued to sit for six months in order to dispose of cases arising prior to the expiration of the convention[71]; and on September 13, both the Rio and the Sierra Leone mixed commissions dissolved. The third question relating to the suppression of the trade disappeared from the stage, leaving behind a legacy of claims that were to vex Anglo-Brazilian relations for decades. In dealing with all three questions, the Rio court revealed a growing spirit of rebellion against political dictation from London.

These three elements of friction in Anglo-Brazilian relations after 1827 were merely phases of the main point at issue between the two governments. As long as the slave trade continued, the question of the equipment clause, the disposal of the *emancipados*, and the validity of the decisions of the Sierra Leone commission remained to vex both countries. When the traffic stopped, with the exception of the legacy of claims, these issues vanished, leaving behind, however, a heritage of bitter recollections in the minds of the South Americans and a tradition of Brazilian procrastination and duplicity in the British Foreign Office. The main problem throughout the period, therefore, was to stop the traffic itself.

Nominally, the slave trade ceased on March 13, 1830, but there is abundant evidence that importations continued steadily after that date. From 1824 to 1827, the period comprised between the success of the revolution in Brazil and recognition by European powers, the average annual importation into Rio[72] was slightly above twenty-five thousand Negroes actually landed. With the announcement of the formal cessation of the traffic set for 1830, the number of Africans brought to the city

[70] F. O. 84/141, Draft, Mattos to Palmerston, November 30, 1833.

[71] F. O. 84/583, Aberdeen to Hamilton, No. 10. June 4, 1845.

[72] The figures for the northern regions are incomplete but the statistics for Rio, gathered by the British consul and faithfully reported to London, may be considered sufficiently accurate.

jumped to 47,450 in 1828; to 57,108 in 1829; and to 32,229 in 1830, a year in which no slaver legally could leave the coasts of Africa later than March 13.[73] For the next few years, the traffic declined since the unusual number brought in between 1827 and 1830 over-supplied the demand.[74] The average price of a young, healthy, male slave previous to the abolition was about £70; in the early months of 1831, the price fell to £55; and by July a low mark of £35 was reached.[75] Yet the illicit importations continued despite the decline in price. The *Aurora Fluminense* complained in November of the same year that Negroes were landed at nearby points, marched through the streets of Rio, and sold at public auction without action being taken by the police.[76]

In 1835 the minister of justice reported regretfully that the traffic continued; the provisions of the treaties were being evaded and the law ignored. The "furor of this barbarous traffic," he lamented, "seemed to progress from day to day with constantly increasing force."[77] The following year the minister[78] confessed to the national Assembly that it was impossible to remedy the evils of the traffic by the methods then in force.

In 1842, twelve years after the nominal cessation of the trade, importations still continued. Exact statistics of course are impossible to obtain and figures vary widely. Christie asserted that over seventy thousand Negroes were imported in that year.[79] The Brazilian government officially estimated the num-

---

[73] These figures are taken from F. O., Brazil, Consular and Diplomatic Reports, General Correspondence, 1825-1830. They do not include the number which died during the passage. In 1827, there died on the voyage over 1,154 with 25,191 landed; 2,539 died on the way in 1828; the number increased to 5,189 in 1829, and fell to 3,332 in 1830.

[74] Alves, "A Questaõ do Elemento Servil," p. 217.

[75] F. O. 84/122, Pennell to Palmerston, No. 7. July 23, 1831. The price of the slave in Africa was £5 (*ibid.*).

[76] Article in the issue of November 30, 1830. Enclosed in F. O. 84/120, Cunningham and Grigg to Palmerston, No. 18.

[77] *Correio Official*, May 20, 1835. Report of Alves Branco to the Assembly.

[78] Antonio Paulino Limpo de Abreo succeeded Alves Branco as minister of justice. The citation is from his report to the Assembly, given in *Correio Official*, May 27, 1836.

[79] *Notes*, pp. 51-53.

ber to be 17,435; and by 1845 the importation crept up to nearly twenty thousand, according to the same authority.[80] Just where the truth lies between Christie's seventy thousand and Rio's seventeen thousand importations, it is impossible to ascertain; but the fact is undeniable that a steady stream of Africans poured into Brazil in spite of the nominal abolition of the trade in 1830. Neither the pressure exerted by Great Britain nor the efforts of the central government at Rio sufficed to stop the traffic between 1830 and 1845.

It is equally certain, however, that both England and the Rio government tried to accomplish the desired result. The persistent, though ineffectual, attempts of Great Britain to secure an equipment clause and the instructions sent to the Sierra Leone commission to act according to the spirit and not the letter of the convention of 1826 demonstrate the determination of the British to employ every means possible to hinder the illicit trade. In addition to the African squadron maintained to prevent the slave traffic, a special fleet was kept off the coast of Brazil. In 1833 Ouseley reported to Palmerston that the Rio government had implied a wish that more British cruisers of a light and small class should be sent to the Brazilian coast. Such vessels should be small enough to follow the slavers into the lesser harbors and mouths of rivers; armed steam vessels independent of the winds would be the most serviceable.[81] In 1839, according to the report of the minister of foreign affairs,[82] British cruisers had captured 1763 Negroes since his last report; and two years later detained slavers were being taken by these cruisers to the Cape of Good Hope or to the Demarara Islands for adjudication instead of to the regular mixed commission at Rio.[83] In 1844 English vessels were detaining ships flying the

[80] Brazil, *Relatorio dos Negocios Extrangeiros*, 1852, xiii. The figures are from a paper ordered printed March 26, 1852, extracts of which are given in this report to the Assembly by the minister of foreign affairs.

[81] F. O. 84/141, Ouseley to Palmerston, No. 8. May 2, 1833.

[82] Brazil, *Relatorio dos Negocios Extrangeiros*, 1839, pp. 4-5. Between 1810 and 1846 English cruisers captured and liberated, from slavers of all nationalities, 116,862 slaves (Mathieson, *Great Britain and the Slave Trade*, p. 123. His authority is a return in Parliamentary Papers, 1847-1848, vol. LXIV).

[83] Brazil, *Relatorio dos Negocios Extrangeiros*, 1841, p. 7.

Brazilian flag within Brazilian ports before they sailed, although the evident destination was another national port; the capture of the *Maria Theresa* by Commander Hoare of the *Dolphin* at Ubatuba was cited as a case in point.[84] The persistence of the British cruisers in Brazilian waters finally became so disturbing to the coastwise trade of the nation that Aberdeen was forced by protests from Rio to issue orders that no seizures should be made in territorial waters without the express approval of the local authorities.[85]

That England was sincere in its efforts to suppress the trade needs little proof; it is more difficult to demonstrate that the central government at Rio likewise endeavored to restrict the illicit importation of Negroes. Yet the Rio authorities were in favor of the abolition of the traffic and took what steps were in their power to make the abolition effective. Ouseley testified in 1833 to the "desire of the Imperial Government to prevent that odious and impolitic traffic" but it was unsupported and found its efforts counteracted in almost every case.[86] When one of the three regents was discovered to be involved in the trade, the other high officials were greatly embarrassed.[87] As a matter of fact, Ouseley reported,[88] the government was "probably sincere in its wish to prevent the introduction of Negroes," but "the feeling against the Slave Trade" was "by no means universal among the Inhabitants generally." To this testimony by a keen British agent of long experience in Brazil may be added the admission of Hamilton-Hamilton that there was no dissenting opinion in the ministry to the prevailing one that there was urgent need for suppressing the slave trade.[89]

This desire of the central authorities to suppress the trade is

[84] *Ibid.*, 1844, p. 4. The *Vencedora*, *Tartaruga*, *Anna*, and *Relampago* suffered the like fate. The Brazilians protested this action as being detrimental to their coastwise trade (p. 18). The case of the *Maria Theresa* was decided in favor of the Brazilians and the captor was censured, but the seizures continued.

[85] *Ibid.*, p. 20.

[86] F. O. 84/141, Ouseley to Palmerston, No. 8.

[87] *Ibid.*, No. 16. Confidential. July 13, 1833.

[88] *Ibid.*, No. 3.

[89] F. O. 13/212, Hamilton to Aberdeen, No. 47. June 8, 1844.

evidenced by the various measures promoted by the government after 1830. That these were inadequate in the first place or were rendered ineffectual after enactment does not prove the want of determination on the part of the Rio court, for circumstances beyond the control of the central power prevented the effective execution of its will until 1848. In spite of public disapproval, the Brazilian government sincerely attempted to make the prohibition of the slave trade effective.

The first of its measures was proposed on the last day of May, 1831, when the Marquez de Barbacena introduced a project into the Senate, which had as its purpose the enactment of the national regulations necessary to make the international agreement effective. It was approved, sent to the Chamber of Deputies in June, and became a law November 7 after having been amended by the lower house.[90] By the terms of the statute, all slaves entering the territory of Brazil in the future were declared free[91]; the importer of illicit slaves was to be punished according to the terms imposed by the criminal code on those who reduced free persons to slavery, with the added penalty of a fine of two hundred milreis per head plus the expense of reëxportation to Africa. "Importers" were defined as the commander, master, and mate of the vessel; the actual owner and the previous title holder in case he was aware of the intended purpose of the purchase; any one who invested in the enterprise or rendered assistance in any way whatsoever in the preparation, the voyage itself, or the landing of the slaves; and anyone who knowingly bought slaves brought in by such importers. In case slavers were captured beyond the territorial waters of Brazil by national vessels the same process would hold as in the case of seizures in national ports. Thirty milreis reward for each person apprehended was granted to informers; the commander, officers, and crew of the vessel effecting a seizure on the seas

---

[90] Alves, "A Questão do Elemento Servil," pp. 206-210. The text of the law is given *verbatim*, pp. 210-211, note 21. It is also to be found in Great Britain, *British and Foreign State Papers*, XX, 165. A printed copy in Portuguese with a translation was enclosed in F. O. 84/120, Cunningham and Grigg to Palmerston, No. 18.

[91] Exception was made of slaves in the service of ships flying the flag of a country where slavery was lawful.

were to divide the fines as a reward. Negroes brought in from Africa as free laborers would not be permitted to land on Brazilian territory, the officials of the vessel importing such Negroes being subject to a fine of a hundred milreis and costs of reëxportation. Any amounts over expenses and rewards accruing from seizures were to be used for foundling asylums or hospitals in the provinces in which the seizures occurred.[92]

Although the bill was a very real effort to comply with the convention abolishing the traffic and was the best that could be done under the circumstances,[93] it was inadequate. The trade was not declared piracy nor was an equipment article included; and the reëxportation scheme, a sincere effort of the Brazilian government to remedy the evils arising from the disposal of freed slaves,[94] was blocked by England as being contrary to the terms of the convention of 1826. Three years later the Senate, influenced by the Regency, attempted to remedy the worst defect of the bill by passing a law in which an equipment article was included, but the Chamber of Deputies killed the project, as we have already noted, by adjourning discussion.[95] The additional articles including the desired clause, negotiated the next year between the foreign offices of Rio and London, failed also.

In 1837 Barbacena again presented a project which, in balancing opposing interests, attempted to secure effective meas-

---

[92] Articles I-IX, respectively.

[93] Alves, "A Questão do Elemento Servil," p. 211.

[94] By decree of April 12, 1832, the Regency attempted to regulate the reëxportation of captured slaves. All vessels should be searched by the police or by a justice of the peace immediately after arrival and before departure for evidence of illicit slave trading; any blacks found on board were to be noted, a minute description of physical characteristics written down, and a check-up on departure to be made by the authorities to see that they left the country; if blacks should prove to be illicit slaves or free laborers, they were to be seized and reëxported at the expense of the importer; deaths of blacks while in port were not to be valid unless the actual body was produced and checked by the description; sales of Negroes recently brought from Africa (the *boçal* was easily distinguished by his state of savagery) should be investigated by the authorities to see if the black was landed before March 13, 1830 (F. O. 84/129, Grigg to Palmerston, No. 7. Enclosure).

[95] The bill passed the Senate on August 21, 1834 (Alves, "A Questão do Elemento Servil," p. 221).

ures for operation on the high seas by relinquishing the gain made within the national territory. The bill, which passed the Senate on August 9, included an equipment clause, but article XIII revoked the law of November 7, 1831. Seizure, therefore, might be made on the high seas in case the vessel was equipped for the trade; but once the slaver was in Brazilian territory, he would be safe as there would be no national law forbidding importation.[96] The Chamber of Deputies once again defeated the project of the Senate.

In the meantime, efforts were made to stop the traffic by propaganda in the government newspapers[97] and by maintaining armed vessels along the coast. In 1833 the minister of marine requested that there be placed at his disposal the "most efficacious means" of stopping the traffic, namely, a sufficient number of small vessels armed and equipped to capture slavers. The two schooners under his orders for that purpose were inadequate and he requested a greater number,[98] the need for which was especially urgent in view of the fact that he had already promised a man-of-war to patrol the coast of the province of São Paulo.[99] In May of the same year Consul General Ouseley reported the sincere lamentations expressed by the Rio ministry over the inadequacy of the means at its disposal and advised the Foreign Office of the desire, implied by the Brazilian minister, to see more British cruisers off the coast of Brazil.[100] Four years later the foreign minister was urging the Assembly to take some action on the articles signed by Alves Branco and Minister Fox on July 27, 1835,[101] while he re-

---

[96] Alves, "A Questão do Elemento Servil," p. 228.

[97] *Correio Official*, February 20, 1836 and May 27, 1836; *Jornal do Commercio*, April 24, 1830 (enclosed in F. O. 84/129, Grigg to Palmerston, No. 7); *Diario do Povo*, April 24, 1832 (enclosed in F. O. 84/129, Grigg to Palmerston, No. 13).

[98] Report of May, 1833. Enclosed in F. O. 84/138, Rio Commission to Palmerston, No. 8. June 17, 1833.

[99] The president of the province wrote to the minister, explaining the hopeless nature of the attempts to prevent the landing of illicit slaves and requesting the man-of-war (F. O. 84/138, Rio Commission to Palmerston, No. 13. November 12, 1833).

[100] F. O. 84/141, Ouseley to Palmerston, No. 8.

[101] *Relatorio dos Negocios Extrangeiros*, 1837, p. 6. The articles referred to were the

gretted the futility of the efforts made by the government to suppress the traffic.[102]

It is clear, therefore, that the Rio government attempted to stop the traffic. Handicapped by popular opinion which favored the importation of Negroes, it was unable to carry out its wish, and Great Britain, by the arbitrary nature of the methods employed to suppress the trade, failed to ease the situation in which the central government found itself. Incapable of stopping the traffic and unable to coöperate with England because such coöperation meant submitting to measures which would make Brazil virtually a British protectorate, the Brazilian authorities were helpless in the face of the dilemma. Although both governments wished to achieve the same object, their common purpose failed to bring united action; instead, the friction which began immediately after the signing of the convention of 1826 increased in bitterness until the crisis of 1845 ended even the pretense of coöperation between London and Rio.

The issue was forced in 1845 by the expiration of the fifteen years during which the convention of 1826 was to be in force. The agreement had never been satisfactory to England and repeated efforts[103] had failed to secure the desired modification; yet the convention was the basis for the existence of the Sierra Leone commission and it granted to British cruisers the precious right to visit and search Brazilian merchantmen in time of peace. If the agreement were allowed to expire, Great Britain, at a time when importations were numbered by increasing thousands, would be deprived of the only two instruments that had yielded results in checking the traffic. On the other hand, Brazil would be freed from the detested legacy inherited from an absolutist prince who had foisted the agreement upon his people under pressure from a stronger power. The issue

---

stipulations contained in the additional convention signed by the plenipotentiaries but unratified due to the refusal of the Chamber of Deputies to accept them.

[102] *Ibid.*, 1838, p. 14.

[103] On an average of every two years between 1827 and 1844 England attempted negotiations with a view to modifying the convention. In 1827, 1829, 1831, 1835, 1837, 1839-40, and 1841-43 more or less formal discussions occurred.

was clearly defined: could England, by repeating the exploit of 1825-27, secure the acceptance of Brazil to a convention which in popular opinion was derogatory to the dignity and national interests of the nation?

A warning was sounded at the time of the Ellis mission in 1842 that a renewal of the 1826 agreement was profoundly distasteful to the Brazilian public. When it was announced that D. Pedro had nominated representatives to treat with the English plenipotentiary, great apprehension was manifested in all classes of society. Brazilians of every rank were anxious to have the convention terminate with the result that public opinion "was energetically resolved to reject any convention whatsoever with England." The minister of foreign affairs, Aureliano de Souza e Oliveira Coutinho, lost popularity and his brother, who was running for election to the Assembly, was defeated, due in large part to the disgust of the public over the conduct of the minister. So uncertain was the Assembly itself over the question of Aureliano's ability to sustain Brazilian rights in the face of British pressure, that it demanded the entire correspondence exchanged between the minister and the English envoy. When his successor, Honorio Hermeto, broke off the negotiations, he won amazing signs of public favor.[104]

No agreement was ever reached, despite long negotiations in Rio and London,[105] and on March 12, 1845, Hamilton received a note from the Brazilian Foreign Office, which stated succinctly that "under the Stipulations for the Slave Trade Convention between Great Britain and Brazil, the Conven-

[104] Pereira da Silva, *Memorias*, I, 99-108. Henry Ellis presented his credentials as envoy extraordinary on November 19, 1842. He continued with Honorio Hermeto Carneiro Leão the negotiations begun by Hamilton for the renewal of the treaty of commerce and the slave trade convention (Brazil, Ministerio das Relações Exteriores, *Relações Diplomaticas do Brasil, contendo os nomes dos Representantes Diplomaticos do Brazil no extrangeiro e dos representantes Diplomaticos dos diversos paises no Rio de Janeiro de 1808 a 1912*, p. 175). Honorio Hermeto succeeded Aureliano as foreign minister on January 20, 1843 (F. O. 13/227, Supplement, Foreign Ministers of Brazil, 1822-1845).

[105] Hamilton continued negotiations in Rio after Ellis' failure, but his efforts dealt largely with the commercial treaty. The details of the negotiations are discussed in the chapter on the economic phase of Anglo-Brazilian relations.

tion of July 28, 1817, would cease to have force and effect from the day following; and that consequently from that date, namely, the 13th of the month, would cease the right of visit and search provided for by the said convention of July 28, 1817," with all the additional articles, instructions, and provisions appended thereto. The mixed commissions would sit for six months longer to finish cases that might be pending, if England agreed to the extension in time.[106] On the following day the minister of justice notified the courts of law of the cessation of the right of visit and search, and informed them that until further instructions captured slavers would be tried in the ordinary courts.[107]

The notice of expiration was received with approval by the Brazilian public. An article in the *Jornal do Commercio*[108] asserted that the cessation of the terms of the convention was "a motive for congratulations as regards" Brazilian "National Commerce, which" was "thus freed from the vexations to which it" had "been subjected by the violence of the British cruisers, and which would have annihilated it entirely; and it" was "also a motive for" Brazilians sincerely "to congratulate the English Merchants established in the Country, to whom the new order of things" could not "but be advantageous." Moreover, the article continued, no one was "ignorant of the progressive prosperity of British Commerce in Brazil since 1808, of the benevolence which Englishmen met with, of the Confidence with which they came to the Country, and of the good reception and preference which they encountered; but everyone" knew "also that from 1835, the period when the violences of the British cruisers commenced, and were exercised without measure, and even in contempt of the Treaties, that confidence and mutual kindly feeling began to be weakened and an irritation of minds appeared, which unhappily manifested itself

[106] F. O. 84/581, Hamilton to Aberdeen, No. 8. The note is given also in *Relatorio dos Negocios Extrangeiros*, 1846, Supplement, Document 1.

[107] F. O. 84/581, Hamilton to Aberdeen, No. 8.

[108] Hamilton sent the article to London as an example of the opinion commonly held by the Brazilians. It was published in the issue of March 19, 1845.

more than once in acts, and which at length might have produced the most fearful consequences."

The article concluded with a significant paragraph. "We who acknowledge," it said, "how advantageous the produce of the Industry of England, and its capital are to Brazil; we who believe that no Foreign Commerce is more useful to the Country, desire that the former good feeling be reëstablished and therefore we sincerely wish that the Right of Visit, happily terminated, be interred forever."

Another illustration both of the resentment felt by the Brazilians against the arbitrary position assumed by England and of their relief over the termination of the Convention occurred in the speeches given in the session of the Assembly of March 31. One speaker[109] pointed out that the offended nationality of the Brazilians appeared desirous of supporting the traffic, "if only in despite of England. If there was not a nation," he said with perhaps more emotion than veracity, "pretending to impose the laws on" Brazilians, certainly their "Christian feelings, their patriotism" would have made them "reflect upon the matter, and it" was "not possible that so many sessions would have passed away without some steps having been taken to put an end to the traffic in some manner or other, but treated" as the Brazilians had been, they had on their part "tried to uphold the traffic if it were only to show" their resistance.

This rejoicing over the termination of the right of visit and search was premature, for Aberdeen had no intention of relinquishing the advantage which England had stubbornly maintained for thirty years. In reply to the Brazilian note of March 12, 1845, advising him of the termination of the convention and the cessation of the right of visit and search, he sent an ominous warning[110] to the government at Rio. In a detailed review of the history of Anglo-Brazilian relations since

---

[109] Junqueira's speech was forwarded to London by Hamilton, F. O. 84/581, Hamilton to Aberdeen, No. 25. April 21, 1845.

[110] F. O. 84/583, Aberdeen to Hamilton, No. 10. June 4, 1845. Instructions for an official communication to be presented to the Brazilian government.

1828 in so far as they related to the slave trade, he pointed out England's efforts to obtain efficient coöperation from the Brazilian government and the failure to reach an agreement which would serve as a basis for the complete suppression of the traffic. When the negotiations of 1840-41 failed, he had warned Rio that if the Brazilian government still declined "to enter with Great Britain into formal engagements calculated to give full effect to the declared intentions of the Parties of the Convention of 1826 for the total and final abolition of the Slave Trade of Brazil," it would "remain for Her Majesty to take alone and by Her Own Means the steps which she" might "feel called upon to adopt for carrying into full and complete effect the humane object of the obligations imposed upon Her Majesty by the first Article of the Convention."[111]

The warning, he continued, passed unheeded, the next communication from the Rio Office being the notification of March 12. He admitted that according to the terms of the agreement, the convention of 1817 with all its annexes terminated on March 13 last; but in that case, he affirmed, England was forced to fall back on the stipulation of the first article of the convention of 1826, "*under which Her Majesty*" had "*acquired the right to order the seizure of all Brazilian subjects found upon the high seas engaged in the Slave Trade, of punishing them as pirates, and of disposing of their vessels in which they*" might "*be captured together with the goods belonging to them as 'bona piratoram'.*" Great Britain had hoped to the very last moment that Rio would not force it to this step; but it now had no alternative but to advise the Brazilian government that the necessary legislation would be proposed in the English Parliament for the complete execution of that article.[112]

In pursuance of the intentions announced in this letter, Aberdeen had a bill introduced in Parliament giving to the courts of admiralty the "power to take cognizance of and to adjudicate upon all" Brazilian "vessels captured for carrying on the

[111] The first article declared the slave trade to be piracy.

[112] Aberdeen agreed to the extension of time granted to the mixed commissions to enable them to close pending cases.

Slave Trade." Cruisers would continue to detain and visit slavers as under the conditions specified by the convention of 1826; but instead of taking prizes to the mixed commission for adjudication, they were to bring them before British admiralty or vice-admiralty courts.[113] At the same time Aberdeen instructed his agent at Rio to inform the Brazilian government that this bill would not be passed, or in case it became law, it would be repealed, if the Brazilian trade should cease entirely or the Rio government should enter into satisfactory agreement with Great Britain.[114]

The bill became law on August 8, 1845, and on the next day, Aberdeen sent Hamilton instructions[115] for concluding a new agreement with Brazil. The annexes and stipulations of Castlereagh's convention of 1817 were to be renewed; seizures by English cruisers were to be authorized on the grounds of equipment for the trade; and the duration of the new agreement was to be for a specified length of time with a stated number of months to pass after the notification of termination by either country. In a confidential aside to his agent, Aberdeen added that in case of abrogation by Brazil, England could again revert to the methods of suppression announced in the bill just passed.

Any hope of a new convention, however, was dissipated by the passage of the Aberdeen Bill. Negotiations for a new agreement were already under way[116] when news of the enactment into law of the warning issued by the English Foreign Office blocked further proceedings. Limpo de Abreu, Brazilian foreign minister, advised Hamilton that the "new act of the British Parliament was virtually a menace" and that a renewal of the old convention would be "inadequate and unprofitable to Brazil unless some stipulation offering more positive security to her Coasting Trade" was included.[117] Full powers were is-

[113] Great Britain, *British and Foreign State Papers*, XXXIV, 1216-1219; F. O. 4/583, Aberdeen to Hamilton, No. 12.

[114] F. O. 84/583, Aberdeen to Hamilton, No. 12.

[115] *Ibid.*, No. 18.

[116] F. O. 83/582, Hamilton to Aberdeen, Nos. 25, 31, and 35.

[117] *Ibid.*, No. 40.

sued to a Brazilian plenipotentiary to negotiate with Hamilton[118] but nothing resulted from the nomination.[119] Hamilton finally gave up hope in December and advised London of the utter failure of his endeavors to obtain a new treaty.[120]

Only an incurable optimist could have hoped for a renewal of the convention in view of the storm which the Aberdeen Bill created in Brazil. An able note[121] written by Limpo de Abreu phrased the point of view not only of the Foreign Office but of the nation as well. In his reply to the act of the British Parliament, he pointed out that no nation had the right to exercise an act of jurisdiction over the property or persons of another country, particularly within the territory of the second nation. Visit and search on the high seas was exclusively a belligerent right and unlawful in time of peace; yet Great Britain by national legislation was proceeding contrary to international usage and was violating the sovereignty and independence of a free nation. Since the convention which declared slave trading to be piracy had expired, that provision terminated also, particularly as no universal consent to treat the traffic as piracy existed. In conclusion he stated emphatically that "the Aberdeen Bill was not based either on the text or on the spirit of the Convention of 1826; it contradicted the clearest principles of the rights of nations, violated the sovereignty and independence of Brazil and of all nations." Therefore Brazil refused to accept responsibility for the consequences of the bill and affirmed its belief that the act was the result "of force and violence." His government at once entered claims for the damages which its subjects might suffer as a consequence of acts performed under the authority of the bill.[122]

---

[118] F. O. 84/583, Hamilton to Aberdeen, No. 42.

[119] *Ibid.*, No. 52.

[120] *Ibid.*, No. 55.

[121] The note was dated October 22, 1845. It is given in Brazil, *Relatorio dos Negocios Extrangeiros*, 1846, Supplement, Document 3.

[122] An acrimonious exchange of letters between the two foreign offices followed the passage of the Aberdeen Bill but neither side moved its opponent to modify his position (F. O. 84/583, Aberdeen to Hamilton, No. 18; F. O. 84/582, Hamilton to Aberdeen, Nos. 25, 35, and 40; Brazil, *Relatorio dos Negocios Extrangeiros,* 1846, Supplement, Document 29).

The issue was clearly defined: the Brazilian government, which thus far had been unable to suppress the slave trade, renounced the convention granting to England the two instruments employed for the abolition of the traffic, namely, the mixed commission at Sierra Leone and the right of visit and search. The utmost pressure by Great Britain failed to modify that determination; hence the London Foreign Office decreed that Brazilian slave ships were to be captured "under the somewhat singular authority of a British statute,"[123] until the Rio government should agree to a satisfactory convention with England. Persuasion had failed; coercion was to be employed to quell the Brazilian revolt against submission to the desires of the London Foreign Office.

It is evident from the foregoing discussion that the twenty years between 1825 and 1845 witnessed a steady decline in the political influence exerted by Great Britain over Brazil. In 1825 the larger power, to all appearances, was beginning to exercise a virtual protectorate over its South American ally, thus carrying on the tradition of Anglo-Portuguese relations in a new setting. But friction that grew more embittered as time passed arose over the continuance of the slave trade. The three allied questions of an equipment clause, the disposal of *emancipados*, and the finality of the decisions of the Sierra Leone commission, increased the ill-feeling between London and Rio, which not even the desire, common to both governments, of stopping the traffic could surmount. The smoldering resentment felt by Brazil over what it termed the arbitrary and dominating action of England broke into open revolt at the expiration of the convention of 1826 when Great Britain, determined on the suppression of the traffic at any cost, employed coercion when persuasion failed. Could that revolt be maintained, or would the Rio government be forced to come to terms with London and sign an agreement satisfactory to the British Foreign Office? The simplest solution to the crisis would be for the Brazilians to stop the traffic by their own efforts, ignore Great Britain's stand, and maintain their attitude of hostility

[123] Mathieson, *Great Britain and the Slave Trade*, p. 130.

until London granted recognition of the fact that the traditional position of England in Portugal could not be continued in Brazilian affairs. Such, as a matter of fact, was to be the solution of the crisis of 1845, as the succeeding twenty years were to show.

CHAPTER X

THE DECLINE OF BRITISH POLITICAL PREËMINENCE

By 1845 the efforts of the London Foreign Office to suppress the slave trade had forced England into an extraordinary position. In that year the means which it had employed to suppress the traffic since 1817 slipped from its grasp, for the international agreements authorizing them terminated. Thus deprived of the only instruments which it considered effective in restraining the traffic, England faced the necessity of withdrawing entirely its opposition to the Brazilian slave trade or of finding a way to impose its will on the empire. The second alternative was chosen, for the Foreign Office announced that it considered the declaration of piracy contained in the first article of the extinct treaty to be perpetual and that it would continue to act against the Brazilian slave trade on the authority not of a bi-partite agreement but of a special statute passed by the British Parliament to cover cases of piracy arising under the declaration. That the Brazilian government denied the perpetual nature of the first article of the treaty of 1826 did not alter the case; the Aberdeen Bill was enacted and seizures continued.

The activity of the British cruisers after 1845 demonstrated the determination of the London Office to check the Brazilian traffic at any cost. Between October 13, 1845, and May 16 of the following year fifteen vessels flying the Brazilian flag were seized by British cruisers and submitted to English admiralty courts for adjudication.[1] The protests of the Rio government elicited the reply that the Aberdeen Act authorizing such seiz-

[1] Brazil, *Relatorio dos Negocios Extrangeiros*, 1847, Supplement, Note 8.

ures would be repealed if the Brazilians would sign an agreement similar to that concluded between England and Portugal in 1842, conceding the right of visit and search with seizure on the grounds of equipment for the trade.[2] Since Brazil made signature of any arrangement whatsoever contingent upon a clause which would grant indemnity for seizures made under the Aberdeen Act, and since the granting of such indemnities by England would be equal to a confession of the illegality of the actions of the cruisers, no agreement was possible[3] and the activity of the British vessels continued.[4] Between August, 1849, and May, 1852, ninety Brazilian ships were seized by British cruisers.[5]

When in 1850 the Rio government again entered a vehement protest against what it termed particularly flagrant breaches of international usage, Minister Hudson made "known to the Brazilian Govt. that the only way to avoid the continuance of such inconvenient questions, and perhaps even of more serious ones, would be for it to execute faithfully and energetically its promises, and to stop entirely the slave traffic in Brazil!"[6] Until such action should be taken, it would be impossible to stop visit and seizure.[7] Moreover, he added by way of admonition, the present state of affairs was "ignominious" and the Brazilian government was "by the violation of its promises, the promoter not only of crime in Brazil but also of desolation and barbarism in Africa."[8]

The repeal of the Aberdeen Bill by the negotiation of another convention was out of the question; the only other possibility lay in the complete extermination of the traffic itself. Yet this

---

[2] *Ibid.*, 1848, p. 6. [3] *Ibid.*, 1847, p. 8.

[4] Early in January, 1850, the *Santa Cruz* was seized between S. Sebastião and Rio by a British cruiser, declared a pirate, burned, and sunk, and its crew set ashore. The *Paquete de Santos* suffered a like fate (*ibid.*, 1850, notes 1 to 6 and 7 to 13).

[5] These are Brazilian figures (Pereira Pinto, *Apontamentos*, I, 364, note 11).

[6] Brazil, *Relatorio dos Negocios Extrangeiros*, 1851, Annex B, No. 4.

[7] *Ibid.*, No. 6. Hudson stated succinctly that when there should be "not one Negro ship to be apprehended by English vessels in these waters, these English ships" would "abstain from making such captures (*ibid.*, No. 20)."

[8] *Ibid.*, No. 8.

avenue appeared as hopeless as the attempt to conclude a new agreement, for the importation of Africans increased astonishingly after 1845. By the official estimates[9] of the Brazilian government the number of slaves brought into the country rose from 19,453 in 1845 to over fifty thousand in 1846, to fifty-six thousand in 1847, and to sixty thousand in 1848. The number dropped to fifty-four thousand in 1849, but that was little consolation to the London Office in view of the extraordinary number of importations made in the years following the termination of the treaty of 1826. Evidently something more severe than the Aberdeen Act itself was needed; and in June, 1850, orders were received by the British cruisers to enter the ports of Brazil and seize all ships fitted out for the slave traffic.[10] Thereafter English war vessels nosed into bays, rivers, and ports of the empire, seizing slavers and carrying them off for adjudication in British admiralty courts or destroying them in case of resistance.[11] These orders were suspended for a few months in 1850, but early in the following year they were declared in full force once more.[12] It was not until June, 1852, that these orders were cancelled and the activity of the British cruisers again limited to the high seas.[13]

The attitude assumed by Great Britain in regard to the Brazilian slave trade was the result of active propaganda carried on in England. Between 1823 and 1838 attention, which had been centered since 1807 on securing agreements with other nations to suppress the traffic,[14] was directed toward the aboli-

---

[9] Brazil, *Relatorio dos Negocios Extrangeiros*, 1852, xiii.

[10] *Ibid.*, 1851, Annex B, No. 19.

[11] One of the interesting incidents which resulted from these orders occurred in Paranaguá where the *Cormorant* entered to destroy a "nest of pirate slave ships" and was fired upon by the Brazilian fort, one seaman being killed and two wounded (*ibid.*, No. 15). Hudson requested the Rio government to issue orders to all fortresses not to fire on English ships making seizures in Brazilian ports (*ibid.*, No. 22). The Brazilian minister refused brusquely as such an order would acknowledge the right of England to make seizures in Brazilian waters on the strength of a British statute (*ibid.*, No. 23).

[12] *Ibid.*, 1851, No. 18. The suspension was due to the Brazilian act of September 4, 1850. The orders were renewed in January, 1851.

[13] *Ibid.*, 1853, Annex, No. 25.

[14] *Supra*, chapter VII.

tion of slavery itself within the British Empire.[15] The abolitionist movement, which succeeded partially in 1833 and completely five years later, gave way in turn to a renewed interest in the international trade when the reformers, finishing one task and realizing the failure of the earlier movement, turned to making the foreign agreements effectual.[16] In 1838 T. F. Buxton, who had inherited the mantle of Wilberforce, proposed a plan of operation to Melbourne, Glenelg, Palmerston, Howick, Hobhouse, Spring-Rice, Grey, Stanley, and others in the ministry; won the approval of the cabinet; organized the Society for the Extinction of the Slave Trade and the Civilization of Africa[17] in 1839; and published his *Remedy* in 1840.[18] In 1839 also, Joseph Sturge started his British and Foreign Anti-Slavery Society in an effort to stop the traffic by abolishing slavery itself in all nations where that institution still remained.[19]

At the same time economic interests became involved in the effort to stop the traffic carried on almost exclusively by Spain, Portugal, Brazil, and the United States. The ten shilling extra duty on Indian sugar was removed in 1836, permitting the cheap-labor product of India to compete with the British West Indies commodity[20]; five years later despite the opposition of the East and West Indian interests and the abolitionists, the government reduced the prohibitive additional duties on foreign sugar.[21] The export of machinery from England to Brazil,

---

[15] T. F. Buxton, *Memoirs*, pp. 383-384, 442-461; W. L. Mathieson, *British Slavery and its Abolition, 1823-1838, passim.*

[16] Buxton laid his first investigation of the slave trade before Parliament, May, 12, 1835, with the recommendation that new efforts be made to stop the traffic which was going on despite the agreements for its suppression (*Memoirs*, pp. 382-384).

[17] At the first meeting Prince Albert presided. Among the four thousand who attended were nobles, prelates, and statesmen (W. L. Mathieson, *Great Britain and the Slave Trade, 1839-1865*, p. 51).

[18] Buxton, *Memoirs*, pp. 447-461, and *The African Slave Trade, The Remedy.*

[19] Mathieson, *Great Britain and the Slave Trade*, pp. 47-48.

[20] In the first year of equal duties 14,000 tons of India sugar entered England; ten years later 80,000 tons entered (Mathieson, *Great Britain and the Slave Trade*, p. 76).

[21] The argument used by the opposition was that foreign sugar was grown by slave labor whereas the British article was produced by free labor (Hansard,

intended largely for sugar-mills, more than doubled between 1845 and 1847; from Bahia in 1846 there were shipped sixty-six thousand sugar barrels and in 1848, ninety-eight thousand. Coincident with this increased demand for sugar came a growth in slave importations, for, as we have seen, from twenty thousand in 1845 the number of Africans brought into Brazil increased to over fifty thousand the next year.[22]

Thus both reformers and economic interests were concerned in stopping the flow of cheap labor to Brazil,[23] and the period of severest measures directed against the slave trade of the empire coincided with the renewed activity of the reformers and the movement toward free trade.[24] The vigorous action of the

---

Debates, 1841, pp. 269, 641). Peel cut down sugar duties until only ten shillings preference remained to the British grown article after the expiration of the Brazilian treaty in November, 1844. In July, 1846, the equalization scheme whereby a uniform duty of fourteen shillings per cwt. was to be levied on all sugar regardless of origin was ordered to be initiated in July, 1847, the plan to be consummated by 1851 (Mathieson, *Great Britain and the Slave Trade*, pp. 82-84).

[22] Mathieson, *op. cit.*, pp. 91-92.

[23] There were certain economic interests which opposed coercion in suppressing the Brazilian traffic. The Aberdeen Act was unpopular in northern England, a member from Manchester moving its repeal in 1849. John Bright called attention to the four or five millions of capital and three millions of export to Brazil and demonstrated the damage done to British interests by the slave trade controversy (Hansard, *Debates*, 1849, pp. 758, 783-787, 800). When a motion to withdraw the whole preventive system and coercive methods was made in 1849 and 1850, Cobden, Bright, and Gladstone voted in favor of the proposal (Mathieson, *op. cit.*, pp. 105-111). The motion was defeated by 232 to 154. A committee of the Lords also supported coercion and reported against the proposal to cease coercive methods.

[24] The detailed study of this activity in England and the steps taken by the British government to suppress the trade have been presented by Mathieson in *Great Britain and the Slave Trade*. The author's point of view is expressed in the preface when he states, "It is a controversial story; but though not without experience in the treatment of such themes, I have found no scope for impartiality." He identifies himself completely with those who attempted to suppress the trade by coercion. Less than one paragraph is devoted to the Aberdeen Bill; no reference is made to the correspondence in the Foreign Office Archives; and no citation from any Brazilian historian or document is given although an entire chapter is devoted to "The Brazilian Crisis." For a brief review of the efforts of England to suppress the Brazilian traffic and for a detailed account of the participation of the United States in that trade see Lawrence F. Hill "Abolition of the African Slave Trade to Brazil," *Hispanic American Historical Review*, May, 1931. Other informative articles are: Jane Addams, "The Abolition of the Brazilian Slave Trade," *Journal*

Foreign Office, which threatened to undermine English influence in the South American empire, was the result of this pressure and of British public opinion created by those interested in suppressing the Brazilian traffic by coercive means.[25]

Just as the London Office shaped its policy under the influence of local conditions in England, so the action of the Rio court reflected the national situation in Brazil. From 1830 to 1848 the ministry admitted year after year its inability to stop the trade; from 1848 to 1850 the ground was prepared for decisive action; in 1850 an effective measure was forced through the Assembly by the cabinet; and by 1853 the traffic ceased. Was the failure of the Rio court from 1830 to 1848 due merely to its supineness and duplicity; was the sudden change of policy to vigorous and effective action after 1848 due solely or even in large part to British coercive measures[26]; or was there some decisive change in national conditions in 1848 which enabled the cabinet at last to enforce its will in regard to the slave trade question?

It will be remembered that the success of the Brazilian struggle for independence was due to the support which both the Portuguese party and the Brazilian patriots gave D. Pedro. It will be remembered also that as success became assured, the young prince inclined to the Portuguese, or absolutist, party and alienated the Patriot, or constitutionalist, party, although, as José Bonifacio admitted, the latter group was the powerful element in the new nation. In 1831 the Brazilians expelled the absolutist prince with the result that thereafter the destiny of the empire lay in the hands of the native aristocracy: Brazil after 1831 was controlled by the Brazilians.[27]

---

of Negro History, October, 1925, and R. W. VanAlstyne, "British Right of Search and the African Slave Trade," *Journal of Modern History*, II, No. 1.

[25] Lord John Russell admitted in 1861 that public opinion was a large factor in the adherence of the government to the policy of coercion (*Parliamentary Debates*, 1861, p. 961).

[26] Mathieson believes that it was due to the pressure exerted by the British that the Rio government was prodded into action after 1848 and especially in 1850 (*Great Britain and the Slave Trade*, p. 133-135).

[27] See *supra*, pp. 188-191, 211-213, 217-219.

The native aristocracy with roots that extended back to the early seventeenth century was based on land. The landowner established his family socially as well as financially while he arrogated to himself absolute power over slaves, dependents, renters, share-croppers, mechanics, overseers, members of his own family—any who existed on his possessions. In the north the basis of this class distinction was the cultivation of sugar; in the south, the plantation of the *bandeirante*[28] or his descendant; in both north and south the labor supply of the *engenho* or plantation was dependent on the slave trade.[29]

It was this native aristocracy dependent on land and slave labor which rose to power in 1831. Opponents of absolutist centralization, this element favored a constitutionalist or even a republican régime; and for the next ten years Brazil passed through a period of severe internal readjustment when the anarchy and chaos which was sweeping over so many of the Spanish republics threatened to dissolve the central government established at Rio.[30] Under various names and led by different figures, two main parties emerged and struggled for control, the liberals and the conservatives.

The liberals favored democratic forms, strove to diminish the authority of the central government, worked to gain more autonomy for the provinces, and appealed to the lower classes and the radicals for support.[31] The *camaras*[32] (town councils) were encouraged to enlarge their powers and decentralization

[28] The *bandeirante* was a member of the famous expeditions called *bandeiras* which explored the interior of Brazil and wrested from the Spaniards three-fourths of what became the Brazil of to-day. These expeditions originated in the captaincy of São Paulo (Alfonso de E. Taunay, *Historia Geral das Bandeiras Paulistas*, 6 vols.).

[29] For a discussion of the rise of this Brazilian aristocracy and the manner in which that class obtained control of the Brazilian government in 1831, see Alan K. Manchester, "The Rise of the Brazilian Aristocracy," *The Hispanic American Historical Review*, May, 1931.

[30] J. M. Pereira da Silva, *Situation Sociale, Politique et Économique de l'Empire du Brésil*, pp. 35 ff.

[31] Oliveira Lima, *O Imperio Brazileiro*, p. 42; Pereira da Silva, *Memorias*, I, 29.

[32] The legal basis for the native aristocracy lay in the right to vote for or sit in the *camara*. The town council had always been the center of the influence and activity of the native aristocracy (See Manchester, "Rise of the Brazilian Aristocracy," p. 145).

followed the absolutism of the exiled prince,[33] the local bodies thus becoming the key to the enforcement of the law with the resultant ability to checkmate the execution of the imperial decrees by the central authority.[34] Thus the *camaras*, which were controlled by the landed aristocracy, or the provincial assemblies, which were responsive to the attitude of the locality, could defy successfully the will of the Rio government in its efforts to suppress the slave trade by serving as the effective vehicles for popular opinion which considered the importations beneficial to the agricultural life of the country.[35] When threatened with defeat by the Conservatives, these Liberals, or decentralists, were ready to resort even to arms in their effort to maintain autonomy in the face of the centralization policy of their opponents.[36] The keynote to the ten years of regency rule following 1831, therefore, was this conflict between the forces of centralization[37]; nor was the issue settled until 1848 when despite the disruptive tendencies manifested in the period between 1841 and 1848, the Rio government was able to extend its authority until it no longer feared the separatist efforts of the Liberals.[38]

The year 1848 was the turning point in the struggle to establish a strong central government. During the four years prior to this date, short-lived, ineffective coalition cabinets consisting of leaders from all groups attempted to manage affairs with no true majority possible in the national Assembly. But in 1848 the abortive revolt of the Liberals in Pernambuco resulted in

[33] Rocha Pombo, *Historia do Brazil*, VIII, 284-285.

[34] *Ibid.*, pp. 299-301.

[35] Brazil, *Relatorio dos Negocios Extrangeiros*, 1832, p. 5.

[36] The liberals were instigators of the revolts in Rio Grande do Sul (1835-1845), in Minas Geraes (1842), São Paulo (1842), and Pernambuco (1848) (Oliveira Lima, *O Imperio Brazileiro*, p. 42).

[37] For a detailed account of the period between 1831 and 1841 with special reference to the decentralization struggle, see Rocha Pombo, *op. cit.*, VIII, pp. 269-391.

[38] The new attitude was illustrated in a striking manner after the abortive revolution in Pernambuco in 1848. After the suppression of the revolt, no one involved in the uprising was sacrificed in vindictive punishment by the central government (Rocha Pombo, *Historia do Brazil*, IX, 5 and note).

their ostracism, and the Conservatives obtained an undisputed supremacy which was to last for many years[39]; in that year also the "personal rule" of D. Pedro II began.[40] Thereafter the governmental institutions, forged in these seventeen years of conflict, were everywhere accepted and only legal and constitutional means of attaining modifications were employed by the opposition. The central government was strong throughout the empire.[41]

Moreover in 1850 the economic revival of Brazil began. The first protective tariff had been passed in 1844 on the expiration of the commercial treaty with England; railroad building began[42]; telegraphs were installed[43]; and private commercial and industrial corporations were organized.[44] Centralization of power and stability of government was followed by a period of economic development.

Under these circumstances the Rio court was able to move toward the realization of the desire to suppress the traffic, which observers as keen and experienced in Brazilian affairs as Consul General Ouseley and Minister Hamilton-Hamilton had noted during the period of instability. The opportunity came in September, 1848, when on the first day of the month the old Senate project of 1837[45] was brought up in the lower house by

---

[39] Oliveira Lima, *O Imperio Brazileiro*, pp. 42-44.

[40] Pedro was not yet six years old when he was proclaimed emperor in 1831. Ten years later the Conservatives proclaimed his majority and strove to centralize power around the monarch. Their restrictions on the provincial assemblies and local bodies resulted in revolts in Minas Geraes (1842), São Paulo (1842), and Pernambuco (1848), but by 1848 opposition was crushed in the provinces and the ten year revolt in Rio Grande do Sul was ended (1845). In 1848 began the "personal rule" of the young emperor, which was to last until 1878 (Oliveira Lima *op. cit.*, pp. 96-107).

[41] Pereira da Silva, *Situation Sociale, Politique et Économique de l'Empire*, pp. 35-51.

[42] The first railroad was inaugurated April 10, 1854; the second, February 9, 1858; and the third, March 29, 1858. The first two were built by English capital, the third by the Brazilian government (Oliveira Lima, *op. cit.*, p. 207).

[43] The first telegraph line was inaugurated in 1857 (*ibid.*, p. 207).

[44] In 1851 eleven of these *Sociedades Anonymas* were incorporated (*ibid.*, p. 207).

[45] This was the project proposed by Barbacena which established the equipment clause for seizure on the high seas, but by Article XIII annulled the Law of 1831. The Senate passed the project in 1837 but it was defeated in the lower house.

the cabinet which insisted on the unmodified acceptance of Article XIII. The chamber adjourned discussion, the cabinet resigned, and the Conservatives with Eusebio de Queiroz as minister of justice came into power. The ministry thereupon called for an election and won a decisive majority in the Assembly convoked for January 1, 1850. Then, overriding the opposition which used England's arbitrary action as the weapon of attack, the Conservative majority, in secret sessions[46] to avoid pressure from public opinion, amended the proposal adjourned two years previously and issued the famous law of September 4, 1850.[47]

The first article of this drastic law established the right of seizure on grounds of equipment for the trade, while Article IV declared the traffic to be piracy. The ships and everything in them were to be sold if they were found to be fitted out for the transportation of Negroes; captured slaves were to be reexported eventually, but in the meantime they could be used in the service of the state, concession of their services to private individuals being expressly forbidden. Shipping papers for vessels bound for Africa were to be granted only to those who gave security to the total value of the ships and goods, the security to be returned only after eighteen months had expired and proof had been presented that no slaves had been received on board. Brazilian admiralty courts were given jurisdiction over prizes and slaves, with appeal to the council of state and over principals and accomplices,[48] with appeal to the Court of

---

[46] Pereira da Silva in his memoirs states that it was only in secret sessions that such a delicate question as the slave trade suppression could be treated. Farmers and rich business men who manipulated public opinion in favor of the traffic exercised too great influence over the representatives who were dependent on the ballot for their next election to allow the necessary independence of action. The law of 1850 was debated and passed in secret sessions therefore (*Memorias*, I, 219).

[47] J. L. Alves, "A Questão do Elemento Servil," *Revista do Inst. Hist. e Geog. Bras.*, Tomo Especial VI, Parte IV, 1916, pp. 234-249. The law is given *verbatim*, p. 250, note 20. It is given also in Great Britain, *British and Foreign State Papers*, XXXIX, 1060-1062.

[48] The principals were captain, owner, mate, pilot, and supercargo; and accomplices were anyone who helped or were implicated in the unloading, hiding, or sale of slaves brought in by the principals.

Appeals. Thus cases were taken from the jury and placed in courts which upheld the authority of the central government. It was an effective measure,[49] placed in the hands of a strong central government which was able to enforce its will.

Eusebio de Queiroz executed the law inexorably.[50] Importations, which in 1849 numbered fifty-four thousand, dropped to twenty-three thousand in 1850, to a little over three thousand in 1851, and to scarcely seven hundred the next year.[51] On June 11, 1852, the British minister advised the Rio government that the orders authorizing British cruisers to make seizures within Brazilian waters was revoked; the next year jurisdiction was given to the Brazilian navy in cases of seizure of traffickers inland as well as on the seas; and in 1854 the final law in the series was enacted with the aim of preventing the disappearance of illicit Africans by indiscriminate mixture with legal slaves.[52] Between 1853 and 1856 only two landings of slaves were recorded, one in Serinhaem[53] (in Pernambuco) and the other in S. Matheus (in Espirito Santo). In June of the latter year, Lord Palmerston announced in the British Parliament that the Brazilian slave trade had ceased.[54]

Was the suppression due to the activity of the British cruisers

---

[49] Two decrees were issued by D. Pedro for the effective execution of the Law of 1831 (Great Britain, *British and Foreign State Papers*, XXXIX, 1062-1074) and of the Law of September 4, 1850 (*ibid.*, pp. 1074-1076).

[50] Alvez, "A Questão do Elemento Servil," p. 253; Pereira da Silva, *Memorias*, I, 219; Joaquim Nabuco, *Estadista do Imperio, Nabuco de Araujo, Sua Vida, Suas Opiniões, Sua Epoca*, I, 225-226.

[51] Pereira Pinto, *Apontamentos*, I, 369; Brazil, *Relatorio dos Negocios Extrangeiros*, 1852, xiii (Report of the minister of foreign relations to the Assembly).

[52] Joaquim Nabuco, *op. cit.*, I, 226-229.

[53] Brazil, *Relatorio dos Negocios Extrangeiros*, 1853, p. 8. The Serinhaem case was serious. On October 13, 1855, some 209 Africans were landed, the importation was detected, but forty-seven Negroes were stolen. By severe measures twenty-one were recovered while families of great importance were implicated. The English consul, Jerningham, threatened to renew the in-shore activity of British cruisers; Nabuco de Araujo, minister of justice, removed or pensioned officials of the court before which the case had been tried and the criminals absolved. Pernambuco protested such high-handed procedure, but illicit importations ceased (Joaquim Nabuco, *op. cit.*, I, 231-241).

[54] Alvez, "A Questão do Elemento Servil," p. 254. The Aberdeen Act was not repealed until 1869 however (Mathieson, *Great Britain and the Slave Trade*, p. 136).

between 1845 and 1853? Christie was quite certain that it was, for he repudiated emphatically the assertion of Queiroz that the Brazilian government stopped the traffic despite the handicap of the arbitrary and unlawful action of Great Britain.[55] Pereira Pinto, on the other hand, pointed out that the largest importations occurred during the years of England's violence while the traffic ceased abruptly when the Rio government was able to take decisive steps.[56] In the opinion of the Brazilian court, the activity of the British cruisers not only failed to stop the traffic, but placed the Rio government in the paradoxical position of protesting against such seizures and thus seemingly adopting a position against the suppression when in reality it was sincerely endeavoring to accomplish that end.[57] At the same time Great Britain could not understand why Brazil did not appreciate England's help since without it the imperial government could not control the traffic.[58]

Regardless of where the credit for suppression lies, the fact remains that the Aberdeen Act embittered Anglo-Brazilian relations until the Christie affair resulted in a diplomatic break between the two countries.[59] The Rio government was convinced that England had acted in a dominating, arbitrary manner and that to Brazil alone was due the credit for the

---

[55] W. D. Christie, *Notes on Brazilian Questions*, pp. 90-92.

[56] *Apontamentos*, I, 369. Alvez ("A Questão do Elemento Servil," p. 253) and Pereira da Silva (*Memorias*, I, 219) agree with Pinto Pereira. Joaquim Nabuco, (*Estadista do Imperio*, I, 226) agrees with Christie to the extent that the terror of the British cruisers aided Queiroz in his successful suppression of the trade. Mathieson (*Great Britain and the Slave Trade*, pp. 123-124) agrees with Christie. In a brief and superficial discussion, Sousa Sá Vianna presents a pro-English version of the diplomatic phases of the suppression of the slave trade ("O Trafico e a Diplomacia Brasileira," *Revista do Inst. Hist. e Geog. Bras.*, Tomo Especial VI, Parte 5, pp. 539-565).

[57] Brazil, *Relatorio dos Negocios Extrangeiros*, 1851. Annex B, Note 7. In proof of the sincerity of the Brazilian government, the foreign minister stated that between October, 1849, and January, 1851, Brazilians had captured 1,200 slaves (*ibid.*, note 19).

[58] *Ibid.*, 1854, Annex B, p. 7. Both John Russell and Palmerston stated in the House of Commons that without the Aberdeen Act the Brazilian slave trade would not have ceased (*ibid.*, 1855, Annex D, p. 6).

[59] Oliveira Lima, *O Imperio Brazilerio*, p. 209; Brazil, *Relatorio dos Negocios Extrangeiros*, 1855, xx, lx, and Annex D, pp. 6-7.

final suppression of the traffic. The feeling of resentment persisted with consequent loss of influence by Great Britain in the political affairs of the empire. Economically, Brazil still leaned toward England; but politically, the Rio court shifted to the United States, and an *entente cordiale* developed between the two American nations which lasted as long as D. Pedro II remained on the throne. Due largely to the arrogant tone assumed by Great Britain in the slave trade controversy, the Brazilian government was alienated from its traditional friendship for England.[60]

The fundamental cause of the irritation which had embittered Anglo-Brazilian relations since 1827 did not cease with the actual suppression of the slave trade; for in addition to the resentment which persisted, there were two types of claims which in the opinion of the Rio court remained to be settled. To the traditional claims for damages arising from the decisions of the Sierra Leone Commission as stated in the formal protest of the Chevalier de Mattos on November 30, 1833, there were now added others arising from the seizure of Brazilian vessels by English cruisers under the authority of a British statute, the Aberdeen Act. Until these claims, which were inextricably bound up with the political relations of the two countries, could be settled or forgotten, amicable coöperation between London and Rio proved very difficult, for the efforts to secure satisfactory settlement caused repeated revivals of the controversy and kept alive the bitterness of the 1845-56 period.

In forcing action in regard to these claims, Brazil was aided by the fact that English subjects were demanding compensation for losses suffered during the revolution for independence and the period of national instability which followed. With the long slave trade controversy apparently settled by the actual termination of the traffic and with a strong, centralized government in command of the situation in Rio, England considered the moment opportune to present these claims. Consequently, P. Campbell Scarlett, envoy extraordinary and min-

[60] Oliveira Lima, *O Imperio Brazileiro*, pp. 210-211.

ister plenipotentiary at Rio, presented a list of the "very numerous and long outstanding British claims against Brazil."[16] The reply of the minister of foreign affairs and Scarlett's comment on that reply present a vivid description of the relations of the two powers in the middle of the century after the slave trade controversy to all appearances had been settled. Scarlett's dispatch to the London Office merits special attention, therefore.

The reply of the Brazilian minister to his note, Scarlett reported,[62] was written in the usual very courteous terms and stated that the more pressing claims specifically alluded to by the British envoy had been referred to the competent department for a solution and the others would be taken up shortly for consideration by the minister for foreign affairs. On the face of it, the reply was satisfactory; but, Scarlett complained, this was merely "one of many of a similar character adopted towards Her Majesty's Ministers at Rio de Janeiro as a convenient form, when the last thing ever contemplated" was "a sincere intention to accede to repeated demands, or to give any definite effect to assurances which" meant "really nothing." For a succession of years the ruling policy of the Brazilian government had been one of courteous delay and civil evasion; note after note had been written without the slightest hope of success. Scarlett, convinced of the futility of continuing such a procedure, requested instructions and hinted at the necessity of "holding firm language" with the Rio government or of "resorting if necessary to still more stringent measures for obtaining reparations for the parties aggrieved." His dispatch shows the growing irritation of the British legation over the polite inertia which was being used to counter the forceful action of a powerful and unwelcome friend.

As a result of this report Scarlett received from Clarendon full powers to negotiate a convention for the settlement of claims existing between the two nations, a printed copy of the instrument recently concluded between England and the

---

[61] F. O. 97/79, Scarlett to Clarendon, No. 62. June 25, 1857.

[62] *Ibid.* A copy of the reply was enclosed in the dispatch.

United States being sent as a model.[63] The Brazilian emperor approved the idea; a plenipotentiary was appointed; and the convention was signed June 2, 1858.[64]

By the convention[65] "all claims on the part of the corporation companies, or private individual subjects" of either country upon the government of the other contracting power presented since the date of the declaration of independence of the Brazilian Empire or to be presented before a given date, were to be referred to two commissioners, one appointed by England and the other by Brazil. Each commissioner would select a permanent secretary who would also act as commissioner in the case of the incapacity or absence of the latter. The commission was to sit in Rio; decisions were to be absolutely final; and in case of disagreement by the two commissioners, they were to select an arbiter, by lot if necessary, who would cast the deciding vote. All claims had to be presented within twelve months, or at the latest, eighteen months from the first meeting of the commission; at least eight sittings a month were obligatory; a final decision on every claim presented was to be rendered within two years; and each government engaged to consider the result of the proceedings of the commission as a final and perfect settlement of every claim prior to the exchange of ratifications whether or not that claim was actually presented.

Great Britain appointed its commissioner and secretary late in September, 1858; in November, the Brazilian representatives were named; the first sitting occurred on March 10, 1859[66]; and claims were received for adjudication. By May 1, 1860, of the fifty-one British and ninety-nine Brazilian claims entered,

---

[63] F. O. 97/79, Scarlett to Clarendon, No. 112, and note dated February 15, 1858. The convention between England and the United States was concluded in 1853.

[64] *Ibid.*, Scarlett to Malmesbury, Nos. 32, 43, 46. The London Office approved of the convention (*ibid.*, Draft to Scarlett, No. 8. July 7) and ratifications were exchanged in London, September 9, 1858 (*ibid.*, Draft to Scarlett, No. 12).

[65] F. O., Treaties, Protocols, 94/477, Brazil. The text is found also in Brazil, *Relatorio dos Negocios Extrangeiros*, 1859, Annex C, Note 5.

[66] F. O. 97/79, Draft to Morgan, No. 1; Stuart to Malmesbury Nos. 83 (1858) and 18 (1859); and Morgan to Malmesbury, March 10, 1859.

five British and eight Brazilian had been decided.[67] Of the ninety-one Brazilian cases remaining for consideration there were fifty-two arising from sentences pronounced by the mixed commissions of Sierra Leone and of Rio, chiefly of the former, sixteen from condemnations by vice-admiralty courts under the Aberdeen Act, and twenty-three miscellaneous cases. The amount claimed by the Brazilians totalled about two millions sterling; if the sixty-eight cases arising from the Sierra Leone commission and the vice-admiralty courts were deducted, the total was about four hundred thousand pounds sterling.

The British claims arose from damages suffered by English subjects during the revolutionary disturbances of 1821 to 1825, or incurred as a consequence of the Brazilian blockade of La Plata in 1825-1827. Some demanded compensation for excess duties levied on imports, others for arrears of allowances or pay due military officers or their widows, and still others for destruction of goods during the numerous revolutions of the period of instability.[68] The total value of claims entered by British subjects was two hundred and fifty thousand pounds sterling.[69]

The proportion of Brazilian claims based on damages for the action of the Sierra Leone commission and seizures made under the Aberdeen Act revealed the purpose of the Rio government to use the claims commission as a means of liquidating the heritage received from the slave trade controversy. In the negotiations leading up to the signing of the convention and the articles of the agreement no mention was made specifically of the status of such claims before the proposed commission; yet the first article provided that any claim could be submitted

---

[67] F. O. 97/80, Christie to Russell, No. 57. Of the five British claims decided, three were granted compensation; of the eight Brazilian, three were granted compensation. The British awards amounted to seven thousand sterling and the Brazilian to fifteen thousand seven hundred. The Brazilian minister of foreign affairs reported to the Assembly that at the first meeting 108 Brazilian and fifty-one English claims were entered (Brazil, *Relatorio dos Negocios Extrangeiros*, 1860, pp. 67-71).

[68] F. O. 97/80, Christie to Russell, No. 57. May 1, 1860.

[69] F. O. 97/84, Christie to Russell, No. 72. A list of these claims with amounts specified is given in Christie, *Notes on Brazilian Questions*, Appendix, pp. 233-236.

"which might have been presented to either government for its interposition with the other since the Declaration of Independence of the Brazilian Empire and which yet" remained "unsettled by either of the two governments." The inference seemed clear that these old claims which the Brazilian government had pressed so often would be permitted.

The English commissioner concurred with the Brazilian opinion that the first article of the convention empowered him to review the decisions of the Sierra Leone court. In an early case decided June 7, 1859, he concurred in the decision that since the vessel in question had been condemned by the mixed commission of Sierra Leone the case had been definitely adjudicated and the commissioners could not take cognizance of it. When the Brazilian government protested this admission of the finality of the sentences of the Sierra Leone court and the Brazilian commissioner argued for a revision of such cases, the English commissioner yielded and in the case of the *Principe do Guiné* concurred in asserting the right of revision. Commissioner Morgan, Christie explained to Lord John Russell, labored under the impression that his oath of office bound him "to act entirely according to his own judgement without reference to the opinions of Her Majesty's Government." Consequently, the wording of the first article of the convention had led him to take, "erroneously and unfortunately," the same position in regard to these slave trade claims as that assumed by the Brazilian government.[70]

Neither the British minister at Rio[71] nor the London office approved of this action of the English commissioner. On February 28, 1860, Morgan presented to his Brazilian colleague a dispatch from the English envoy stating that Lord John Russell had issued instructions not to deal with any more cases arising from the decisions of the Sierra Leone commission or from seizures made under the Aberdeen Act until further notice.

---

[70] F. O. 97/84, Christie to Russell, No. 81. June 24, 1860 (see particularly Morgan's letter of explanation to Christie, enclosure); Brazil, *Relatorio dos Negocios Extrangeiros*, 1860, pp. 67-71.

[71] *Ibid.*, No. 57. May 1, 1860.

Such an order, the Brazilian commissioner maintained, made a suspension of the sittings unavoidable; Morgan concurred; and work was interrupted. Toward the end of March when the English envoy tried to force the required eight sittings for that month by inviting the Brazilian commissioner to act within the limitation imposed by the London office, the Brazilian government refused unless the motive for the suppression were removed, and Morgan again concurred in the continued cessation of the work of the commission. The success or failure of the claims commission now rested on the question as to whether the disputed slave trade cases would be made subject to revision or ruled out of consideration.[72]

The decision of the British Foreign Office in regard to the question was communicated to Christie under the date of July 18, 1860.[73] As to the admission of claims arising from the action of the Sierra Leone commission, England had uniformly refused to have the decisions of the mixed courts reviewed and had considered as absolutely final the sentences imposed by that commission; neither government had a right, therefore, to require that such cases be reopened. As to the second set of claims, those arising from seizures made under the authority of the Aberdeen Act, London could not admit that Brazil had "any just foundation whatever on which to rest any remon-

[72] *Ibid.*, No. 81. June 24, 1860; and No. 61. May 5, 1860. During the period when the sittings were interrupted, the Rio government and the British legation agreed that no new cases were to be received after March 10, 1860 (*ibid.*).

[73] *Ibid.*, Draft to Christie, No. 51. July 18, 1860. A draft of a tentative reply was first submitted to the law officers (see F. O. 97/84, Draft to Christie, June, 1860—Draft as submitted to the law officers, June 22, 1860); two minutes by Lord Wodehouse, dated July 6 and 14, suggested certain changes; and Lord Palmerston and the queen passed on the final draft. The suggestions of Lord Wodehouse, which were incorporated in the final draft, excluded "the argument introduced by the Law Officers as to there being an appeal from Vice-Admiralty courts to which the Bras. did not resort," and included in the British refusal "all Slave Trade Claims, whereas the draft as allowed by the Law Officers would confine" British "objections to cases adjudicated, and would allow claims to be discussed arising out of capture where the vessels were released without sentence—claims which" England "had always refused to discuss . . . and which it would be most dangerous now to admit." He also changed the language somewhat (see F. O. 97/84, Draft to Christie, No. 51, July 18, 1860. Two minutes by Lord Wodehouse).

strance against the action of the British cruisers under that bill." Consequently, Great Britain could not admit that the Brazilian government was justified in attempting to treat as "unsettled" claims which England had "invariably treated as settled and into the merits of which it had always, upon this very ground, refused to enter."

Christie was to acquaint the Rio government with the decision. If Brazil should concur with this interpretation of the convention of 1858, the commissioners were to resume work with an extension of time; or if the Rio court wished to submit a list of claims excluding those of the two types under discussion, England would consent to a new convention, which would specify in detail the character of the claims to be considered; but if the Brazilian government adhered to its present view, England would have no alternative but to allow the commission to expire. Whatever inconvenience might result would be regrettable but Great Britain could not "yield to a pretension on the part of Brazil which would involve a departure from the settled policy" of the London office.

Christie delivered the note as instructed,[74] although he had already learned that the Brazilian government was firmly determined to adhere to its point of view. The cases to which the protest of the Chevalier de Mattos of November 30, 1833, referred and other similar cases since that date "were naturally considered by the Brazilian government as still pending"; the Rio court, therefore, held that "they were necessarily proper to be referred to the Claims Commission and that the reconsideration of these cases and of the cases adjudicated by British Admiralty courts under the provisions of the Aberdeen Act in defiance of the protests of the Brazilian Govt. was the advantage which induced the Bras. Govt. to agree to the convention."[75]

Since neither London nor Rio would yield, the suspension of the claims commission continued indefinitely with scarcely more than a dozen cases actually adjudicated and no warrants for payment issued even for those claims awarded.[76] Thus as

[74] Brazil, *Relatorio dos Negocios Extrangeiros*, 1861, Annex, Notes 45-56.

[75] F. O. 97/84, Christie to Russell, No. 72. June 2, 1860.

[76] *Ibid.*, No. 123. September 24, 1860.

far as the settlement of the long-standing claims was concerned, the work of the commission was absolutely void of results. The Brazilian government used every influence to prevent the expiration of the convention by insisting that the sittings were suspended not terminated, until England could "decide the question in consonance with justice"; but Lord John Russell merely reiterated the stand taken in the instructions sent to Christie and on February 24, 1862, announced that Great Britain considered the claims commission to have expired by virtue of the two years time limit specified in the convention.[77] Thus the whole question of claims reverted to the status so bitterly complained of by P. Campbell Scarlett in 1857. Both governments were forced to resort again to settlement of separate claims taken up individually with the competent department through the respective foreign offices.[78] The shadow of the slave trade controversy still poisoned Anglo-Brazilian relations.

The failure of the claims commission served to increase the tension already existing between the London and Rio courts. Thus in the early 1860's relations were so strained that a relatively minor incident would precipitate an explosion of serious proportions. In the delicate state of affairs caused by the cumu-

[77] F. O. 97/85, Christie to Russell, No. 91. June 24, 1861; Draft to Christie, No. 48. July 5, 1861; Baille to Russell, No. 13. August 24, 1861; Moreira to Russell, Brazilian Legation at London, November 20, 1861 (this dispatch gives the final stand of Brazil in regard to the point at issue. It is a reply to Christie's note of September 11, 1860, containing Russell's instructions); Draft to Christie, No. 5. February 24, 1862; Brazil, *Relatorio dos Negocios Extrangeiros*, 1862, Annex, Notes 46-56.

[78] Despite repeated efforts to revive the claims commission method of settlement, the question dragged on for years. It was not possible to follow the point to its conclusion in the records of the British government as the Foreign Archives are closed to research in the later period. In 1871, 1872, 1873, 1874, 1875, 1883, and 1884, the report of the minister of foreign affairs of Brazil revealed that attempts to submit the matter to arbitration, to revive the commission, or to negotiate a new convention failed. The difficulty arising from the two types of claims, those resulting from the action of the Sierra Leone mixed court and from seizures made under the Aberdeen Act prevented a satisfactory settlement (Brazil, *Relatorio dos Negocios Extrangeiros*, various dates). No record of a settlement by a claims convention is given in the check list of diplomatic agreements compiled from official Brazilian sources by José Manoel Cardoso de Oliveira (*Actos Diplomaticos do Brazil, 1493-1912*).

lative friction of the past thirty years, England needed a cool, able diplomat in Rio to prevent a total loss of that political influence which had been so dominant in 1827; but unfortunately W. D. Christie, minister from 1860 to the break in 1863, was impulsive, precipitate, and totally out of sympathy with the point of view of the Rio government. How hostile his attitude was may be seen in his letters and in the prefaces to his books dealing with the Brazilian crisis.[79] The opinions expressed by him in those publications furnish a striking arraignment of a friendly government by a high official in the British diplomatic service.

The letters and prefaces were written to offset the "paid puffers of Brazil and the lacqueys of its legation" who had "had it too much their own way in the English press and with the general public." Since no trustworthy book in English existed on Brazil[80] and a general ignorance as to South America and a general indifference to Brazil prevailed, it was "time that some truth about the Brazilian government should be told."[81] Christie, therefore, enlightened the British public on the subject of the empire.

In the first place, he reviewed the slave trade controversy. The cessation of the traffic was due, in his opinion, not to an aversion to slavery or to a sense of moral wrong but to external pressure and public opinion.[82] Moreover, the liberation of the *emancipados* was a mockery: "the course of the Brazilian Government about the Emancipados" had "been like that which it pursued about the slave trade. Left to itself, it did nothing:

[79] These letters appeared in the *Daily News* from July 2 to October, 1864, over the signature C. They were collected and published by Christie in 1865 under the title of *Notes on Brazilian Questions* with a long preface. In 1863 he published *The Brazil Correspondence in the Cases of the "Prince of Wales" and Officers of the "Forte," Reprinted from Papers Laid before Parliament*, containing "an introduction telling some truths about Brazil." The following discussion of the Christie affair is based largely on these two publications and on the documents and correspondence in the foreign relations reports of Brazil.

[80] Christie termed Kidder and Fletcher's *Brazil and the Brazilians* an "elaborate fulsome puff of Brazil which" had "done much mischief" (*The Brazil Correspondence*, p. iii).

[81] *The Brazil Correspondence*, p. iii. [82] *Ibid.*, p. ix.

it treated for a long time with neglect representations of the English Government; it did not answer notes. When obliged to reply, it protested that its dignity did not allow it to act while pressed by a foreign government; it resented interference, and claimed to be left free to execute its own laws, forgetting that treaty stipulations gave a right to England to interfere. At last after force had been used, and the English government was known to be serious, and there seemed no help for it, it" had "done what it ought to have done long before."[83] As for the Aberdeen Act, it still remained on the English statute books because Brazil had refused to make a new treaty, as other nations had done, which would enable Great Britain to maintain the suppression of the traffic. The act was continued as security against the renewal of the Brazilian trade. England could not "abandon in South America the privilege, which Mr. Bright freely" used "in the north of 'teaching the nations how to live'."[84]

The English merchants in Brazil, Christie contended, needed "the strong arm of their government to protect them," as fear was "the only effectual security for justice" and the British navy was "the right arm of the merchants. The gross amount of commerce" would be "regulated by wants, without treaties, which wants dispense with, and in spite of bad legislation, which wants baffle. But individuals from time to time" needed aid and protection: this their government must give them.[85] When he went to Brazil, Christie confessed, he was favorably inclined toward it, just as was the general public of England; but slowly by contact with the Rio court "he swung to the other side, since he saw that the government would do justice only through fear and that all reasonable demands were met with excuses and delays, evasions, subterfuges, and unfounded assertions."[86] In the end he became convinced that as England was necessary to Brazil, if the Brazilian government found "that they *must* behave properly," they would "take care so to behave." As long as the Rio court was "just and becomingly mod-

---

[83] Christie, *Notes on Brazilian Questions*, p. xxxv.
[84] *Ibid.*, pp. xlvi, lii-liii.
[85] *Ibid.*, p. liii.
[86] *Ibid.*, p. lxvii.

est and respectful," it need not fear "violence and want of moderation" by England against a weaker nation; but any deviation from the path of justice, modesty, and respectfulness would bring down upon Brazil the power of the British navy.[87]

These were the opinions of the diplomat in charge of the English legation at Rio during the crisis of 1863. He arrived at the time when the claims commission had reached the *impasse* resulting from the dispute over the slave trade cases. A firm believer in fear as the only effective security for justice and in force as the only instrument by which Brazil could be kept in hand thus became the crucial factor in Anglo-Brazilian relations at a time when thirty years of growing irritation and critical tension required the utmost tact to avoid a complete break between the two countries. The failure of the claims commission with the revival of the slave trade controversy greeted the impulsive Christie on his arrival; the habitual easy procrastination of the Latin irritated the envoy imbued with British ideas of energetic promptness; and no comprehension of the internal problems confronting the Brazilian government relieved the severity of his judgment. It was unfortunate that the course of Anglo-Brazilian relations depended on the action of a diplomat of Christie's bent.

Two incidents served as the occasion for the break in diplomatic relations which occurred in 1863. The first arose from the shipwreck of the *Prince of Wales*, out of Glasgow, on the desolate coast of the province of Rio Grande do Sul near a place called Albardão. Rumors of robbery and murder in connection with the disaster reached Consul H. P. Vereker who demanded an investigation of the "savage and wicked proceedings of the natives." At the inquest held on June 24, 1861, seventeen days after the wreck, only four bodies were produced, the burial place of six more having disappeared in the shifting sands of the deserted coast. The physician pronounced drowning as the probable cause of death in two cases; the other two bodies were in too bad a state to enable him to render any decision. But several facts pointed to robbery, or perhaps murder,

[87] *Brazil Correspondence*, pp. xxix and xxx.

and the possible complicity of the local officials in the crime. The sub-chief of police, a local officer who had arrived on the spot five days after the wreck, failed to inspect the bodies although ten could have been produced in good condition at that time. Many empty crates of crockery, many barrels, chests, and cases lay scattered on the beach with contents pillaged although nothing could be found except a Bible and some empty packing boxes which were unearthed in the house of the chief landed proprietor of the district. Moreover, the affair was aggravated by the distance of the wreck from any center of civilization, the quality and condition of the inhabitants of that region, and the prolonged time necessary to effect communication between Rio and the province.[88]

The imperial government, after receiving reports of the incident through regular channels, ordered a thorough investigation. When on October 25, the British envoy presented his official complaint, it was passed on to the provincial authorities by the Rio officials who entertained suspicions of robbery but denied the possibility of murder.[89] On September 6 a request to the Admiralty by the British Foreign Office asked that a war vessel be detached from the Rio squadron and sent to Rio Grande do Sul[90] where the inadequacy of the investigation carried on by the Brazilian authorities and the improbability of bringing the individuals involved to justice was disturbing Consul Vereker.[91]

---

[88] *Brazil Correspondence*, No. 1 and Enclosure 1, No. 2; Christie, *Notes*, pp. 177-179; Brazil, *Relatorio dos Negocios Extrangeiros*, 1862, pp. 56-57. R. P. Stephens of the Steampacket Company of Glasgow demanded £5,500 exclusive of the ship, plus £1,025, 19s for freight by way of damages, urged that a warship be sent to demand restitution, and insisted that "no more humbugging on the part of the Brazilian authorities be allowed" (*Brazil Correspondence*, Nos. 6 and 11).

[89] Brazil, *Relatorio dos Negocios Extrangeiros*, 1862, p. 57, and 1863, pp. 10-11; Christie denied that any action was taken until he forced the issue at Rio (*Brazil Correspondence*, No. 41).

[90] *Brazil Correspondence*, No. 4.

[91] *Ibid.*, No. 19. The chief of police pointed out the wealthiest inhabitants of the coast as the principal criminals (*ibid.*). Rio Grande do Sul was a frontier province, the traditional center of revolt against the authority of Rio. Public order was largely a question of local action among these independent plainsmen who recognized little authority beyond their own wills.

The president of the province refused to allow Captain Saumarez of the gunboat *Sheldrake*, sent as a result of the above request, to participate in the investigation,[92] while Consul Vereker reported that the action of the local authorities was entirely inadequate, the investigation being conducted not to ascertain the truth but to satisfy the British and the Rio governments.[93] By May 23, fifteen days less than a year after the wreck, seven culprits had been ascertained but none prosecuted.[94] At the same time Foreign Minister Taques declared to Christie that although the imperial government was free from any responsibility for acts ascribed to the inhabitants of the coast of Albardão, it intended to exert every effort to bring the culprits to justice.[95]

Just as Christie had reached the point of advising his home office that "as much pressure as possible" be exerted on the Brazilian government, a second incident occurred to aggravate the situation. According to Christie's version, three officers, a chaplain, a lieutenant, and a midshipman, of the crew of the British naval vessel, the *Forte*, on their return from a pleasure jaunt to Tijuca outside the city of Rio de Janeiro, were set upon by a Brazilian sentry, seized, forced to walk to the city as culprits, thrown into the worst prison of the capital, changed to a better and again to a better, and finally were released without cause shown for the detention. The reasons given later by the Brazilian authorities were that the officers were drunk and disorderly on the road; they had attacked the sentry without provocation and had been arrested on just cause. They were not in uniform and as soon as the fact was ascertained that they belonged to the English navy, they were released. Thirteen depositions were produced as evidence of this version

---

[92] Russell sent instructions to Christie insisting that a British officer should be on the spot at the time of the investigation (*Brazil correspondence*, No. 29).

[93] *Ibid.*, No. 33.

[94] *Ibid.*, No. 37.

[95] *Ibid.*, No. 27. For a detailed story of the events which occurred in Rio Grande do Sul and of the efforts of the Rio government to execute justice, see Brazil, *Relatorio dos Negocios Extrangeiros*, 1863, Annex, Documents Nos. 1-15. For texts of notes exchanged between the Brazilian Foreign Office and Christie, see *ibid.*, Nos. 16-29.

of the story. The officers swore, on the other hand, that they were the sober victims of an unprovoked attack by a sentry on the road to Rio.[96]

Both Christie and Admiral Warren, who credited the story of the three officers, considered that an insult had been offered the British navy. They recommended to London that the ensign in charge of the post and the sentry who started the row ought to be punished and that the Imperial Government should express regrets over the affair and apologize for the conduct of the prison officials of the capital.[97] Lord John Russell accepted the version of the minister and instructed him to demand the dismissal of the ensign, the punishment of the sentry, an apology by the Brazilian government, and a censure of the chief of police of Rio and the officials of the prison. He also demanded restitution and indemnity in the *Prince of Wales* case, the amount to be decided by arbitration.[98] On November 4, 1862, Russell authorized Christie to resort to reprisals in case Brazil refused to comply with these demands, although the minister was to refer any proposal of arbitration made by the Imperial Government to London. Later he suggested that the reprisals be in the form of seizure of property such as a government ship or, better, of private property in order to avoid a clash between the two governments.[99]

When Marquez de Abrantes, foreign minister, attempted to transfer the question to London where the Brazilian legation could confer directly with Lord John Russell, Christie pointed

---

[96] *Brazil Correspondence*, No. 45. Christie to Russell, August 7, 1862. For documents and correspondence exchanged between the Brazilian Foreign Office and Christie on the case of the *Forte*, see Brazil, *Relatorio dos Negocios Extrangeiros*, 1863, Annex, Nos. 30-34.

[97] *Brazil Correspondence*, No. 48.

[98] *Ibid.*, Nos. 52 and 53. On August 23, 1862, Christie reported that the subchief and the inspector of the district in the province had been dismissed for complicity or neglect of duty; eleven arrests had been made; fugitives to Montevideo were being sought; and prosecutions were being arranged. No admission by the Brazilian authorities as to the possibility of murder had been made and the action had been delayed until conviction would be difficult (*ibid.*, No. 49).

[99] *Brazil Correspondence*, Nos. 61 and 62. Orders were sent to Admiral Warren to carry out the reprisal orders (*ibid.*, No. 66).

out that unless satisfaction were given to him in Rio, he would be forced to resort to reprisals; if on December 27, no satisfaction had been received, he warned, recourse would be had to the navy.[100] On the twenty-ninth Abrantes refused to accede to the demands made by Lord John Russell; on the thirtieth Christie advised the minister of his order to Admiral Warren authorizing reprisals; from December 31 to January 5, Rio was blockaded; and Admiral Warren seized and held five merchant vessels flying the Brazilian flag.[101]

The notice of the blockade and the manner in which the five vessels were seized set the capital in a turmoil. Furious crowds gathered in the streets, on the squares, hills, and beaches, shouting curses and threats at the English, while some threatened to attack the British consulate and legation. Christie kept discreetly within doors and sent heated notes to the Brazilian foreign minister in regard to statements allowed to appear in the Rio papers. Both police and regular troops were required to prevent violence while only the popularity of the emperor and of João L. Viera Cansancão de Sinimbú (minister of commerce) enabled them to quiet the threatened riots by appealing to the crowds in person.[102] Forced to submit to superior force, Brazil yielded on the fifth and promised to pay whatever indemnity England might demand in the case of the *Prince of Wales*, without, however, recognizing the principle of responsibility which was an attribute to such acquiescence and against which it protested categorically. The demands in regard to the *Forte* were rejected outright but Rio consented to arbitration of the case.[103] The reprisals were stopped and the king of Belgium was chosen arbiter.

The Brazilian government immediately ordered its minister in London, Carvalho Moreira (later Barão de Penedo) to demand satisfaction from Great Britain for the seizure of the five vessels within Brazilian territorial waters and their detention

---

[100] *Brazil Correspondence*, No. 71; Brazil, *Relatorio dos Negocios Extrangeiros*, 1863, p. 12.

[101] Brazil, *Relatorio dos Negocios Extrangeiros*, 1863, Annex, Nos. 39 and 40; *Brazil Correspondence*, No. 72.

[102] Pereira da Silva, *Memorias*, I, 311; *Brazil Correspondence*, No. 72.

[103] Brazil, *Relatorio dos Negocios Extrangeiros*, 1863, pp. 12-13, and Annex, No. 53.

within the bay of Rio.[104] On February 23, 1863, Moreira remitted a check to Lord John Russell for £3,200 in payment for the damages caused by the loss of cargo and personal effects of the crew of the *Prince of Wales*, together with a heated protest reserving the right to require satisfaction for the seizures made in Rio. Two months later he demanded an expression of regret by England for violations of the national territory of Brazil and a recognition of the obligation to pay compensation, the amount of which would be determined by an arbiter. Russell refused; Moreira requested his passports and left England June 4, 1863.[105] One month later Cornwallis Eliot, *chargé* in the absence of Christie who had returned to England, obtained passports and left Brazil.[106]

Leopold of Belgium announced his acceptance as arbiter early in March before Moreira requested his passports[107] and in June rendered the decision that "in the manner in which the laws of Brazil were applied to the English officials, there was no offense, either premeditated or intended, to the British navy."[108] Thus the initiative in healing the breach between the two countries was left to England. Russell announced in Parliament his desire to renew relations; Portugal offered its mediation; and Brazil consented.[109]

Negotiations began in London in May, 1864, when the Conde de Lavradio, plenipotentiary mediator, proposed that England send a special envoy to Rio to declare: first, that the British government had no intention of offending the dignity nor of violating the territorial sovereignty of Brazil; second, that in view of King Leopold's decision, England deplored all acts

---

[104] *Ibid.*, 1863, Annex, No. 56.

[105] *Brazil Correspondence*, Nos. 78, 79, 81, 83-86, 88-91; Brazil, *Relatorio dos Negocios Extrangeiros*, 1863, Annex, Nos. 74-79; and 1864, Annex, Nos. 3-9.

[106] R. A. Campos, *Relações Diplomaticas do Brazil*, p. 176. A list of all the cabinets with dates of formation and changes from July 17, 1823, to March 7, 1871, is given in A. J. Mello Moraes, *Historia do Brazil-Reino e Brazil-Imperio*, I, 425-441.

[107] *Brazil Correspondence*, No. 87. Lord Howard de Walden to Russell, Brussels. March 4, 1863.

[108] The text of the decision is given in Brazil, *Relatorio dos Negocios Extrangeiros*, 1864, Annex I, No. 10. It may be found also in Pereira Pinto, *Apontamentos*, II, 316.

[109] Brazil, *Relatorio dos Negocios Extrangeiros*, 1864, pp. 8-9.

which had been practiced to revenge an offense which did not exist; third, that the British government lamented certain facts which had accompanied the reprisals; and fourth, that England admitted the obligation of paying the claims arising from the seizure of the five ships and would accept the decision of a mixed commission as to the amount due. Lord John Russell refused, but proposed that Edward Thornton, minister in Buenos Aires, should go to Brazil on a special mission to solicit an audience with the emperor when he would "express the sorrow with which the Queen" had "considered the circumstances which accompanied the suspension of friendly relations." England would disavow "in a most solemn manner every intention of offending the dignity of the Empire of Brazil"; it would accept unreservedly the sentence of the king of Belgium and would be pleased to nominate a minister to Brazil as soon as the emperor would consent to renew relations. The indemnity for seizures was refused, but in view of the threatened war with Paraguay and the delicate international situation created by Emperor Maximilian in Mexico, the Rio government yielded on that point. Thornton, who hastened from Buenos Aires to Uruguayana (in the province of Rio Grande do Sul) to present the apology to the emperor as agreed upon by the terms of the mediation, was received officially on November 14, 1865, as minister of England, while Carvalho Moreira was received in London in March of the next year.[110]

The interruption of diplomatic relations did not break the traditional economic connections between England and Brazil. On the contrary, in the words of a foreign minister of the Rio cabinet, they had "continued so closely allied in reciprocal interests that it could scarce be imagined that the two governments were separated by a question of so great an importance and difficulty."[111] During the period of suspension of formal relations two loans were floated in England by Brazil, Rothschild with Lord Palmerston's backing handling the bonds which

[110] Brazil, *Relatorio dos Negocios Extrangeiros*, 1866, pp. 1-5, and Annex I, Nos. 1-50; Nabuco, *Estadista do Imperio*, II, 317-318.

[111] Brazil, *Relatorio dos Negocios Extrangeiros*, 1866, p. 2.

were quickly absorbed by the British public.[112]

"Trembling, hoping, or grateful holders of Brazilian investments" which under the propaganda directed by a Brazilian agency in England had rapidly accumulated in the years preceding the crisis, socially prominent capitalists involved in loans and speculations, eminent Britishers on boards of directors of Brazilian railways and other companies, bankers, and merchants protested the action of the Foreign Office in the Christie affair.[113] Their position was stated in a *Daily News* article on February 12, 1863, by a writer who complained: "who of us, we ask Lord Russell, can trade safely with Brazil or any other country, who can buy Brazilian or foreign bonds of any kind, who can with common prudence invest his money in the railway shares of small and defenseless states . . . if mines like this are to be sprung under his feet by his own government"?[114] It was not economic interests that forced the crisis of 1863; on the contrary it was a question almost exclusively of the perpetuation or failure of the traditional political influence of Great Britain in Portuguese America.

In the contest Brazil yielded only when superior force was actually employed and severed relations when the pressure was removed, thus consummating the revolt against the political preëminence of England. It was definitely determined that the traditional political dependence which had existed for centuries between England and Portugal in Europe was not to be continued between Great Britain and Portuguese America. The trans-

---

[112] Nabuco, *Estadista do Imperio*, II, 319-320.

[113] Christie, *Notes*, p. lxix.

[114] *Brazil Correspondence*, pp. xvi-xvii Christie gives a detailed account of the means employed by the Brazilian government to spread favorable propaganda in England and of the agencies, newspapers, and persons connected with that effort. Letters in the *Daily News*, inspired articles in the *Edinburgh Review*, the *Morning Herald*, *The Brazil and River Plate Mail*, *The News*, and *The Star;* the attacks of Cobden, Bright, Lord Palmerston, Mr. Bramley Moore, and others; the conferring of degrees on Brazilian ministers by Oxford; and the expenditure of large sums (Christie estimated the amount spent yearly in foreign countries by Brazil for this purpose to be £30,000) by Brazilian agents were pointed out as evidences of the effort to create a favorable reputation for the empire (see the prefaces and letters in *Notes* and *Brazil Correspondence*, *passim*).

fer of that dominance to the new world effected between 1808 and 1825 and the virtual protectorate begun in the new empire between 1825 and 1827 failed to last. In the words of a writer[115] in the *Daily News*, "what English interests" had the succession of foreign ministers "promoted in Brazil?" They had not obtained a treaty of commerce nor a consular agreement such as France had secured; and they had not produced a settlement of the claims which the subjects of each country had on the government of the other, as the United States long since had obtained. In the opinion of the author, "a very different policy in Mr. Canning's time made Brazil an Empire almost dependent on England. A subsequent policy of 'taunting' " had "converted it into an Empire on which the English Government" had "not a particle of influence."[116]

In the first quarter of the century Brazil had been obliged to yield to the forceful diplomacy of the able ministers, Viscount Strangford and Lord Gordon, who were acting under the keen direction of Castlereagh and Canning. By 1850 the incipient empire was stabilized, confident with reference to the future, and divorced from the old idea of maintaining close relations with the European powers. Thirty years of continued friction, arising principally from the slave trade controversy, and the marked national and economic development of the empire had weaned Brazil from its political allegiance to Great Britain. In 1860 it was strong enough to sustain its revolt; thereafter friendly relations were to exist between the two governments, but the thread of political control by England in Portuguese territory—a thread which runs back in a remarkably clear fashion to 1640—was definitely broken in Brazil.

[115] The author, who signed as a "Friend of Both Countries," was W. H. Clark, formerly registrar of the Great Northern Railway, member of the Reform Club, paid correspondent of the Rio *Jornal do Commercio* (*Brazil Correspondence*, p. xiii), and coffee broker for a Rio firm (Christie, *Notes*, p. xxxiii).

[116] The article appeared in the *Daily News* of August 23, 1864, signed by a "Friend of Both Countries," quoted by Christie, *Notes*, pp. 105-106.

CHAPTER XI

THE ABOLITION OF SPECIAL PRIVILEGES

THE ATTITUDE which led the Rio government to resist British economic preëminence differed somewhat from that which prompted its revolt against the political dominance threatened by Great Britain. In the latter case, Brazil sought to eliminate English influence outright and, by cutting the traditional thread which had linked the British and Portuguese empires politically for centuries, to terminate the virtual protectorate, the foundations of which had been established in Brazil between 1808 and 1827. The economic phase of the revolt, on the other hand, aimed not at severing connections with England, but at placing that country on an equal footing with other nations by abolishing the special privileges granted by the treaty.

Evidence of this point of view may be found in the protests of Brazilian writers, which are directed, not against British economic enterprise, but against the vexatious restrictions imposed by the stronger on the weaker nation. Pereira Pinto, who was so severe in his criticism of the arbitrary and arrogant attitude of England in political matters, commended the aid which British capital had rendered Brazil in opening roads and developing national industries.[1] Dunshee de Abranches[2] interpreted the action of the Brazilian statesmen who negotiated the treaties of 1825-1827 as an effort to free Brazil from the humiliating position of Portugal which had always lived "un-

[1] Antonio Pereira Pinto, *Apontamentos para o Direito Internacional*, I, 386.

[2] Dunshee de Abranches, authority on foreign affairs, member of the Assembly, and at one time chairman of the Committee on Diplomacy and Treaties of the National Assembly, was a severe critic of Great Britain in its dealings with Brazil. For an expression of an opinion see his speech reprinted with a bitter preface by an unsigned author under the title *A Inglaterra e a Soberania do Brazil.*

der the mailed fist of old England."[3] Although the effort failed and a mortifying reproduction of the 1810 treaty was forced upon the empire, it was not the preëminence of English capital and commerce which provoked his criticism but the extraterritorial privileges, consular concessions, and restrictions on the sovereignty of the nation imposed by the terms of the treaty.[4] Oliveira Lima summarized the attitude of Brazil in regard to this phase of the revolt against British preëminence in his statement that England enjoyed in the empire privileges which called to mind those imposed by European powers on far-Eastern nations.[5]

The desire to abolish those privileges and restrictions inspired the revolt of Brazil against British economic preëminence, this issue thus becoming another phase of the movement described in the preceding chapters. The aim of the Brazilians was not to eliminate British interests in their foreign commerce, capital investments, or domestic enterprises, but to free themselves from economic restrictions imposed by England and to open their country to the competition of other nations. As long as Great Britain could maintain its paramount position by economic superiority, its preëminence in Brazilian commerce, investment, and shipping would be assured. If a competitor should come to rival the advantages offered by England, no exclusive privileges obtained by political pressure would remain to bolster Britain's position. The story of Anglo-Brazilian economic relations after 1827 thus centers, first, in the efforts of the Rio government to free itself from the restrictions imposed by England during the period from 1808 to 1827, and second, in the rise of competitors who were to challenge Britain's position.

The main obstacle which barred the path to freedom from restrictions was the commercial treaty negotiated by Lord Gordon in 1827.[6] That agreement was objectionable for several

---

[3] Dunshee de Abranches, *A Expansão Economica e o Commercio Exterior do Brazil*, p. 70.

[4] *Ibid.*, pp. 70-71.

[5] Manoel de Oliveira Lima, *O Imperio Brazileiro*, p. 208.

[6] See *supra*. pp. 208-210.

reasons. In the first place, although the constitution of the empire had expressly abolished all special jurisdiction, the English were granted a continuation of the century-old right to maintain judges conservators or special magistrates, before whom cases involving British subjects might be tried. The right was to continue until a satisfactory substitute could be established; yet despite the criminal code and the judicial system inaugurated by the empire, England refused to relinquish the extra-territorial privilege and in 1835 the council of state in Rio announced formally that it was "prudent to yield to the demands" of the British government "since it refused to recognize as satisfactory the judges instituted under the Constitution of the Empire."[7]

A second objection arose from the right granted to English consuls not only to administer the property of British subjects who died intestate in Brazil[8] but also to sign clearance papers and handle complaints in the customs houses on the same plane as native administrators. A third objection resulted from the fifteen per cent. maximum import duties levied on English goods. By most favored nation clauses this rate was granted at once to certain other countries which signed commercial treaties with the empire; and by the decree of September 28, 1828, it was extended to include all goods imported into the country irrespective of the nationality or origin of the commodities. Thus although the market of Brazil was thrown open to the competition of all nations despite the efforts of England and France to maintain an exclusive field for their efforts, the empire was limited to a maximum tariff of fifteen per cent. Since the revenue from the customs houses furnished the chief income of the imperial government, the Rio court in 1836 was forced to impose an export tax of eight per cent. when growing expenses created a deficit.[9]

---

[7] Dunshee de Abranches, *Expansão Economica*, p. 73.

[8] This point rose to importance after the abolition of the judge conservatorship at the expiration of the treaty in 1844. It is discussed in detail in connection with Anglo-Brazilian relations of that period. See *infra*, pp. 298 ff.

[9] Dunshee de Abranches, *A Expansão Economica*, pp. 71 and 132; Oliveira Lima, *O Imperio Brazileiro*, pp. 199-200.

Moreover, under the treaty the manufacturers of Brazil were hopelessly handicapped by the lack of protection and British articles had practically free entrance into the empire; yet the principal exports of coffee and sugar from the South American nation were excluded from England by prohibitive duties. Brazilian shipping was also sacrificed in benefit of the English merchant marine; and the coastwise trade, by right the exclusive privilege of the native, was endangered by the pretensions of British shipping interests.[10]

The irritation which resulted in Brazil from these privileges granted to a foreign power and from the restrictions imposed on the sovereignty of the empire were aggravated by the tone assumed by the London Foreign Office.[11] The opinion was current among Brazilians that the English cabinets and foreign ministers adopted as the only method of treating with the Rio government a note of disdain on the one hand or threats of armed intervention on the other; their attitude was the same as that assumed toward the uncivilized or semi-barbarous nations of the South Seas or Africa. In the words of Minister Macedo, "it was always with a threat on its lips that the English Government spoke to Brazil."[12]

By Article XXVIII the obnoxious treaty of 1827 was to remain in force for fifteen years from the date of ratification,[13] with the understanding that it would continue to operate thereafter unless one of the contracting parties should give notice of its termination. In case of such notification two years were to elapse before the treaty became void. Thus in 1842 England was faced with the necessity of renewing the existing treaty, concluding a new agreement, or allowing the privileges obtained in 1827 to expire.

Consequently, early in 1842 Aberdeen sent[14] a draft of a new treaty to be negotiated by Minister Hamilton-Hamilton at Rio.

---

[10] Dunshee de Abranches, *A Expansão Economica*, p. 73; and *supra*, pp. 208-210.

[11] Dunshee de Abranches, *op. cit.*, p. 74.

[12] Letter of Minister Sergio de Macedo to Lord Clarendon, May 16, 1854, quoted by Dunshee de Abranches, *op. cit.*, p. 75.

[13] Ratifications were exchanged in London on November 10, 1827.

[14] F. O. 131/12, Aberdeen to Hamilton, No. 2. February 1, 1842.

The diplomat, in the first place, was to insist that the treaty of 1827 was to be valid until 1844[15] in order to give time for the negotiation of a new agreement. The draft sent to the minister as a basis for his efforts was a reproduction of the old treaty with two important innovations. By Article IX of the new project the emperor of Brazil was to engage "to take into His consideration the question of abolishing Slavery throughout the whole of His Dominions" and in the meantime to decree, within two months from the date of ratification, that all children born in Brazil whether of slave parents or free should be free subjects of the empire. Thus he would settle effectively the vexing question of the slave trade by abolishing the incentive of the traffic. In return for that concession on the part of the emperor, England (by Article XV of the project) undertook to lower its duties on Brazilian sugar and coffee six months after the decree granting freedom to all children had been issued. Furthermore, reductions on Brazilian nuts, cocoa, untanned hides, bones, ostrich feathers, sarsaparilla, woods, and other articles would be conceded. In other respects the draft resembled the treaty then in force.[16]

If, however, Hamilton found it impossible to secure the new clause as to slavery, he was to warn the Rio government that England would "never relax in any effort which Her treaties and Her power" might "enable her to apply" in stopping the traffic. Then he was to secure an extension of the old treaty intact.[17]

When the envoy proposed negotiations, he was informed that the Brazilians intended to treat with Aberdeen direct through their minister at London. Yet on April 10, undaunted by this

[15] The Brazilian government insisted that the treaty terminated outright in 1842 but England maintained that notification of expiration could not be given until November of that year, which would cause the agreement to terminate two years later, or in November, 1844. After consulting the ministers of France and the United States, the Rio government consented to the extension of time (F. O. 131/12, Ellis to Aberdeen, No. 30. February 20, 1843).

[16] F. O. 131/12, Aberdeen to Hamilton, No. 2. Enclosure: draft of proposed treaty.

[17] *Ibid.*, No. 2. Instructions to Hamilton.

initial check, he opened the subject of the commercial treaty with Foreign Minister Aureliano; on May 18, however, he reported to the London Office his impression that Brazil would conclude no commercial treaty with England or anyone else.[18] In July Aberdeen modified his instructions so as to leave three options open to his agent: first, an arrangement which, in addition to the advantages of the second and third options, included the slavery and sugar claims; second, an arrangement with no mention of slavery or sugar but with guaranties of special privileges such as the admission of Brazilian coffee (not sugar) at reduced import duties into England and the fifteen per cent. on English articles taken into Brazil; and third, a simple reciprocity agreement with a most favored nation clause.[19] The first option was the paramount point to be obtained. Two months later, however, he modified these instructions still further by authorizing the signature of an agreement which omitted any reference to sugar or slavery, those subjects to be left for a separate convention at a later date.[20] Thus Aberdeen gradually reduced his original demands to the simple extension of the existing treaty.

Despite Hamilton-Hamilton's pessimistic report, the London Office considered the question of the commercial agreement important enough to warrant a special envoy. Henry Ellis, therefore, was sent to negotiate in place of the diplomat stationed at Rio. On his arrival he was "met with ceremonial pomp, received by the emperor and his sisters, saluted by all the war vessels at anchor in the port of Rio de Janeiro, and applauded and hailed by the English merchants residing in the capitol." His ostentatious magnificence with guards at the door of his residence, his splendid carriages with eight thoroughbred horses brought from England, his liveried servants and sumptuous mode of living made him the object of universal curiosity.[21]

---

[18] F. O. 131/12, Aberdeen to Henry Ellis, No. 2. August 26, 1842, and enclosures.

[19] *Ibid.*, Aberdeen to Hamilton, No. 14. July 6.

[20] *Ibid.*, Aberdeen to Ellis, No. 7. September 28.

[21] J. M. Pereira da Silva, *Memorias do Meu Tempo*, I, 98-99.

Yet his task was a difficult one; for despite the splendor of his reception, he faced the apprehension and even the hatred of the public and the press. As he reported to Aberdeen,[22] the language of the newspapers of Rio was "absurdly violent and impertinent." One journal[23] pointed out that the emperor could not act as D. Pedro I had done in signing the 1827 agreement, as by Paragraph 8 of Article 102 of the constitution any treaty which set new rates for imports must be approved by the Chamber before it could become law. Thus the empire could defend itself against the determination of England "not to lose the power which she" had "of enslaving Brazil with treaties . . . after the same manner as she" had "accomplished with regard to Portugal during the long intercourse of two hundred years" since the separation from Spain in 1640. The history of Anglo-Portuguese relations was clear evidence, the article continued, of Britain's systematic policy of utilizing occasions when its allies were in difficulties to increase its own power. That "political leech" was now talking of renewing a treaty which had made of Brazilian commerce an English monopoly; no such agreement should be signed.

In addition to the opposition of public opinion[24] Ellis was faced with the ill will of the ministry. He reported that it was hopeless to propose in the actual temper of the Brazilian government any comprehensive scheme such as that laid down in the instructions to Hamilton. Moreover, it was futile even to attempt to fix a set rate of import duties on British articles entering Brazil as the cabinet then in office, as well as any other that might succeed to power, was opposed to fettering the cus-

---

[22] F. O. 131/12, Ellis to Aberdeen, No. 11. November 26, 1842.

[23] *O Pharol Constitucional* of November 12. Translation was enclosed by Ellis (*ibid.*). Translation of another article of similar vein, published in *Diario do Rio* on November 22, was enclosed also. In a later dispatch Ellis enclosed a vicious attack on him personally, published in *O Brazil* (*ibid.*, No. 21).

[24] For a detailed exposition of the attitude of the public toward the ministers who negotiated with the English agent, see Pereira da Silva, *Memorias*, I, 100-108. At one time the Chamber of Deputies became so uncertain as to the ability of the foreign minister to sustain Brazilian rights in the face of Britain's attitude that it demanded the entire correspondence exchanged between the minister and the envoy (*ibid.*, p. 106).

toms house with permanent maximum rates. The only recourse left was to secure a treaty which would guarantee the individual rights of the persons and property of British subjects, thus putting Great Britain on an equality with other nations in Brazil.[25]

As a matter of fact, he reported, the British merchants in Rio did not require more than that guaranty of equality. He had learned this to his surprise at a meeting wherein he had discussed the situation with the merchants themselves. They revealed to him quite clearly that they linked no importance to the continuation of the treaty of 1827. Under various forms English goods were paying twenty-one per cent., some as high as forty per cent., and Brazil would be stupid, said the merchants, to load any more duties on suddenly. Nor were they solicitous about maintaining the conservatorial courts, for, as they reported, traders of other nations were not suffering injustice in the administration of the law although only the British had the privilege of extra-territorial jurisdiction. They accepted the customs rates then in operation and merely desired a guaranty of the status of equality of all nations for the future. A simple reciprocity treaty with a most favored nation clause would suffice for their desires, but even that would be difficult to secure as the action of the British government in suppressing the slave trade had created such antagonism that any agreement whatever was very uncertain.[26]

Ellis, therefore, decided to sacrifice the fifteen per cent. rate and the conservatorial courts and to present terms so free from objectionable points that their rejection could occur only in case the Rio court was determined "to stand aloof from all connection with Great Britain." But when he proposed to Foreign Minister Aureliano a treaty granting England equality with other nations, France for instance, the minister parried by insisting that something would have to enter as to the conduct of British cruisers in Brazilian waters. When Ellis suggested that the slave trade and commercial treaties were sepa-

[25] F. O. 131/12, Ellis to Aberdeen, No. 16. December 16. 1842.

[26] *Ibid.*, No. 15.

rate negotiations and should not be confused, Aureliano, silenced but unconvinced, returned to the point at a later date.[27]

In January, 1843, the envoy learned that the Assembly opposed any treaty with any nation which refused to allow Brazilian produce to enter on the same basis as produce from the colonies of that nation.[28] Soon afterward the new foreign minister[29] announced that the conditions on which he proposed to treat were the admission into England of Brazilian produce on the same footing as goods introduced from British colonies, and, despite the warning by Ellis that such conditions would terminate negotiations, persisted in his stand.[30] The British envoy thereupon advertised his furniture for sale, had one more conversation with the minister, closed the negotiation, and sailed for home.[31] In a confidential report Ellis interpreted the action of the Rio court as an attempt to force England to send another special minister who should bring larger powers enabling him to grant the concessions required by Brazil in regard to the entrance of its chief exports, sugar and coffee, into England. In Honorio Hermeto's opinion Great Britain would be forced eventually to concede those terms in view of the large credits granted to Brazil by English interests.[32]

Without waiting for that second mission to materialize, the Rio office ordered José de Araujo Ribeiro, Brazilian minister at Paris, to negotiate a treaty at London.[33] On November 3, 1843, he presented two projects, one of commerce and the other of limits,[34] with the statement that he was authorized to sign

---

[27] *Ibid.*, No. 16 (December 16) and No. 19 (December 23). Ellis stated that he was empowered also to close a slave trade convention but the two negotiations were to be kept distinct.

[28] *Ibid.*, No. 23. January 14, 1843.

[29] Honorio Hermeto Carneiro Leão followed Aureliano de Souza e Oliveira Coutinho as foreign minister on January 20, 1843. He was also prime minister (Mello Moraes, *Historia do Brazil-Reino e do Brazil-Imperio*, I, 435).

[30] F. O. 131/12, Ellis to Aberdeen, No. 27.

[31] *Ibid.*

[32] *Ibid.*, No. 28. February 20, 1843.

[33] Brazil, *Relatorio dos Negocios Extrangeiros*, 1844, pp. 7-8.

[34] The second project was an attempt to settle the boundary between British Guiana and Brazil.

both or neither.[35] The first was unacceptable in Aberdeen's opinion as it was more restricted in its terms than any treaty then in force between Great Britain and any other power in any part of the world; and the second was not a matter to be confused with commercial questions. Hence England could not accept these terms; Ribeiro could not grant others; and negotiations again broke down.[36]

In his reply to Ribeiro, Aberdeen revealed the motives underlying Britain's actions during the negotiations. Brazil, he said, was demanding entrance into England of its chief raw materials, sugar and coffee principally, on the same terms that such imports from British colonies enjoyed, and in return was willing to grant only most favored nation treatment to England in the matter of importations of manufactured articles. Such an arrangement would mean that while England would be forced to compete with other foreign nations for the Brazilian market, the empire would be allowed to compete with English colonial possessions in the British market, a situation which was quite inadvisable. In the first place, no real reciprocity was possible under those conditions, for whereas Brazil, by imposing a high tariff on all nations and thereby fostering its own manufacturing interests, could limit British imports, England could not restrict Brazilian importations without prejudicing *ipso facto* imports from its own colonies.

In the second place, as long as slavery and the slave trade persisted in Brazil, the entrance of raw products grown in the empire would have to be excluded from British markets. This was necessary for two reasons: first, the admission of Brazilian sugar into England would tend to increase the traffic and to strengthen slavery by the increased demand for the product; and second, it would not be "just to expose the West Indian planters, the cost of whose production" had "been greatly enhanced by the emancipation of the negroes,[37] to a competition

---

[35] F. O. 131/15, Aberdeen to Hamilton, No. 1. January 3, 1844. Enclosure 1.

[36] *Ibid.*, No. 1. Enclosure 2.

[37] On the margin opposite this statement in Aberdeen's letter there is an unsigned, uninitialed comment, "a dangerous admission." It will be remembered

upon terms nearly approaching to those of absolute equality with the Sugars of a Country in which labour" was "obtained at a much lower charge and from very different sources." To replace the advantageous treaty of 1827 with an agreement so unfavorable to England's interests was quite impossible.

Thus the initial efforts of Hamilton, the special mission of Ellis, and the London negotiations failed to secure even a simple renewal of the treaty which was to expire in November, 1844. In a last futile effort Aberdeen sent Hamilton instructions to sign an agreement in Rio which, though not as desirable as England could desire, might save the situation. He was authorized to propose a treaty in every essential point similar to the commercial draft presented by Araujo Ribeiro in London.[38] Great Britain would be content to remain on a footing of equality with other nations, provided that status could be guaranteed by treaty.

But even this moderate wish proved impossible of attainment, due largely to the shadow cast by the slave trade controversy. In the five months prior to the date when Hamilton received instructions to close any treaty which would grant England parity with other nations,[39] three assaults on British naval officers occurred in different sections of the empire. On January 5 at Santos the commander, the master, and the steward of the *Frolic* were severely beaten on their way from the town to the beach where their gig was awaiting them. All three were in uniform. On March 4 the envoy reported an assault on the crew of the *Growler* at Pernambuco; and on February 27 he reported the imprisonment of the sailors and the seizure of the gig of Lieutenant Hoare of the *Dolphin* when he went ashore for supplies at Ubatuba. In all three cases the cruisers had been

---

that the apprenticeship period in the British possessions ended in 1837 when complete emancipation was granted.

[38] F. O. 131/15, Aberdeen to Hamilton, No. 7. April 3, 1844. Aberdeen stated that a refusal to sign the commercial treaty would be "little short of actual hostility" and that England had a right to demand a continuation of the old slave trade convention (J. F. Cady, *Foreign Intervention in the Rio de la Plata, 1838-50,* p. 132).

[39] The instructions were sent April 3 and were received May 16, 1844 (F. O., 131/15, Aberdeen to Hamilton, No. 7).

active in suppressing the slave traffic in the vicinity where the assaults occurred.[40] So sensitive had public opinion become on the subject of Anglo-Brazilian relations, or so the Brazilian foreign minister interpreted the situation, that any negotiations had to be kept a profound secret in order to prevent the opposition from utilizing the issue to carry the next election.[41] In the provinces the opposition was raising the cry of "subserviency to England" as the outstanding dishonor of the present ministry,[42] and was preaching a crusade against the venality of the cabinet in its devotion to Great Britain.[43]

On May 18 Hamilton broached the subject of the proposed treaty,[44] yet no plenipotentiary had been named to treat with him by October, although the existing agreement would expire the following month.[45] On November 9 the minister of foreign affairs notified the provincial authorities that the Anglo-Brazilian treaty of 1827 had expired and the conservatorial courts were abolished.[46] Plenipotentiaries were appointed to treat with Hamilton late in November,[47] full powers were exchanged in January, 1845, and there the matter rested[48] until in June the Brazilian minister submitted two conditions as the *sine qua non* of any commercial treaty. In the first place, England must grant indemnities for seizures made by British cruisers under the illegal interpretation of the convention existing between the two countries; and second, the boundary dispute over the British Guiana frontier must be settled.[49] Since England consistently refused to recognize the illegality of the seiz-

[40] F. O. 13/211, Hamilton to Aberdeen, Nos. 13, 17, 21, and 35.

[41] F. O. 13/212, Hamilton to Aberdeen, No. 48.

[42] *Ibid.*, No. 50.

[43] F. O. 13/213, Hamilton to Aberdeen, No. 73.

[44] F. O. 13/212, Hamilton to Aberdeen, No. 42.

[45] F. O. 13/214, Hamilton to Aberdeen, No. 75.

[46] Hamilton attempted to secure the continuance of the courts as a perpetual institution until a satisfactory substitute could be secured. Neither the Brazilian government nor his own Foreign Office consented to this view, however, and the courts were abolished definitely (F. O. 13/214, Hamilton to Aberdeen, No. 88, and F. O. 13/224, Aberdeen to Hamilton, No. 23, April 21, 1845).

[47] F. O. 13/214, Hamilton to Aberdeen, No. 89.

[48] F. O. 13/215, Hamilton to Aberdeen, No. 5.

[49] F. O. 13/224, Hamilton to Aberdeen, No. 46. June 21, 1845.

ures in question, negotiations terminated, this time indefinitely.

The Aberdeen Act of 1845 was a climax to the negotiations just as it was to the attempts to conclude a slave trade convention. In reporting the situation in December, 1845, Hamilton, after enclosing a very bitter attack on England published in a Pernambuco newspaper, stated that it was not alone in that city or province that the Brazilian press indulged "in such virulent invective against England, her Government, and her people." Wherever a provincial press existed, the same feeling was manifested in its publications and that hostile attitude was spreading and acquiring day by day, greater intensity. The moving principle at that time, he explained, was the so-called "Piratical Act of Parliament"[50] and England's "intrusive intervention" in the affairs of South America.[51] In the face of that universal opposition no cabinet dared enter into a treaty with Great Britain.

As a matter of fact, no treaty of commerce and amity was concluded, nor has one ever been signed between Brazil and England since that date. The empire, liberated at last from the restrictions imposed by Great Britain as the price of recognition in 1827, was free to develop a national foreign policy unhampered by international complications of a political character. The key to this independence of action was Great Britain, for that country with its extraordinary privileges had served as the basis for the most favored nation treatment extended to other powers. Thus with the termination of the Anglo-Brazilian treaty, the Rio government was free to establish a new basis for its commercial relations with all foreign countries. Extra-territorial jurisdiction was materially restricted; the continuance of the British monopoly was henceforth to depend on England's economic superiority over its rivals; and tariffs could be adjusted to the needs of the em-

[50] The "Piratical Act" referred to the Aberdeen Act.

[51] F. O. 13/227, Hamilton to Aberdeen, No. 84. December 6, 1845. A detailed account of this intervention of Great Britain in South America may be found in John F. Cady, *Foreign Intervention in the Rio de la Plata, 1838-50*. The relations of Brazil and England during that intervention, particularly between 1838 and 1846, are discussed in chapter V.

pire as understood by the Rio government.

Yet despite the successful revolt against special concessions there still survived one form of extra-territorial jurisdiction which Brazil found it extremely difficult to abolish. By Article II of the Anglo-Brazilian commercial treaty of 1827, consuls were granted the right to administer the properties of the citizens of their respective countries, who died *ab intestato*, in so far as the laws of each nation permitted such action.[52] The stipulations which defined that right were so vague, however, that innumerable controversies arose in relation to the collection, the care, and the final disposal of the possessions of British subjects dying in Brazil, the consular jurisdiction over the property of the deceased being extended eventually to include all cases of goods left by foreigners whether or not wills existed or relatives or heirs were present to serve as administrators.[53] The article was interpreted by one English envoy to mean that British citizens although living in Brazil could dispose of their properties strictly according to the laws of England without any reference whatever to the national laws of Brazil.[54]

With the expiration of the commercial treaty in 1844, the jurisdiction of English consuls over the property of their fellow citizens dying intestate terminated, and all possessions of deceased British subjects were administered by the judge of orphans (*juiz dos orfãos*) if the deceased left no will or if there was no heir or relative to administer the estate. Minister Hamilton admitted the legality of the new régime, but lamented the harm which the change in administration would do to the commercial relations of the two countries. It was unfortunate, he contended, that the English should be subjected to national jurisdiction in these cases whereas the French were exempt forever from any interference by local authorities in the disposal of goods left by their citizens, and he requested that the law grant-

---

[52] Treaty of Friendship, Navigation, and Commerce, signed August 17, 1827. See *supra*, pp. 208-210.

[53] Pinto Pereira, *Apontamentos*, II, 286-288.

[54] Brazil, *Relatorio dos Negocios Extrangeiros*, 1854, Annex A, Henry Howard to Limpo de Abreu, April 24, 1854.

ing jurisdiction to the judge of the orphans not be enforced.[55]

The law was enforced, however, and as far as England was concerned, the consular jurisdiction over the estates of deceased citizens dying intestate in Brazil was ended for the time being. Since the stipulations contained in the Anglo-Brazilian commercial treaty served as the basis of the demands of other foreign powers to similar jurisdiction, it was to be expected that after 1844 all consular jurisdiction of this nature would terminate regardless of the nationality of the consul or of the deceased. France, nevertheless, flatly refused to consider the privileges terminated, successfully retained jurisdiction by its consuls over the property of French citizens dying in Brazil, secured a consular convention in 1860, and by keeping alive the privilege, eventually enabled England to recover the right lost in 1844. It was not until 1907 that the Rio government succeeded in throwing off this form of extra-territorial jurisdiction. The story is a curious one, illustrative of the long struggle required of Brazil in its efforts to free itself from the tutelage of European powers.

The commercial treaty[56] signed by D. Pedro I and Charles X of France on January 8, 1826, did not grant judge conservatorships to the French, but by Article IV consuls were granted the same privileges in protecting the interests of their fellow citizens as those which were or had been granted to the consuls of the most favored nation. They were thus conceded the right to collect, administer, and liquidate the inheritances of French citizens who died intestate, unhampered by any interference from the local Brazilian authorities.

In an attempt to clarify the whole question of the adminis-

---

[55] Brazil, *Relatorio dos Negocios Extrangeiros*, 1847, Annex, No. 93, Hamilton to the Imperial Government, April 2, 1846. The envoy was protesting against the administration of the goods left by one John George March, a British subject who died on his farm in the Organ Mountains in 1845. Despite the protests of Hamilton and his successor, James Hudson, the Brazilian authorities, not the English consul, administered the goods of the deceased British subject (*ibid.*, Nos. 94-96, 98). Protests on other cases which terminated in the same way as the March question were entered also (*ibid.*, Nos. 99-110).

[56] The treaty was ratified by Brazil on June 6 and by France on March 19. The text is given in Pereira Pinto, *Apontamentos*, II, 43-56.

tration of properties left by deceased, whether natives of Brazil or foreigners, the Rio government in 1842 and 1845 issued regulations respecting the collection and disposal of the goods of deceased persons or of persons whose whereabouts was unknown. In these regulations were included certain stipulations regarding the administration of properties of foreigners dying without a will or without heirs present to take charge of the inheritance. Such properties were defined and ordered liquidated and the proceeds turned over to the national treasury in case of escheat; a system of bookkeeping was established; the duties and pay of officials were specified; and provisions for methods of sale and liquidation drawn up. Then by Article XLIII it was declared that the unclaimed inheritances (*bens jacentes*) and escheats (*bens vagos*) belonging to foreigners dying in Brazil with or without testament who were not citizens of nations signatory to conventions containing stipulations to the contrary should be subject to the terms of these regulations. All judicial and administrative acts relative to such goods should be performed in Brazilian courts with the assistance of the respective consuls or of some person authorized by them to act in their place.[57]

France protested immediately and effectively.[58] The following September the Rio court issued a circular letter to the governors of the provinces explaining that the decrees of 1842 and 1845 did not apply to the unclaimed inheritances or escheats belonging to French subjects who died with or without testament,[59] although the Anglo-Brazilian treaty which had served as the most favored nation basis for these claims of France had

[57] Pereira Pinto, *Apontamentos*, II, Documentos A, pp. 70-88, and B, pp. 89-92. Properties of deceased and absent were defined as: goods of deceased with or without wills when it is known or presumed that there are heirs who are absent; goods of absent persons, whose whereabouts are unknown or whose existence is undetermined. Such goods were to be administered until the heirs appeared or until they escheated to the state. Escheated goods were defined as: properties without established owners; properties belonging to a deceased who left no relative nearer than the tenth degree, or whose heirs repudiated the inheritance.

[58] Dunshee de Abranches, *Tratados*, p. 42.

[59] The text of the circular is given in Pereira Pinto, *Apontamentos*, II, note 6, pp. 17-18.

expired. Again France protested, this time against the fact that merely unclaimed inheritances and escheats were excluded from the operation of the decrees; France maintained that all inheritances whether heirs were present and known or absent and unknown fell under the exclusive jurisdiction of French consuls.[60] The right to this jurisdiction was based on Article XXV of the commercial treaty of 1826 which stated that consular privileges granted in the terms of the agreement were perpetual. The Rio government on the other hand maintained that although by the perpetual nature of the privileges granted by the 1826 treaty France did possess the right to administer the unclaimed inheritances and escheats of its subjects, no further jurisdiction was justified under the agreement. In the case where heirs were present to receive and administer inheritances, legal proceedings must conform to Brazilian law and all taxes, tithes, and expenses paid as stipulated in the decrees of 1842 and 1845. Moreover, since the Franco-Brazilian treaty called for perfect reciprocity, Brazil recommended that France establish similar regulations with reference to the jurisdiction of Brazilian consuls, pointing out at the same time that the exemptions conceded the Paris government established France as the most favored nation in Brazil in view of the expiration of the agreement with England.[61]

A second difficulty complicated the situation, for in addition to the question of jurisdiction over inheritances, there arose the problem of nationality. By the constitution of the empire[62] all persons "born in Brazil, whether free-born or freedmen, even of foreign fathers" were Brazilian citizens, "so long as these" were "not in residence in the service of their country." France, backed by England and other powers, denied cate-

[60] *Ibid.*, II, 19. Note of the French minister dated March 4, 1846.

[61] Reply of Barão de Cayrú to the French minister, October 21, 1846. Text is given in Pereira Pinto, *Apontamentos*, II, note 7, pp. 19-21. Councillor Alves Branco stated the grounds on which Brazil could contest the perpetual nature of the consular privileges in an opinion rendered as a member of the Council of State, January 27, 1847 (*ibid.*, IV, Note 5, pp. 228-231).

[62] Title II, Article 6, Paragraph 1. Text of the constitution is given in H. G. James, *The Constitutional System of Brazil.*

gorically the loss of citizenship by the son of a foreign national born in Brazil and maintained the right of consular jurisdiction over the property of such children, whereas Brazil asserted that the mere fact of the place of birth irrevocably determined Brazilian citizenship and established the right of national jurisdiction over such persons.[63]

In order to clarify the situation and in response to the protests of the foreign powers, the Rio government promulgated the decree[64] in 1851 by which it clearly specified the exemptions and prerogatives of the consuls and the manner in which they should collect, administer, and liquidate the inheritances of subjects of their respective nations. By this decree consuls were granted jurisdiction in case the deceased died intestate without legal heirs present or in case there was a will but no heir present to claim the inheritance. In case one of the heirs, whether present or absent, was a Brazilian citizen, however, jurisdiction fell to Brazilian courts.

Liberal as the decree was,[65] it still left the question of nationality on the basis established by the constitution and restricted the jurisdiction of consuls to the administration of one type of inheritance. The powers of Europe demanded complete and exclusive jurisdiction over all kinds of inheritances and insisted pertinaciously in a reinterpretation of the disputed article of the constitution.[66] The inheritance law of 1851, Minister Howard pointed out, worked great injury to English subjects since if they had any capital invested in Brazil, they were forced to dispose of their property and make their wills in accordance with Brazilian laws instead of British regulations. If any error

[63] By a joint note signed by the entire consular body at Rio, dated January 11, 1845, an interpretation of this article of the constitution was requested. The consuls asserted that this stipulation was optional, not imperative, the choice of citizenship being left to the person born on Brazilian soil of a foreign father (Brazil *Relatorio dos Negocios Extrangeiros*, 1847).

[64] Pereira Pinto, *Apontamentos*, II, Documento C, pp. 93-102.

[65] The French minister commented specifically on the liberality of the regulations in respect to the entire range of consular activity (Pereira Pinto, *Apontamentos*, II, Note 10, p. 23). It was the position assumed in regard to inheritances and nationality to which the powers objected.

[66] Dunshee de Abranches, *Tratados*, p. 43.

was discovered in the will, the deceased was declared to have died *intestate*, his goods were sold and estate liquidated to the great damage of heirs in England, to business partners, or to anyone investing in the company. Moreover, many vexatious delays and losses resulted from the local jurisdiction of the *juiz dos orfãos* and the expenses of administration under Brazilian laws were so great that often there was nothing left for the heirs. And finally, every member of an English family when only one child was born in Brazil became subject to Brazilian jurisdiction although the parents and other children were still natives of England. Surely, the minister concluded, the Rio government would not refuse to remedy a situation so prejudicial to Anglo-Brazilian commercial relations.[67]

In the face of similar protests the imperial government gradually shifted its attitude in regard to the question of inheritances and nationality of foreigners. At first, from 1842 to 1857, the Rio court vigorously defended its right to extend national jurisdiction over inheritances of foreigners and maintained the principles of nationality enunciated in the Constitution.[68] But after 1857 a distinct change occurred in the language of the reports of the foreign minister to the Assembly and in the measures adopted by the Rio government. When early in that year the French opened negotiations intended to settle disputed points in regard to consular jurisdiction over properties of deceased citizens and to the nationality of French children born in Brazil, it was discovered that no solution was possible until the legislative body should modify the stipulations concerning Brazilian nationality.[69]

On June 13, 1859, Councillor Pimenta Bueno, therefore, pre-

---

[67] Brazil, *Relatorio dos Negocios Extrangeiros*, 1854, Annex A, Henry Howard to Limpo de Abreu, April 24, 1854. The minister also complained of the fact that by the Brazilian law of nationality minors of foreign parents were liable to compulsory military service. This point was still in discussion in 1877 when the son of an English citizen was forcibly called to the colors (*ibid.*, 1877, p. 25, and Annex 1, Nos. 101-104). The question of nationality of children was important in Brazil in view of the large immigrant population and the relatively small number who were natives of a third or fourth generation.

[68] See the report of the foreign minister in *Relatorio dos Negocios Extrangeiros*, 1847.

[69] Pereira Pinto, *Apontamentos*, IV, 234.

sented a project to the senate regulating the nationality of children of foreigners[70]; and on September 10 of the following year, the project became a law. By the terms of this new interpretation of nationality, children of foreign subjects born in Brazil retained the citizenship of the father until they were twenty-one when they automatically became Brazilians. In case a Brazilian woman should marry a foreigner, she lost her nationality until she became a widow, when she could recover her former citizenship if she so desired; foreign women marrying Brazilians acquired the civil status of the husband.[71]

This law enabled the Foreign Office to sign consular conventions which contained stipulations satisfactory to France. Three months to a day from the date of the final approval of the law of 1860, a convention was signed with France[72] conceding to French minors the same civil rights as those enjoyed by their fathers until they were twenty-one, and by 1863 similar conventions were concluded with Switzerland, Italy, Spain, and Portugal. England was not included in the list of European powers which secured such agreements.

Almost immediately trouble arose over the interpretation of the law of 1860, as the consuls of the powers signatory to conventions stretched the privileges obtained by the agreements to lengths unauthorized by any clause or understanding between the governments in question. Consequently, on January 27, 1864, a circular was sent to the governors of the provinces of the empire which specified the only cases in which consular intervention would be allowed. These cases were: when there were no heirs or executors by the will and when the heirs were

---

[70] Two members of the Senate committee on the constitution reported favorably on the bill, one member, the Marquez de Olinda, opposed the project as unconstitutional (Pereira Pinto, *Apontamentos*, IV, Note 8, p. 234, and Brazil, *Relatorio dos Negocios Extrangeiros*, 1860, Annex C).

[71] The text of the law is given in Pereira Pinto, *Apontamentos*, IV, Note 1, p. 226. Formerly Brazilian women retained their original citizenship although married to a foreign husband. Pereira Pinto asserts that the law of 1860 was unconstitutional since by legislative act a constitutional provision was modified. Only a constitutional amendment could effect the modification legally (*op. cit.*, IV, 238-239).

[72] The convention is given in Pereira Pinto, *op. cit.*, IV, 259 ff.

unknown, legally incapable, or were absent.[73] In protest against this interpretation of the consular conventions signed between 1860 and 1863, the five powers signatory to those agreements sent a joint note to the imperial government[74] demanding exclusive jurisdiction over all minors of foreign parents, over all types of inheritances, and over all expenses and fees involved in the administration of these cases. The Rio government refused to yield; Barão de Penedo was sent to France to arrange matters if possible; and on July 21, 1866, a declaration interpretative of the consular convention was signed, in which the Rio court while yielding on some points maintained the ciples enunciated in the circular.[75] Yet the intervention of foreign consuls in Brazil continued in regard not only to inheritances but also to the loading and unloading of ships, customs matters, damages, and other questions.[76]

In 1872 the Rio government notified the five powers with which it had signed agreements that the conventions would terminate at the time limit specified in the terms thereof.[77] France accepted the announcement but fell back at once on the perpetual clause of the 1826 treaty, thus forcing Brazil to renew in a slightly modified form the convention which had expired.[78] In the meantime Great Britain at last secured the coveted convention on April 22, 1873,[79] and Spain and Portugal renewed their old agreements.[80] But again when the time limit of these conventions was reached in 1887, Brazil declared them expired and refused, this time successfully, to sign re-

[73] Brazil, *Relatorio dos Negocios Extrangeiros*, 1865, pp. 43-49, and Annex, pp. 15-157.

[74] The note was dated May 1, 1864. It is given in Pereira Pinto, *Apontamentos*, IV, Note 16, pp. 248-249.

[75] The text of the declaration is given in Brazil, *Relatorio dos Negocios Extrangeiros*, 1867, Annex I, No. 87, pp. 144-149.

[76] Dunshee de Abranches, *Tratados*, p. 43.

[77] The time of duration was for ten years.

[78] The renewal occurred after Spain and Portugal had accepted a modified form of the old conventions and after England secured an agreement (Dunshee de Abranches, *op. cit.*, p. 45).

[79] Brazil, *Relatorio dos Negocios Extrangeiros*, 1873, p. 3, and 1874, Annex, Nos. 114-116.

[80] *Ibid.*, 1875, p. 15; 1877, p. 23 and Annex, No. 94.

newals.[81] Great Britain, in accepting the annulment, suggested a treaty to cover maritime and commercial affairs, but the Rio government politely refused. Three-quarters of a century of experience with European entanglements had demonstrated the inadvisability of commercial treaties and consular conventions. In replying to the proposal of the London Office, the Rio court stated laconically that the policy had been adopted to conclude agreements of that nature only with countries which bordered on Brazilian territory.[82]

Thus terminated the long struggle by which Brazil freed itself from the obligations incurred by the treaties concluded during the first decade of its national existence. The extra-territorial privileges, consular concessions, and restrictions placed on the sovereignty of the nation by the Anglo-Brazilian treaty of 1827 terminated in 1844; but by a rather curious turn of affairs, certain of the privileges granted by that agreement were perpetuated in Franco-Brazilian relations and eventually were renewed between Great Britain and the empire. These restrictions were thrown off finally in 1887 with the termination of the consular conventions; thenceforth Brazil was free, definitely and permanantly, from the last vestiges of the traditional privileged position of Great Britain in the political affairs of Portuguese America.[83]

Two incidents in later Anglo-Brazilian relations illustrate the changed attitude assumed by the London Office toward the empire. Both were disputes over territory; one arising over the

---

[81] Brazil, *Relatorio dos Negocios Extrangeiros*, 1887, p. 11, and Annex, Nos. 25-43. It was not until 1907, however, that Brazil denounced the perpetual articles of the 1826 commercial treaty with France. All provisions based on the perpetual stipulations of that treaty as well as the additional articles ceased on June 13 of that year (Cardoso de Oliveira, *Actos Diplomaticos do Brazil*, I, 101).

[82] Brazil, *Relatorio dos Negocios Extrangeiros*, 1887, p. 12, and Annex I, Nos. 48-55; and Dunshee de Abranches, *Tratados*, p. 45.

[83] The agreements in force between Brazil and Great Britain in 1924 were: 1) delivery of deserters from merchant ships (signed 1888), 2) arbitration convention (1909), 3) peace commission (1919), and 4) domestic postal rates, (1921). The complementary declaration to the Treaty of Arbitration for the solution of the boundary dispute over British Guiana (1901) was still in force (Hildebrando Accioly, *Actos Internacionaes Vigentes no Brazil*).

determination of a boundary line between Brazil and British Guiana, and the other over the possession of a small group of islands off the coast. The first,[84] which was the more serious of the two, became an international question in 1838 following a scientific expedition sent by the English into territory claimed by the empire. Robert Schomberg, a German in the service of Great Britain, traversed the region between Demerari and the Rio Branco in 1836, and two years later after repeating his exploit, this time penetrating to the Rio Negro, sailed for London to report and to receive his reward of promotion to a colonelcy. Soon after his departure, a missionary, one Thomas Yowd (or Youd), of the Methodist Society, entered the disputed region of the upper Rio Branco with the purpose of converting the Indians to loyalty to Methodism and the British Empire. A Catholic priest, backed by the Brazilian governor of the province, forced him to withdraw until Schomberg returned from England with orders to take possession of the region to the west of the river called Rupunuri and east of the Rio Branco, a section which had been neutral ground between territory recognized as belonging to England and Brazil respectively. The Methodist missionary then returned, expelled the Catholic, and occupied the mission of the Carmelite friar. The priest appealed to the governor of the province, who in turn presented the case to the national government for solution.[85]

The London Office, after appointing a commission to determine the true boundary, delivered a note through its agent in Rio, laying claim to a frontier quite beyond the historic limits. On March 24, 1841, the Rio court stated its position in an able dispatch written by Aureliano de Souza e Oliveira Coutinho, and by refusing to treat as long as the military occupation continued, forced England to order the withdrawal

---

[84] One of the conditions, it will be recalled (*supra*, p. 293) which Minister Araujo presented as the price of a commercial treaty in 1843 was a proposal for the settlement of a boundary line between Brazil and British Guiana.

[85] Antonio L. Monteiro Baena, "Memoria," *Revista do Inst. Hist. e Geog. Bras.*, 1841, pp. 322-332. Explorations and demarcations of limits in this region had been accomplished by Brazil between 1754 and 1823. The claims of the Rio government were based on the charts and maps resulting from these expeditions.

of the expedition. In September of the next year an accord was signed which declared the region in question to be neutral until some decision could be reached as to the true boundary. Until the line could be determined, the Indians were to be sole possessors of the land and no armed force of either nation should enter the disputed territory.[86]

Schomberg, however, continued the occupation, erected signs asserting the ownership of Great Britain, and maintained an armed force in support of the missionary, Thomas Yowd. The Rio court protested; London ordered the signs removed and recalled the expedition[87]; and the dispute slumbered until 1895 when a rumor of another invasion of the neutral territory by Great Britain disturbed Rio.[88] Three years later when the Brazilian minister at London protested the expedition promoted by the authorities of British Guiana, Lord Salisbury replied that the English official who had entered the neutral zone was merely on a visit of inspection and had not raised the British flag nor proclaimed title of sovereignty. London, so the minister reported, had already ordered the withdrawal of the only post established by the expedition.[89]

In 1901 the long dispute was settled when the case was submitted to the arbitration[90] of the king of Italy for a definitive decision as to the location of the boundary line. The arbiter in rendering his decision June 6, 1904, stated that since neither Brazil nor England had established indisputable rights of sovereignty over the territory in litigation and since it was impossible to divide the region into equal portions, either in extent or value, he had based his judgment on natural geographic features. By the boundary which followed the watersheds of the disputed region, Great Britain obtained the major part of the territory in question, but both powers accepted the deci-

---

[86] Cardoso de Oliveira, *Actos Diplomaticos*, I, 130.

[87] For a summary of the dispute of 1842, see Pereira Pinto, *Apontamentos*, II, Note 31, pp. 311-314.

[88] Brazil, *Relatorio dos Negocios Extrangeiros*, 1896, Annex I, Nos. 21-23.

[89] *Ibid.*, 1898, p. 20 and Annex I, No. 62.

[90] The treaty was signed November 6, 1901, and ratifications were exchanged January 28 of the following year (*ibid.*, 1902, Annex, No. 3).

sion and the question was definitely settled.[91]

The second incident concerned the possession of a group of small islands located 1,112 kilometers off the coast of Brazil in the latitude of Espirito Santo. Discovered in 1501 by the Portuguese, they remained unoccupied until 1700 when Edmund Halley took possession in the name of England. No settlement was made, however. Seventy-five years later J. Cook touched at the islands and in 1781 the British attempted to colonize the group. Portugal protested, and when England withdrew, sent an expedition of military and agricultural colonists to occupy the territory. In 1797 the attempt was abandoned as the unfertile, volcanic soil proved incapable of supporting the population. No further attempt was made to establish settlements although throughout the nineteenth century occasional visits were paid the islands by the French (in 1817, 1825, and 1829) and by the Brazilians (in 1825, 1846, 1871, and 1873).[92]

In 1895 England secretly but officially occupied Trindade, incorporating that island and the smaller Martim Vaz into British territory. When the news reached Rio six months later, a vigorous protest was made to the British legation by the foreign minister.[93] Lord Salisbury for England offered to arbitrate or to return the islands at once if Brazil would guarantee to utilize them as a station for a cable which an English company wished to lay; but Foreign Minister Carlos de Carvalho re-

[91] The boundary followed the watershed to the Mahu river and thence to the Tacutu (Rocha Pombo, *Historia do Brazil*, X, 452). Later the line was corrected in view of certain errors made in the decision as to the location of the source of the Cotingo River (Cardoso de Oliveira, *Actos Diplomaticos*, II, 323). For details of the dispute see: Joaquim Nabuco, *Primier Mémoire* (7 vols.), *Second Mémoire* (6 vols.), and *Troisième Mémoire*, in which the case for Brazil was presented to the arbiter; Barão do Rio Branco, *Mémoire sur la question des limites entre les Etats-Unis du Brésil et la Guyane Britannique;* and Paul Fauchille, "Le Conflit de limites entre le Brésil et la Grande Bretagne et la Sentence arbitrale du Rio d'Italie," *Revue Generale de Droit Internacional Public*, January-February, 1905, pp. 25-142.

[92] Rocha Pombo, *Historia do Brazil*, X, 445; and Brazil, *Relatorio dos Negocios Extrangeiros*, 1896, Annex I, Supplement, Correspondencia e Documentos Diplomaticos sobre a occupação da Ilha da Trindade, Nos. 13 and 14.

[93] Brazil, *Relatorio dos Negocios Extrangeiros*, 1896, p. 57, and Annex I, Supplement, Nos. 13 and 14.

fused to arbitrate or to condition the return of territory, the ownership of which was clearly demonstrated by document in the archives of four nations, Brazil, England, Portugal, and Spain. He refuted energetically the argument advanced by Lord Salisbury that in cases where the well-being and interests of a densely populated nation required the use of certain places for purposes for which that nation had shown special aptitude, the owners of the localities in question had no right to prohibit the proposed use or to retire those places from the service of humanity. That doctrine, in the opinion of the Brazilian minister, was a very serious threat to the sovereignty of those nations which combined extensive territories and inadequate resources.[94]

Through the mediation of Portugal, in which the traditional ally of Great Britain explained the basis of Brazil's claim to ownership, England yielded. By orders from London the *Baracouta*, the same vessel which had taken the expedition to the islands, was sent to remove all signs of occupation and in January, 1897, a Brazilian cruiser placed a bronze plaque on the largest island of the group as evidence of ownership.[95]

The methods of solution and the outcome of these two incidents offer a striking contrast to the story of Anglo-Brazilian relations during the first half of the nineteenth century. The days of privileged position and practical tutelage established by Viscount Strangford and Lord Gordon were past; the revolt against the preëminence of Great Britain in the political affairs of the empire and the attempt to abolish the special privileges secured in the early years of national existence had liberated Brazil from the traditional position maintained by England in Portuguese territory. The dream cherished by George Canning of attaching the South American empire to Europe by close political ties failed of realization, for not even England,

[94] Brazil, *Relatorio dos Negocios Extrangeiros*, 1896, Annex I, Supplement, No. 49.

[95] *Ibid.*, 1897, Annex I, Nos. 1 and 2 and p. 8; and Rocha Pombo, *Historia do Brazil*, X, 446. For description and history of the islands see "Memoria historica e geographica da ilha da Trindade. Organisada e dedicada ao Exmo. barão da Ponte Ribeiro, pelo bacharel Pedro Torquato Xavier de Brito," *Rev. do Inst. Hist. e Geog. Bras.*, 1877, pt. II.

the traditional privileged power in Portuguese territory, could maintain the concessions won in Brazil between 1808 and 1827. By a struggle which lasted for nearly three-quarters of a century, the tutelage of Europe was renounced by the Rio government while at the same time the position of Great Britain was reduced to a plane of equality with other foreign powers. Preëminence in the markets, investments, and shipping business of the empire thus became a question not of privileged position but of economic superiority over rivals.

CHAPTER XII

THE CHALLENGE TO BRITAIN'S ECONOMIC SUPREMACY

THE PREËMINENCE of Great Britain in Brazilian markets, investments, and shipping was already an established fact when the colony became an independent empire. The favored position in Portuguese territory during colonial times; the successful transfer of the historic privileges enjoyed on the European continent to the South American possession when the seat of the monarchy was shifted to Rio de Janeiro; the period of monopolistic participation in Brazilian commerce while Europe was at war; the great advantage resulting from the fifteen per cent. import tax as against twenty-four for all other foreign powers; the economic penetration carried forward under favorable circumstances between 1808 and 1825; and the final consolidation of these advantages in the young empire by the treaty of 1827 all worked together to secure for Great Britain the favored position in Brazilian economic life.

Statistics for the early period of the empire are uncertain or non-existent, but there is no doubt that in 1827 England was the greatest foreign supplier of the markets of Brazil.[1] In the number of ships entering the port of Rio, where more than half of the imports of the empire was landed, Great Britain was far in the lead. In 1821 for instance, there were reported 124 ships flying the Portuguese flag, 192 British, fifty-four American, and thirty-one French. Five years later only seventeen Portuguese vessels entered whereas in 1828, some 260 British ships were registered.[2] No figures are available as to the amount of

[1] Centro Industrial do Brazil, *O Brazil: Suas Riquezas Naturaes, Suas Industrias,* I, 275.

[2] *O Brazil, Suas Riquezas,* I, 276. In 1842 the port of Rio returned to the treasury

foreign capital invested in the empire in 1827, but it is more than probable that British investments exceeded those of other foreign powers.[3]

Yet competition began at once. For coincident with their recognition of the independence of the empire, France, the United States, the Hanseatic Cities, Holland, and Sweden initiated the long struggle which eventually was to result in the successful rivalling of Britain's favored position. In the early period France was most active despite very serious handicaps which resulted in part from French colonial laws and in part from lack of capital and industrial development.[4] Due to this competition the number of British ships entering Rio in 1837 fell to 110 whereas French vessels numbered sixty-eight and American ships (in 1836) almost equalled the British with 102.[5]

This competition proved futile, however, as long as the market in which it occurred remained comparatively stationary in the value of goods imported. That condition existed from 1827 to 1850 due to the disturbed conditions of the last years of the reign of D. Pedro I and the internal disorder of the period of

---

in import duties one and a half times as much as did all other ports combined (Diogo de Soares da Silva de Bivar, "A Chronica do Anno de 1842," *Revista do Inst. Hist. e Geog. Bras.*, V [1843], 388-389).

[3] The only foreign loan contracted by the empire had been floated in London and the economic penetration of the preceding twenty years would indicate an influx of British capital.

[4] By the colonial laws France prohibited entrance of nearly all Brazilian products, for coffee, sugar, and tobacco came from the French West Indies. Freights from France were very high as a result, for the return voyage was usually in ballast (*O Brazil, Suas Riquezas*, I, 275). In 1839 Horace Say in his *Histoire des Rélations Commerciales entre la France et le Brésil* accused the Brazilians of favoring British articles from force of long habit. A committee composed of Bento da Silva Lisbôa and J. D. de Attaide Moncorvo after studying the criticism advanced by Say reported to the Instituto Historico e Geographico that low cost and superior goods could undermine England's position but France did not have either the vast capital of England, nor mechanics and engineers as expert as the British, nor machines capable of putting as excellent goods on the Brazilian market as cheaply as did Great Britain. France, in the opinion of the committee, was essentially agricultural, as was Brazil, whereas England had a manufacturing and business interest which obtained for it the favored position in Brazilian markets (report of the committee found in *Revista do Inst. Hist. e Geog. Bras.*, 1839).

[5] *O Brazil, Suas Riquezas*, I, 276.

the Regency and of the first years of the rule of the second Pedro.[6] During that period, Great Britain not only maintained a fairly level average of exports to Brazil but even increased its annual sales slightly. The fact that the income from the fifteen per cent. duties on British goods rose from £321,735 in 1832 to £393,876 in 1841[7] indicates this gradual increase. Thus there was little chance for the rise of a successful rival.

By far the largest item in the list of British exportations to Brazil during this period was cotton manufactures with woolens a poor second. Then followed, in order of value, linens, hardware and cutlery, Irish butter, iron of all sorts, hard soap, common earthenware, copper goods, stationery, glass, silk goods, beaver hats, beer and ale, gunpowder, lead and shot, painters colors, umbrellas, steam engines and machinery, musical instruments, and military stores. In 1835 the value of all exports from the British Islands to Brazil was £2,553,203.[8]

Of the imports received by England in exchange for these articles, raw cotton led the list with coffee a poor second. Then followed, in order, sugar, hides, woods, and cocoa.[9] The total value of imports from the empire into the British Islands was £1,479,588.[10]

As these figures show, British sales to Brazil greatly exceeded British purchases. In 1842, whereas over fifty-one per cent. of the total importations received at the port of Rio came from Great Britain and its possessions, only twenty per cent. of the

---

[6] *O Brazil, Suas Riquezas*, I, 277.

[7] F. O. 131/12, Aberdeen to Ellis, No. 2. August 26, 1842. Enclosure: Letter from Board of Trade. An estimate taken from official figures of British exports is given of what the fifteen per cent. tax should have returned annually to the Brazilian Exchequer between 1831 and 1842. In 1836 the duties were £454,576; in 1837 they were £273,612; and in 1839 they were £397,605.

[8] Customs 8/42, British Exports by Countries. Value of cottons was £1,501,689; of woolens £338,698; of linens (British and Irish) £157,273; of hardware and cutlery £85,096; of Irish butter £82,052; of iron £67,850; of hard soap £50,689. Other items were below £50,000 in value. These are values for 1835.

[9] Customs 4/30, British Importations by Countries. The value of items mentioned were: raw cotton, £806,852; coffee, £275, 318; sugar, £111,852; hides, £110,000; woods, £98,155; cocoa, £37,472. The values are for 1835.

[10] *Ibid.*

exportations were destined for English ports.[11] As explained to Henry Ellis by the Rio merchants, this unbalanced trade was completed in a triangular exchange. Goods were sent by consignment to Brazil on long term credit, the only kind of credit under which Brazilian buyers could operate. After selling his articles, the British merchant loaned the proceeds of his sales to non-British foreign merchants, taking bills of exchange on London in return. These non-British agents used the money so obtained to buy Brazilian articles for shipment to their respective countries, where English purchases equalized the bills of exchange drawn on London. Thus by means of British capital Brazilian trade with Sweden, Denmark, Hamburg, Trieste, and other places was helped materially.[12]

Moreover in 1843 approximately three-eighths of the sugar, one-half of the coffee, and five-eighths of the cotton exported from Pernambuco, Bahia, and Rio de Janeiro were shipped on British accounts although, except for cotton, very little of these products were actually landed in England.[13] Of the coffee shipped from Rio, for example, over three hundred and fifty thousand sacks were sent to the United States alone whereas the British Isles took less than two hundred thousand. Hanseatic towns received some three thousand sacks less than England while Austria imported over one hundred and twenty thousand sacks. Thus although less than one-fifth of the total coffee export was shipped to England, one-half of the crop, by

---

[11] Silva de Bivar, "A Chronica . . .," pp. 395 and 396. Minister Hamilton reported to Lord Aberdeen that the statistics in this report, which was presented to the Historical Society, were as reliable as any that could be obtained (F. O. 13/211, Hamilton to Aberdeen, No. 38. May 13, 1844). He enclosed the article. France was second with 14.64 per cent., Portugal third with 9.01 per cent., and the United States fifth with 6.10 per cent., in the list of exporters to Brazil. As buyers the United States led with 26.09 per cent.; England followed with twenty per cent., with the Hanseatic Cities, Austria, Belgium, Portugal, and France in the order named. These percentages were for Rio only.

[12] F. O. 131/12, Ellis to Aberdeen, No. 15. December 10, 1842. Leland H. Jenks in *Migration of British Capital to 1873*, pp. 68-70, describes the part played by British capital in the United States-Brazil trade.

[13] F. O. 131/12, Letter from Ellis to Honorio Hermeto, February 22, 1843. Enclosure No. 2 in Dispatch of February 22, 1843.

the estimate of Henry Ellis, ordinarily was handled through British accounts.[14] Consequently in the evaluation of Anglo-Brazilian economic relations, there must be added to the actual commercial interchange carried on between the empire and Great Britain the participation of British agents and capital in the trade of Brazil with other foreign powers.

No less commanding was England's position in the investment field in 1842. Of the internal funded debt British subjects held over eight times as large a share as citizens of all other foreign powers combined.[15] In addition, all foreign loans since the declaration of independence had been floated in London, a new loan of £732,600 being secured in 1843.[16] As to the value of British capital employed in private enterprise in Brazil, there are no figures available for the 'forties, but in shipping England still maintained its lead, although the United States was a close rival.[17]

The cessation of the commercial treaty in 1844 did not alter England's preëminent position in Brazilian economic life. On the contrary, during the last days in which the fifteen per cent. import duties operated every facility was accorded the British merchants in their effort to clear their goods before the expiration of the treaty. As Minister Hamilton reported to Aberdeen, there were only two instances at the port of Rio where any particular hardship was experienced and even these cases were not such as to warrant formal complaints.[18] The mer-

[14] The total export of coffee in 1842 from Rio was 1,161,436 sacks plus 574 barrels (Silva da Bivar, "Chronica . . .," p. 391). Of this amount 548,903 bags were shipped on British accounts (F. O. 131/12, Letter of Ellis to Honorio Hermeto, February 22, 1843, Enclosure No. 2).

[15] The internal debt amounted to approximately 38.134:419$000 (read thirty-eight thousand, one hundred thirty-four contos, four hundred nineteen milreis). Of this British subjects held 8.491:000$000 and subjects of all other foreign nations only 979:000$000 (Bivar, "Chronica . . .," pp. 385-386).

[16] Four loans were contracted between 1824 and 1843; namely, £3,686,200 (1824), £769,200 (1829), £411,200 (1839), and £732,000 (1843). See Liberato de Castro Carreira, *Historia Financeira e Orçamentaria do Imperio do Brazil*, p. 656.

[17] In 1842 of the 695 foreign merchant vessels which entered Rio, 167 were British, 164 American, 65 Danish, 58 Swedish, 47 from Hamburg, 42 Sardinian, 34 Portuguese, 28 French, and 27 Spanish (Bivar, *op. cit.*, p. 397).

[18] F. O. 13/214, Hamilton to Aberdeen, No. 88, and F. O. 13/222, Hamilton to Aberdeen, No. 2.

chants themselves placed slight importance on the continuation of the treaty if they could be assured of equality of treatment with other foreign agents,[19] and the percentage of British goods in the import values of the empire in 1854 revealed no loss by England of the preëminent position maintained prior to the expiration of the treaty.[20]

During the period when the trade of the Portuguese empire was a monopoly of the mother country, these special privileges had played a useful part in opening colonial possessions to British trade, while their continuation in the early years of the independence of Brazil had guaranteed a low import tax during the critical transition period and at the same time had prevented the granting to other foreign powers of special favors adverse to British interests. Their usefulness, however, was past, for as long as all competitors were placed on a basis of equality and Brazil continued to be essentially an agricultural country, the economic superiority of England would guarantee its preëminent position in the markets of the South American nation. The historic privileges enjoyed by England in Portuguese possessions for centuries ceased to exist in Brazil without damage to British trade.

The year 1850 marked a turning point in Brazilian economic development.[21] The centralization of power in the hands of D. Pedro II, who began his personal rule two years earlier, the restoration of order after the revolutions of the preceding twenty years, and the extension of the authority of the national government to the provinces introduced a period of economic expansion which in turn increased the purchasing power of the empire. The federal income, which had grown from twenty to forty thousand contos of reis between 1838 and 1850, leaped

---

[19] F. O. 131/12, Ellis to Aberdeen, No. 15.

[20] The relative position of the principal countries in value of goods imported into Brazil during the fiscal year 1854-1855 was: Great Britain 54.6 per cent., France 11.6 per cent., the United States 8.3 per cent., Portugal 6.9 per cent., Argentina 6.3 per cent., and the Hanseatic Cities 5.6 per cent. (Brazil, *Relatorio á Assemblêa Geral pelo Ministro e Secretario de Estado dos Negocios de Agricultura, Commercio e Obras Publicas*, 1866, p. 118).

[21] Pereira da Silva, *Situation de L'Empire du Brésil*, p. 58.

to one hundred thousand contos in 1858.[22] Deficits ceased, Brazilian credit abroad became more firmly established,[23] and import taxes trebled between 1836 and 1856[24]—an increase which was due in part to the higher rates imposed when the commercial treaty with England expired, and in part to the fifty per cent. rise in the value of goods brought in. In the same period exports more than doubled.[25]

In the years immediately following 1850 commercial and industrial corporations began to be organized for the first time[26]; the Bank of Brazil was founded with numerous state and private banks appearing immediately after the authorization of the national banks[27]; the first telegraph line began operation in Rio with extensions to various points in the provinces; and the first railroad was inaugurated.[28] Although the preëminence of north Brazil in the production of articles for export still continued, the south was rising to importance as the province of

[22] Pereira da Silva, *L'Empire du Brésil*, p. 59.

[23] The loan of 1839 was contracted for 76 per cent., that of 1842 at 85 per cent., that of 1852 at 95 per cent., that of 1858 at 95½ per cent., and that of 1859 for 100 per cent. The interest rate was lowered from 5 per cent., which hitherto had been charged on all loans, to 4½ per cent. for the 1853 and 1858 loans (Castro Careira, *Historia Financeira*, p. 656).

[24] Pereira da Silva, *op. cit.*, p. 64.

[25] Pereira da Silva, *op. cit.*, p. 70.

[26] A mutual benefit society (1838) and three banks (1842, 1845, 1850) had been organized but the movement really began in 1851 when eleven commercial and industrial companies were incorporated. Between 1851 and 1860 some 148 corporations were formed. These *sociedades anonymas* were founded to promote banks, railroads, steamship lines, insurance agencies, manufacturing enterprises, city traction and gas works, mining, colonization, and other activities (Antonio de Barros Ramalho Ortigão, "Surto de Cooperativismo," Chapter V of "Contribuições para a Biographia de D. Pedro II," in *Rev. do Inst. Hist. e Geog. Bras.*, Tomo Especial, IX, Pt. I, pp. 290-291).

[27] This was the third bank of Brazil. The first, organized in 1808, suspended operations in 1828; the second, authorized in 1833, was never incorporated. When the third bank was authorized, only four banks existed in Brazil, all in the north. Bahia had two, Maranhão one, and Pará one. By 1858 eight more banks were founded and in 1859 alone sixteen appeared. Private banks as commercial corporations and mutual benefit societies swelled the number of such institutions. The London and Brazilian Bank was installed in Rio in 1862 with branches (1863 and 1864) in Pernambuco, Bahia, Santos, Rio Grande do Sul, and Paraná (Ortigão, *op. cit.*, pp. 292-293).

[28] Ortigão, *op. cit.*, pp. 289, 309-311, 295-308. By 1889 there were 8,966 kilometers of railroads actually in operation in the empire (*ibid.*, p. 308).

São Paulo began its striking development.[29] Sugar, cotton, cacao, coffee, hides, and tobacco with two new articles, rubber and *matte*, were the chief exports of the country just as in the first quarter of the century[30]; it was in the quantity of production of these articles that 1850 differed from 1827.

The significance of this economic revolution in the social life of Brazil was described by Joaquim Nabuco who returned to Rio in 1843 after a long absence. As it appeared to him, the old social order of the time of the first Pedro was being supplanted by a new nobility based on political position and wealth. The old habits, etiquette, principles, and education were disappearing and new fashions, instituted by leaders who had risen through the revolutions or become rich through commerce, were coming into vogue—politics and money had become the two wheels of the social cart. The essential morality, almost ostentatious honesty, and simplicity of life exemplified in the leading men of the old régime were yielding to the luxury of the 'fifties, as the "elegant vices" crept in to accompany the "French veneer" so long affected by the Rio court.[31]

Thus in the social life as well as in economic development of the empire the year 1850 marks a transition from the customs and manners of the first half of the century. The political independence gained in 1825 did not produce an immediate revolution in the social and economic life of Brazil, for the succeeding twenty years revealed slight differences in the conditions which had existed prior to the formation of the empire. But by 1850 with stability and order came prosperity and a striking economic development which in turn reacted on the social life and national consciousness of the Brazilians.

---

[29] In 1808 almost the entire exportation of the colony was produced in the north and as late as 1852 Bahia and Pernambuco each exported over five times the value of goods shipped out of São Paulo. It was not until 1872 that the latter province exceeded the northern cities in value of exports (Agenor de Roure, "Eleição Direita-Ensino Publico," Chapter IX in "Contribuições para a Biographia de D. Pedro II," in *Rev. do Inst. Hist. e Geog. Bras.*, Tomo Especial, IX, Pt. I. p. 709). A large part of these exports were sent to Rio for reëxportation.

[30] Agenor de Roure, *op. cit.*, pp. 709-710.

[31] Augusto Olympo Viveiros de Castro, "Emancipação Gradual . . .," Chapter VIII in "Contribuições para a Biographia de D. Pedro II," in *Rev. do Inst. Hist. e Geog. Bras.* Tomo especial, IX, Pt. I, pp. 540-542.

These changes made the empire a more desirable market than before, with the result that England encountered severer competition in this traditional field of interest. Partly as a reply to the threat of other nations and partly as the natural result of the increased purchasing power of the Brazilians, England increased its activity in the empire. In 1851 the first mail steamboat line to England was inaugurated by a special convention signed by the two governments. The Royal Mail Steam Packet Line was granted the contract, two-thirds of the expenses to be paid by the British and one-third by the Brazilian government. Special exemptions from port taxes and quarantine laws were specified and the postage rates agreed upon. The vessels which carried the mail averaged eight hundred tons burden.[32] The advantages accruing to England from the arrangement were visible immediately, for, in the opinion of the British legation at Rio, the inauguration of this steampacket line was a strong contributing factor in the sudden growth of British exports which occurred after 1850.[33]

As an indication of the trend of international relations existing between Brazil and foreign powers the number of consuls maintained by other countries in the empire and by the Rio government abroad is suggestive. In 1853 England outranked all other nations with the exception of Portugal in the number of consuls serving in Brazil while the Rio government maintained its greatest number of representatives in Great Britain and its possessions.[34] By 1870 the relative position in regard to

[32] Brazil, *Relatorio dos Negocios Extrangeiros*, 1851, Notes 8-16, and 1852, p. x. The first concession granted to any steamship company was conceded to France by an agreement closed November 21, 1843. France was to maintain a steamship line for travellers and official correspondence with regular sailings. The vessels were to be French warships moved by steam. A monthly service from St. Nazaire by Lisbon, Cape Verde, Pernambuco, and Bahia to Rio was specified (Rocha Pombo, *Historia do Brazil*, IX, 451, note 3).

[33] Great Britain, *Commercial Reports-Diplomatic*, 1861, pp. 461-462. Exports from England to Brazil grew from a little over £2,500,000 in 1850 to £5,500,000 in 1856.

[34] In 1853 England had fifteen consuls in Brazil, France fourteen, Hamburg twelve, Spain and Austria eleven each, the United States eight, and Portugal thirty-five (Brazil, *Relatorio dos Negocios Extrangeiros*, 1853, Annex, No. 4). In England and all dominions Brazil maintained thirty-six consuls; in Portugal and pos-

foreign consuls in Brazil was modified considerably, for Spain (with twenty-six), the United States (with eighteen), France (with seventeen), and Portugal (with ninety-one) had increased the number of their representatives whereas the consular body of Great Britain (sixteen in number) remained stationary. In 1880 Germany (with twenty-one) demonstrated its interest in the empire by maintaining more consuls than did England, only Portugal (with ninety-eight) and Spain (with twenty-six) outranking it while Great Britain (with twenty) came fourth. In 1888, just before the fall of the empire, Portugal (with 107), Spain and the United States (with twenty-five each), Germany (with twenty-three), and Italy (with twenty-two) exceeded Great Britain (with twenty-one) in the number of representatives appointed to Brazil, a position which England maintained more or less constantly until just prior to the World War, when it increased the number of its consuls appointed to Brazil.

On the other hand, by far the largest representation of the Rio government abroad was maintained in Great Britain and its possessions: in 1870 there were fifty-one Brazilian consuls in English territory to thirty-one in Portugal, with Italy, France, and Spain following; in 1880 there were seventy-two in English territory to forty-four in Portugal, with Spain, France, and Italy following; in 1888 the same relative positions held except that the United States supplanted France; and in 1912, just prior to the World War, there were 109 Brazilian consuls in British territory, to fifty-one in France, with Spain, the United States, Italy, Portugal, and Germany following close behind.[35]

These figures are indicative of the particular phases of interest felt by foreign powers in Brazil. Great Britain as the greatest supplier of the South American country received a large body of Brazilian consuls within its territory in order to furnish the necessary invoices, whereas Portugal and Spain,

---

sessions, twenty-four; in Spain and possessions, eighteen; in France, fourteen; and in the United States, eleven (*ibid.*).

[35] Brazil, *Relatorio dos Negocios Extrangeiros*, 1870, Annex II, pp. 34-51; 1880, Annex II, pp. 34-46; 1888, Annex II, pp. 48-78; 1900, Annex II, pp. 78-114; 1912, Annex B, pp. 137-166.

and later Italy and Germany,[36] required a large representation in Brazil to care for the emigrants who settled there and to supply invoices for purchases. The United States as the greatest buyer of all foreign countries maintained an increasing number of consuls.

These figures are also indicative of the growth of British exports to Brazil. In 1835 the value of goods sent to the empire from Great Britain was a little over two and one-half million pounds sterling[37]; by 1854-5, exports doubled in value[38]; by 1863-4 they were forty-one per cent. over the 1854-5 figure[39]; by 1874-5 they were fifteen per cent. above the value of the previous decade[40]; by 1905 a decrease occurred when the average exports from England fell to the 1854-5 period[41]; but by 1912, just prior to the World War, British sales to Brazil not only recovered from the depression of the early years of the twentieth cenutry but reached the highest figure ever attained.[42]

---

[36] In 1882 of the 25,845 immigrants who landed at Rio, 10,562 were Italians, 9,269 were Portuguese, 3,738 were Spanish, 1,538 were Germans, and 249 were French (Great Britain, *Commercial Reports, Consular*, 1884 [1-4], p. 13). Consul Cowper in 1886 reported a tide of hardy Italian immigrants who were replacing the slaves as laborers (*ibid.*, 1886, pp. 211-212). Germans settled in the south in Rio Grande do Sul, Santa Catharina, and Paraná (Great Britain, *Commercial Reports, Diplomatic and Consular*, 1886, pp. 1-11). After the abolition of slavery São Paulo became a favorite destination for Italian immigrants (*ibid.*, 1889, Report No. 498, by Consul Cowper).

[37] Customs 8/42. The exact figures are £2,630,767.

[38] Brazil, *Relatorio á Assembléa Geral pelo Ministro e Secretario do Estado*, 1866, p. 116. By these Brazilian figures, British exports to Brazil in 1854-5 were valued at 46,-565:000$000. At the rate of exchange of 1854-5 (27 5/8 d per milreis) this is equivalent to about £5,000,000.

[39] Exports to Brazil in 1863-4 were valued at 65.678:800$000 (*ibid.*), at the exchange rate of 27d per milreis, about £7,400,000.

[40] The figures for 1874-5 were 76.750:000$000, at the rate of exchange of the period (26d per milreis) equivalent to more than £8,300,000 (*O Brazil, Suas Riquezas, I, 295*).

[41] According to Brazilian figures, the average importation from England for the years 1902-5 was 63.407:610$000 gold milreis or at par of 27d per milreis, £7,124,450 (*O Brazil, Suas Riquezas, I, 296*).

[42] The value of imports into Brazil from Great Britain was placed at 239.554:-161$000 by official Brazilian figures (Brazil, *Annuario Estatistico do Brazil, 1° Anno*, II, 102-103). With exchange at 16d per milreis this sum is equivalent to a little over £16,000,000. During the same period, however, the total of Brazilian imports increased nineteen times. Imports in 1842 (estimate by Silva de Bivar, "A

Thus Great Britain, although it was the leading supplier of Brazil in the early period with a relative high value of exports, succeeded in increasing its sales six hundred per cent. between 1835 and 1912.

To accompany this growth in exports, British enterprise in Brazil was intensified after 1850. Although the first railroad inaugurated in the empire was constructed by Brazilians with national capital,[43] English capital and agents were a large factor in the expansion of railroad building which occurred during the last half of the nineteenth century.[44] In 1856 a company was incorporated in London with British capital to construct a line from Santos up the mountain to the city of São Paulo and down to Jundiahy, a town which lies at the point where the vast inner plateau joins the mountains.[45] The first railways in Pernambuco[46] and Bahia[47] were constructed by English companies. In the case of the Pernambuco line all the plant, ma-

---

Chronica," p. 395) were 30.000:000$000 or at 27d per milreis, £3,370,000; imports in 1912 were 951.369:556$000, or at 16 5/32d per milreis, about £64,000,000 (Brazil, *Annuario Estatistico, 1° Anno*, II, 102-103).

[43] An English engineer, Thomas Cochrane, secured a contract with the Rio government in 1840 to construct a railroad from Rio to the province of São Paulo, but he was unable to initiate construction. In 1855 a national company operating under the supervision of the government began construction of the line which today links the cities of Rio de Janeiro and São Paulo. The first to operate was a short line from Rio to Petropolis, where the mountain palace of the emperor was located, constructed without guarantee by a famous Brazilian engineer, Irineu Evangelista de Souza, later Visconde de Mauá. The first section of the Rio-São Paulo project was inaugurated in May, 1854 (Rocha Pombo, *Historia do Brazil*, IX, 444-446). It soon became the most important railroad of Brazil and has continued to hold that position.

[44] For a detailed account of the lines constructed or projected during the empire régime, see Ramalho Ortigão, "Surto de Cooperativismo," Chapter V of "Contribuições para a Biographia de D. Pedro II," *Rev. do Inst. Hist. e Geog. Bras.*, Tomo Especial, IX, Pt. I, pp. 295-308.

[45] This road was a remarkable engineering feat as the abrupt rise from the port of Santos to the summit of the ridge necessitated the use of a cable section for the severest part of the incline. It still serves as the funnel through which the imports and exports of the state of São Paulo pass. Financially, it has been extremely successful. The line from Santos to Jundiahy was in operation by 1867 (Rocha Pombo, *Historia do Brazil*, IX, 447).

[46] Capital £1,200,000 with an increase of £485,000 later. The line extended from Recife to São Francisco. It was inaugurated 1875 (*ibid.*, p. 448, note 1).

[47] From Bahia to São Francisco (*ibid.*, note 2).

terials, and labor were imported from England; costly and complete locomotive workshops were constructed with a staff from Great Britain; and the road was administered by British subjects. A telegraph line built along the right of way was opened to public use.[48]

In the province of São Paulo railroad expansion was rapid and profitable. By 1877, ten years after the line was open to traffic, the Santos-Jundiahy road not only dispensed with the government guaranty of seven per cent. but returned a profit to the government in excess of the specified returns to the company. By connections with other lines a continuous road penetrated 170 miles into the interior with numerous offshoots to the most productive sections. In 1877 between seven and eight hundred miles of line were either in operation or under construction or survey. All lines seemed prosperous.[49]

The greatest activity in railroad construction occurred in the provinces of Pernambuco, Bahia, Rio de Janeiro, Minas Geraes, and São Paulo, although lines were built in other sections.[50] The extent to which Great Britan contributed to that phase of economic life is indicated by the estimate compiled by Acting Consul General Rhind in 1901. In railway enterprises throughout the republic there was invested according to his figures, about thirty million pounds sterling of British Capital.[51]

It was not only in railroad construction and management that British enterprise was manifested in the years following 1850.[52] In 1863 an English company was installing gas works to

[48] The Brazilian government guaranteed seven per cent. on the capital invested. The line which was inaugurated in November, 1862, made a profit of less than £3,500 during 1862-3. The 77½ English miles of road and the workshops, stock, etc., cost £1,800,000 (Great Britain, *Commercial Reports, Consular*, 1863-4, pp. 49-51). As the line did not pay, the company obtained authorization to continue this first stretch of 77½ miles to São Francisco, 230 additional miles, in an effort to secure increased traffic. The government guaranteed £350,000 yearly for construction although it had already paid a sum equal to the original cost of the road as a result of the seven per cent. guaranty (*ibid.*, 1877 [4-5], p. 1185).

[49] Great Britain, *Commercial Reports, Consular*, 1877 (4-5), pp. 1206-07.

[50] Rocha Pombo, *Historia do Brazil*, IX, 448-451.

[51] Great Britain, *Commercial Reports, Diplomatic and Consular*, 1901, Report No. 2724.

[52] The first mail steamship line inaugurated by England in 1851 was followed by

light the city of Pará[53] while a Manchester firm under the direction of British engineers was completing a similar plant in the city of Pernambuco. A reservoir and connections had just been completed in the latter place at a cost that was below the estimate and the enterprise was yielding fifteen per cent. profit. A drainage contract signed with a Frenchman had not been executed, although, the consul reported, since the contractor had gone to London to raise two hundred thousand pounds sterling to float a company, something might yet result from it.[54] Several years later a dry dock cut from solid rock and large enough to accommodate the largest vessels afloat was constructed and operated in the Rio harbor by an English company.[55]

In 1875, at the invitation of the Brazilian government, a group of British engineers, headed by Sir John Haupshaw, visited Pernambuco and other ports of the country with a view to suggesting plans for improvements, while English contractors were building a magnificent bridge to connect the mainland on which part of the city of Pernambuco was situated.[56] That region was a special center of English interest: for more than half a century the greater part of the commerce of that port had been carried on by the English; large British import and export houses prospered there; two English telegraph companies, the Western Brazilian and the Brazilian Submarine, had stations there; two English banks maintained branches in the city; a long railroad constructed with British money joined the capital to the interior; regular steamship lines picked up a sizable volume of business at the port; the light, gas, and sewerage works were in the hands of an English company; and many millions of pounds sterling were invested there.[57] The tramways

the Liverpool, Brazil, and River Plate Steam Packet Company, the Pacific Steam Navigation Company, the London, Belgium, Brazil, and River Plate Steam Packet Company, the Lamport and Holt Company, and others (Great Britain, *Commercial Reports, Consular*, 1870, p. 242).

[53] *Ibid.*, 1863-64, p. 6.

[54] *Ibid.*, pp. 55-56.

[55] *Ibid.*, 1870, p. 424. The dry dock was the property of Hett, Wilson, and Co.

[56] *Ibid.*, 1875 (4-6), p. 1424.

[57] Brazil, *Relatorio dos Negocios Extrangeiros*, 1877, Annex, I, Document 107.

were owned and operated by the British and a steam cotton press was under British control.[58]

The drainage contract not only for the city of Rio but for outlying districts was secured by one Joseph Hancox, an engineer who had acquired a favorable reputation in the country by his public improvements work.[59] In Bahia two English companies, one of which had already constructed the "stupendous" bridge which connected the two sections of the city,[60] secured concessions from the imperial government to construct eight sugar factories when Brazil endeavored to rejuvenate that historic business. By the law of 1875 the government had authorized a guaranty of six and seven per cent. on capital, not to exceed three millions sterling, which was to be invested in sugar factories throughout the northern and central provinces. By 1884 fifty factories with a capital of £2,965,000 were set up under this plan while eleven more without guaranty were in operation. Most of the capital employed in these enterprises was British.[61]

In the São Paulo region the British were equally prominent. In the words of one of the chief local authorities, the Brazilian might be jealous of the foreigner but he could "not do without the English." The São Paulo Railway from Santos to Jundiahy, the Cities Improvement Company of the capital supplying gas, water, and tramways, the Western and Brazilian Telegraph, the English banks, all were owned and administered by British subjects and all were prospering.[62] By one estimate over six million pounds sterling of English capital were invested in São Paulo by 1888,[63] while by another estimate over twelve

---

[58] Great Britain, *Commercial Reports, Diplomatic and Consular*, 1889, Report No. 606.

[59] Great Britain, *Commercial Reports, Consular*, 1878 (4-5), pp. 1415-1416. This enterprise was successful. By 1895 nearly two millions sterling, all English, had been invested in the sewerage project (Great Britain, *Commercial Reports Consular and Diplomatic*, 1895, Report No. 1531).

[60] *Ibid.*, 1884 (8-10), p. 1594-1619. The companies were Dennis Blair and Company, and Hugh Wilson and Son. The latter company constructed the bridge. The eight factories constructed by Dennis Blair failed (Great Britain, *Commercial Reports, Diplomatic and Consular*, 1890, Report No. 793).

[61] Great Britain, *Commercial Reports, Diplomatic*, 1884, pp. 352-353.

[62] Great Britain, *Commercial Reports, Diplomatic and Consular*, 1888, No. 315.

[63] *Ibid.*, 1889, No. 498.

millions were employed in the state in 1890.[64] The strong financial and commercial position acquired by the English in São Paulo was due, in the opinion of the consul, to the fact that they were the first to develop its resources. The marvelous prosperity noticeable in 1890 from the seacoast to the interior had its inception "with the advent of the English merchant, engineer, and capitalist."[65]

As might be surmised, British banks were numerous in Brazil. The London and Brazilian Bank with a capital of a million and a half sterling, all British, was established at Rio in February, 1863, with branches in Bahia, Pernambuco, Santos, and Rio Grande do Sul. During the first year it did business to the amount of more than two million sterling. At the same time the Brazilian and Portuguese Bank was incorporated, with headquarters in London, its million sterling capital being all English.[66] By 1913 the assets of the British banks operating in Brazil constituted almost thirty per cent. of the total assets of all banks, national and foreign, and over fifty-seven per cent. of the assets of all foreign banks operating in Brazil.[67]

The opportunities which the growth of Brazil offered to British economic interests are seen in the report of Consul Cowper in 1884.[68] After describing the prosperous trade which had begun to pass through Santos to and from the interior of São Paulo, the consul predicted that this embryonic trade was but the first flow of the sap from a few incisions which would become channels of incalculable commerce. To reach and utilize the regions of future wealth two things were required; first, a solid and abundant immigration; and, second, the resources of foreign industries and civilization. The first would be supplied from Germany, Italy, and Spain; the second,

[64] *Ibid.*, 1890, No. 693.

[65] *Ibid.*, 1890, No. 693.

[66] Great Britain, *Commercial Reports, Consular*, 1863-64, p. 73.

[67] Brazil, Ministry of Agriculture, Industry and Commerce; *What Brazil Buys and Sells*, pp. 98-99. The figures are: assets of British banks $304,620,000 (gold dollars); all foreign banks $532,548,000; total assets of all banks, $1,047,956,000.

[68] Great Britain, *Commercial Reports, Consular*, 1884 (1-4), pp. 261-262.

which comprised the principal factors of development of a new country, would be derived from England. Many thousands of miles of railroads would have to be built and immense supplies of rails, rolling stock, and supplies furnished; new lands would be brought under cultivation and agricultural interests promoted; new industries requiring the most improved machinery would be started; and many thousands of pounds sterling would be required to carry out urban improvements and rural developments. This activity had its basis in gold, coal, and iron—factors of which Great Britain possessed a virtual monopoly. As long as England controlled these three factors, its supremacy in Brazil would remain unrivaled.

But the consul warned his government that already the United States had entered a thin wedge by furnishing some of the new railroads with rolling stock while American farm machinery was beginning to attract notice. The British manufacturer should break that entering wedge by supplying the market with the most suitable materials of that nature before the Americans obtained too strong a leverage, for once lost, a trade was exceedingly difficult to regain.

The consul was right, for Britain's strength lay in its abundant capital and excellent manufacturing ability. As long as England commanded the necessary capital to be invested in this virgin field, maintained its leadership in the manufacturing of those articles which Brazil needed but did not make, and controlled the foreign shipping business of the South American nation, its preëminent position in Brazilian economic life would remain intact. But, as the consul intimated, that position was not to be maintained without a struggle, for since the founding of the empire other nations had attempted to rival England's favored place and as the century wore on, that competition grew more keen.

That rivalry, as we have seen, was futile in the first half of the nineteenth century. France, the greatest threat to England's supremacy, supplied less than twelve per cent. of the total imports of Brazil in 1854-5 as against nearly fifty-five per cent.

by Great Britain.[69] English shipping represented more than one-third of the total foreign tonnage entering Brazilian ports,[70] and British capital and enterprise were the first to enter the field when the rapid economic development of the empire began in 1850.

The first rival to threaten Britain's position in a serious way was Germany. As early as 1873 German tonnage was threatening to displace the United States, which held third place among foreign nations trading with Brazil,[71] while the consul at Santos, a British stronghold, was complaining that the German crews were better trained, made a better appearance, and were far more sober than their English rivals. Shippers, to his distress, were beginning to prefer German and Norwegian boats, as rumor had it that they took better care of the cargo and charged lower rates.[72] By 1885 German tonnage to Brazil was rivalling the French[73] and by 1912 it was second only to England.[74]

It was in the competition for the markets of Brazil, however, that the threat of Germany was most pronounced. In the northern and central sections of the country, long the favored localities for English interests, an increasing chorus of warning was raised by British consuls as the nineteenth century ended, while in the south, German interests drove their English rivals from the field.[75]

---

[69] Brazil, *Relatorio á Assembléa Geral pelo Ministro de Agricultura, Commercio e Obras Publicas*, 1866, p. 118. The United States came next with 8.3 per cent. and Portugal next with 6.9 per cent.

[70] British tonnage was given as 225,674, American as 145,802, Portuguese as 82,713, and French as 59,780. The total of all foreign vessels was 764,217 (*ibid.*, Supplement R. Table No. 6).

[71] Great Britain, *Commercial Reports, Consular*, 1876 (4-6), p. 787. England was easily first and France second.

[72] *Ibid.*, 1877 (4-5), pp. 1209-1210. The same complaint was repeated by the consul at Rio (*ibid.*, 1878 [4-5], p. 1420).

[73] *Ibid.*, 1886, pp. 195-196.

[74] Brazil, *Annuario Estatistico*, 1° Anno, II, p. 18. Britain was first with 8,748,770 tons net. Germany next with 3,520,328, and France third with 1,222,122. England's margin thus was still quite large.

[75] See Great Britain, *Commercial Reports, Consular*, 1881 (7-8), p. 1430; 1884 (8-10),

One of the principal causes of German success in the markets of Brazil was stated by a vice-consul in Porto Alegre, one of the principal towns of Rio Grande do Sul, the southernmost province of the empire. In his opinion, the stubbornness of the English manufacturer in clinging persistently to old forms and styles, quite in defiance of their suitability to the special requirements of the market, contributed largely to England's downfall in that region. The German, and American, manufacturer studied the predilections of the particular market for which the goods were intended, and sought to follow out as closely as possible the suggestions and wishes of the customers, even in relatively small orders. The English manufacturer, however, seemed to consider that the people ought to want what the manufacturer produced; he disregarded special recommendations or suggestions made by his customers and acted on the theory that what had been good enough to gain a fortune fifty years before must still be good.[76] The glassware trade in the province of São Paulo was an illustration of the argument advanced by the Porto Alegre consul; for although Great Britain at one time supplied that region, Germany preempted the trade by introducing lighter, more novel, more attractive forms to compete with the old style English article.[77] Crockery and earthenware were other examples.[78]

To this complaint which cropped out in report after report sent by British consuls from every section of Brazil to the London office,[79] were added other causes for the successful competition of the Germans. In the two southernmost provinces, Rio Grande do Sul and Santa Catharina, the German popula-

p. 1594; 1886, pp. 210-211; *Diplomatic and Consular*, 1886, Rio Grande do Sul, Report No. 32; 1887, Santos, Report No. 168, and Rio Grande do Sul, Report No. 216; 1888, Pernambuco, Report No. 374, and Rio Grande do Sul, Report No. 323; 1892, Rio Grande do Sul, Report No. 1077; 1897, Rio, Report No. 1874; 1898, Rio, Report No. 2058; 1901, Porto Alegre, Report No. 2602; 1902, Sergipe, Report No. 2740; and Porto Alegre, Report No. 2859; 1903, Porto Alegre, Report No. 2996; 1906, Santa Catharina, Report No. 3737.

[76] Great Britain, *Commercial Reports, Consular*, 1881 (7-8), p. 1430.

[77] *Ibid.*, 1886, pp. 210-211.

[78] *Ibid.*, *Consular and Diplomatic*, 1887, Santos, Report No. 168.

[79] See references, *supra*, note 74.

tion, which by virtue of an extremely pronounced immigration toward the end of the century became very numerous, demanded German-made articles. By 1886 British exporting houses were reduced to one and importing houses to two with the importing trade of the city of Rio Grande (the port of the province) almost entirely in the hands of the Germans who supplied their countrymen.[80] In other sections of Brazil, where the German population was not numerous, commercial travellers were sent from Europe who by virtue of a command of Spanish or Portuguese could treat directly with Brazilian buyers, discover their likes and dislikes, and guarantee an article that would please. Catalogues of German and American firms were printed in Portuguese or Spanish also, whereas English travellers could not speak either language, and advertising literature was sent from England printed in a tongue absolutely foreign to the vast majority of the commercial element of Brazil.[81]

There were other ways in which the Germans showed a progressiveness foreign to the British manufacturer. In the matter of candlesticks, for instance, the Germans made a light weight, showy article which came within the tariff minimum exemptions, while the British article by its old-fashioned solidity exceeded the weight limit; consequently German agents sold candlesticks and the English firms lost the market. Moreover, the German and American houses were content with smaller profits if they could secure the market for their goods, while the British agent demanded larger returns.[82] Sheffield knives, packed without oiling, often arrived too rusty to be salable, although such ignorance of shipping technique was unknown in goods from Germany and the United States.[83]

By 1904 Germany had taken the leadership in the importation of several articles which previously had been received

---

[80] Great Britain, *Commercial Reports, Diplomatic and Consular*, 1886, Rio Grande do Sul, Report No. 32.

[81] *Ibid.*, 1892, Rio Grande do Sul, Report No. 1077.

[82] *Ibid.*, 1898, Rio, Report No. 2058.

[83] *Ibid.*, 1899, Bahia, Report No. 2282.

chiefly from Great Britain. These were: tanned hides and leather, plated ware, iron wire, earthenware and china, sewing machines, printed matter, lighting apparatus, rubber manufactures, and rice. In wool embroidery, cement, lace, and ammunition, German importation was superior to England but below the figures for other countries; and in pig and sheet lead, cutlery, iron nails and screws, locomotives, and books and periodicals, it was threatening British supremacy.[84] From 1893 to 1912 the value of German importations, which throughout the period was second only to that of Great Britain, grew at a threatening rate, for whereas in 1895 the value of English goods sold in Brazil was over two hundred per cent. greater than that of German articles, in 1912 it was less than fifty per cent. greater. In 1850 British goods comprised over half of the total imports of the empire; in 1912 they comprised only 25.18 per cent.[85] Thus in the period just prior to the World War the competition of Germany in the Brazilian market had developed into a serious threat of British preëminence.

The cataclysm of 1914 eliminated Germany as a rival in the South American republic; and yet it prepared the way for another competitor which was to succeed where others had failed. Until 1914 the United States was never a serious contender for economic preëminence in Brazilian markets, shipping, or investments. In 1854-5 the value of American goods imported into the empire constituted a small fraction of the total value[86]; twenty years later the United States was in fourth place among importers with less than one-seventh of the value of British goods[87]; thirty years later it was still

[84] Great Britain, *Commercial Reports, Diplomatic and Consular,* 1906, Rio, Report No. 3521.

[85] Brazil, *Annuario Estatistico,* 1° Anno, II, pp. 102-103, and Bureau of American Republics, *The United States of Brazil,* p. 138.

[86] Importations from the United States were valued at 7.073:000$000, or 8.3 per cent. as against 54.6 per cent. for Great Britain (Brazil, *Relatorio á Assembléa Geral pelo Ministro da Agricultura, Commercio, e Obras Publicas,* 1866, p. 118). The figures given in United States, *Statistical Abstract of Foreign Countries,* 1909, p. 59, are taken from Brazilian sources, the original figures in milreis being converted to dollars on the basis of rates of exchange on London.

[87] The figures are: Great Britain, 76.750:000$000; the United States, 10,813:-000$000 (*O Brazil: Suas Riquezas,* p. 295).

fourth with a fraction over ten per cent. of the total imports[88]; and in 1912 it was third with 15.61 per cent. of the total value of goods brought into Brazil as against 25.18 per cent. for Great Britain and 17.20 per cent. for Germany.[89]

As for shipping, the Yankee clipper with its threat to the preëminence of British navigation interests in the 'forties, faded into the background with the innovation of steam vessels. In 1842 only three more English vessels entered the harbor of Rio than did American ships,[90] and yet twelve years later British tonnage recorded as entering the ports of the empire was fifty per cent. greater than American,[91] and in 1912 the tonnage of vessels registered under the flag of the United States was in fourteenth place among the arrivals of foreign ships.[92] The same inferiority was visible in the participation of American capital in the field of Brazilian investments, for prior to the World War the total amount of American money so invested scarcely exceeded fifty million dollars.[93]

There was, however, one field in which the United States surpassed all foreign countries. Late in the 'fifties the North American republic had increased its purchases from the empire so rapidly that it was on the point of superseding Great Britain as the largest consumer of Brazilian exportations. The Civil War checked the rise for a decade but by the 'seventies the United States had become the largest foreign buyer of Brazilian products, a position which it has maintained ever since.[94] Great Britain, however, has never made a question

[88] *Ibid.*, p. 301.

[89] Brazil, *Annuario Estatistico do Brazil*, 1° Anno, II, 102-103.

[90] Silva de Bivar, "A Chronica," p. 397.

[91] Brazil, *Relatorio á Assembléa pelo Ministro de Agricultura, Commercio, e Obras Publicas*, 1866, Supplement R, Table 6.

[92] Brazil, *Annuario Estatistico do Brazil*, 1° Anno, II, 18-19.

[93] Max Winkler, *Investments of United States Capital in Latin America*, p. 91.

[94] Great Britain, *Commercial Reports, Diplomatic*, 1861, p. 463; Brazil, *Relatorio á Assembléa pelo Ministro da Agricultura, Commercio e Obras Publicas*, p. 119; *O Brazil: Suas Riquezas*, pp. 295 and 296; Brazil, *Annuario Estatistico do Brazil*, 1° Anno, II, 100-101. In 1912 the United States purchased three times as much as did England. The figures are: The United States, 438,008:906$000; Germany, 160.272:207$000; Great Britain, 136.789:709$000 (Brazil, *Annuario Estatistico do Brazil*, 1° Anno, II, 101).

of maintaining its early supremacy in the field of Brazilian exportations: it is primarily interested in Brazil as a market for English goods, not as a supplier of raw materials for home consumption.

Thus despite the occasional warning voiced by British consuls,[95] the United States figured as a minor competitor of England until the World War, when it supplanted Great Britain as the principal supplier of the South American republic.[96] The failure of England to maintain its traditional position during the years following 1914 was merely the natural result of war conditions and, to the Britisher, a temporary eclipse which would be rectified at the proper moment. Consequently, the real struggle for supremacy came after 1918.

For three years after that date the United States continued to command the situation in both the buying and selling markets of Brazil; but in September of 1922 E. Hambloch, commercial secretary to the British legation at Rio, reported with intense satisfaction that Great Britain had "been slowly but surely overhauling her American commercial rival and the official statistics for the first quarter of the current year [1922]" showed "that Great Britain once more" occupied "its original position as the most important of Brazil's suppliers." The next year he failed to mention Yankee competition, confining his warnings to alarming reports of Germany's extraordinary

[95] The consuls included the American manufacturer and merchant in their warnings against the rise of German competition (Great Britain, *Commercial Reports, Consular*, 1885 [8-9,] p. 1664; *Commercial Reports, Diplomatic and Consular*, 1888, Pernambuco, Report No. 374; 1889, Rio de Janeiro, Report No. 504, Rio de Janeiro, Report No. 1531; 1897, Rio de Janeiro, Report No. 1874; 1899, Rio de Janeiro, Report No. 2284; 1908, Pernambuco, Report No. 4139. See also references, *supra*, note 74). An attempt at a reciprocity agreement between the United States and Brazil, concluded in 1891, failed and was revoked by the United States (Great Britain, *Commercial Reports, Diplomatic and Consular*, 1892, Porto Alegre, Report No. 1077; 1893, Rio Grande do Sul, Report No. 1263, and Bahia, Report No. 1290; Brazil, *Relatorio dos Negocios Extrangeiros*, 1891, July, text, p. 6; and Annex I, pp. 3-30; 1893, June, text, p. 5 and August, text, p. 43; 1895, May, text, pp. 20-22; 1900, August, text, p. 52.

[96] For 1917 and 1918 see Brazil, Directoria de Estatistica Commercial, *Commercio Exterior do Brasil* (*Resumo por Mercadorias*), January to December of 1917 and 1918, pp. 18-19.

recovery; but in 1925 he announced laconically that figures for the previous year revealed that the United States had again surpassed Britain in the value of goods sold to Brazil.[97]

In that year the superiority of the North American rival was slight, a matter of some two hundred thousand pounds sterling in excess of the value of Britain's sales; but in 1925 the lead was increased to two million pounds sterling and in 1926 the United States was furnishing over twenty-nine per cent. of Brazil's imports to nineteen per cent. for Great Britain and nearly thirteen per cent. for Germany.[98] Thus, after having lost the lead in 1922, the United States not only regained it but by 1926 furnished a greater proportion of imports to Brazil than did Great Britain in 1912. In the opinion of the commercial attaché, the explanation of this rapid increase in exports from the United States to Brazil lay in the extraordinary demand for American motor cars, gasoline, and electrical material. Largely as a result of increased purchasing power on the part of Brazil, for imports in 1929 were nearly sixty per cent. greater than in 1923, United States sales in these and other articles[99] grew from slightly over eleven millions

[97] Great Britain, *Diplomatic and Commercial Reports*, September, 1922, Department of Overseas Trade, "Report on Economic and Financial Conditions in Brazil," by E. Hambloch, p. 24; *ibid.*, September, 1923, p. 40; *ibid.*, September, 1925, p. 22; *ibid.*, October, 1926, p. 23.

[98] The figures are, in pounds sterling: 1924: United States, 16,543,809 and Great Britain, 16,346,931; 1926: the United States, 23,308,962; Great Britain, 15,207,-459; and Germany, 10,129,524 (Brazil, Directoria de Estatistica, *Commercio Exterior do Brasil*, 1927, pp. 12-13). In 1929 the percentage of imports from these three countries in relation to the total importation of Brazil were: the United States, 30 per cent.; Great Britain (including all possessions) 20½ per cent.; and Germany 12¾ per cent. (Brazil, Departamento Nacional de Estatistica, *Commercio Exterior do Brasil-Importação por Paizes de Procedencia, Janeiro a Dezembro, 1926-1930*).

[99] The principal articles in which the United States was competing with Great Britain in the Brazilian market were: coal, iron bars and plates, steel bars and plates, railway material, telegraph and telephone posts, staples, screws and rivets, tubes and pipes, wire, cutlery, tin plates, tools and utensils, motor cars and accessories, gasoline, scales, hydraulic pumps and boilers, cranes, sewing machines, industrial and agricultural machinery, copper plates and electric copper wire, soda ash, paints and varnishes, caustic soda, drugs and chemicals, electric cables, electrical apparatus, dynamos, motors and transformers, lubricating oils, photographic apparatus, rubber tires, and skins and hides (E. Hambloch, "Report on Industrial and Financial Conditions in Brazil," September, 1926, p. 23).

sterling in the earlier period to over twenty-six millions in 1929, whereas Great Britain was able to increase its sales by less than one-third of the value of the earlier period.[100]

Thus by the end of 1929 the United States was successfully rivalling Great Britain in the buying and selling markets of Brazil.[101] On the other hand, in the fields of shipping and investments, English preëminence was still virtually unchallenged. In 1926 the tonnage of vessels flying the British flag was almost twice as large as that of its nearest competitor, Germany.[102] In investments, of the estimated two billion, five hundred million dollars of foreign capital invested in Brazil in 1929 half was British.[103] In 1927 there was four times as much British as American money invested in Brazil, and over one and one-half times as much as all other foreign capital combined.[104] In two of the three traditional fields of British interest in the South American republic, England was still preëminent at the end of the last decade.

Will the United States be able to maintain its paramount position as the successful rival of the British in the markets of Brazil, and perhaps even displace England in the investment field as well? Or will Great Britain be able to regain its traditional position of absolute economic preëminence in Brazil? These are questions to which only the future can reveal answers.

---

[100] Exports from Great Britain in 1923 were £13,427,738 and from Great Britain and all possessions in 1929, they were £17,850,514 (Brazil, Directoria de Estatistica, *Commercio Exterior do Brasil*, 1927, pp. 12-13, and Departamento Nacional de Estatistica, *Importação por Paizes de Procedencia, Janeiro a Dezembro*, 1926-1930).

[101] It would be premature to assert that the preëminence of the United States in Brazilian markets was permanently assured. Due to the unsettled conditions resulting from the revolution, United States sales dropped fifty per cent. in 1930, although it still maintained its leading position (Brazil, Departamento Nacional de Estatistica, *op. cit.*).

[102] Brazil, Directoria de Estatistica, *Commercio Exterior do Brasil*, 1927, p. 174.

[103] Winkler, *Investments of United States Capital in Latin America*, p. 88. For a detailed statement of United States capital in Brazil see *ibid.*, pp. 86-93.

[104] *South American Handbook for 1928*, p. 188.

SUMMARY

THE FOUNDATIONS of British preëminence in Portuguese America were laid before Brazil became a nation, for the line of continuity may be traced to the Anglo-Portuguese treaties of 1642-'54-'61. By those agreements practices which had become recognized by custom and by the decrees of Portuguese kings were legalized, and additional privileges in Portuguese economic life demanded by English merchants were guaranteed to them. Methuen's solution of the crisis of the last decades of the seventeenth century established a lucrative economic exchange between the two countries which the British exploited under the special privileges obtained by the earlier series of agreements. So valuable to Englishmen were the commercial relations which developed after 1703 that Portugal outrivaled France in the esteem of the British merchant and industrial class. Consequently, by the middle of the eighteenth century English penetration developed to such a degree that Portugal became the economic vassal of its ally. To the British merchant, the principal factor in this Anglo-Portuguese exchange was the colony of Brazil, for the mother country served as the *entrepôt* for the streams of merchandise which flowed from England to the Portuguese colonies and from these colonies back to England.

The industrial revolution in Great Britain, which was coincident with the effort of the Marquez de Pombal to free his country from its economic vassalage, almost severed the connection between the two allies; but raw cotton from Brazil and the wars with France reëstablished the intimate relations which had been threatened with dissolution. When the invasion of the French forced D. João to flee to Rio under the protection of England, the opportunity came for Great Britain to transfer its old privileges and preëminent position in Portugal to the colony itself. Strangford, by his treaty in 1810, succeeded in this task beyond the expectations of the London court.

From 1808 to 1821 the relations between the two countries were conducted on the traditional European basis, although the Portuguese court was residing in the colony. During these thirteen years English penetration into Brazil assumed formidable proportions, for, encouraged by the special privileges, immunities, and guaranties specified to them by treaty, British capital and enterprise were enticed into the huge colony, ripe for exploitation. When the cry of independence was raised in 1822, these interests had become so important that Great Britain forced the revolting colony to accept as binding upon itself the obligations which Portugal had incurred by the treaty of 1810, despite the fact that Brazil had renounced the authority of the government which had negotiated that agreement. This transfer of the traditional English privileges so long enjoyed in Portugal to the independent empire of Brazil was completed by the commercial treaty of 1827, by which the new state paid a debt due Great Britain for its services in securing the entrance of the empire into the family of European nations.

Two currents of interest threatened to disrupt the transfer of traditional British privileges in Portugal to the new state. One was the desire of the Rio court to absorb the north bank of the Plate River, but under British mediation the question was settled in 1828 without fundamentally disturbing Anglo-Brazilian relations. The other problem, the suppression of the slave traffic, was far more serious and proved impossible of solution during the formative period of the empire, although Great Britain succeeded in forcing Brazil to sign agreements which nominally abolished the slave trade under conditions which would enable the English to employ their cruisers to enforce the prohibition. The history of the Portuguese and Brazilian slave traffic between 1808 and 1827 presaged the difficulties which were to confront the London court in its relations with Brazil during the succeeding forty years. The fact that the empire in 1827 acceded to the demands of England in regard to the slave trade is evidence of the preëminence of Britain in Brazil, but persistence in those demands constantly threatened during the first three-quarters of the century to destroy the good relations which existed between the two governments.

Between 1825 and 1827 British preëminence in Brazil reached its zenith. In shipping, commerce, and investments Great Britain enjoyed the paramount position among foreign powers interested in Brazil, and politically the London Office was beginning to exercise a virtual protectorate over the empire. Yet the twenty years following 1827 witnessed a steady decline in the political influence exerted by Great Britain over Brazil. Friction which arose from England's efforts to suppress the slave trade embittered Anglo-Brazilian relations and led to a revolt by the South American nation against the traditional position of Great Britain in Portuguese affairs. The smoldering resentment felt by Brazil over what it termed the arbitrary action of England came to a crisis in 1845 at the expiration of the convention of 1826 when Great Britain, determined on the suppression of the traffic at any cost, employed coercion when persuasion failed.

The revolt against British preëminence in the political affairs of Brazil was carried to a successful conclusion in the two decades following 1845. By 1850 the imperial government, which in the first quarter of the century had been forced to yield to the commanding diplomacy of British agents, was stabilized, confident of its future, and divorced from the old idea of maintaining close relations with the European powers. Irritated by forty years of friction arising mainly from the slave trade controversy, and aided by the marked national and economic development of the empire, Brazil was able to throw off its political subjection to Great Britain. In 1860 it was strong enough to sustain its revolt; thereafter friendly relations were to exist between the two governments, but the thread of political control by England in territory possessed by the Portuguese race was definitely broken in Brazil.

A different phase of this revolt against British preëminence was revealed in the efforts exerted by the South American empire to free itself from the extra-territorial privileges, consular concessions, and economic favors imposed by England during the period from 1808 to 1827. The aim of the Brazilians was not to eliminate British interests from their foreign commerce, capital investments, and domestic enterprises, but to open their country to the competition of all other nations, and thus to make the paramount position of England dependent not on special favors but on economic superiority over rivals. That objective was attained by the middle of the century.

Yet Great Britain was able to maintain its position of economic supremacy in Brazilian shipping, markets, and investments throughout the nineteenth century. The traditional privileges, won in Portugal centuries earlier and transferred to South America between 1808 and 1827, were abolished at the expiration of the treaty in 1844 without altering England's preëminence in Brazilian economic life. During the period when the trade of the Portuguese empire was a monopoly of the mother country, these special privileges had played a useful part in opening colonial possessions to British trade and their continuation in the early years of the independence of Brazil had guaranteed a low import tax during the transition period and at the same time had prevented the granting to other foreign powers special favors adverse to British interests. By the middle of the century, however, their usefulness was past, for in open competition Great Britain was superior to any rival.

That superiority was threatened seriously for the first time when Germany appeared to challenge England's position as the chief supplier of Brazilian markets. By 1914 it had risen to second place in the carrying trade and in exports to Brazil, only to drop out of the race when the World War started. For the next eight years the United States, which since the late 'sixties had been the largest buyer of Brazilian products, occupied Great Britain's place as chief foreign exporter to the South American nation. In 1922 England regained the lead only to lose it again two years later to the same rival. The

United States not only succeeded to first place but by 1926 furnished a greater proportion of imports to Brazil than did Great Britain prior to the outbreak of the World War.

Yet England still retains a commanding position in the fields of investments and shipping, despite the fact that the United States is the largest buyer of Brazilian products and the principal supplier of foreign goods to the South American republic. Thus the historic preëminence of Great Britain in Portuguese domains has been challenged successfully in only one of its three principal economic phases. Politically, British preëminence in Brazil has disappeared; economically, it is still a decisive factor in the life of Portuguese America.

BIBLIOGRAPHY OF CITATIONS

I. SOURCES

A. Manuscript materials

In the British Museum:

Papers of the Commission of the English Council of State. Add. Ms., 4192.

Newcastle Papers. Add. Ms., 32795.

Eden Correspondence. Add. Ms., 34420.

Evidence for the Commercial Treaty with France taken before the Board of Trade, 1785-1786. Add. Ms., 34462.

Coxe Papers. Add. Ms., 9252.

Miscellaneous Papers of Lord Bexley, 1796-1844. Add. Ms., 31237.

Birch Manuscript, 4155.

In the Catholic University of America, Washington, D. C.:

Cartas a Suas Magestades—Anno 1661—do Conde da Ponte.

In the Public Record Office, London:

Customs and Excise:

Customs 8, vols. 1-42. Ledgers of Exports of British Merchandize, 1812-1835.

Customs 4, vols. 8-30. Ledgers of Imports into Great Britain, 1812-1835.

Foreign Office:

Claims Commissions 97, vols. 79-85, Rio Mixed Commission of 1858.

Embassy Archives, Brazil, 131, vols. 12, 15, 211-215.

General Correspondence, Portugal, 63, vols. 6-8, 54-279. Correspondence between London, Lisbon, and Rio de Janeiro, 1785-1786, 1807-1824.

General Correspondence, Brazil, 13, vols. 1-50 and 211-

227. Correspondence between London and Rio de Janeiro, 1825-1828 and 1844-1845.

General Correspondence, Brazil, 97, vol. 76. Brazil and Buenos Aires Memorandum. Montevideo. 1811-1824.

Secretary of State's Office, 95, vol. 183. 1806-1808.

Slave Trade, 84, vols. 5-17. London and Rio Commissions. 1819-1822.

Slave Trade, 84, vols. 23-145. Rio Commission and reports of consuls, *chargés*, ambassadors, agents. 1823-1833.

Slave Trade, 84, vols. 581-583. Correspondence between London and Rio, January-December, 1845.

Treaties, Protocols, Portugal, 93/37, vols. 1B-16. 1807-1823.

Treaties, Protocols, Brazil, 93/9, vol. 1. 1826.

Treaties, Protocols, Brazil, 94/55. 1826.

Treaties, Protocols, Brazil, 94/477. 1858.

State Papers, Foreign, Portugal:

Treaty Papers, 103, vols. 57-58. 1673-1777.

Foreign Ministers, 100, vol. 37. 1648-1710.

General Correspondence, 89, vols. 4, 5. 1634-1660.

General Correspondence, 89, vols. 17, 18. 1690-1705.

General Correspondence, 89, vols. 36-39. 1728-1737.

General Correspondence, 89, vols. 54-64. 1761-1767.

State Papers, Foreign, Spain:

General Correspondence, 94, vols. 122-127. 1735-1737.

B. Official Published Documents

Brazil

Annaes do Parlamento Brazileiro. Assembléa Constituinte. 1823. 6 vols., Rio de Janeiro, 1874.

Archivo Diplomatico da Independencia. 6 vols., Rio de Janeiro, 1922.

Annuario Estatistico do Brasil, 1° Anno, 1908-1912. Rio de Janeiro, 1917.

Directoria de Estatistica, *Commercio Exterior do Brasil.* Rio de Janeiro, 1927.

Directoria de Estatistica Commercial, *Commercio Exterior do Brasil (Resumo por Mercadorias) Janeiro-Dezembro, 1917-1918.* Rio de Janeiro, 1919.

Ministry of Agriculture, Industry, and Commerce, *What Brazil Buys and Sells*. Rio de Janeiro, 1918.

Ministerio das Relações Exteriores, R. A. Campos (ed), *Relações Diplomaticas do Brazil, contendo os nomes dos Representantes Diplomaticos dos diversos paizes no Rio de Janeiro de 1808 a 1912*. Rio de Janeiro, 1913.

Ministerio das Relações Exteriores. *Relatorio da Repartição dos Negocios dos Estrangeiros, apresentado á Assembléa Geral Legislativa.* Rio de Janeiro, 1837—.

Ministerio do Trabalho, Industria e Commercio, Departamento Nacional de Estatistica, *Commercio Exterior do Brasil, Importação por Paizes de Procedencia, Janeiro a Dezembro, 1926-1930.* Rio de Janeiro, 1930.

Relatorio á Assembléa Geral pelo Ministro e Secretario de Estado dos Negocios de Agricultura, Commercio e Obras Publicas, 1866.

Great Britain

British and Foreign State Papers. London, 1841—.

Calendar of Patent Rolls. London, 1891.

Commercial Reports, Diplomatic, 1858-1866.

Commercial Reports, Consular, 1862-1866.

Commercial Reports, Diplomatic and Consular, 1866—.

Department of Overseas Trade, Reports on the conditions in Brazil by commercial secretary of the Embassy at Rio de Janeiro. Various dates.

Journals of the Commissioners for Trade and Plantations. London. 1920—.

Journals of the House of Commons.

Journals of the House of Lords.

Parliamentary Debates from the Year 1803 to the Present Time. London (Hansard), 1812—.

Portugal

Collecção Chronologica de Leis Extravagantes, Posteriores á nova Compilação das Ordenações do Reino Publicados em 1603. Collected by J. I. de Freitas. 7 vols., Coimbra, 1819-1833.

Quadro Elementar das Relações Politicas e Diplomaticas de Portugal com as diversas potencias do Mundo. Collected and written by Visconde de Santarem by order of the Portuguese government.

Last two volumes finished by L. A. Rebello da Silva. 18 vols., Lisbon, 1842-1860.

United States

Department of Commerce and Labor, Bureau of Statistics, *Statistical Abstract of Foreign Countries*, October, 1909. Washington, D. C., 1909.

C. Other Sources

Accioly, Hildebrando, *Actos Internacionaes Vigentes no Brasil.* Rio de Janeiro, 1927.

Aguiar, Antonio Augusto de, *Vida do Marquez de Barbacena.* Rio de Janeiro, 1896.

Republica Argentina, *Tratados, Protocolos, Actos y Acuerdos Internacionaes.* 11 vols., Buenos Aires, 1911.

William, Lord Auckland, *Journal and Correspondence.* 4 vols., London, 1861-1862.

Azeredo Coutinho (Bishop of Pernambuco), *An Essay on the Commerce and Products of the Portuguese Colonies in South America, especially in the Brazils.* London, 1807.

Borges de Castro, José Ferreira, *Collecção dos Tratados Convenções, Contratos e Actos Publicos celebrados entre a Corôa de Portugal e As Mais Potencias desde 1840 até ao Presente.* Lisbôa, 1856-1863.

Boyer, Abel, *The History of the Reign of Queen Anne.* 11 vols., London, 1703-1713.

Bureau of American Republics, *The United States of Brazil.* Washington, 1899.

Calvo, Carlos, *Anales de la Revolución de la América Latina.* 5 vols., Paris, 1864.

————, *Colección Completa de los tratados . . . de todos los estados de la América Latina.* 10 vols., Paris, 1862-1864.

Cardoso de Oliveira, José Manoel, *Actos Diplomaticos do Brazil, 1493-1912.* 2 vols. Rio de Janeiro, 1912.

Centro Industrial do Brasil; *O Brazil: Suas Riquezas Naturaes, Suas Industrias.* Rio de Janeiro, 1907.

Chalmers, George, *A Collection of Treaties between Great Britain and other Powers.* 2 vols., London, 1790.

Charlevoix, José, *Historia del Paraguay, Collección de Libros y Documentos referentes a la Historia de América.* 5 vols., Madrid, 1910.

Christie, W. D., *The Brazil Correspondence in the Cases of the*

"Prince of Wales" and Officers of the "Forte." Reprinted from Papers laid before Parliament. With an introduction telling some truth about Brazil. London, 1863.

———, *Notes on Brazilian Questions*. London, 1865.

Cobbett, William, *Parliamentary History of England*. 36 vols., London, 1806-1820.

Debrett, J., *A Collection of State Papers*. 7 vols., London, 1794-1799.

Hertslet, L., *A Complete Collection of Treaties and Conventions and Reciprocal Regulations between Great Britain and Foreign Powers*. London, 1841—.

Historical Manuscripts Commission,
Bath Papers, vol. 1.
Mss. of the House of Lords, vol. 5.
Townshend Papers, vol. 1.
Rutland Papers, vol. 2.
Dropmore Papers, vols. 1-3.
Buckinghamshire Papers.
Portland Mss., vols. 1-5.
Egmont Papers, vol. 2.

Howell, Thomas B., *A Complete Collection of State Trials and Proceedings for High Treason and other Crimes and misdemeanors from the earliest period to the year 1820*. 34 vols., London, 1816-1826.

Hyde, Edward, Earl of Clarendon, *State Papers*. 3 vols., Oxford, 1767.

Leonard, Peter, *The Western Coast of Africa, Journal of an Officer, 1830, 1831 and 1832*. Philadelphia, 1833.

Lunan, John, *An Abstract of the Laws of Jamaica, relating to Slaves with the Slave Law at length. Also an Appendix containing an Abstract of the Acts of Parliament relating to the Abolition of the Slave-Trade*. Jamaica, 1819.

Luttrell, Narcissus, *A Brief Historical Relation of State Affairs*. 6 vols., Oxford, 1857.

MacPherson, David, *Annals of Commerce*. 4 vols., London, 1805.

Malmesbury, *Diaries and Correspondence of James Harris, First Earl of Malmesbury*. Edited by the Third Earl. 4 vols., London, 1844.

Martens, F., *Recueil des Traités des Puissances e États de l'Europe depuis 1761*. Gottengue.

Mascaró, Pedro, *Revista del Archivo, General Administrativo, Colección de Documentos.* Collected by Mascaró. Montevideo, 1885.

Mawe, John, *Travels in the Gold and Diamond Districts of Brazil.* London, 1825.

Mello e Torres, Francisco, Conde da Ponte e Marquez de Sande, *Relaçam da Embaxaida do Conde da Ponte.* Lisbôa, 1661.

Molinari, Diego Luis, *Antecedentes de la Revolución de Mayo.* 3 vols. Buenos Aires, 1923-1926.

Nabuco, Joaquim, *Primier Mémoire* (Le Droit du Brésil and Annexes). 7 vols.

————, *Second Mémoire* (La Prétention Anglais and Annexes). 6 vols.

————, *Troisième Mémoire* (La Construction des Mémoires anglais and an atlas).

Núñez, Ignacio, *Río de la Plata.* London, 1824.

Parish, Woodbine, *Buenos Aires and the Provinces of the Rio de la Plata.* London, 1st edition, 1839; 2nd edition, 1852.

Pedro I, *Cartas de D. Pedro Principe regente do Brasil a Seu Pae D. João VI, rei de Portugal.* São Paulo, 1916.

Pereira Pinto, Antonio, *Apontamentos para o Direito Internacional, ou Collecção Completa dos Tratados celebrados pelo Brazil com differentes Nações Estrangeiros.* 4 vols., Rio de Janeiro, 1864.

Pereira da Silva. J. M., *Memorias do Meu Tempo.* 2 vols. Rio de Janeiro and Paris. N. D.

Pitt, William, *Correspondence between William Pitt and Charles, Duke of Rutland, 1781-1787.* Edinburgh and London, 1890.

Presas, José, *Memorias Secretas de la Princesa del Brazil, actual reina viuda de Portugal, La Señora Doña Carlota Joaquina de Borbon.* Burdeos, 1830.

Privileges of an Englishman in the Kingdoms and Dominions of Portugal. Done in Portuguese and English. London, 1730.

Privilegios da Nação Britanica em Portugal . . . extrahidos por ordem do Consul Geral de S. M. B. Lisbôa, 1814.

Rio Branco, Barão do (José María da Silva Paranhos), *Mémoire sur la Question des limites entre les États-Unis du Brésil et la Guyanne Britannique.* 1897.

Rymer, Thomas, *Foedra.* 5 vols., The Hague, 3rd edition, 1740.

Smith, John A., Count da Carnota, *Memoirs of the Marquis of*

Pombal, with Extracts from his Writings and from Dispatches in State Paper Office. 2 vols., London, 1843.

South American Handbook for 1925 (J. H. Hunter, ed.). London.

South American Handbook for 1928 (J. H. Hunter, ed.). London.

Stapleton, A. G., *George Canning and His Times.* London, 1859.

Tracts Relating to Various Trades. . . .

"The State of the English Sugar Trade, with that of Portugal." (About 1670)

"The Case of their Majesties' Sugar Plantations." (About 1688)

Swift, Jonathan, *Prose Works.* 12 vols., London, 1897-1908.

Thurloe, John, *A Collection of State Papers of John Thurloe, Esq.* 7 vols., London, 1742.

Tomline, George, *Memoirs of the Life of William Pitt.* 2 vols., Boston, 1821.

Welsh, Rev. R., *Notices of Brazil in 1828-1829.* 2 vols., Boston, 1831.

Whitelocke, Bulstrode, *Memorials of English Affairs.* London, 1732.

II. SECONDARY MATERIALS

A. Books

Altamira, Rafael, *Historia de España y de la Civilización Española.* 4 vols., Barcelona, 1914.

Angell, Hildegarde, *Simón Bolívar, South American Liberator.* New York, 1930.

Armitage, John, *The History of Brazil.* 2 vols., London, 1836.

Baril, V. L., Comte de la Hure, *L'Empire du Brésil.* Paris, 1862.

Beverina, Juan, *La Guerra contra el Imperio del Brasil.* 2 vols., Buenos Aires, 1927-1928.

Biographie Universelle. Paris, 1823.

Bowden, Witt, *The Rise of the Great Manufacturers of England. 1760-1790.* University of Pennsylvania, 1919.

Buxton, Charles (ed.), *Memoirs of Sir Thomas Fowell Buxton.* London, 1851.

Buxton, Thomas Fowell, *The African Slave Trade.* Pt. II. *The Remedy.* London, 1840.

Cady, John F., *Foreign Intervention in the Rio de la Plata, 1838-50.* Philadelphia, 1929.

Carvalho, Augusto de, *O Brazil, Colonização e Emigração*. Porto, 1876.

Carvalho, Delgado de, *Geographia do Brasil*. Rio de Janeiro, 1929.

Castro Carreira, Liberato de, *Historia Financeira, e Orçamentaria do Imperio do Brazil*. Rio. 1889.

Chapman, Charles E., *A History of Spain*. New York, 1927.

Clarkson, Thomas, *History of the Abolition of the African Slave-Trade by the British Parliament*. Abridged by Evan Lewis. Wilmington, 1816.

Cunningham, W., *The Growth of English Industry and Commerce in Modern Times*. 2 vols., Cambridge, 1903.

Davenport, Francis, *European Treaties Bearing on the History of the United States and its Dependencies to 1648*. Washington, 1917.

Dictionary of National Biography. Editors, Leslie Stephen and Sidney Lee. 66 vols., New York and London, 1885-1901.

Dominguez, Luiz, *Conquest of the River Plate*. Hakluyt Society Publication, London, 1891.

Dunshee de Abranches, *A Espansão Economica e O Commercio Exterior do Brazil*. Rio de Janeiro, 1915.

————, *A Inglaterra e a Soberania do Brazil*. Rio de Janeiro, 1915.

————, *Tratados de Commercio e Navigação do Brazil*. Rio de Janeiro, 1909.

La Grande Encyclopédie. 31 vols., Paris, N. D.

Feiling, Keith, *A History of the Tory Party, 1640-1714*. Oxford 1924.

Grant, Andrew, *History of Brazil*. London, 1809.

Humboldt, F. H. Alexander, *Essai Politique sur le royaume de la noveau espagne*. 2 vols., Paris, 1811.

Innes, Arthur D., *Britain and Her Rivals in the 18th Century*. London, 1895.

————, *A History of England and the British Empire*. 4 vols., New York, 1915.

James, Herman G., *The Constitutional System of Brazil*. Washington, 1923.

Jenks, Leland H., *The Migration of British Capital to 1875*. New York and London, 1927.

Keller, Albert G., *Colonization: A Study of the Founding of New Societies*. New York, 1908.

Mathieson, William Law, *British Slavery and its Abolition*. New York, 1926.

————, *Great Britain and the Slave Trade, 1839-1865*. New York, 1929.

Mello Moraes, A. J., *Historia do Brazil-Reino e Brazil-Imperio*. 2 vols., Rio de Janeiro, 1871.

Monteiro, Tobias, *Historia do Imperio: A Elaboração da Independencia*. Rio de Janeiro, 1927.

Morse, Jedidiah and Sidney E., *A New Universal Atlas of the World*. New Haven, 1822.

Moses, Bernard, *Spain's Declining Power in South America, 1730-1806*. University of California Press, 1919.

Nabuco, Joaquim, *Estadista do Imperio, Nabuco de Araujo: Sua Vida, Suas Opiniões, Sua Epoca*. 3 Tomos. Rio de Janeiro-Paris, 1897.

Oliveira Lima, Manoel de, *Dom João VI no Brazil, 1808-1821*. 2 vols., Rio de Janeiro, 1908.

————, *O Imperio Brazileiro, 1822-1889*. São Paulo, 1927.

————, *O Reconhecimento do Imperio*. Rio de Janeiro and Paris, 1902.

————, *Relação dos Manuscriptos de Interesse para o Brazil no Museo Britannico em Londres*. Rio de Janeiro, 1903.

Oliveira Màrtins, J. P., *O Brazil e as Colonias Portuguesas*. Lisbôa, 1920.

————, *Historia de Portugal*. 2 vols., Lisbôa, 1927. 11th Edição.

Packard, Laurence B., *The Commercial Revolution. 1400-1776*. New York, 1927.

Pereira da Silva, J. M., *Historia da Fundação do Imperio Brazileiro*. 7 vols., Rio de Janeiro, 1864.

————, *Situation Sociale, Politique, et Economique de l'Empire du Brésil*. Rio de Janeiro, 1865.

Pitman, Frank W., *The Development of the British West Indies, 1700-1763*. New Haven, 1917.

Prestage, Edgar, *The Diplomatic Relations of Portugal with France, England and Holland from 1640 to 1668*. Watford, 1925.

Quesada, Vicente G., *Historia Diplomática Latino-Americana*. Vol. II, *La Política del Brasil con las Republicas del Río de la Plata*. Buenos Aires, 1919.

Ragatz, Lowell Joseph, *The Fall of the Planter Class in the*

Caribbean. 1763-1833. New York and London, 1928.

Rippy, J. Fred, *Latin America in World Politics.* New York, 1928.

————, *Rivalry of the United States and Great Britain over Latin America (1808-1830).* Baltimore, 1929.

Robertson, William S., *History of the Latin American Nations.* New York, 1927.

Rocha Pombo, José F. da, *Historia do Brazil.* 10 vols., Rio de Janeiro, N. D.

Rubio, Julián María, *La Infanta Carlota Joaquina y la Política de España en América (1808-1812).* Madrid, 1920.

Sorel, Albert, *L'Europe et la Révolution française.* 8 vols., Paris, 1903.

Southey, Robert, *History of Brazil.* London, 1822. 2nd edition.

Stanhope, Earl, *History of England Comprising the Reign of Queen Anne. 1701-1713.* London, 1870.

————, *Life of William Pitt.* 4 vols., London, 1861.

Taunay, Alfonso E., *Historia Geral das Bandeiras Paulistas.* 6 vols., São Paulo, 1925-1929.

Temperly, Harold, *Foreign Policy of Canning, 1822-1827.* London, 1925.

Thiers, M. A., *Histoire du Consulat e de l'Empire.* 21 vols., Paris, 1849.

Trevelyan, G. M., *England Under the Stuarts.* New York and London, 1912.

Varnhagem, Frc°. Adolpho, Visconde de Porto Seguro, *Historia Geral do Brazil.* Rio de Janeiro, 1854.

Villanueva, Carlos A., *Bolívar y el General San Martín.* Paris. 1911.

————, *Napoleón y la Independencia de América.* Paris, 1911.

Ward, A. W. and G. P. Gooch, *Cambridge History of British Foreign Policy. 1783-1919.* Cambridge, 1922.

Webster, C. K., *Foreign Policy of Castlereagh, 1815-1822.* London, 1925.

Winkler, Max, *Investments of United States Capital in Latin America.* Boston, 1929.

B. Periodicals and Newspapers

Addams, Jane, "The Abolition of the Brazilian Slave Trade," *Journal of Negro History*, October, 1925.

Alvez, João Luiz, "A Questão do Elemento Servil. A Extincção do Traffico e a Lei de Repressão de 1850. Liberdade dos Nascituros," *Revista do Instituto Historico e Geographico Brasileiro.* Tomo Especial 6, Parte IV (1916), pp. 188-257.

Baena, Antonio L. Monteiro, "Memoria," *Revista do Instituto Historico e Geographico Brasileiro.* 1841, pp. 322-332.

Bevilaqua, Clovis, "As Capitanias Hereditarias perante o Tratado de Tordesillas," *Revista do Instituto Historico e Geographico Brazileiro,* Tomo Especial, Parte II, Rio de Janeiro, 1915.

Bourne, E. G., "The History of the Determination of the Line of Demarcation Established by Pope Alexander VI," American Historical Association, *Reports,* 1891.

Bowden, Witt, "The English Manufacturers and the Commercial Treaty of 1786 with France," *American Historical Review,* XXV (1920).

————, "The Influence of the Manufacturers on some of the Early Policies of William Pitt," *American Historical Review,* XXIX (1924).

Browning, Oscar, "The Treaty of Commerce between England and France in 1786," *Transactions Royal Historical Society,* New Series, II.

Chapman, A. B. W., "Commercial Relations of England and Portugal, 1487-1807," *Transactions Royal Historical Society,* Third Series, I.

Dubois, W. E. B., "The Enforcement of the Slave-Trade Laws," American Historical Association, *Reports,* 1891.

Fauchille, Paul, "Le Conflit de limites entre le Brésil et la Grande Bretagne et la sentence arbitrale du Roi d'Italie," *Revue Generale du Droit Internacional Public,* Jan.-Feb., 1905.

Hill, Lawrence F., "Abolition of the African Slave Trade to Brazil," *Hispanic American Historical Review,* May, 1931.

Jones, Guernsey, "The Oldest European Alliance—England and Portugal, 1640 to 1661," American Historical Association, *Reports,* 1916. Pt. I.

Manchester, Alan K., "The Rise of the Brazilian Aristocracy," *Hispanic American Historical Review,* May, 1931.

————, "The Paradoxial Pedro, First Emperor of Brazil," *Hispanic American Historical Review,* May, 1932.

Pinto da Rocha, "A Politica Brazileira do Prata até á Guerra contra Rosas," *Revista do Instituto Historico e Geographico Brasileiro,* 1917, Tomo Especial V.

Ramalho Ortigão, Antonio de Barros, "Surto de Cooperativismo," Chapter V in *Contribuiçoes para a Biographia de D. Pedro II*, Pt. I, *Revista do Instituto Historico e Geographico Brasileiro*, Tomo Especial IX, Pt. I.

Roure, Agenor de, "Eleição Direita—Ensino Publico—," Chapter IX in *Contribuiçoes para a Biographia de D. Pedro II*, Pt. I. *Revista do Instituto Historico e Geographico Brasileiro*, Tomo Especial, IX, Pt. I.

Shillington, Miss Violet, "The Beginnings of the Anglo-Portuguese Alliance," *Transactions Royal Historical Society*, New Series, XX.

Silva de Bivar, Diogo de Soares, "A Chronica do Anno 1842," *Revista do Instituto Historico e Geographico Brasileiro*, 1843.

Sousa Sá Vianna, Dr. Manoel Alvaro de, "O Traffico e a Diplomacia Brasileira," *Revista do Instituto Historico e Geographico Brasileiro*, Tomo Especial, V. 6, Pt. 5 (1917), pp. 539-565.

Van Alstyne, "British Right of Search and the African Slave Trade," *Journal of Modern History*, II, No. I.

Viveiros de Castro, Augusto Olympo, "Emancipação Gradual," Chapter VIII in *Contribuições para a Biographia de D. Pedro II*, Pt. I, *Revista do Instituto Historico e Geographico Brasileiro*. Tomo Especial, IX, Pt. I.

Xavier de Brito, Pedro Torquato, "Memoria Historica e Geographica da Ilha da Trindade," *Revista do Instituto Historico e Geographico Brasileiro*, 1877, pt. 2.

Aurora Fluminense. Rio de Janeiro, November 30, 1830.

Correio Braziliense ou Armazen Literario. 29 vols., London, 1808-1822.

Correio Official. Rio de Janeiro, 1833, 1835, 1836.

Diario do Povo. Rio de Janeiro, April 24, 1832.

Diario do Rio. Rio de Janeiro, 1825, and November 22, 1842

Journal do Commercio. Rio de Janeiro April 24, 1830 and March 19, 1845.

The Historical Register. London, 1735.

The London Magazine. London, 1735.

O Pharol. Rio de Janeiro, November 12, 1842.

The Political State of Great Britain. 26 vols., London, 1711-1741.

The Present State of Europe. London, 1688-1736.

INDEX